The Book of Baldwin

The BOOK *of* BALDWIN

KENNETH E. BURCHETT

Amity America
Branson, Missouri

Library of Congress Control Number: 2025919863

ISBN: 978-1-7350442-7-9

On the cover: John Calvin Baldwin.
W. H. Chaney, Photographer.
Jerico Springs, Missouri.

*Amity America, Publishers
One Seventeen Westwood Drive
Branson, Missouri 65616*

In Memory of
Anna Eliza

Contents

Contents

Preface

Genealogy is art more than it is science. Documents and records are the facts of a family tree, but the art of interpretation of facts gives the tree its shape. Like pieces in a jigsaw puzzle, the full picture only emerges if the pieces fit together. A picture puzzle usually includes a picture guide as the desired outcome of the finished puzzle; genealogy has no outcome guide. Yet, the true picture of a family tree depends on how its pieces fit together. Genealogy is subject to the same temptations that scientific inquiry often encounters because too often the genealogist has a picture of a desired outcome in mind and fits the facts into an imagined family tree that may or may not represent reality. The Baldwin name is commonplace in such well-known items as the Baldwin Piano, Baldwin Locomotive, Baldwin Apple, and the occasional Baldwin celebrity. Yet, it is not by fame and fortune that we know the Baldwins best but by their pioneering spirit in the building of America. Family historian Frank C. Baldwin wrote, "We erect monuments to our soldiers and sailors, which is right and as it should be, and neglect to honor our Pioneers. While they built up our country, war devastated it. When one goes into the wilderness to hew them out a home, it is no small undertaking. When the task was completed it made the country better for future generations."

In about the year 1841, Thomas Lee Baldwin moved to Sangamon County, Illinois. A short time later, he moved again to Macoupin County, near Carlinville, Illinois, where he established the Baldwin Horse Ranch, one of several Macoupin County horse breeders in the 1840s. The ranch flourished. Thomas Lee and his sons bought several farms in the county. They remained there until about the time of the Civil War. In 1858, Thomas Lee sold the farm he lived on in Illinois and bought land in Kansas. His son, John Calvin, went to Kansas, where he opened the Baldwin Horse Ranch. Thomas Lee's sons, Thomas Jackson and Caleb J., remained in Macoupin County to manage the other branches of the horse ranch business.

During the Civil War, Thomas Jackson and Caleb J. stayed on the horse ranches and out of the war. John Calvin fought for the Kansas Militia. Sons Joshua L., James W., and Jeremiah Washington all fought for the 122nd Illinois Infantry. After the War, Thomas Lee and his wife, Nancy, moved the Horse Ranch to Cedar County, Missouri, where they settled on the O'Connor Prairie. By 1867, six of the seven Baldwin sons were in or near Linn Township of Cedar County. Henry was the lone son who remained in Illinois, near his sister, Sarah Baldwin Worth. Sarah and her husband, William Worth, remained in Sangamon County, Illinois. Thomas Lee's daughter, Lucinda Baldwin, died at the age of 21 in Illinois; the other daughter, Nancy J., married J. B. Walters and also remained in Illinois.

The Horse Ranch was located south of Stockton, Missouri, and later became the John Calvin Baldwin Horse Ranch. Thomas Lee Baldwin remained on the ranch until his death on November 26, 1879, at the age of 83. His burial was in Gum Springs Cemetery, south of Stockton. His wife, Nancy J. Brizendine Baldwin, died on February 14, 1881. Her burial was also in Gum Springs Cemetery. Gum Springs Cemetery is in Linn Township, Cedar County, Missouri, 3.5 miles south of Stockton on Highway 39, south of the 39 and 215 junction. The cemetery is on the west side of the highway. The old church still stood in 2025.

Several genealogies of the Baldwin name have appeared over the years, representing different branches of the Baldwin family. Each one contributes important elements to a large and multifaceted family tree that is Baldwin history. *The Book of Baldwin* is a history and genealogy of Thomas Lee Baldwin, his ancestors, and descendants who embodied the pioneer spirit of early frontier America. In doing so, they were central to the overall Baldwin family story and the establishment of the Baldwin name in Middle America. This book begins with the ancestral past of the Baldwins in England and Pennsylvania, and then proceeds to trace the family roots of Thomas Lee in North Carolina and Virginia, before chronicling his life and descendants in Indiana, Illinois, Kansas, and Missouri. My great-grandmother was Anna Eliza Baldwin, the third child of John Calvin Baldwin, and the granddaughter of Thomas Lee. Accordingly, the book devotes more space to her line of heritage.

Minnie Baldwin Cornwall and Jimmy O. Baldwin did much to preserve the legacy of the Baldwin name. What they wrote about Thomas Lee was accurate. It only needed an enlargement of detail to paint a bigger picture of the Baldwin family. Minnie and Jimmy died in 1998, having spent many years researching and exploring the Baldwin story. This book honors their memory and recognizes the many genealogists and historians who have contributed and continue to contribute to the preservation and celebration of the Baldwin name.

Medieval England

1

A Brief History of Baldwin

The following brief history of Baldwin comes primarily from the writing of John D. Baldwin's 1880 *Record of the Descendants of John Baldwin,* and from Charles C. Baldwin, who in 1881 published his monumental *The Baldwin Genealogy from 1500 to 1881.*[1] Additional material is from Frank C. Baldwin's 1935 manuscript of *History of the Baldwins in Europe and England from 672 A.D. to 1640,* and the research of George R. Baldwin.[2] Early accounts of the Baldwin name are from *Medieval Lands: A Prosopography of Medieval European Noble and Royal Families* by Charles Cawley[3]

The name Baldwin is very old. There was in England a Baldwin as early as 672. The name was in Flanders, too, in Normandy, and elsewhere in France. People knew the family in the province of West Flanders, in the Flemish region of Belgium, as "Baldwin of the Iron Arm." In 862, Baldwin—he then being the hereditary Grand Forester of Flanders—became the first ruler of Flanders and later Count of Artois,

---

[1] Baldwin, John D. *A Record of the Descendants of John Baldwin of Stonington, Conn. with Notices of Other Baldwins Who Settled in America in Early Colony Times.* Worcester Mass.: Printed by Tyler & Seagrave, 1880; Baldwin, Charles C. *The Baldwin genealogy from 1500 to 1881.* Cleveland, Ohio: [Leader Printing Company], 1881. Charles C. Baldwin interviewed more than 22,999 individuals and spent 20 years and much of his own fortune to research his book, which mostly covers Baldwins in Massachusetts, Pennsylvania, and Connecticut.

[2] Baldwin, Frank C. *History of the Baldwins in Europe and England from 672 A. D. to 1640.* Manuscript–January 1, 1935.

[3] Cawley, Charles, *Medieval Lands: A Prosopography of Medieval European Noble and Royal Families* [online 4th edition], 2022.

in northern France, named by his father-in-law, Charles II the Bald, Emperor of the Romans and King of the Franks. It was to Charles II's daughter Judith that Baldwin became her third husband. The legend of their marriage tells how Baldwin spirited his young bride off to Lorraine, much to the chagrin of Charles II. However, Charles relented, welcomed the marriage, and entrusted the outlying borderland of Flanders to the care of Baldwin against invading Norsemen. Frank C. Baldwin, in his genealogy of the Baldwin family, claimed that Baldwin I, who became the Count of Flanders, was the great-grandson of Lyderick. Lyderick was the governor of Flanders and the King of the Franks in 621.

Baldwin II, son of Baldwin I, and successor Count of Flanders, married Elftrudis of Wessex, the youngest daughter of Alfred the Great, King of the Anglo-Saxons from whom many of the English Kings since William the Conqueror trace their descent.

The Baldwin dynasty lasted for several generations, expanding their

Baldwin I of Flanders and his wife Judith of France. This portrait is one of 28 full-length portraits of all counts of Flanders that decorate the Gravenkapel (Counts Chapel), a medieval chapel in Kortrijk, Belgium, constructed during the reign of Count Louis II of Flanders and finished around 1374. The Flemish painter Jan van der Asselt painted this imaginary portrait of Baldwin I and Judith between 1372 and 1373, long after they died. Source: Gravenkapel (Kortrijk).

influence in France and Germany, and enjoying virtual independence from French and German kings into the early twelfth century. Several generations of Baldwins served as King of Jerusalem from 1100. Another Baldwin, known alternatively as Baldwin VI or Baldwin IX, was also Count of Flanders, led the Fourth Crusade in 1202, inherited the throne of Jerusalem, and became the first Latin emperor of Constantinople (retitled as Baldwin I) in 1205. He ruled large parts of the Byzantine Empire.

The name, Baldwin, served as a hereditary title, which identified the person's rank and not necessarily their ancestral lineage. The same person might acquire a different number depending on the office he held. Accordingly, for example, the same Baldwin VI was the son of Baldwin V, became Baldwin IX as Count of Flanders and leader of the Crusades, and was Baldwin I, Emperor of the East in Constantinople.

There have been numerous claims regarding the origin of the name Baldwin. Scholars guess it to be of Danish origin, coming to Flanders and Normandy with the Norse invasions, and hence to England. At the same time, near the town of Coblenz in western Germany, on a stream flowing into the Rhine River, is Balduinstein—Baldwin Stone—the name of a castle and a town, which Archbishop Baldwin of Trier began work on in 1319. Spreading outward from the Baldwin seat in Flanders and northern France, the Baldwin name has a long tradition of Saxon origin. Baldwin, when broadly interpreted, signifies "Bold Winner." In German, Baldwin means the speedy conqueror, or victor, from the German *Bald*, meaning soon, quick or speedy, and *win*, an ancient word signifying victor, or conqueror, all of which relates back to the early generations of Baldwins of Flanders as protectors of the king's territory.

Notwithstanding Danish ancestral Baldwin roots in France and Saxony, the Baldwins who immigrated to America originated in England. A Baldwin was one of the favorites of the Anglo-Saxon king, Edward the Confessor, the last king of the House of Wessex who ruled from 1042 until he died in 1066. Wessex was an Anglo-Saxon kingdom in the south of Great Britain, located across the English Channel from Flanders and northern France. Baldwin is a common name in England, seen there as early as the Conquest of England, which followed the death

William the Conqueror Invading England. In 1066, William, Duke of Normandy, sailed from northern France and challenged Harold II King of England, culminating in the Battle of Hastings and the Norman Conquest of England. This scene from the Bayeux Tapestry dating to the 11th century is one of 58 scenes depicting events leading up to and during the battle. Bayeux Museum.

of Edward the Confessor. The name Baldwin appears in the roll of Battle Abbey, the Benedictine abbey in East Sussex, England, built on the site of the Battle of Hastings by William the Conqueror, who led the Norman Conquest of England. Baldwin, of the Battle of Hastings in English history, ties to the Baldwins who held offices as Counts of Flanders, contemporary with Alfred the Great, king of the West Saxons and Anglo-Saxons until 899. When Baldwin II, Count of Flanders, married Elftrudis, daughter of Alfred the Great, the succeeding Baldwin generations eventually led to Matilda, daughter of Baldwin V, in the fifth generation. She married William the Conqueror in 1053. The Baldwin name appears often in the Domesday Book, the book of the Great Survey of English inhabitants in 1086.

English history runs rich in the Baldwin name. A Baldwin was among the first to lead a revolt against Stephen of Blois, the controversial king of England from 1135 until he died in 1154. The uprising marked the Anarchy, a civil war between Stephen's cousin and rival, the Empress Matilda, namesake of Matilda, wife of William the Conqueror. Her son, Henry II, succeeded Stephen as the first of the Angevin kings of England, ruling roughly half of France and all of England, and establishing the House of Plantagenet. Meanwhile, Baldwin of Exeter, England, was Bishop of Worcester in 1180 and Archbishop of Canterbury between 1185 and 1190.

Surnames did not appear in England until after the Conquest. Early societies used only first names, usually extended by title, geographic location, or occupation, such as Baldwin I, Baldwin II, etc., or Baldwin of Essex, Baldwin of the Iron Arm, Baldwin son of Harluin, and so on. Surnames were not necessarily from sire, but became superadded to the Christian name. Thus, finding the names of Baldwins, for example, in the same locality, even after the Conquest, is no proof of a Baldwin family connection. Genealogist Charles Baldwin said that he never could find a hereditary Baldwin name in England before the Conquest, causing him to conclude that first and last names did not widely appear among the common people until about the time of Edward II, around 1300. Nevertheless, there were early examples of the surname Baldwin in England. Historic documents name Robert Fitz Baldwin in 1198, John Baldwin 1252 to 1272, Adam Baldwin 1277, and Richard Baldwyne in 1342. The Hundredorum Rolls of 1273 list Stephen filius Baldewyn (son of Baldwin) in Cambridgeshire, Thomas Baldwyn in Oxfordshire, and Robert Baldewyne in Cambridgeshire. Later, the Yorkshire Poll Tax Rolls of 1379 list Johannes Bawdwyn, all of which indicates that the Baldwin surname, or a similar version of it, was in use very early, at least within certain parts of England.

The Baldwin surname comes in a multitude of spelling variations. Changes in surnames resulted from the Old and Middle English languages' lack of definite spelling rules. Moreover, the introduction of Norman French to England, combined with the official court languages of Latin and French, influenced the spelling of surnames. Medieval scribes and church officials recorded names as they sounded, rather than adhering to specific spelling rules. Documents frequently show the same individual referred to with different spellings. Thus, the name Baldwin may appear as Bauldin, Baldwine, Baldwyn, Baldwyne, Baldwynn, Bawden, Bawdwin, Bawdwen, Bawdweyn, and others, including French variations of Baudin, Boudin, and Boudoin.

Charles Baldwin began his genealogy in County Herts (Hertfordshire County), in Brickenden, a village and civil parish in southern England. Baldwin, a certain servant of the king in the time of King Edward I, in about the year 1300, kept a manor in this location. Mr. Baldwin further refined the geography to focus on Buckinghamshire County (Bucks County), immediately north of Herts, in southeast England. Here, in the time of Edward III, we find Henry Baldwin in 1340; Walter Baldwin and

Medieval England and France. This map shows the dominions of England and France in 1259. It also shows lands belonging to Scotland and to the Danish or Norse. Included is Flanders, seat of the Baldwin Counts of Flanders in northeastern France. Following the Norman invasion of England in 1066, the greater concentration of Baldwin families was in southern England. From Gardiner, *School Atlas of English History,* 1914, Map 33, Hathi Trust.

his wife Gunneva at about this same time having land in Honeyborn. John Baudwyn and Elizabeth, in 1358, executed a land transaction in Nether Winchendon, a village in the Aylesbury Vale district of

Buckinghamshire, and John Baldwin of Aylesbury appeared as a party to a land conveyance in 1429. John Baldwin Senior and John Baldwin Junior were founders of the fraternity of the town of Aylesbury in 1429.

Going forward a couple of generations, we find that Richard Baldwin, son of Robert of Aylesbury, died in Aylesbury, Bucks County, September 21, 1485, leaving a modest estate to his next heir, his brother John, probably the same John named in Richard's will, who paid a relief upon the Baldwin manor in 1492. These were two of the descendants of John Baldwin of Aylesbury, named in 1429. John of 1485, brother of the deceased Richard, was age 16 at the time of his brother's death. The two brothers had an annual agreement with the court of Henry VII to see to the comfort of the king at their manor on the king's annual visits to Aylesbury, a tradition that originated with previous Baldwin generations.

The Baldwin property at Aylesbury, Bucks County, remained in the family through many generations. The most eminent Baldwin of Bucks County, England, was Sir John Baldwin, Chief Justice of the Common Pleas of England from 1536 until he died in 1545. One cannot tell whether the earlier Baldwin history directly connects to Sir John. Genealogists believe he was the son of William Baldwin by William's wife Agnes Dormer, daughter of William Dormer, of West Wycombe, Buckinghamshire, and a very old and wealthy family. Whether Sir John was a descendant of past Baldwin generations of antiquity is speculation with no traceable records of connection. However, common sense suggests that he was of the family of Richard and John Baldwin of 1485, based on geographic proximity and perhaps a generation removed. There is sufficient evidence to name brothers, Richard and John Baldwin, and by familial relation, their father, Robert of Aylesbury, as the ancestors of many of the Baldwin descendants of southern England, and likely ancestors of Sir John Baldwin of Aylesbury.

Sir John's manor home seems to have been in Aylesbury, where he was lord of the manor of Aylesbury. He was a very rich man because of his lucrative office. In 1540, Henry VIII granted Sir John the home and site of Gray Friars in Aylesbury, the site of the Franciscan Order known for their gray-colored religious habit. Sir John's association with the

A MAPP OF
Ÿ COVNTY OF
BVCKINGHÃ

Radical King Henry VIII is a marker in Baldwin history, and a key to Sir John Baldwin's great wealth.

Sir John Baldwin died on October 24, 1545, and left a large estate. Besides Aylesbury and Walton, he owned several parishes. Additionally, courtesy of King Henry VIII, he owned Missenden Abbey and held the fee of Dundridge. In a historical side note, Sir John acquired some of his property from Sir Thomas Boleyn, father of Anne Boleyn, she being one of the unfortunate wives of Henry VIII, and mother of Queen Elizabeth I. Sir John Baldwin allegedly presided over the trials and executions of Sir Thomas More and Anne Boleyn.

Historic Map of Buckinghamshire, England. Several of the places associated with the early Baldwins of Buckinghamshire are on this 1673 map of the county. Located on the map, roughly in line with the direction symbol, across to the border with Part of Hartford Shire, is St. Leonard's. Above that is Cholesbury and Vale Aylesbury to its left, to name some. Above Vale Aylesbury is the town of Aylesbury, the family seat of Sir John Baldwin. Richard Blome. *Britannia or, a Geographical Description of the Kingdoms of England, Scotland, and Ireland, with the Isles and Territories Thereto Belonging*. Printed by Tho. Rycroft for the engraver, Richard Blome, 1673.

2

Ancestral Home of the Baldwins

Prominently linked to the history of the Baldwin family in England is Bucks County, aka Buckinghamshire County, in southeast England. Buckinghamshire, abbreviated Bucks, borders Greater London to the southeast. Place names within Bucks County associated with the Baldwin family include Aylesdale, Aylesbury, Dundridge, Great Missenden, St. Leonard's, Aston Clinton, and Cholesbury, to name a few.

Buckinghamshire County, England. The ancestral home of the Baldwin family in Buckinghamshire County is in southern England, about 40 miles west of London. Ordinance Survey of Great Britain National Geospatial-Intelligence Agency.

The geographic region called Buckinghamshire originated in about the sixth century, as part of the Anglo-Saxon occupation of England. It emerged as a county sometime in the 12th century and was important in English history throughout the reign of various English monarchs, especially during the times of King Henry VIII and King Charles I in the 16th and 17th centuries. Their reigns linked the periods marked by the reign of Queen Elizabeth I and the settlement of the first English colonies in North America under King James I, in 1607. It was during the reign of Queen Elizabeth I that England sent its first colonial expedition to North America.

In the middle of Bucks County, at Aylesbury and Dundridge, were two of the ancestral seats of the many Baldwins who came to America. Baldwin family historian Frank C. Baldwin, on a visit to England in 1870, described Bucks County as "a quiet, picturesque place, the green grass everywhere, leaving no bare earth." The farms and estates of Aylesbury had an enjoyable air about them, Mr. Baldwin said. "They are fertile, celebrated long ago as that pleasant vale of 'Aylesdale that walloweth in wealth.'" Baldwin characterized the locality as pleasant and healthy. He did not comment on the boys of Aylesdale, but remarked that the little girls were stout and rosy, "prospectively stout women well fitted for severe life in a new land."

The headwaters of three streams that rise within the Vale of Aylesbury, on the northwest side of the Chiltern Hills, join to form the River Thame east of the village of Hulcott, and north of Aylesbury. It was at Holman's Bridge on the Thame that Sir John Baldwin and a force of Parliamentarians defended Aylesbury in the English Civil War in 1642. The River Thame runs generally southwestward across Buckinghamshire and Oxfordshire counties to its confluence with the River Thames.

The town of Aylesbury, in Aylesbury Parish, was one of the strongholds of the ancient Britons. In Anglo-Saxon times, it was a major market town. At the time of the Norman Conquest, in 1066, the king made the manor of Aylesbury his occasional home and enlisted Baldwin to maintain it as a comfortable way station of his travels. Generations passed, and Henry VIII declared Aylesbury the county town of Buckinghamshire in 1529, which was at the time owned by Thomas Boleyn, father of Anne Boleyn and future father-in-law of Henry VIII. The town played a large part in the English Civil War of 1642 when it became a stronghold for Parliamentarian forces, and was a breeding ground of Puritan sentiment.

In this same locality is Dundridge, a small hamlet, but more correctly a single farm, near the village of St. Leonard's, south of Aylesbury. According to historian Samuel Lewis, Dundridge (Duddridge, Dunriche, Dunrigge, Dunrig) was the name of a manor located within sight of the Chapel of St. Leonard's. Dundridge and the surrounding tenements came into Baldwin's hands in 1544 by way of a grant from

King Henry VIII to Sir John Baldwin, who held a seat in Parliament in 1529. There were many transactions from Henry VIII to Sir John Baldwin beginning as early as 1509, including Dundridge. Sir John bequeathed Dundridge to one of his daughters in 1545. In 1577, it returned to the Baldwin name, to Henry and Richard Baldwin, and remained associated with the name Baldwin thereafter until 1748. Dundridge also lies near Cholesbury, another location where Baldwins were well known.

Four miles from Aylesbury and three miles northwest of St. Leonard's lies Wendover, and a little further to the west is Great Hampden. Great Hampden was the paternal home of John Hampden, who died in 1643, and in his will remembered John Baldwin (not Sir John, who died in 1545, but a probable descendant). This John Baldwin

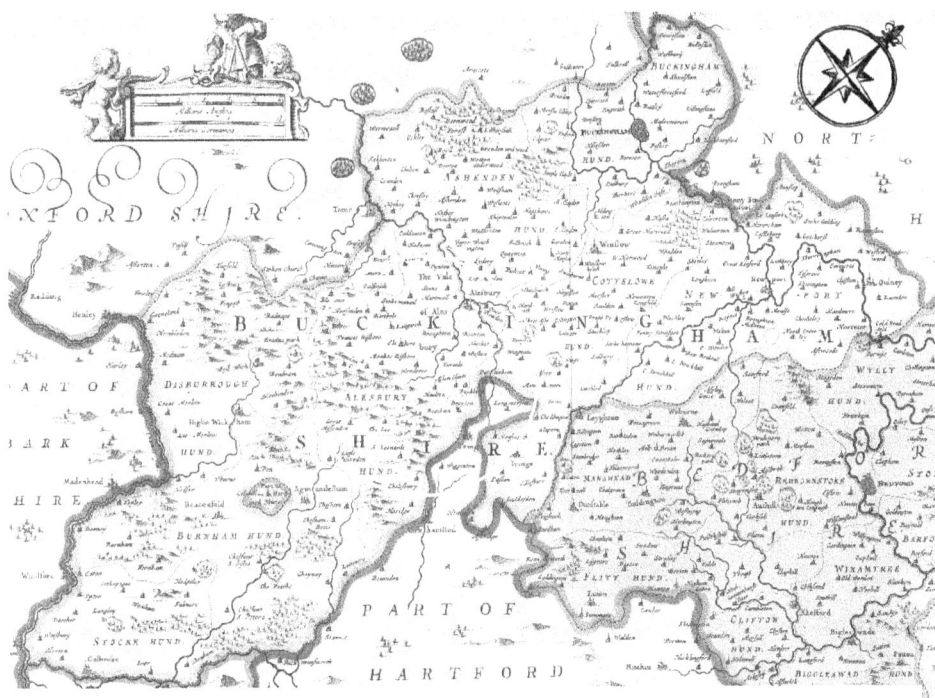

The Baldwin Ancestral Home in Buckinghamshire, England. The lands traditionally associated with Baldwins in England covered an area approximately 10 miles in diameter, in Buckinghamshire County. Place names frequently mentioned in Baldwin documents include the Vale of Ayles and Aylesbury in the north of Aylesbury Parish, and Cholesbury and St. Leonard's about 10 miles south of Aylesbury. Other names connected to Baldwin settlements indicated on the map are Great Hampden, Wendover, Aston Clinton, and Great Missenden. Not shown on the map was the hamlet of Dundridge near St. Leonard's where Baldwins also lived. Excerpt from a map by Gerard Valck & Peter Schenk dated ca. 1646.

of Wendover is of interest. He was the son of Thomas Baldwin of Cholesbury and owner of the manor of Wendover Borough. In 1660, he represented Wendover in Parliament.

According to Lord Nugent, in his *Memorial of Hampden*, John Baldwin of Wendover once had an intention to immigrate to New England, America. However, the project of emigration ended upon an order of the King's Council in 1638. This was a time of political strife in England. The order of the King's Council intended to stifle the escape of the king's political enemies to America. The edict restrained all masters and owners of ships from setting forth any vessels with passengers for America without a special license. The immediate effect of this decree was to restrain eight ships with respectable emigrants on board, which at the time lay in the Thames River bound for the new colony. On one of these ships were John Hampden, and his relative Oliver Cromwell. We do not know if John Baldwin was on the detained ships. The Council relented and named only two ships of the eight as the target of the restraining order.

The 1638 date on which the order took place coincides with the year that the Baldwins immigrated to New England. The date of the edict of the King's Council was 6 April 1638. In that year, many from the immediate vicinity of John Hampden's home, in Bucks County, immigrated. Among them was Sylvester Baldwin who died on the ship *Martin* in June or July 1638. Sylvester and his family were likely on one of the eight ships initially banned from travel by the King's Council but subsequently released to sail to America. Assuming this story to be true, one wonders what would have been the outcome of English history had John Hampden, Oliver Cromwell, and perhaps John Baldwin been allowed to sail for the New World. All were instrumental in the English Civil War of 1642 to 1651, and in the overthrow of King Charles I and the British monarchy, which created the Commonwealth of England, Scotland, and Ireland in 1649. John Hampden died in 1643. Cromwell ruled the Commonwealth until he died in 1658 and never lived to see Parliament restore the monarchy in 1660. An embittered John Baldwin left public life, lived the last 30 years of his life in seclusion, and died in 1691.[1]

Meanwhile, Aston Clinton is a village and a quiet little parish in the Vale of Aylesbury, about four miles from the town of Aylesbury. Aston Clinton was yet another place in Bucks County frequently mentioned in Baldwin lore, along with Great Missenden, a village in the Misbourne Valley, a couple of miles south of Aston Clinton. At Great Missenden, which is also near Dundridge, stand the remains of the Missenden Abbey, on a rising slope back from the road. The Missenden Abbey dates to the time of the Baldwins. Demolished in 1574, rebuilt in its place was St. Leonard's, a small church or chapel in the old English style, and characterized as the chapelry of Aston Clinton. Erected in 1278 on the hermitage site of Missenden Abbey, St. Leonard's roof burned during the Revolution of 1640 before the citizenry rebuilt it. The Chapel Farm, formerly in the tenure of Sylvester Baldwin, lay directly across the street from the chapel. The rolling, grassy farm extended out to a small forest named Baldwin Woods. The poor of Great Missenden were often recipients of gifts in the wills of the Dundridge Baldwins. For example, in the year 1539, Alice Baldwin, the last Abbess of Burnham Abbey and daughter of Sir John Baldwin, surrendered her house to the church at Missenden in exchange for a pension.

---

[1] Oliver Cromwell came to prominence during the 1639 to 1651 Wars of the Three Kingdoms. He advocated for the execution of Charles I, in 1649, which led to the establishment of the Republican Commonwealth of England, Scotland, and Ireland, where Cromwell ruled as Lord Protector from 1653 until his death in 1658. John Hampden was one of the leading architects of the resistance to Charles I's arbitrary rule during the years leading up to the outbreak of the English Civil War. Hampden came from an ancient Buckinghamshire family. He was one of the Five Members whom King Charles I tried to arrest for high treason in 1641, which led to the civil war in England. Hampden went on to play an important part in the impeachment and execution of the King's chief minister, the Earl of Stratford.

3

Out of England

In 1552, Richard Baldwin, yeoman of Dundridge, in the parish of Aston Clinton, county of Bucks, died leaving a brother John. His death in that year repeated a similar generational relationship of 1485 when another Richard Baldwin died leaving as his heir a brother John. Historian Frank Baldwin supposed that the Richard and John of 1485 were nephews of Sir John Baldwin, based on their associations with their country estate at Dundridge, and the fact that both families had considerable property in proximity. Records show that Dundridge and other lands of Aylesbury went to Henry Baldwin and Richard Baldwin in 1577, two of the seven children of the deceased Richard Baldwin of 1552, and nephews of Richard's brother John.

When Richard Baldwin died in 1552, he left his wife Ellen and seven children, three sons and four daughters. His eldest living son, Henry, was the executor of his will in 1552. Henry was almost certainly the progenitor of one company of Baldwins who later settled in America, in Connecticut. Henry died in 1599, and his son, also named Richard, was executor of his will in 1602. In turn, the will of Richard identifies him as Richard Baldwin, yeoman of Dundridge, in the parish of Aston Clinton, in the County of Bucks. Richard died childless in 1636. His older brother Sylvester apparently preceded him in death because the Baldwin properties in Aston Clinton passed from Richard to Henry, son of the deceased Sylvester, and nephew and nearest heir of the childless Richard of 1636. Sylvester, being the eldest brother of Richard, would ordinarily have been Richard's heir; however, Sylvester appears to have died before 1636. Henry, Sylvester's son, received the title to the manor at Dundridge and other lands. The court proved the will of Richard in 1636, attested by Sylvester Baldwin (Jr.), Henry's younger brother, son of Sylvester, Sr., and nephew of Richard. By his will, Henry then passed Dundridge to his son, Edward, in 1661. It remained in the Baldwin family for many years before being transferred out of the family and thereafter sold in 1748, at which time it ceased to be a seat of Baldwin property. Dundridge passed out of Baldwin's hands after ownership of 170 years, and the home of Baldwin tenants, making up two centuries of Baldwin occupation.

BALDWINS OF BUCKINGSHIRE, ENGLAND
1552-1676

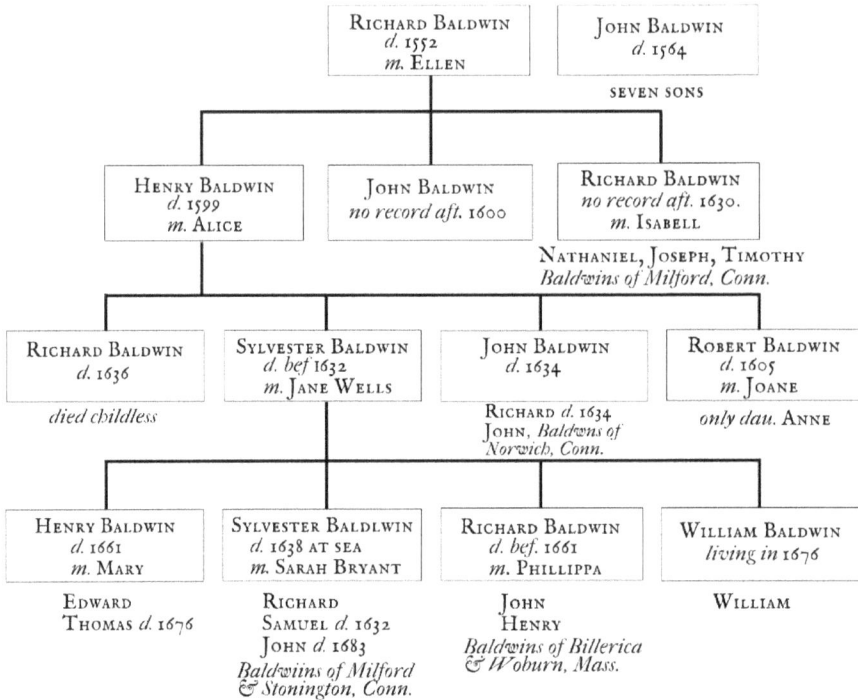

RICHARD BALDWIN *d.* 1552 *m.* ELLEN	JOHN BALDWIN *d.* 1564

SEVEN SONS

HENRY BALDWIN *d.* 1599 *m.* ALICE	JOHN BALDWIN *no record aft.* 1600	RICHARD BALDWIN *no record aft.* 1630. *m.* ISABELL

NATHANIEL, JOSEPH, TIMOTHY
Baldwins of Milford, Conn.

RICHARD BALDWIN *d.* 1636	SYLVESTER BALDWIN *d. bef* 1632 *m.* JANE WELLS	JOHN BALDWIN *d.* 1634	ROBERT BALDWIN *d.* 1605 *m.* JOANE
died childless		RICHARD *d.* 1634 JOHN, *Baldwns of Norwich, Conn.*	*only dau.* ANNE

HENRY BALDWIN *d.* 1661 *m.* MARY	SYLVESTER BALDLWIN *d.* 1638 AT SEA *m.* SARAH BRYANT	RICHARD BALDWIN *d. bef.* 1661 *m.* PHILLIPPA	WILLIAM BALDWIN *living in* 1676
EDWARD THOMAS *d.* 1676	RICHARD SAMUEL *d.* 1632 JOHN *d.* 1683 *Baldwins of Milford & Stonington, Conn.*	JOHN HENRY *Baldwins of Billerica & Woburn, Mass.*	WILLIAM

Baldwin Immigrants to America. Separate groups of the Baldwin family of Buckinghamshire, England, immigrated to America at different times in the 1600s. They were cousins and relatives of each other who settled first in New England, in Connecticut, Massachusetts, and Delaware. Chart by K. Burchett.

Family historian Charles Baldwin connected the family of Richard Baldwin of 1552 to the Baldwins of Connecticut through a conveyance made in New England of interests revised in subsequent wills, and recorded in New Haven Colony Records. When Richard, of 1636, died childless, making his nephew Henry his sole heir, it had the effect of complicating the Baldwin heritage. A line of the Baldwin family, which had continued from Richard of 1552 through his oldest son, Henry, to Richard of 1636, transferred to Richard's brother, Sylvester Baldwin, likewise a descendant of the Baldwins of Dundridge. Sylvester married Jane Wells at Cholesbury in 1590, and they had several children. When he died prematurely, his wealth went to his oldest son, Henry, the heir of the childless Richard, and brother of Sylvester, thus, giving Henry two inheritances of the Baldwin fortune.

Among Sylvester's sons was Sylvester (Jr.), the executor of his Uncle Richard's estate in 1636 but not Richard's heir. That went to Sylvester's older brother, Henry. Thus, the heritage of Baldwin continued through Sylvester, Jr., but not the inheritance. Sylvester Baldwin, Jr., left England in 1638 with his family, which made up one segment of the Baldwin immigrants that came to America. Sylvester, Jr., the immigrant to New England, died on board the ship *Martin* in June 1638. He made his will "On the main ocean, bound for New England" on 21 June 1638. His widow, Sarah Bryant Baldwin, with her six children, continued to New Haven, Connecticut, where, as Widow Baldwin, she enrolled among the first planters.

Meanwhile, another brother of John Baldwin and Henry Baldwin was Richard Baldwin of Cholesbury, a weaver, and uncle of Richard the childless. Richard the weaver made his will in 1630 and named three sons: Timothy, Nathaniel, and Joseph. No trace of these sons exists in England after the probate of the Will of Richard the weaver of Cholesbury in 1633. Genealogists believe they are the same three brothers who immigrated to New England, appearing there in 1639, in Milford, Connecticut, with the other Baldwins from Dundridge and Aston Clinton. Thus, the three Baldwin brothers constitute another segment of Baldwin immigration that dates to the period of settlement of the Baldwin estate in Bucks County, England.

Yet another Baldwin immigrant of this time was John Baldwin, son of John Baldwin of Bucks, England, who died in 1634. The younger John was the brother of Sylvester Baldwin, Sr., Robert Baldwin, and the childless Richard Baldwin of 1636. Like his brother Sylvester, John appears to have preceded his father Richard in death. Consequently, his son, John, was not a legatee of the Dundridge estate. John Baldwin who witnessed the will of Sylvester (Jr.), the Sylvester who died at sea, suggests that they younger John joined Sylvester's family on the voyage to New England in 1638. He settled in Norwich, Connecticut, and was the progenitor of many generations of Baldwins.

There were multiple clans of Baldwin immigrants sailing for America at about the same time. A family tradition among several branches of the Baldwin name says that the first to leave England for America were three brothers. Among the possibilities were the three sons of Richard Baldwin the weaver of Cholesbury, namely, Timothy, Nathaniel, and Joseph. They were in Buckinghamshire County, England, in 1633. Baldwin immigrants bearing their names appeared in 1639 in Milford, Connecticut. The Baldwins of Dundridge and Aston Clinton left England and arrived in New England at approximately the same time in 1638.

There is another tradition among certain branches of the Baldwins that says three brothers came to America after being disowned in England. Through a maze of confusing inheritances, Sylvester Baldwin, Sr., made no will or other provisions for his children. Thus, his estate passed to his oldest living son, Henry, who also received the inheritance of his Uncle Richard Baldwin. Sylvester's sons Richard, William, and Sylvester Baldwin (Jr.) received nothing. Hence, the claim by tradition that the Baldwins who came to America were, by English law, effectively disinherited. Sylvester died on board the ship *Martin* en route to America in 1638, never having received a legacy to pass on to his children. At the same time, the sons of Richard Baldwin, the weaver of Cholesbury—Timothy, Nathaniel, and Joseph—and the cousins of the Dundridge Baldwins settled in the same area of New England at almost the same time. Thus, from about 1630 forward, Baldwins in America accounted for a large part of colonial settlement.

Genealogists draw a connection between the Baldwins of Bucks County, England, and the American Baldwin immigrants through a repetition of the Coat of Arms of Sir John Baldwin, Richard Baldwin, and the Coat of Arms used in America. All have the same crest, a squirrel, sitting upright with oak leaves or oak branches in the shield. The Coat of Arms of Sir John Baldwin appears in William Dugdale's *Origines Juridiciales* of 1666 as three oak leaves, sometimes with acorns in natural color, in the shield. In ancient times, Coats of Arms evolved as different lines of heraldry intermarried and combined Arms. Thus, it is impossible to make much of a Coat of Arms as verification of lineage in a family tree. Moreover, the general ideas of Americans about Arms are very loose, and lead to such a plethora of seals and other matters enough to startle a diligent scholar. In any event, the sacrosanct value of heraldry in old Europe did not survive the passage to the New World. In America, being the descendant of a titled family carried little weight on the farms of New England and in the tobacco fields of Virginia.

Most of the Baldwin families who left England for America came from Buckinghamshire County. It is likely that the Baldwin family grew from its ancient roots in the Vale of Aylesbury

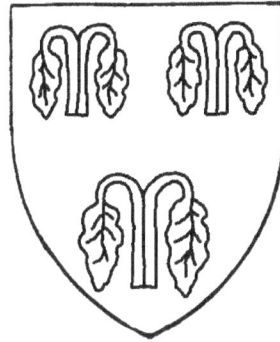

Coat of Arms of Sir John Baldwin. This sketch of the escutcheon of the coat of Arms of Sir John Baldwin first appeared in William Dugdale's *Origines Juridiciales,* published in 1666. The ancient Baldwin motto of Je n'oublierai pas [I will never forget] was originally a war cry or slogan, which originated in the 14th and 15th centuries but did not come into general use until the 17th century. Mottoes seldom formed part of the grant of arms and rarely accompanied the oldest coats of arms. From the third edition of 1680, p. 330.

between the cities of Oxford and London. However, this is not to say that all of them emigrated from that location. For example, General William Baldwin was born in Hook Norton, Oxfordshire, England. He commanded the Left Wing of Cromwell's army in the Battle of Marston Moor in 1644. After the Restoration of the monarchy in 1660, the Baldwins in England were political targets of Charles II. Tradition has it that General Baldwin, with three of his sons, left England in 1668 for America. General Baldwin supposedly died on the voyage, a story with familiar elements in the story of the emigration of the Baldwins of Buckinghamshire. General Baldwin's sons—Thomas, Francis, and

John—appear in records in Pennsylvania in the 1680s.[1] Meanwhile, some records show the Baldwins were in America before the 1630s. In any event, one of these or another line of Baldwins left England for America, later settled in North Carolina, moved to Virginia, and from there westward, and into the Midwest.

---

[1] US Passenger Arrival Records of Immigration Ships [online]. The immigration date of 1668 for John, Thomas, and Francis Baldwin is at odds with the date in the Passenger and Immigration Lists, 1500s-1900s, which gives an arrival date of 1686, in Pennsylvania. However, the 1668 date coincides with the era of King Charles II in England after the Restoration of the Crown in 1660.

4

Voyage to America

One of the ships that first carried the Baldwins from Buckinghamshire, England, to the New World was allegedly the *Martin*, which probably sailed in late April 1638, bound for Massachusetts with the family of Sylvester Baldwin, Jr., and perhaps a cousin, John Baldwin, aboard. History knows of the voyage of the *Martin* only through the death of Sylvester Baldwin, Jr., and the settlement of his estate by depositions of witnesses to his will. Sylvester wrote his will on June 21, 1638, aboard the *Martin* "On the main ocean, bound for New England." It was proved on July 13, 1638, and administered by the general court in Boston on September 7, 1638. The ship arrived in Boston Harbor before July 13.

It took about six weeks to make a trip from England to Virginia, more or less depending on the weather and the type of ship. For example, the Pilgrims' voyage took ten weeks. Some vessels completed the northern route to Newfoundland in less than thirty days, and then worked their way down the Atlantic coast to New Amsterdam (New York), Boston Harbor, or the Chesapeake, Virginia. Most Virginians, however, opted for the longer southern route and a more direct line to the southern colony.

Onboard conditions were crowded. The first migrant ships were relatively small. Some were not much larger than the *Santa Maria*, the original flagship of Columbus, which measured less than eighty feet in length. Likewise, the ship *Mayflower* that sailed from Plymouth, England, to America in 1620 measured approximately ninety feet in length with a deck about twenty-five feet in width, onto which were crowded one hundred two passengers and a crew of about twenty sailors. Passenger ships were wider, which kept them slow and made them handier to navigate. English craft were generally more sea-worthy, less castle-like than their other European counterparts, and better decked than the old exploration models of Columbus's time.[1]

Immigrant Ship. Colonial ships, which brought the first European settlers to the New World, were very small. Passengers spent weeks or months crossing the Atlantic on these vessels. Arthur C. Perry. *American History,* 1913.

Thousands of adventuring travelers made the dangerous journey to the New World and lived to tell the tale. John Josselyn, a London Gentleman, kept a diary of one such trip to New England in 1638 aboard the ship *Nicholas,* aka *New Supply.* The ship carried one hundred sixty-four passengers and forty-eight sailors.[2] Josselyn's voyage took many weeks and was typical of colonial immigrant travel. We may assume the Baldwin voyage in the same year as Mr. Josselyn's trip in 1638 was a similar journey.

---

[1] Smith, *Colonists in Bondage,* 210; Martinez-Hidalgo, *Columbus' Ships,* 42; Bathe, *Seven Centuries of Sea Travel,* 34.
[2] Josselyn, *An Account of Two Voyages to New-England,* 5.

A traveler might spend considerable time on the England inland waterways, as Josselyn did on his Journey, before finally reaching the open sea for the trip across the Atlantic. Leaving from London, it took more than a week of sailing, riding the falls of the tide down the Thames past Gravesend, before setting a westward course. Once on the open water, there was much to write about along the way. Josselyn's striking account of the sailors and their day-and-night work to keep the ship at sail dispels any thought that these were easy trips.

Although most ships sailed well provisioned, travelers were skilled at eating off the sea. They depended on a steady diet of fish and the occasional catch of ocean fowl. On board, anything could happen, and usually did. Disease was common. Josselyn writes of a case of smallpox not long after his ship departed from England. Four people died and were buried at sea before the ship reached America. The number who did not survive a voyage was often much greater than the four lost on Josselyn's trip, sometimes catastrophically high. We do not know the circumstances of the death of Sylvester Baldwin, Jr., on board the *Martin*. However, he likely succumbed to one of the diseases that plagued the Atlantic crossing.

Meanwhile, there was discipline to perform for the crew and passengers. A large crowd of people sharing a space for weeks on end, about the size of a tennis court, presented a unique social environment. Perhaps the most unusual of Josselyn's entries on punishment was his description of a young male traveler whipped for stealing and eating nine lemons. Lemons, it seems, were a prized cargo among individual passengers as a hedge against scurvy.

Josselyn's ship, *Nicholas,* hit Newfoundland on June 16, 1638, after a journey of forty-four days and more than six hundred leagues. However, the ship did not reach its final destination until much later as it meandered down the Atlantic coast. The total time of Josselyn's trip from England—in this case to Boston—took seventy-five days door-to-door, a normal time of passage in the early seventeenth century. He reckoned the trip slightly greater, including brief side trips on both ends of his journey, "which makes my voyage 11 weeks and odd days," he wrote.[3] For those making the journey back to England, the trip was usually shorter, anywhere from four to six weeks.[4]

It came to be standard practice for those who became familiar with the voyage to the New World to give advice to new travelers, having

Map of Immigration Routes. Ships plying the Atlantic followed one of two sailing routes between England and America, the northern route or the southern route. A journey could take anywhere from five to eleven weeks. The return trip was usually shorter. Based on a map by Arnoldi of Siena, Italy, ca. 1600. Library of Congress.

made the trip themselves on more than one occasion. Several publications appeared concerning how to provision passage across the Atlantic, and arrive in America prepared to begin life as a planter. John Smith, the organizer of Jamestown, wrote extensively on the matter, and others did as well.

Josselyn made his trips in 1638 and again in 1663, but did not publish his advice until 1672. No doubt, earlier colonists sought him out for advice. Ship's fare, Josselyn noted, comprised the staples of beef or pork, fish, butter, cheese, "pease" [beans], pottage, water-gruel, biscuit, and beer. He recommended augmentation of the ship's provisions with

---

[3] Josselyn, *An Account of Two Voyages to New-England,* 20.

[4] Barbour, *The Jamestown Voyages under the First Charter,* xxiv.

personal caches of conserves, spirits, and various spices; and, of course, a good supply of lemons. In addition, he gave suggested remedies for seasickness.

To live one year in the colony, an individual was advised to take from England eight bushels of meal, two bushels of "pease," two bushels of oatmeal, one gallon of "Aqua-vita," one gallon of "oyl," two gallons of vinegar, and various sundry other items, altogether about a half ton of freight. Josselyn recommended the purchase of sugar in America because it was cheaper than in England, but he advised purchasing spices beforehand.

The well-prepared traveler also came with a skillet and a few pots and pans. Basic clothing and personal items included coarse canvas ticking filled with straw for a bed, and a coarse rug to soften the discomfort of many hours spent sitting on ship planking. For those voyagers intent on making America their new home, which included almost everyone who made the trip, lists were drawn up of tools and weapons, a not-too-subtle reminder that the destination was hostile territory.

On the open sea, one expected to see many ships encountered in route, going and coming, and giving a clear impression that the Atlantic Ocean was a busy place in the seventeenth century, particularly so at the ports of England and more and more so in America. Up and down the Atlantic coast, European ships mingled with the native craft. Josselyn wrote, "In the afternoon I returned to our Ship, being no sooner aboard but we had the sight of an Indian-Pinnace sailing by us made of Birch-bark, sewed together with the roots of spruce and white Cedar (drawn out into threads) with a deck, and trimmed with sails top and top gallant, very sumptuously."[5]

---

[5] Josselyn, *An Account of Two Voyages to New-England,* 25.

Colonial America

5

Baldwins in America

There can be little doubt that the Baldwins of colonial America originated in southern England, probably from Buckinghamshire County, and possibly descended from Sir John Baldwin of Buckinghamshire, who died in 1485. Exactly how his lines of decent connect, no one knows. Genealogists have built multiple branches of the Baldwin family tree, some more convincing than others, but none that directly tie to Sir John, and none that extends the present genealogy of the Midwest Baldwins to before the mid-eighteenth century in America. Nevertheless, there is enough circumstantial evidence to suggest a strong familial connection among the various early Baldwin immigrants to the New World, and their first settlements in New England and Virginia.

Records of the Baldwin family in colonial America are numerous, some dating from the earliest times of colonial settlement, and in both New England and Virginia, the two colonies most often the destination of English migrants. For example, George Baldwin settled in Boston, Massachusetts, in 1620, well before the Baldwins of Buckinghamshire arrived in New England in 1638.

The earliest destination of Baldwins to America, however, was not New England, as in the case of George Baldwin, but the Virginia Colony, the first colony established in the New World in 1607. Hugh Baldwin and Thomas Bouldin [*sic*] were in Virginia before 1615.[1] At about the same time, we find Nicholas Baldwin, John Baldwin, and William Baldwin there in 1622. Among John Baldwin's children upon his death in 1564 were George, Nicholas, Thomas, and Hugh, all relatively unique

---

[1] Cridlin, William B. *A History of Colonial Virginia: The First Permanent Colony in America, to Which is Added the Genealogy of the Several Shires and Counties and Population in Virginia from the First Spanish Colony to the Present Time*. Richmond, Va.: Williams Printing Co., 1923, 110.

names in the taxonomy of American Baldwin names except for Thomas, which appears often and rather early. The name Thomas is prominent among the earliest proven ancestors of the Midwest Baldwin lineage.

Charles Baldwin, in his detailed and exhaustive genealogy of the Buckinghamshire Baldwins, accounts for a large part of this Baldwin branch, and appears to suggest that most of them—although he does not account for all of them—remained in England.[2] Nevertheless, one cannot rule out that these early Virginia Baldwins of unique identity were descendants of John Baldwin, the brother of Richard of 1552. In all of Mr. Baldwin's 996 pages of genealogy, he mentions the name of Hugh Baldwin only once in connection with John Baldwin, brother of Richard of 1552. Yet, there was a Hugh Baldwin in Virginia by 1615 of possible age to be the grandson of John Baldwin of 1564.

King James I granted two proprietary charters in 1606 for London companies to do business in America, one charter to Plymouth, Massachusetts, and the other to the London Company in Virginia. The Plymouth Colony did not initially succeed, leaving Virginia the destination of most early adventurers. Under the Great Revised Charter of 1618, settlement in Virginia entitled all who came and stayed to tracts of land. Accordingly, we find among the earliest settlers of Virginia Nicholas Baldwin, Hugh Baldwin, John Baldwin, William Baldwin, and Thomas Baldwin, all recorded in the Chesapeake between 1622 and 1635, the years that were some of the most trying times in the establishment of the Virginia Colony.

After the Indian Princess Pocahontas died in 1617, while visiting England, the calming effect of her personal diplomacy that had kept an uneasy peace between the Indians and colonists in America soon vanished. Her father, Chief Powhatan, died shortly thereafter, and in 1622, his brother led the Powhatan Confederacy in a surprise attack on the colony. Three hundred forty-seven settlers were killed, about one-third of the total community.[3]

---

[2] Baldwin, *The Baldwin Genealogy from 1500 to 1881*, 55-66.
[3] Dabney, *Virginia, the New Dominion*, 31, 35-36.

Historian Matthew Andrews described the attack. "In concerted action, the attack began at hundreds of homesteads on both sides of 'Powhattan's river' at eight in the morning of April 1 (March 22, O. S.) …Not a few of the natives had spent the night within the hospitable

Warfare between Virginia Colonists and Native Americans. In this scene, Indians attack Virginia settlers in 1622, while the inhabitants dined and worked. The Indians massacred 347 English men, women, and children. Edward Waterhouse created this woodcut engraving and published it in 1622. Historians consider it largely conjecture. Courtesy of John Carter Brown Library, Brown University.

shelter of English households; and when the fatal moment came, they rose up to slay men, women and children alike."[4] The following account appeared in the *William and Mary College Quarterly*. "Some miraculous escapes are reported in the Warrosquyoake settlement. The Indians came to one Baldwin's house and wounded his wife; but Baldwin, by repeatedly firing his gun, so frightened them as to 'save both her, his

---

[4] Andrews, Matthew P. *Virginia, the Old Dominion.* New York: Doubleday, Doran, 1937, 104.

house, himself and divers others.' About the same time, they appeared at the house of Mr. Harrison, half a mile from Baldwin's, where was staying Thomas Hamor, a brother of Capt. Ralph Hamor, who also lived nearby.... Then the savages set the house on fire, whereupon Hamor, with twenty-two others, fled to Baldwin's house, leaving their own burning.... The consternation produced by this horrid massacre caused the adoption of a ruinous policy. Instead of marching at once, bold to meet and drive the Indians from the settlement, or reduce them to subjection by a bloody retaliation, the colonists were huddled together from their eighty plantations into eight. Works of great public utility were abandoned and cultivation confined to a space too limited merely for subsistence. These crowded quarters produced sickness, and some were so disheartened that they sailed for England."[5]

We do not know exactly which Baldwin or Baldwins were the subjects of the above description. We do know that soon after the massacre, there was a muster of the inhabitants of Virginia settlements on February 16, 1622/23. Settlers living at the plantation at "Basses Choyce" on the lower south side of the James River, near the Indian village of Warrosquyoake, were Thomas Baldwin, William Baldwin, and a second William Baldwin, possibly William Jr., all three living near each other at "Basses Choyce." Meanwhile, listed as a survivor of the massacre of March 22, 1622, and living "In the Maine" was Hugh Baldwine [sic] and his wife.[6] In addition, "at the Plantation over against James Cittie" was John Baldwine [sic].[7] These two plantations lay on the

Baldwins Living in Virginia in 1623. Seven colonists of the Baldwin name resided at various plantation locations along the James River, depicted in this inset of John Smith's Map of Virginia. Circle A, Thomas Baldwynne at "Chaplains Choyce." Circle B, John Baldwine and Hugh Baldwine and his wife "In the Maine and the plantation over against James Cittie," and Circle C, William Baldwin, Thomas Baldwin, and another William Baldwin at "Basses Choyce Plantation." Adaptation of *John Smith's Map of Virginia*, 1624. Library of Congress.

---

[5] Isle of Wight County, Va., Records; *William and Mary College Qrtly*, Vol. 7, No. 4, 1899, 205 249, 207; Morrison, E. M. *A Brief History of Isle of Wight County, Virginia 1608-1907*, Library of Congress, 1907, 9-10.

[6] Hotten, *The Original Lists of Persons of Quality*, 84 188.

[7] Lists of The Living and Dead in Virginia, February the 16th, 1623, 177, 180, 185, 186.

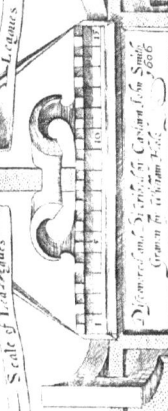

north bank of the James River about seven miles upriver from Thomas Baldwin and the two Williams on the south bank of the James. Meanwhile, a Thomas Baldwynne had a home at "Chaplains Choyce" plantation, further upriver, some five miles west of Hugh and John Baldwine. We find these Baldwins again in these same locations in a 1624 listing of early Virginia pioneers. Notwithstanding variations in name spellings, it is clear that Baldwins were among the earliest settlers of the Virginia colony, arriving in the colony well before the Baldwins of Buckinghamshire, England, who settled in New England, beginning in 1638. However, this is not to say that the Baldwins of New England and of Virginia did not originate from the same Baldwin roots of southern England. On the contrary, all likely descended from Sir John Baldwin, or one of his ancestors.

English retaliation for the Great Massacre was equally bloody. The settlers carried out raids against the Indians in a desperate grasp for survival, despite the grievous depletion of their ranks by illness and hunger, as well as by the loss of nearly one-third of their number in the massacre.[1] The colonists prevailed, and Native American resistance ended for the time being.

Throughout the colony, disease continued to take a heavy toll that became far heavier during the winter of 1622. On the heels of the Great Massacre, more than five hundred more colonists died from an outbreak of 'pestilent fever.' From the earliest days of settlement, disease came into the colony from Europe in carriers called 'pestered ships.' These vessels often were germ-laden and wholly unsanitary. In one instance, a ship lost one hundred thirty of its one hundred eighty passengers and crew on its way to Virginia. Upon arrival, it doubtless spread the lethal malady to the mainland.[2] Death from disease in the winter of 1622 was greatly augmented by near starvation because of poor plantings the previous spring and the loss of cattle that had been driven away or slaughtered by the Indians.

The settler population in the beginning, in 1620, had been close to 900 persons. Despite an immigration of more than 3,500 people in the

---

[1] Dabney, *Virginia, the New Dominion*, 38.
[2] Ibid, 39.

intervening four years, by 1624 the population stood at no more than 1,275. Some of the migrants returned home, but the great majority died in Virginia.[3] More than 850 died in 1622 alone. The writer, Virginius Dabney, saw the beginning of the Virginia colony as an improbable triumph. He wrote, "The ghastly mortality figures for the entire period from 1607 through 1624 are almost incredible. In February 1625, only 1,095 settlers were alive in Virginia of the 7,549 who had come to the colony since 1607. In other words, not one in six had survived. The death rate was less staggering thereafter, but for many years, Virginia was a hazardous place in which to live."[4]

Despite the perseverance of the colonists and the steady growth of the settlement, the Virginia Company itself failed to prosper to the satisfaction of its stockholders. In 1624, the British Crown dissolved the beleaguered company, beset by internal dissension, and ordered it to surrender its private charter.[5] Virginia thus passed from private ownership to become the first Royal government colony in English history. Starting at Roanoke, after four decades of failure and precarious success, the British were in America to stay. By 1641, the colony was well established and extended on both sides of the James River up to its falls.

Meanwhile, from 1629 to 1651, during the personal reign of Charles I, England remained in a state of turmoil, which led ultimately to civil war. Many English families immigrated to the North American colonies to escape the political chaos in Britain at the time. Many families made the trip to the New World under harsh conditions. Overcrowding on the ships caused many of the immigrants to arrive diseased, famished, and destitute from the long journey across the stormy Atlantic. Such was the experience of the Sylvester Baldwin, Jr., family in 1638 when Sylvester died while en route to Boston.

Meanwhile, of the Baldwin families who journeyed to New England in the 1630s, the three sons of Richard Baldwin, the weaver of Cholesbury and Aston Clinton, Buckinghamshire, England, appear to have arrived first, sometime between 1633 and 1639, and settled at Milford, Connecticut. Richard died in England in 1630 and did not

---

[3] McFarlane, *The British in the Americas,* 45.

[4] Dabney, *Virginia, the New Dominion,* 39.

[5] Marshall, *A History of the Colonies,* 62.

accompany his three sons. Timothy Baldwin, the eldest son, produced no male heir and no descendant of his bears the Baldwin name. Joseph Baldwin, the second son of Richard, the weaver, removed from Milford after 1663 to Hadley, Massachusetts. His descendants settled in Massachusetts and New Jersey. Meanwhile, Nathaniel Baldwin, of Milford, Connecticut, and later of Fairfield, Connecticut, the third son of Richard, produced a Baldwin line that distinguished itself in Newark, New Jersey. There can be little doubt that these were the three sons of Richard, the weaver, of Cholesbury, England. It seems equally unlikely, however, that their descendants migrated out of New England to North Carolina and Virginia to continue the line of Baldwins who later migrated to Middle America.

Meanwhile, the family of Sylvester Baldwin—the Sylvester, Jr., who died on the trip from England to America—arrived at Boston in the summer of 1638, coming from Aston Clinton, Buckinghamshire. Family historians conclude that he had six surviving children who settled with their mother, the Widow Sarah Bryant Baldwin in New Haven, Connecticut. Documents record Sarah as the Widow Baldwin in New Haven in 1643, as one of the city's wealthiest proprietors. She later married Mr. Astwood and died in Milford, Connecticut, in 1669. Among Sarah's six children were two sons, Richard and John. Richard was about 16 years old, and John, about three years old, at the time of the family's ocean crossing to New England. Richard, eventually settled in Milford, Connecticut, was the town clerk, and died there in 1665. John Baldwin, the youngest son of Sylvester and Sarah, settled first in Milford, moved to New London, Connecticut, and then to Stonington, Connecticut, where he owned a large tract of land. He died in 1672. It is impossible to determine whether the descendants of Sylvester Baldwin, Jr., through his sons, Richard and John, account for the Baldwin family branches that migrated to North Carolina and Virginia. Historian John D. Baldwin found that families collected in his genealogy were scattered through every part of the country. For example, not many of the descendants of Richard Baldwin's son John, of Aston Clinton, England, remained in Connecticut, although it was only after the close of the Revolutionary War that they began to emigrate out of New England, according to Mr. Baldwin. There is no evidence that any migrated to Pennsylvania, the ancestral home of the Midwest Baldwins.

However, there is evidence that in addition to the immediate family of Sylvester Baldwin, Jr., there were on board the ship *Martin* at least one other Baldwin, and possibly tow, each of the name John.[6] It is of interest to examine how these Johns may fit into the Baldwin family puzzle and, at the same time, bridge the connection between the Baldwins of Buckinghamshire, England, the Baldwins of Pennsylvania, and the Baldwins of Middle America.

The earliest record of Sylvester Baldwin, Jr., and his family in America comes from his will, written on the ship *Martin* on June 21, 1638. Among the witnesses to the will was John Baldwin. Sylvester had a son, John, but he was too young—three years old—to witness the will of his father. Family historian Charles Baldwin concluded, also, that another John Baldwin of Buckinghamshire, who could have been on the ship, was likewise too young, at about age six or seven. No record of a ship's manifest exists that lists the passengers of the *Martin,* or that verifies its passage from London to Boston, only the will of Sylvester. Whether John was with Sylvester's family or came later, he immigrated to America sometime, married twice, had fifteen children, and died in Milord, Connecticut, on June 21, 1681. Among his children was a son, John, who settled in Newark, New Jersey. Certain branches of the Baldwin family tree claim John of Newark as the progenitor of descendants among the Virginia Baldwins. Some of this family also migrated to Pennsylvania, but there is no evidence of a Thomas Baldwin in the family during the prescribed period. There is a family tradition among some branches of the Baldwin family that their ancestor came to America with a Baldwin family that settled in Milford, Connecticut. The family with which he came was apparently the family of Sylvester, Jr., on board the ship *Martin.* However, as a young boy, John could not have been a witness to Sylvester's will.

That leaves John Baldwin, the witness, who came to America at the same time as the Sylvester Baldwin, Jr., family, and was the witness to

---

[6] *Topographical Dictionary of 2885 English Emigrants to New England 1620 - 1650* by Charles Edwards Banks, Edited and Indexed by Elijah Ellsworth Brownell, Southern Book Company, Baltimore, 1957 (Lady Anne's Library).

Sylvester's will on board the ship *Martin* in 1638. We do not know exactly how he connects to the Baldwins of Buckinghamshire, England, except that his presence on the same ship and his witness to the Baldwin will suggest a likely family connection. Mr. Baldwin concluded that John was the son of John of Dundridge, England. John of Dundridge was the brother of Sylvester, Sr., thus making his son, John, the cousin of Sylvester, Jr. The elder John Baldwin, brother of Sylvester, Sr., died in England in 1634, potentially causing his son, John, to join his cousin on the journey to America in 1638. He, too, appears to have settled with Sarah Bryant Baldwin in Milford, Connecticut. In 1653, he went from Milford to Guilford, Connecticut, where he married Hannah Richard, and in 1662, settled in Norwich, Connecticut, where he died. He had sons, but apparently, none of them left New England for Virginia or Pennsylvania.

Other late-arriving immigrant Baldwins are possible bridges between the Baldwins of England and the Baldwin line of Pennsylvania and Middle America. For example, the large wave of Quaker immigrants that came to America in the late seventeenth and early eighteenth centuries included two brothers, John Baldwin and William Baldwin, who settled in Bucks County, Pennsylvania. William was an esteemed Father in the Truth and an eminent minister of the Society of Friends. His brother, John, married Ann Scott and was ancestor to a large number of Quaker Baldwins in the Midwest. They had a son, William, who later moved to Virginia and then North Carolina, and who was likely the ancestor of the Baldwins who settled first in Frederick County, Virginia, about 1751, and then in Rowan County, North Carolina, but neither of which appears to have produced the line of the present Midwest genealogy. Although their presence pre-dated that of our Baldwin family, John Baldwin did not have a son named Thomas, Nevertheless, some of his descendants migrated to Wayne County. Indiana, in 1825, the future home of our Baldwins of the Midwest.

6

Virginia and New England

The Baldwin family tree in America has many branches. Most if not all descendants of the Baldwin family likely originate with the same Baldwin ancestors of southern England, more or less with a particular generation, and at least as far back as the 16th century. Following the migration to colonial America, multiple lines of the Baldwin family trace to various locations. Exactly which Baldwin line connects the Baldwins of England with the Baldwins of Middle America in the present genealogy is speculative. However, among the possibilities are three options: 1) the early Baldwins of the Virginia Tidewater, 2) the Baldwins of New England, and 3) late-arriving immigrant Baldwins. These three options comprise theorized ancestral links to the Baldwins of Middle America and the evidence, or lack thereof, of family connections to Thomas Baldwin of North Carolina and Grayson County, Virginia, the first proven ancestor of the Baldwin family and the subject of the present genealogy.

It is unrealistic to think that genealogists have accounted for every Baldwin who immigrated to New England within the broader context of population across the thirteen American colonies. Nevertheless, Baldwin family historians rarely mention, let alone document, the migration of Virginia Baldwin descendants to New England, or vice versa. There is, however, evidence to suggest that the Baldwins later migrated from Virginia to North Carolina, and there is strong circumstantial evidence that some of them eventually lived concurrently with our Baldwins in Grayson County, Virginia. Although apparently not all closely related, the Baldwins of Virginia made up a potpourri of kin that likely shared the same English roots as the New England Baldwins. Absent any irrefutable proof of family connections, it is fair to suggest that Thomas Baldwin of Grayson County, Virginia, and some of his Baldwin neighbors were plausible kin of the first Baldwin immigrants who settled along the James River during the earliest days of colonial America.

The will of Thomas Baldwin, Sr., written in 1826 in Grayson County, Virginia, identified three generations of the Baldwin family: Thomas Baldwin, Sr., his son Thomas Baldwin, Jr., and grandson Thomas Lee Baldwin, the latter being the ancestor of our branch of the Baldwin family of the Midwest. In his will, Thomas, Sr., expressly named his daughter, "be it understood that my daughter's children, Rebecca Jackson, deceased, to have the same share that she would be legally entitled to provided she was living."[1] Rebecca Baldwin married Joseph Jackson. Several land transactions recorded in the Grayson County, Virginia, Deed Book name Joseph and Rebecca Jackson. For example, Deed Book 1-427 23 Feb 1802 "Joseph & Rebekah Jackson of Grayson $200 to: Greenberry G. McKenzie 164 acres on the east side of Chestnut Creek (Ref D. B. 1-77)." Joseph and Rebecca had a son, Thomas B. Jackson, who migrated to the upper Midwest. When he died in 1877, the Minnesota Register of Deaths for Rice County, Minnesota, recorded the names of his parents as "Joseph and Rebecca Jackson," both born in Pennsylvania.[2] Therefore, Thomas Lee Baldwin was the nephew of Rebecca Baldwin Jackson, whose genealogical roots trace to Pennsylvania. More of Rebecca and Thomas Lee further on.

The connection of the Baldwin line of Middle America to Pennsylvania provides a genealogical starting point but does not definitively link the family to the Baldwins of southern England, nor does it explain how they came to be in Pennsylvania in the first place.

1759 Map of North America Comprehending New England, Pennsylvania, Virginia, and Carolina. Immigrants of the Baldwin name were early arrivals to America. They settled in colonies up and down the Atlantic Coast from Pennsylvania to North Carolina. Most if not all of them came originally from southern England. John Barrow, *New Geographical Dictionary, London,* 1759-60.

---

[1] Grayson County, Virginia Wills 1793-1849. Will of Thomas Baldwin, Sr., Will Book #1, Grayson Co., Virginia, 1826, 309.

[2] Thomas B. Jackson 18 Aug 1877 Death Info Minnesota Rice Co. Deaths 1850-2001, Register of Deaths, 25-26. Mother and father Joseph and Rebecca both born in Penn. Thomas B. Jackson died at the age of 82, calculated birth in 1798.

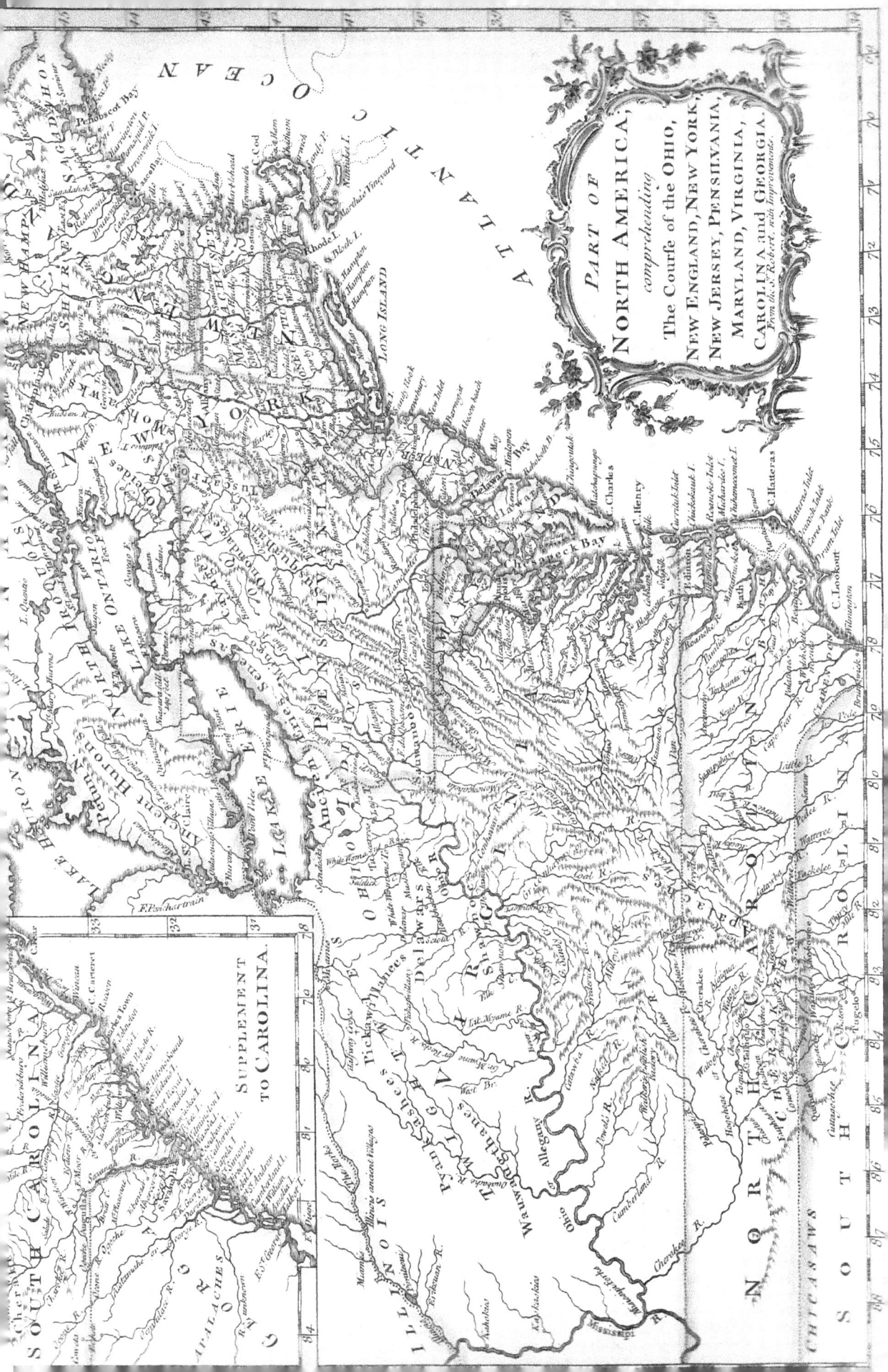

PART OF
NORTH AMERICA,
comprehending
The Course of the OHIO,
NEW ENGLAND, NEW YORK,
NEW JERSEY, PENSILVANIA,
MARYLAND, VIRGINIA,
CAROLINA, and GEORGIA.
From the S.t Robert, with improvements.

SUPPLEMENT
TO CAROLINA.

Nor, for that matter, does it tell us much about the circumstances of the Baldwin removal from Pennsylvania to North Carolina, which occurred sometime around 1790. However, a few possibilities merit attention.

We begin with the early Baldwins of the Virginia Tidewater. Hugh Baldwin was in Virginia as early as 1615. He came on board the ship *Tryall,* which made several trips from England to the Virginia Colony starting about 1610. The ship's rolls suggest that Hugh came first, followed by his wife, Susan, on a later voyage. It was probably Hugh and Susan Baldwin who successfully defended against the Indian massacre of 1622.[1] However, historian Matthew Andrews concluded, it was not Susan Baldwin but Mrs. John Baldwin who, though wounded, held the Indians at bay by shooting at them from within her house until a rescue party arrived from the plantation of Thomas Hamor. Andrews correctly noted, "Several women were triumphant defenders of their households, thus leading, in point of time, to others of their sex who, likewise, became heroines in American history."[2]

Meanwhile, John Baldwine [*sic*] arrived in Virginia in 1622, on the ship *Tyger.* He came as a servant to George Sands of the Mathews Plantation. He was among the musters of inhabitants in Virginia in 1624/1625.[3] At the same time, Nicholas Baldwin also arrived in Virginia in 1622. He came on the ship *Truelove.* He died at the hands of Indians at Chaplains' Choice in 1624.[4] Three additional early immigrants to the Virginia Colony were John Baldwyn [*sic*], John Baldwynn [*sic*], and William Baldin [*sic*]. [5] The two Johns arrived together on the ship

---

[1] John Camden Hotten: London, 1874, (Reprint by Empire State Book Co., New York, ca. 1940s.) (in Lady Anne's library), citing Hotten book 8a from the Musters of the Inhabitants in Virginia 1624/1625 chapters, pages 201 thru 265, which lists the muster captain, and what ship the individual arrived on. Baldwine, Hugh. Wife Susan on an unknown ship.

[2] Andrews, Matthew P. *Virginia, the Old Dominion.* New York: Doubleday, Doran. 1937, 105.

[3] Hotten: London, 1874, 201 thru 265

[4] Ibid, 201 thru 265, Baldwin, Nicholas, on 1622 voyage, "slaine by Indians at Chaplains Choice 1624."

[5] Peter Wilson Coldham's *The Complete Book of Emigrants,* 117, 158, "The underwritten names are to be transported to Virginea imbarqued in the *Primrose* Capten Douglass Mr p Certificate under ye Ministers hand of Gravesend, being examined by

Primrose in 1635, the same year that William Baldwin came on the *Merchant's Hope*.[6] The ships' records do not give much information about the origin of these immigrants, except that they sailed by way of Gravesend on the Thames River, which was the embarkation route of most immigrant ships sailing out of England.

Whether any of these early Virginia Baldwins or their descendants migrated to Pennsylvania cannot be determined. Anecdotal evidence suggests that the early Baldwin descendants who settled in Virginia remained there through most of the colonial period. While it is possible that one or more of them removed to Pennsylvania before 1790 and account for the Baldwin descendants of Middle America, the record does not point to such a likelihood.

Many descendants of the Baldwin name continued to populate the Virginia Colony, some returned to England, and others of the name came on later voyages. Deed books, tax rolls, court records, and church registers document an ongoing presence in the Tidewater of Virginia, much of which reaffirms the locations of the earliest arriving Baldwin colonists. For example, William Bauldwin [*sic*] obtained a land grant of 600 acres on the Charles River, in York County, in 1652.[7] In 1656, John Bauldwin [*sic*] bought land in James Island.[8] An entry for a William Baldwin in the Vestry Book of Christ Church Parish, in Lancaster County, Virginia, in 1664, contains elements of what it could be like to live in colonial America. "When…widower William Baldwin died in 1664, before the formation of Middlesex [County], a neighbor seems to have taken in his children. The Lancaster court subsequently assumed responsibility for their care, ordering that the children remain 'where

---

him touching their Conformitie to the Church Discipline of England. The Men have taken the oaths of Allegeance & Supremacie. Jo Baldwyn, Jo Baldwynn 27 July 1635."
[6] Hotten, *The Original Lists of Persons of Quality*, 116–117. The *Merchant's Hope* sailed July 1635 from Gravesend to Virginia under Master Hugh Weston. The *Merchant's Hope* was owned in 1635 by a wealthy English ship owner William Barker. "Ultimo Julij 1635 Theis under-written are to be transported to Virginea, imbarqued in ye Merchant's Hope Hugh Weston Mr. p examinacon by the Minister of Gravesend touching their conformities to the Church discipline of England & have taken the oaths of Alleg: & supreme." [*sic*]
[7] Virginia State Land Office. Patents 1 42, reels 1 41 [microfilm].
[8] Ibid, Patents 1 42, reels 1 41.

they are' until arrangements could be made to bind them out as servants. One of the children, however, had a 'scald head.' Henry Corbin's Lancaster Parish vestry paid Henry Pickett for curing him, and then bound the child to Pickett... The minor child of William Baldwin, 'being Cast on the Parish,' was simply bound out a servant to Henry Pickett."[9] Middlesex County, Virginia, appears to have been the home of multiple generations of Baldwins in the 17th and 18th centuries. From 1733 to 1749, John Baldwin was Clerk of the Upper Chapel of Christ Church Parish in Middlesex. The Vestry paid him 1,000 pounds of tobacco. During that time, Judith Baldwin was sexton of the same chapel from 1743 to 1746, for which she received 600 pounds of tobacco. Similarly, Isle of Wight County was home to successive generations of Baldwins. Isle of Wight County was the original Warrosquyoake Shire on the James River, where the first Baldwin immigrants to America settled. In 1679, in Isle of Wight, we find the marriage of William Baldwin to Elizabeth Barlow, widow of Thomas Barlow. William Baldwin was witness to a deed in the county in 1724/5[10] A John Baldwin still resided in Isle of Wight County, Newport Parish, as late as 1755.[11] The same applies to the Baldwins found in Surry County, Virginia, once part of James City County, another original seat of the first Virginia Baldwins. For instance, we find William Baldwin, of Surry County, in 1684 and 1694.[12] Part of the family was still in Surry County in 1746, according to a land grant that mentions a William Baldwin.

---

[9] Darrett B. Rutman & Anita H. Rutman. *A Place in Time: Middlesex County, Virginia, 1650-1750*. New York: Norton, 1984, 129, 195-196; Lancaster Orders, 1655-1666, 323; Middlesex Wills, 1675-1798, 146-47; Middlesex Deeds, 1679-1694, 80; C. G. Chamberlayne, Ed. *The Vestry Book of Christ Church Parish*, 4.

[10] Virginia and New York Genealogy Virginia Marriages 1670-1679 [online].

[11] Newport Parish Vestry Book, 1752 1760 Isle of Wight Co. Va., 231. John Baldwin listed as processioner by order of Vestry dated 17 Oct 1755.

[12] Land Office Patents No. 7, 1679 1689 (Vols. 1 & 2, 1 719), p. 376 (Reel 7). "William Baldwin 20 Apr 1684 Land Grant Surry County Va. Description Grantee(s): Baldwin, William and Duce, John. Description: 2600 acres on the southwest side of the Cypress Swamp. Beginning at the mouth of Tyases Branch; William Baldwin 20 Apr 1694 Land Grant Surry County Va. Description 100 acres on the northeast side of Clayes Branch. Beginning at a pine Roger Dolks beginning tree in the said Baldwins line of his old land."

There is no credible proof that any of the Baldwins of the Chesapeake migrated to Pennsylvania; nor is it possible to say they did not. However, the migration patterns of colonial America argue against Virginia being the original seat of the Baldwins of Pennsylvania. Several conditions support such a position. First, Pennsylvania did not become a popular immigrant destination until 1681, although European activity in the region preceded that date. The Dutch first colonized the area in 1643. Nevertheless, Pennsylvania did not become an English colony until William Penn received a royal deed from King Charles II of England in 1681. A second consideration regarding Pennsylvania migration is that the Virginia and Pennsylvania colonies were vastly different in character. The Virginia tobacco trade subsisted on the land of the Chesapeake and the free labor of indentured servitude, and black slavery. Pennsylvania did not have a tobacco economy until the 1700s, and then nothing on the scale of the Virginia plantations. Moreover, many Pennsylvanians avidly opposed slavery. While the colony had indentured servants and a slave trade, both diminished over time until Pennsylvania became the first state in the Union to abolish slavery, before the Civil War. Throughout the history of the Baldwin family that migrated to the Midwest, there is no evidence that any owned slaves. On the contrary, there is a family tradition that claims that one of the reasons the family later left Virginia for Indiana was to escape slavery in the South. While many Virginians did not own slaves, Virginia existed and prospered on a slave culture. Meanwhile, a third argument against the migration of the Virginia Baldwins to Pennsylvania rests on the migration patterns of Virginians before the American Revolution. Land and labor to sustain the Virginia tobacco economy steadily declined. Each new generation further divided the land that became increasingly less available. New generations began to seek other opportunities. While some of the colonists of the Chesapeake and the Tidewater migrated north up the Northern Neck of Virginia toward New England, the general direction of migration was westward toward the Piedmont, at the base of the Appalachian Mountains, and beyond, and not toward New England and Pennsylvania. The flow of migration instead was from Pennsylvania south to Virginia and North Carolina, and west to the Ohio Valley.

We turn next to the Baldwins of New England as the possible origin of the Pennsylvania Baldwins, and hence their appearance in North Carolina and Virginia. It fell to the younger branches of the Baldwin line of Buckinghamshire, England, to perpetuate their race in New England. The older branch, which remained in Buckinghamshire, faded out entirely in about a hundred years after the Great Emigration to America. Genealogist Charles Baldwin named nine Baldwins who came to America in early colonial times, and who arrived in New England at about the same time. However, he makes no connection between the immigrant Baldwins to the Baldwins of the Midwest, or to the families of Buckinghamshire, England, except for the extended family of Sylvester Baldwin. Aside from Mr. Baldwin's impressive genealogy of the descendants of Sylvester in America, he was unable to expand the Baldwin presence in Virginia or elsewhere, except to acknowledge the probabilities that all Baldwins descended from the Baldwins of southern England.

Some of those of the Baldwin name living in New England predate the family of Sylvester Baldwin, who arrived in America in 1638. Previously mentioned was one George Baldwin, who settled in Boston in 1620, who was probably the George Baldwin who came from Great Missenden, Buckinghamshire.[13] Additionally, William Baldwin arrived in 1635 on board the ship *Plain Jane* and apparently disembarked at Providence, Rhode Island.[14] Meanwhile, we find two boys named John Baldwin, aged 13, and William Baldwin, aged nine, arrived on the ship *Pied Cow* in 1635 under the charge of William Harrison and settled at Woburn, Massachusetts.[15] Mr. Baldwin, in his genealogy, absent any subsequent documentation of these two boys, assumed, perhaps incorrectly, that they either died or returned to England. Later, a Henry

---

[13] Charles Edward Banks. *Topographical Dictionary of 2885 English Emigrants to New England 1620-1650* (3rd ed, edited by Elijah E. Brownell). Baltimore: Genealogical Publishing, 1963. (originally published 1937), #55, p. 9.

[14] Hotten, *The Original Lists of Persons of Quality*, 78-80.

[15] Banks, *Topographical Dictionary of 2885 English Emigrants*. The *Pied Cow* (Pide Cowe) left London, England, July 23, 1635, with her Master Mr. Ashley, arriving in New England. Oath taken July 18 or 23, 1635. Baldwin, John. Originally Baldin (Possibly from Ashton Clinton, Buckinghamshire bound for Norwich, Conn. 36 p. 7). Baldwin William, citing Hotten, pp. 106, 110.

Baldwin appeared at Woburn in 1640, and a John Baldwin, of Billerica, Massachusetts, was one of the "petitioners for Chelmsford," Massachusetts, in 1653, but disappeared from the records thereafter. A Richard Baldwin was at Mount Wollaston, Braintree, Massachusetts, in 1637, likewise believed to have returned to England.

The Baldwins of Middle America were certainly in Pennsylvania at least by 1790. The possibilities from whence they migrated are, however, extensive. Of the three possibilities set forth at the beginning of the chapter, viz., 1) the early Baldwins of the Virginia Tidewater, 2) the Baldwins of New England, and 3) late-arriving immigrant Baldwins, there is no definitive record of a family connection in any of these three possibilities before 1790. Nevertheless, circumstantial evidence suggests late-arriving Baldwins settled in Pennsylvania as early as the 1680s.

7

Three Baldwin Brothers

There is a theory among Baldwin family historians that the Baldwins of Middle America were the offspring of a late arriving branch of the Baldwin family that settled in Chester County, Pennsylvania in the 1680s.[1] The lineage of the present genealogy comes from a branch of the southern Baldwin family, which family tradition says emigrated from Pennsylvania to North Carolina and Virginia.

Most of the Baldwin families who came to America came from Buckinghamshire County, England, between Oxford and London, England. A notable exception was William Baldwin from Oxfordshire, England. He no doubt shared ancestral roots with the Baldwins of Buckinghamshire because Oxfordshire County is immediately west of Buckinghamshire County, with which Oxfordshire shares a common border. William Baldwin had three sons. A legend among his descendants is that his three sons arrived in America before the year 1686, which coincides with the arrival date of the Baldwins in Pennsylvania in the 1680s. The story of these three Baldwin brothers has many of the same qualities as other Baldwin traditions; namely, that the Baldwins in Middle America descended from brothers who came from England. The three Baldwin brothers—Thomas, Francis, and John— matching the descriptions of William's sons of Oxfordshire, first appeared in records in Pennsylvania in the 1680s. Descendants of one of the sons allegedly moved to North Carolina after the American Revolution. Genealogists point to his migration south as an indication of the ancestry of the Baldwins of North Carolina and Virginia, and hence the Midwest.

The Baldwins of Pennsylvania became a numerous family. Of the three brothers, John Baldwin seems to have been the most successful.

---

[1] Passenger and Immigration Lists, 1500s-1900s.

He was born in Hook Norton, Oxfordshire, England, in 1657, and arrived in America around 1683. He settled originally in Northley Township, Chester County, Pennsylvania, which became Aston Township, named for Aston, Oxfordshire, England, in present Delaware County, Pennsylvania. A carpenter by trade, he became a merchant in Chester, Pennsylvania, and acquired a large and valuable estate.[2] In his religion, he was a believer in the doctrines of the Friends' faith, as was his wife, who, before her marriage to John in 1689 in Philadelphia, was the widow of Edward Turner; her maiden name was Katherine Carter.[3] John and Katherine acquired land in Chester County, and in 1694, they sold property located there.[4] Records suggest that John and his brothers acquired land through the headright indenture system of free labor.[5] In 1702, John claimed 100 acres on the north side of Brandywine Creek on behalf of himself and his wife in Cain Township.[6] According to the conditions of the time, those who came as servants with the first adventurers to Pennsylvania received 50 acres of land each at the end of their service. In time, John became a wealthy man. He purchased another 600 acres in 1702 and bought land in Chester in 1705, 1709, and more.[7] He had extensive land holdings in Chester, Kennett, and East Cain Townships. In a 1722 assessment of his estate, his holdings stood third in value in a list of over sixty taxables in Chester Township.[8] John died in 1731/32.[9] In his will, he left legacies to his grandsons, John and

---

[2] Baldwin, *The Baldwin Genealogy from 1500 to 1881*, p. 735; Futhey, J. Smith, and Cope, Gilbert. *History of Chester County, Pennsylvania*. Philadelphia: Louis H. Everts, 1881; Cope, Gilbert, and Ashmead, Henry G. Eds. *Chester and Delaware Counties, Pennsylvania* (Vols. 1 & 2). New York: Lewis Publishing, 1904.

[3] Cope and Ashmead, *Chester and Delaware Counties,* pp. 275-277.

[4] Chester County Deed Book B, p. 181.

[5] Martin, John Hill, *Chester (and its vicinity,) Delaware County, in Pennsylvania: with genealogical sketches of some old families*, Philadelphia: [Printed by W. H. Pile & Sons], 1877, p. 479.

[6] Chester County Deed Book N, p. 414.

[7] Chester County Deed Book F, p. 363, Book B, p. 320, Book N, p. 414.

[8] Futhey, J. Smith, and Cope, Gilbert. *History of Chester County, Pennsylvania*. Philadelphia: Louis H. Everts, 1881, p. 154.

[9] Martin, John Hill, *Chester (and Its Vicinity,) Delaware County, in Pennsylvania: with Genealogical Sketches of Some Old Families*, Philadelphia: [Printed by W. H. Pile & Sons], 1877, p. 479.

Joshua Baldwin, and a stipend of £5 per year to his brother Thomas, payable for life.[10] He gave £20 to his nephews Thomas and Anthony, sons of Thomas, and £10 each to Thomas and John, sons of his brother Francis Baldwin. John owned a black servant woman, which was at odds with strict Quaker beliefs against slavery. Upon his death, he instructed his executors to set her free. Extensive genealogies exist that trace the descendants of the immigrant John Baldwin, most, if not all, of whom remained in Pennsylvania and New England.[11] None is known to have migrated to North Carolina.

Meanwhile, Thomas Baldwin was the brother of John, and the eldest of the three sons of William Baldwin and his wife Mary of Sussex, England. He was born in December 1657 in Hook Norton, Oxfordshire. Thomas most likely came to America about 1683, also, because Michael Izard, of Philadelphia, conveyed to him land in Chester County on June 2, 1684.[12] His name first appeared in Fenwick's Colony, in the Township of Penn's Neck, Chester County, Pennsylvania, as one of the earliest English immigrants to purchase land in the Upland district known as Weston.[13] Baldwin Run traversed this property from east to west, and retains to this day the Baldwin name.[14] Thomas settled near the Delaware and Brandywine Rivers near his brother John. He married Mary Hart, widow of Richard Linvill, on December 16, 1684, in Chester, Pennsylvania. She was born in the Parish of Macefield, in the county of Sussex, England, in 1653, the daughter of Thomas Hart and Mary Wrenn, and the widow of Richard Linville.[15] Thomas and Mary Baldwin raised four sons, twins Joseph and Thomas born in 1685, William born in 1687, and Anthony born in 1690. They had three daughters, Mary born 1692, and twins Martha and Elizabeth born 1694.

---

[10] Ibid, p. 480.

[11] Futhey, J. Smith, and Cope, Gilbert. *History of Chester County, Pennsylvania*. Philadelphia: Louis H. Everts, 1881, pp. 469-470.

[12] Chester County Deed Book A, p. 158.

[13] *History of Chester Co., Pa*, p 471.

[14] Ashmead, Henry Graham. *History of Delaware County, Pennsylvania*. Philadelphia, Penn.: L. H. Everts, 1884, p. 425.

[15] C. C. Baldwin's *Supplement to the original Baldwin Genealogy from 1500-1881*.

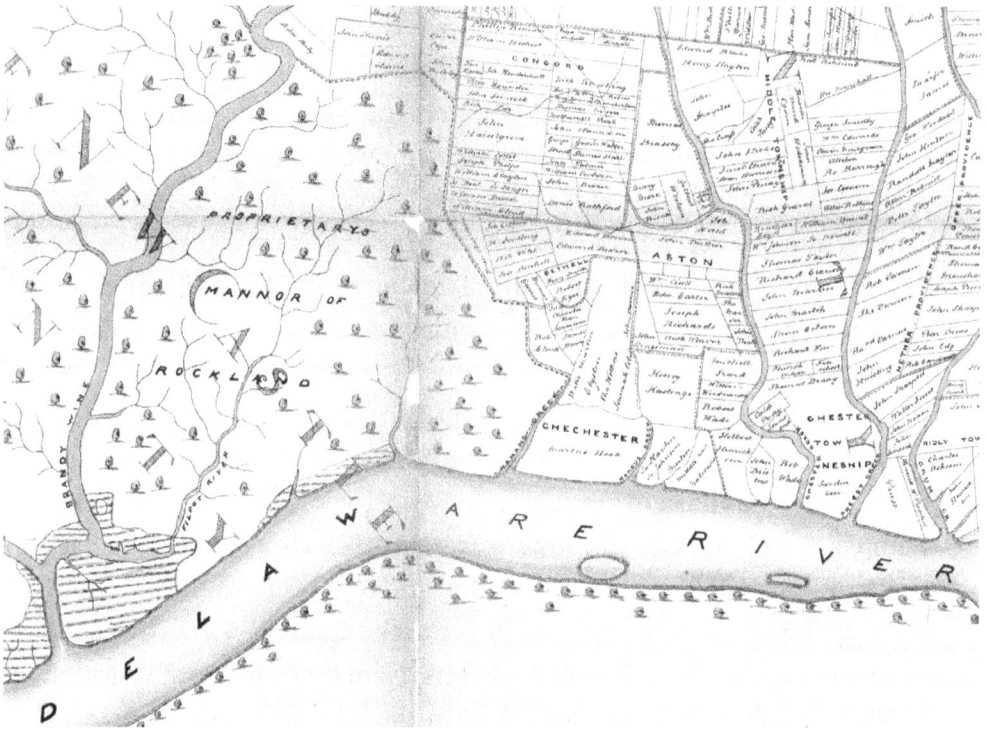

Province of Pennsylvania begun by William Penn. Except of a map showing part of the province of Pennsylvania from Brandywine Creek to Chester Creek, the general locations of the Baldwin family. It shows the names of the original purchasers from 1681 to 1687. Francis Baldwin, although not an original purchaser, took up residence southwest of Chester Creek, near Caleb Pusey in the Township of Chester. John Baldwin lived near Brandywine Creek. Original map created by Robert Greene, Thomas Holme, Lloyd Smith, and John Thornton in 1687. Philadelphia Library.

In the year 1693, Thomas Baldwin's name appeared on the List of Taxables for the Township of Chester, assessed there again in 1715. His brother Francis appeared on the same list, each with taxes of about 2 shillings.[16] In 1693, Chester County levied a provincial tax of one penny per pound of tobacco on estates and six shillings per head upon freemen.[17] In 1697, Thomas resided on the southwest side of Chester Creek above Chester Mills.[18] He received land grants in 1698 and 1699

---

[16] Futhey, John Smith, Cope, Gilbert, *History of Chester County, Pennsylvania; with Genealogical and Biographical Sketches,* Philadelphia: L. H. Everts, 1881, pp. 33.

[17] Futhey, J. Smith, and Cope, Gilbert. *History of Chester County, Pennsylvania.* Philadelphia: Louis H. Everts, 1881, p. 33.

[18] Smith, George, *History of Delaware County, Pennsylvania,* p. 443.

Opposite Top, Chester County as constituted in 1690 with inset of modern Pennsylvania outline map showing the location of the county. Below, Chester County as constituted in 1790. Maps modified from maps courtesy of the Chester County Archives, 2017, 2023.

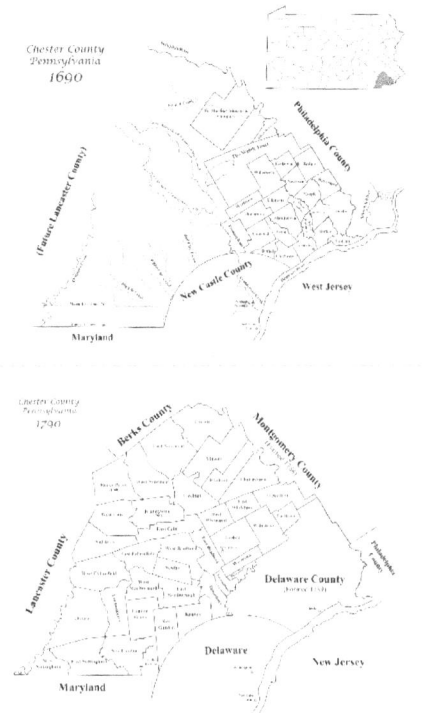

from Thomas Coebourne and Jasper Yeates, respectively.[19] He lived in Chester and helped lay out Chichester Road in 1704. He helped clear a 50-foot-wide road from Aston to Chester in 1706, which cut across his property.[20] He was a court supervisor in 1708 for the lower part of Chichester Township.[21] He witnessed the will of William Baldwin, a mason, in 1722, in Chester.[22] We do not know the relationship of Thomas to this William. However, Thomas had a son named William who predeceased him. The relationship of Thomas as one of the three original brothers of Oxfordshire is confirmed in the will of his brother John Baldwin, in 1731, in which John states, "to the children of brother Thomas and brother Francis, 5 shillings each. Thomas Baldwin was a blacksmith by trade who lived most of his life in Chester Township of Chester County, Pennsylvania. He owned land in several Townships, listed on tax rolls first as a Freeman and then as a Landholder in Chester, Kennett, Conestoga, and Newlin Townships. His Will, dated March 17, 1730, gave to his son Thomas [Jr.] in place of his deceased older sons Joseph and William, the

---

[19] Chester County Deed Book A pp. 163, 226.

[20] Dorothy Lapp, Trans., *Records of the Courts of Chester County, Pennsylvania* (Vol. 2), Danboro, Penn.: Richard T. and Mildred C. Williams, 1972, a2:155.

[21] Ibid, 2:178.

[22] Chester County Will Abstracts and Administrations 1713-1825, Index Will Book A, pp. 100-199, Baldwin, William, Chester, June 2, 1722, A, p. 135.

rightful heir of his property.[23] The elder Thomas died on July 2, 1731, at age 73, in Chester County, Pennsylvania. His burial was at St. Paul's Episcopal Church, Chester, in present Delaware County, Pennsylvania.[24] St. Paul's was for many years the only non-Quaker church in Chester County before that part of Chester County became Delaware County in 1789. Therefore, unlike his brother John, who was a Quaker, it appears that Thomas was Episcopalian.

Of the children of Thomas Baldwin, Joseph, his eldest and his rightful heir, married Elizabeth Mealis in 1712/13, and died young in 1715. He received one shilling in the will of his father, the colonial sign that, although deceased, he was not forgotten. Thomas' son, William, likewise died young.[25] His son, Thomas [Jr.], was alive in 1753 when his brother Anthony named him in his will. Family historian Gilbert Cope believed that this Thomas [Jr.], son of Thomas the Immigrant, was doubtless the Thomas of Conestoga, in Lancaster County, Pennsylvania.

---

[23] Martin, John Hill, *Chester (and Its Vicinity,) Delaware County, in Pennsylvania: with Genealogical Sketches of Some Old Families*, Philadelphia: [Printed by W. H. Pile & Sons], 1877, p. 481. The geography of Chester County, Pennsylvania, can be confusing. Originally there were three counties in Pennsylvania; namely, Philadelphia, Bucks, and Chester, created by William Penn in 1682. Chester County bordered Philadelphia County on the south, extended approximately to the Susquehanna River to the west, and the Delaware River to the east. The colonies of Delaware and Maryland lay to the south across the Delaware River. Lancaster County, Pennsylvania, formed from Chester in 1729; Berks County broke off from Chester County in 1752; and the eastern part of the county separated and formed Delaware County in 1789, which contained the town of Chester. The town of West Chester became the county seat of Chester County. Place names mentioned in records associated with the Baldwin family often mention locations in Chester County from Brandywine Creek to Chester Creek, in a region bordering the Delaware River. Townships within a county were common references in Pennsylvania records, which add to the potential confusion of locations because frequently a township and borough had the same or a similar name, and generally was adjacent within the county. A township partially or wholly might surround a town of the same name. For example, the city of Chester (present West Chester) lies within Chester Township in Chester County, Pennsylvania, while Chester after 1789 became part of Chester Township in Delaware County, Pennsylvania.

[24] Smith, George *History of Delaware County, Pennsylvania*, p. 443.

[25] Martin, John Hill, *Chester (and Its Vicinity,) Delaware County, in Pennsylvania*, p. 479.

Meanwhile, the youngest son of Thomas the Immigrant, Anthony Baldwin, married first Hannah Coebourne before 1712. A Quaker, the Society of Friends admonished her for marrying "one who does not any way profess the truth with us," meaning Anthony was not a Quaker.[26] Anthony married secondly Margery Hannum, daughter of John Hannum and Margery Sothery, of Concord.[27] Court records identify Anthony as a yeoman in cases where he appeared in 1747 and again in 1757 as a defendant in a debt suit. Lawsuits were common in colonial Pennsylvania. After the Court of Common Pleas rendered a judgment, the debtor had to satisfy the judgment debt and other costs. If he did not comply with the judgment, the court would proceed with a writ of *fieri facias* commanding the sheriff to levy and sell as much of the defendant's personal estate as necessary to pay the debt. We do not know if the court ordered a judgment in Anthony's case. He died in 1760, providing in his will for his wife Margery, eldest son William, and daughter Elizabeth Baldwin Daugherty with the balance of his estate divided among his nine youngest children, viz., Anthony, George, John, Thomas, Martha Nichols, Hannah Keach, Robert, Ann Clark, Margery Gray, and Sarah Walker.[28] He left to his brother Thomas [Jr.] and wife six acres on which to live for the duration of their lives.[29]

Meanwhile, of the daughters of Thomas Baldwin, the immigrant, Mary Baldwin Lewis died in 1754, leaving a legacy to William and Thomas Baldwin, each to receive £12 upon reaching the age of 21. She also left £10 each to Mary, Lydia, and Hannah. The twin daughters of Thomas and Mary Baldwin—Martha and Elizabeth—are absent from the record, except that Martha married John Grice, and Elizabeth married Richard Weaver.

---

[26] Shourds, Thomas. *History and Genealogy of Fenwick's Colony, New Jersey.* Bridgeton, N.J., G. F. Nixon, 1876, p. 411.

[27] Will of Margery Baldwin 22 Feb 1786, Newlin, Chester, Pa. Executor son John mentioned and still living after 1786.

[28] Will of Anthony Baldwin 5 Sep 1760, Newlin, Chester, Pa. Mentions a grandson, William Edwards. The Executors wife and son, Anthony.

[29] Chester County Will Abstracts and Administrations 1713-1825, Index Wills Proved 1760-1, Baldwin, Anthony, Newlin, June 9, 1753, proved September 5, 1760.

Concerning the descendants of Thomas the Immigrant, it is possible that one or more of his descendants migrated south. However, analyses of the records imply that his son, Thomas [Jr.], could not be the Thomas of North Carolina, the progenitor of the Midwest Baldwins, because Thomas [Jr.] appears in Chester County, Pennsylvania, records well after Thomas of North Carolina appeared in the South. Nor could it be his son Thomas [III] of Newlin Township, because he died in Chester County in 1809. Meanwhile, if Mr. Cope is correct, neither can Thomas of North Carolina be Thomas, the son of Anthony. Nonetheless, the prodigious nature of Baldwin offspring doubtless connects the Baldwins of Chester County, Pennsylvania, to the Baldwins of the South and the Midwest. We cannot claim a direct connection to the descendants of Thomas the immigrant, nor to his brother John Baldwin. Nevertheless, Baldwin descendants greatly populated the environs of Chester County. For example, when Lydia, the wife of Thomas the Immigrant's grandson Thomas [III], departed life in 1832, at age 93, she left 10 children, 89 grandchildren, and 177 great-grandchildren, or a total of 276 Baldwin descendants. In the words of family historian, Hadley Baldwin, "the descendants are too numerous to particularize."[30]

The third immigrant brother of Oxfordshire, England, was Francis Baldwin, brother of John and Thomas. He arrived in America aboard the ship *Amity*, which docked in Upland, Pennsylvania, in the summer of 1682. The three brothers may have immigrated at separate times; a second voyage of the *Amity* departed from England, sailed to Rotterdam, The Netherlands, and arrived in Philadelphia in the spring of 1686.[31] Like his brothers, Francis was a Freeman who owned indentured servants. Francis settled in the neighborhood of West Chester County, Pennsylvania, as early as 1686.[32] He was a miller who later lived on 100 acres of land on Chester Creek, in Chester, Pennsylvania, near Kings Road and the town of Chester. He married Cicely Coebourne, daughter of Thomas and Elizabeth Coebourne, in

---

[30] Futhey, J. Smith, and Cope, Gilbert. *History of Chester County, Pennsylvania.* Philadelphia: Louis H. Everts, 1881, p. 471.

[31] Passenger Lists of Chester County, [online].

[32] Martin, John Hill, *Chester (and its vicinity,) Delaware County, in Pennsylvania.* p. 479.

1691, in Chester County.[33] She was originally from Berkshire, England. The Coebourne Christian name of Thomas Coebourne reinforces the name "Thomas" found in many Baldwin generations, when offspring took the name of a paternal or maternal grandparent.

Francis and Cicely Baldwin appear many times in Chester County Court records. Francis was witness to deeds in 1691, 1697, 1699, and 1700. He was one of the proprietors of the Mill on Naaman's Creek, requesting a grant of 100 acres for a slip of land on the south side of the creek as far up as the King's Road.[34] His father-in-law conveyed to him 100 acres of land on Chester Creek in Chester Township in 1695/6.[35] Francis died in New Castle County in 1702. After his death, his wife appeared multiple times in court as both a plaintiff and a defendant in her duties as the Executrix of his will.[36] Court appearances were a regular occurrence for members of the Baldwin family. From 1700 to 1760, Baldwins were part of 57 lawsuits in the Chester County Court of Common Pleas. Moreover, court minutes frequently referenced the names of the Baldwin brothers, often for their service on juries, sometimes brothers serving on the same jury.

Francis and Cicely Coebourne Baldwin had four children: a daughter, Anna, and three sons, Thomas, William, and John.[37] It is this Thomas who historian Charles Baldwin says "must be, I think, the Thomas who, with his brother William, was by tradition from the vicinity [of Chester], and settled in Virginia; said to have lived in Philadelphia for a while." This Thomas—son of Francis, born about 1692—married Mary Beal on March 29, 1714 [*op cit* 1712/13], in St.

---

[33] Will Book page A 444, 21 3 1697, proved 6 3 1698 [ID I2694] attributes will to Francis' son Francis Hackney Baldwin but it is clearly Thomas Coebourne, probably father-in-law of Francis Baldwin.

[34] Minute Book "G" Minutes of Property Commencing Ye 19th 9th ber., 1701. This is Book G in the Secretaries Office. [date indicated Quaker month "ber"]

[35] *Record of the Courts of Chester County, Pennsylvania*, 1681-1697, Philadelphia: Colonial Society of Pennsylvania, 1910, 1:375.

[36] Lapp, *Records of the Courts of Chester County, Pennsylvania* (Vol. 2), 2:103, 2:111.

[37] A possible fifth child of Francis and Cicely Baldwins appeared in the 1715-1764 Chester County Tax Index from 1735 to 1740, in Kennett Township listed as Baldwin, Francis, Freeman, Book C-13B, p. 13; Book C-15, p. 10; Book C-16, p. 15.

Paul's Episcopal Church, Chester.[38] She was the daughter of John Beal of Chester County, who received a legacy in the will of Thomas Coebourne in 1697. Thomas Baldwin's name appeared in the 1715 Tax List of Chester Township. In the summer of 1717, a county land record named Thomas Baldwin heir-at-law of Francis Baldwin who assigned the right to William Baldwin who assigned it to John Baldwin. Thomas was Church Vestryman from 1717 to 1727 at St. Paul's Episcopal Church, Newlin Township, in Chester County.[39] Speculation is that this Thomas was the Thomas Baldwin of Kennett, where there was a Thomas

Caleb Pusey House. This is the second oldest English-built house in Pennsylvania, and the only remaining house in Pennsylvania where William Penn visited in 1683. Caleb Pusey was a Quaker lawmaker, friend and business associate of Penn. Built in a vernacular English yeoman's style, it stood on 100 acres where Pusey owned a mill on Chester Creek near the Baldwins. Pusey's name appears in numerous court documents alongside the Baldwin name. The National Register of Historic Places added the site to the National Collection in 1971. Friends of the Caleb Pusey House, Inc.

---

[38] Pennsylvania, Historical Society of Pennsylvania, Marriage Records, 1512-1989; Pennsylvania, Church Marriages, 1682-1976; Marriage Record of St. Paul's Episcopal Church, Chester, Pa. 1704 1733, Pennsylvania Archives, Second Series, Vol. 8.
[39] Wardens and Vestrymen of St. Paul's Episcopal Church (1704 1727), Chester Co., Pa.

in 1738. His Uncle John Baldwin named him in his will. Thomas was the eldest son of Francis. He turned down his legacy in his father's mill on Naaman's Creek in favor of farming in Kennett Township. He later resided near Wilmington, Delaware, where his children married in Holy Trinity Church. He died about the year 1752. Notwithstanding Mr. Cope's theory that he migrated to the South, dates and records make it implausible that he was the Thomas who migrated to North Carolina. However, it could have been his son or grandson. In any event, Mr. Cope concluded that the descendants of Francis Baldwin the Immigrant were those "probably in the South and West."[40] Genealogist C. C. Baldwin concurred in Mr. Cope's speculation.[41]

While Thomas Baldwin, son of Francis, could have been the ancestor of Thomas Baldwin of North Carolina and Virginia, there is no certain proof of that. Mr. Baldwin's theory that these were the Baldwins of Virginia is conjectural because he admitted he could not identify the several Thomases who descended from Francis.[42] Nevertheless, there is reason to speculate that Thomas Baldwin of North Carolina was a fourth-generation descendant of Francis Baldwin the Immigrant. The arrival date of Francis in America in about 1682 and his marriage in 1691 allow for a great-grandson born about the approximate date of Thomas of North Carolina, born about 1754. A span of 4 generations would bridge Francis the Immigrant [1], son of Francis [2], grandson of Francis [3], and Thomas of North Carolina [4]. However, other candidates among the sons of Francis besides Thomas may fill the gap of missing generations. For example, William Baldwin, the second son of Francis, was by family tradition from near Philadelphia. He married Ann Lucas. They had several children before 1734. Their descendants were among those who migrated to Virginia and later moved to Georgia and Ohio. Finally, John Baldwin, third son of Francis the Immigrant, was probably the John Baldwin, yeoman of the Christina Hundred, of New Castle County, Delaware. He married twice, first to Sarah Cloud

---

[40] Futhey, J. Smith, and Cope, Gilbert. *History of Chester County, Pennsylvania*, p. 471.

[41] Baldwin, *The Baldwin Genealogy from 1500 to 1881*, p. 735.

[42] Ibid, p. 729,

and secondly to Hannah Cloud. He died in Delaware in 1745. He had at least eight children about whom we know little.

Notwithstanding the scramble of Baldwin genealogy, based on the Pennsylvania birthplace of his children, there can be little doubt that the migrant, Thomas, Sr., of North Carolina was one of the many Thomas Baldwins of Chester County, Pennsylvania. He was the probable great-grandson of one of the three Baldwin brothers, likely Francis Baldwin the Immigrant, who arrived in America in 1682, the son of William Baldwin of Oxfordshire, England, and descendant of the ancient ancestry of the Baldwins of Buckinghamshire, England.

8

Revolutionary War

The momentous events of 1776, and after, which resulted in the American Revolution, caught the Thomas Baldwin family in a hiatus of traceable movements. Based on obtainable records of the period, the family was in either Pennsylvania or in the South. They did not leave Pennsylvania until after 1776, perhaps as late as around 1786, according to available birthdates and birthplaces of the Baldwin children. Assuming the earlier date, they could have been in North Carolina or Virginia during the War, while the later date would place them in Pennsylvania. Baldwins from all three localities of Pennsylvania, North Carolina, and Virginia served in the Revolutionary War, including several of the name Thomas Baldwin. So far, records do not confirm that our Thomas served, although the possibility exists that he was one of the Thomas Baldwins from Virginia or Pennsylvania who fought in some of the key battles and survived the awful winter with George Washington at Valley Forge in 1777-1778.[1]

The Revolutionary War came on slowly. For several years, there had been talk among the colonies of dissatisfaction with the British Crown over taxes. The British Parliament said it had a right to tax colonists; the colonists saw taxation without representation in Parliament as illegal. The issue galvanized around the Stamp Act of 1765, a particularly egregious tax placed on paper products. The Parliament repealed that tax the following year under pressure, but further resistance to British intrusion in colonial affairs continued. The American boycott of the tax on British tea led to the Boston Tea Party in 1773.[2] The following year saw the creation of the Continental Congress. The next year, Patrick Henry made his immortal speech on March 23, 1775, at Richmond,

---

[1] Valley Forge Muster Roll Project, ID: VA14213.
[2] Revolutionary War Pensions Richard Bettisworth S36410.

Chester County Courthouse. This building served as the Chester County, Pennsylvania, Courthouse from 1724 to 1789. Built before the Revolutionary War, it is the oldest public building still standing in the United States. It is the site of many court meetings and events associated with the Baldwin family, everything from court appearances to jury duty. The building is 2 ½ stories with 2-foot thick walls. Quaker influence on the design of the building is in its two entry doors, one for men, and the other for women. The interior measures 31 by 36 feet. The jury room was on the second floor. The National Register of Historic Places added the building to the National Collection in 1971. Photo National Register of Historic Places.

before the Virginia Convention.[3] Henry, who a decade earlier had led the fight against the Stamp Act and survived the crown's accusation of treason against him, fired the revolt.[4] "I know not what course others may take," he said, "but as for me, give me liberty, or give me death." Remembered as the greatest American orator of all time, his words resonate through history.[5] The Convention enacted legislation placing

---

[3] Van Schreevan, et al, *Revolutionary Virginia* (Vol. 1), 221, 331-332; Lancaster, *A Sketch of the Early History of Hanover County*, 30, 50. Profoundly moved by the death of his wife the month before after a long struggle with mental illness, Patrick Henry threw himself fervently into the call for independence.

[4] Lancaster, *A Sketch of the Early History of Hanover County*, 27.

[5] Ibid, 28.

Virginia on a war footing.[6] The buildup of colonial militias began shortly thereafter in anticipation of trouble.

In April 1775, some 700 of the King's troops advanced on Concord, in the Massachusetts Bay Province, to confiscate Massachusetts militia supplies. The militia met them at sunup. The exchange of shots and ensuing pitched battle marked the opening of armed hostilities and the beginning of the colonies' war of independence.[7] On May 10, 1775, the Continental Congress convened in Philadelphia to coordinate efforts of the thirteen colonies to secure British recognition of American rights.[8] Hardly had their work begun when on June 17, the first major battle of the Revolutionary War took place at Bunker Hill, where colonists of New England met British forces laying siege to Boston. That month, the Congress formed the Continental Army and unanimously chose General George Washington its commander-in-chief.[9]

During the summer of 1775, as the Continental Congress pursued its work in Philadelphia, the Virginia Convention met to begin creating Virginia militia regiments. Virginia raised its first militia regiments with a term of service not to exceed one year.[10] The recruits tended to come from the poorer elements of American society, to whom the army offered greater opportunity than did civilian life. Enlisted men were young, averaging about age twenty-two when they enlisted, and mostly common laborers.[11]

The Continental Congress authorized the Fourth Virginia Regiment of the Continental Army in December of 1775, saw it organized at Suffolk Court House, Virginia, and accepted it into the Continental Army on February 13, 1776. It was with this unit that Thomas Baldwin/Baulding [sic] saw action assigned to the Third Division of Major General Marquis de Lafayette at the Battle of Trenton, Battle of

---

[6] Wingfield, *A History of Caroline County*, 136.

[7] Sanchez-Saavedra, *A Guide to Virginia Military Organizations,* 7; Ward, *Charles Scott*, 10.

[8] Wright, *The Continental Army*, 21.

[9] Wright, *The Continental Army*, 23-25; Waldenmaier, *Some of the Earliest Oaths of Allegiance*, 1.

[10] Virginia's Soldiers in the Revolution, 19:408.

[11] Wright, *The Continental Army*, 184.

Princeton, Battle of Brandywine, Battle of Germantown, Battle of Monmouth, and the Siege of Charleston, South Carolina, not to mention the hardship of Valley Forge.[12] The regiment formally disbanded on January 1, 1783.

On July 2, 1776, the few dozen members of the Second Continental Congress crowded into the Pennsylvania State House, in Philadelphia (hence Independence Hall), to declare that the thirteen colonies they represented would no longer be part of the British Empire but a new nation independent of British rule. Two days later, the Congress ratified the eloquent text of Thomas Jefferson's declaration, an audacious piece of prose filled with self-evident truths but no certain promise of real success.

The Pennsylvania Militia was organized on March 7, 1777. The law required all able-bodied men between the ages of 18 and 53 to enroll. Observers have described the Pennsylvania Militia as easy-going duty. The men seldom drilled, and when called upon to perform during the war, it was usually for short tours of active duty, two or maybe three times. Many men who enrolled never saw a single day of active duty. A militiaman called for active duty could hire a substitute to fight in his place. The conduct of the Pennsylvania Militia, however, was not necessarily so with the Pennsylvania divisions of the Continental Line, which saw some of the toughest fighting of the War. Nevertheless, here, too, Pennsylvania lagged the other colonies to the point that troops mutinied against their officers. Pennsylvania was one of the stingiest when it came to paying its soldiers, many of whom served for three years for a $20 bounty.

A contributing issue for the organization of Pennsylvanians arose from the enrollment of militiamen on a geographical basis. Throughout the first two years of the war, most Pennsylvanians did not want to fight. For many, serving tours was not worth risking losing their crops. Moreover, the population of Pennsylvania was heavily Quaker, who opposed war and remained pacifistic throughout much of it. This was especially true in Chester County, which was almost entirely Quakers

---

[12] Revolutionary War Service Records, No. M881 Record Group 93, The National Archives.

and was the home of the Baldwin family. Although there were Baldwins who did not adhere to the Quaker faith, the Quakers cast out of favor those of other religions in the community if they participated in the War.

The area in and around Chester County saw some of the key events of the Revolutionary War. Philadelphia, immediately east of Chester County, was the site of both Continental Congresses as well as the de facto capital of the colonies. Valley Forge was on the Schuylkill River, which ran near the east boundary of the county. The Battle of Brandywine occurred on September 11, 1777, virtually in the backyard of the Baldwins in Chester County. The three original Baldwin brothers settled on and near Brandywine Creek. British forces overwhelmed General George Washington's Continental Army at Brandywine. Historian Henry S. Canby, in his analysis of the battle, blamed it on the strict neutrality of the Quakers. Quaker farms surrounded the site of the battle. The local population called Brandywine Creek the Quaker stream. When the battle appeared imminent, for the most part, Quaker men stayed quietly at home attending to their business. The movements of British Army General Charles Cornwallis' troops around the Continental right flank interrupted the quiet of a Fifth-day morning meeting. When the British occupied the meetinghouse, the Quakers hauled their benches to a grove of trees and held services in the shade. Their sincere dedication as noncombatants prevented them from intervening in the battle on either side. No one alerted Washington to the British movements around his right flank because that would be against their religion.[13]

There were others of the Baldwin name connected to the War. By 1777, eight militia companies had been organized in Connecticut. One of the soldiers mustered in was Sergeant Thomas Baldwin. He is of interest because he was from Westmoreland County, Connecticut, which once encompassed present Luzerne County, in northeast Pennsylvania. He was 22 years old when the army arrived at Valley Forge. However, he cannot be our Thomas Baldwin because Sergeant Baldwin died in 1819 in New York. Mention should also be made of one

---

[13] Canby, *The Brandywine*, 179, 193, 207-208, 218.

Captain Thomas Baldwin, who saw service along the Yadkin River, in Guilford County, North Carolina.[14] Regrettably, it is not possible to determine how he or any of the Thomas Baldwins who served in the Revolutionary War may or may not connect to the Baldwins of Pennsylvania, North Carolina, or Virginia, except to say that they and many of the Baldwin name answered the call to fight for American independence.

It is debatable whether the Baldwins migrated south before or after the Revolution, and likewise whether they came first to North Carolina or to Virginia. However, the family most certainly left Pennsylvania sometime after 1777 and was in North Carolina by 1796. The conclusive documentation of the birth of Rebecca Baldwin Jackson in Pennsylvania is sufficient to establish this claim.[15] Circumstantial evidence regarding her assumed siblings, Sarah and Jeremiah Baldwin, is further corroboration. Sarah married Samuel McClure. He was born in Chester County, Pennsylvania.[16] The couple was married in Virginia, and documents sometimes give Sarah's birthplace as Virginia. However, it seems likely that, like Samuel, she, too, was a native of Pennsylvania. Moreover, Jeremiah Baldwin, who appeared in tax records with Thomas, Sr., and was likely his youngest son, also had a son named Thomas who indicated in 1880 that his father—Jeremiah—was born in Pennsylvania.[17]

At the close of the Revolutionary War, multiple migration routes connected Pennsylvania and New England with the southern states. The preferred route south was the Great Warrior's Path, which was originally a network of ancient Indian paths, later known as the Great Wagon Road. Other roads also existed, such as the Fall Line, Upper

---

[14] Pension Applications of the Guilford County, N.C., Soldiers of the Revolutionary War, Pension Application of Isaac Jones, Natl. Archives Microseries M804, Roll 1439, Application #S31777, The Society of the Descendants of Washington's Army at Valley Forge.

[15] Find a Grave Memorial ID 74484468.

[16] 1850 US Census, Fairfield, Highland, Ohio, Record Group Number: 29, Series Number: M432, Roll: 694, p. 130b, National Archives; see also *History of Ross and Highland Counties Ohio.* Cleveland, Ohio: Williams Bros., 1880, pp. 96, 402, 414-415.

[17] 1880 US Census, Scioto, Ross, Ohio, Roll: 1063, p. 354B, Enumeration District: 155, NARA.

Road, and others. These roads ran mostly along a line north and south within the coastal areas of the colonies and connected to the highly traveled King's Highway, which ran south along the coast. The inland path of the Great Wagon Road offered a more direct connection between eastern Pennsylvania and North Carolina, along the Appalachian Valley to Virginia, and connecting Philadelphia with the North Carolina settlements via a journey of some 750 miles.[18] It could be a dangerous route. Many families who traveled it fell victim to the Indians in the early years, and it was not passable for wagons until the 1790s. Private contractors authorized to keep up sections of the road charged tolls for their use.

The diverse backgrounds of the immigrants who came down the Great Wagon Road shaped the North Carolina backcountry into a patchwork of religious and cultural enclaves. A large number of newcomers from Pennsylvania were Quakers; German families were predominantly Lutheran, except for the German Moravians; and immigrants of Scotch-Irish heritage were invariably Presbyterian.

Moreover, the Great Awakening, a religious revival that swept the English colonies in the mid-eighteenth century, resulted in the founding of several Baptist churches in the Carolina backcountry.[19]

Most of the Baldwins of the present line were not members of the Society of Friends, i.e., Quakers. However, some were, and others married into Quaker families. Even for those who did not openly profess the Quaker faith, there is ample evidence that the Baldwin family closely interacted with their Quaker neighbors, generally agreed with Quaker

The Great Wagon Road. The white overlay line on the opposite 1755 map traces the path of the Great Wagon Road from Philadelphia to Anson County, North Carolina. Anson County originally occupied a vast territory with indefinite northern and western boundaries. Once home to the Catawba Siouan tribe, the area became the destination of large numbers of migrants after the Revolutionary War. Joshua Fry, *A Map of the Most Inhabited Part of Virginia* [Containing Parts of Pennsylvania and North Carolina], [1755]. Library of Congress Geography and Map Division Washington, D.C.

---

[18] Joe A. Mobley, Ed., Elizabeth A. Fenn, et al., *The Way We Lived in North Carolina*, 2003. Chapel Hill, N.C.: University of North Carolina Press, 2003.

[19] William S. Powell, Ed., *Encyclopedia of North Carolina*, Chapel Hill, N.C.: University of North Carolina Press, 2006.

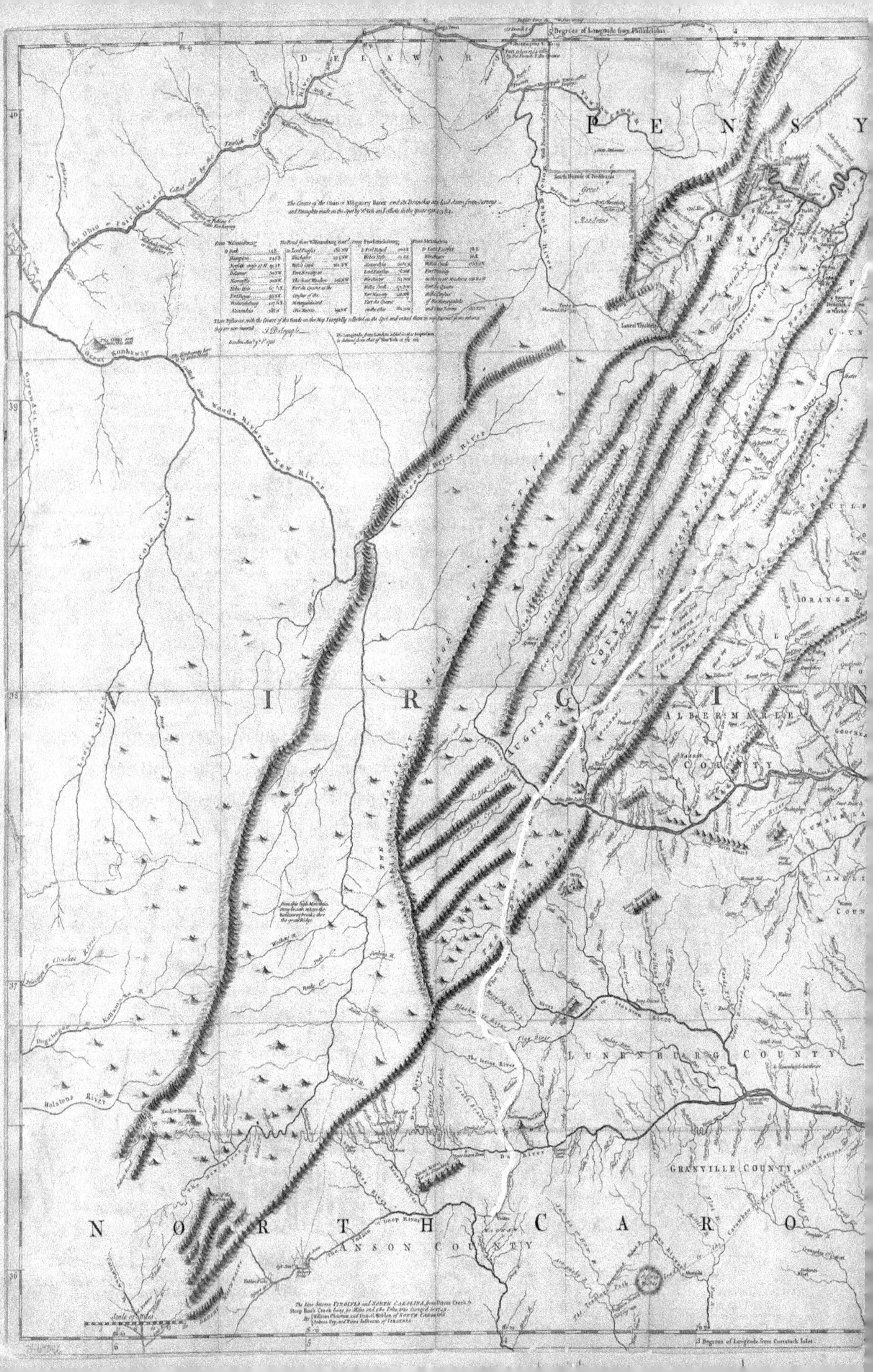

DELAWAR

PENSY

South Branch of Petomack

Great Meadows

The Courſe of the Ohio or Alligany River, and its Branches my laid down from Surveys
and Draughts made on the Spot by W Gist an Elliots in the year 1753, 54.

The Ohio or Fair River

VIRGIN

Woods River and New River

THE GREAT RIDGE

AUGUSTA COUNTY

ALBEMARLE
COUNTY

ORANGE

Greenbryar River

Cole River

Louisa River

NORTH CARO

ANSON COUNTY

LUNENBURG COUNTY

GRANVILLE COUNTY

Holstons River

Great Konhaway

A MAP of
the most INHABITED part of
VIRGINIA
containing the whole PROVINCE of
MARYLAND
with Part of
PENSILVANIA, NEW JERSEY and NORTH CAROLINA
Drawn by
Joshua Fry & Peter Jefferson
in 1751

To the Right Honourable, George Dunk Earl of Halifax, First Lord Commissioner, and to the Rest of the Right Honourable and Honourable Commissioners, for Trade and Plantations, This Map is most humbly Inscribed to their Lordships, By their Lordships Most Obedient & most devoted humble Servt. Thos. Jefferys.

PENSILVANIA

MARYLAND

VIRGINIA

NEW JERSEY
EAST PART OF NEW JERSEY
PART OF

NORTH CAROLINA

DE LA WAR BAY

CHESAPEAKE BAY

BALTIMORE COUNTY
ANN ARUNDEL COUNTY
CHARLES COUNTY
DORCHESTER CO.
TALBOT COUNTY
KENT ISLAND
SUSSEX COUNTY
NEW CASTLE COUNTY

FAIRFAX COUNTY
PRINCE WILLIAM COUNTY
STAFFORD COUNTY
HANOVER COUNTY
GLOUCESTER COUNTY
CHARLES CITY COUNTY
PRINCE GEORGE COUNTY
SURREY COUNTY
SOUTHAMPTON COUNTY
BRUNSWICK COUNTY
NANSEMOND COUNTY
PRINCESS ANN COUNTY
NORFOLK COUNTY
ISLE OF WIGHT COUNTY

ACCOMACK COUNTY
NORTHAMPTON COUNTY

BERTIE PRECINCT
CHOWAN PRECINCT

LANCASTER CO.
CHESTER COUNTY
GLOUCESTER COUNTY
SALEM COUNTY
CUMBERLAND COUNTY
CAPE MAY COUNTY

THE DISMAL SWAMP

ALBEMARLE SOUND

CAPE HENLOPEN
CAPE MAY
CAPE CHARLES
CAPE HENRY

The Line between Virginia and North Carolina from the Sea to Peters Creek, was Surveyed in 1728, by the Honble. Wm. Byrd, Wm. Dandridge and Richard Fitzwilliams Commissioners, and Mr. Alexander Irwine and Mr. W.m. Mayo, Surveyors.

Engraved and Published according to Act of Parliament by Thos. Jefferys, Geographer to His Royal Highness the Prince of Wales at the Corner of St. Martins Lane, Charing Cross, London.

dogma opposing slavery, and joined in mass Quaker migrations to the South and, later, to the Midwest.

The Society of Friends originated in England in 1650 as an alternative to the Puritans. Their strict dogma declared, "One must tremble at the mere mention of the word of the Lord;" hence, the label Quakers or Shakers. One of the most famous among the sect was William Penn of Pennsylvania. They suffered great persecution for their beliefs. A massive exodus of the midland Quakers of England brought them to America in 1681, the large majority of them settling in Pennsylvania. From there, they migrated south into Virginia and North Carolina, and later to Indiana. They did not believe in a formal clergy or weekly service. Instead, they required Monthly Meetings at designated meetinghouses, at which they recorded events and actions of each Monthly Meeting. Monthly Meetings often required long journeys by members not living in proximity to a meetinghouse. The first Quaker establishment in Chester County, Pennsylvania, was in 1718 at New Garden Monthly Meeting. The Society of Friends had settled in Chester County by 1712, meeting in homes until a meetinghouse went up in 1717 on land patented by William Penn. The New Garden Monthly Meeting name—originally in remembrance of New Garden Meeting, in County Carlow, Ireland—became the name of New Garden Meeting places in North Carolina, and later in Indiana.

One of the earliest Quaker meeting sites in Virginia was at Hopewell Monthly Meeting, in Frederick County, Virginia, established about 1734. Baldwins were early residents of Frederick County, although not necessarily associated with Hopewell. Nevertheless, one of the founders of Hopewell was one Thomas Thornbrough, a name often found in the marriage records of our Baldwin family and a name prominent in Pennsylvania, North Carolina, and Virginia Quaker history. For example, Jeremiah Baldwin, son of our Thomas, Sr., married Hannah Thornbrough. This has prompted some genealogists to speculate that the present line of Baldwins passed through Frederick County, Virginia. However, records do not specifically support such a claim.

Meanwhile, the Quaker presence along the migration trail extended to North Carolina. In 1754, there was a New Garden Monthly Meeting in Guilford County, North Carolina. The Guilford County reference by historians is somewhat misleading because Guilford County did not form until 1770 out of Rowan and Orange counties. Nevertheless, it was to the western part of this region that our Baldwin family migrated about 1795. Rowan later branched off into Surrey County. In 1786, Quakers created Westfield Monthly Meeting in Surrey County, not far from the Virginia line. Westfield Monthly Meeting was on the northern border of North Carolina, on the eastern border of Surry County, approximately 25 miles east of what became Ashe County in 1799, and where the Baldwins lived in 1796. The meetinghouse was 5 miles from the Virginia border and about 25 miles southeast of where the Baldwins later settled in Grayson County, Virginia.

It was to Westfield Monthly Meeting that Hannah Ricks Baldwin— not to be confused with Hannah Thornbrough Baldwin—requested a transfer from Springfield Monthly Meeting, a request granted by certificate in September 1797. Springfield was part of the New Garden Quarter established in 1790. Springfield Monthly Meeting condemned Hannah for her marriage out of unity to Thomas Baldwin on January 2, 1796, in Guilford County. Hannah was born on February 23, 1771, the eldest daughter of Jonas Ricks.[1] Circumstantial evidence suggests that she was the wife of our Thomas Baldwin, Jr. Her age coincides with the estimated age of Thomas, Jr., and there were Hannah Baldwins in the family. Moreover, her requested transfer from Springfield Monthly Meeting to Westfield on the Virginia Border coincides with the movements of the Baldwin family from North Carolina to Virginia. Ironically, the same Quaker admonishment against out-of-faith marriage befell the probable ancestor of Thomas, Jr., when Hannah Coebourne received the same punishment for marrying Anthony Baldwin in 1712, in Chester County, Pennsylvania.

---

[1] Donald M. Ricks, *The Descendants of Jonas Ricks and Other Ricks Families in America*, Dexter, Mich. 1998, pp. 87, 96.

Southern Roots

9

Baldwins of North Carolina

The children of Thomas Baldwin, Sr., Rebecca and Joshua, were born in Chester County, Pennsylvania. The family left Pennsylvania sometime after the Revolutionary War. The marriages of his children indicate that by 1798, Thomas had settled in Grayson County, Virginia. The birthplace of his grandson, Thomas Lee Baldwin, in Ashe County, North Carolina, in 1796, suggests the family migrated first to North Carolina before settling permanently in Grayson County. They likely followed the Quaker migration route along the Great Wagon Road to Ashe County. The heavily traveled Great Wagon Road extended from Philadelphia to the Yadkin River in North Carolina, a journey of more than 500 miles. From Ashe County, they then moved nearby across the Virginia border to Grayson County, Virginia.

Movement of the Baldwin family from Pennsylvania to North Carolina followed the trend of southward migration after the Revolutionary War, when large numbers of Pennsylvanians—mostly Quakers—left their homeland for the adventures of the open frontier. The major incentive of early pioneers was the promise of cheaper land and the opportunities that it offered. At the same time, however, many adventurous souls longed to escape the religious and political domination of their ancestral roots for the choice of religious freedom. We do not know the religion to which Thomas Baldwin and his family subscribed, if any. They appear to have descended from an Episcopalian family but with strong ties to the Quaker faith, a few at least being of the Quaker Society of Friends Church. A brief overview of the religious climate into which Thomas moved suggests a plethora of religious choices.

The religious history of Ashe County, North Carolina, and the territory of Grayson County, Virginia, adjacent to it, was free from domination of any particular religious sect for many years. The earliest religious group to explore the region that became Ashe County was the Moravians—German-speaking protestants—looking for a new home for the group in 1752.[1] They found Ashe County unsuitable for their purpose and in 1772 settled in Winston-Salem, North Carolina. However, some of the party returned a decade later to the Ashe County vicinity where, with a handful of other pioneers, which included Daniel Boone, they established families. Boone, a Quaker, spent time in the eastern part of Ashe County, near present-day Obids, before moving on to other pioneering adventures.

J. F. Fletcher, in his book on the history of Ashe County, concluded that the majority of pioneers who first settled in the county were not Quakers but either Presbyterians or Episcopalians, followed by the Baptists.[2] "The earliest Baptists in the region organized in Grayson County, Virginia," he wrote. Hardly any churches of any kind lay west of the Blue Ridge Mountains. This famous range of mountains served to cut off all of the territory lying west of it, from Wilkes County and the remainder of North Carolina, and allied it with Virginia. Church history does not easily separate Ashe County, North Carolina, from Grayson County, Virginia. For example, Fletcher tells the story of the alleged organization of a Baptist church in Grayson County known as the "North Fork of New River Church," in 1796, at about the same time the Baldwins coincidentally arrived in North Carolina from Pennsylvania. Historically aligned with Grayson County, this 1796 Baptist church was undoubtedly in Ashe County, North Carolina, and not Virginia, according to Fletcher, "as no part of the north fork of New River touches Grayson County anywhere. All of it lies in Ashe County. The church had thirteen members." Meanwhile, Meadow Creek Baptist Church, in the lower end of Grayson County, Virginia, also organized in 1796. The Baptist churches in Ashe County, North Carolina, associated themselves with the Virginia Baptists, and they remained so allied for a hundred years.[3] The history of the growth of the Baptists in Ashe and Grayson

---

[1] The Moravians are one of the oldest European Protestant denominations, which originated in Bohemia in 1457. Primarily a German speaking sect, there is no evidence that the Baldwins had Moravian affiliations.

[2] J. F. Fletcher, *A History of Ashe County*, p. 8.

[3] Fletcher, *A History of Ashe County*, p. 10.

counties included the highly respected Rev. Noah C. Baldwin, who served the church in the mid-19th century.

Meanwhile, the Methodists were the next to organize in this territory, after the Presbyterians, Episcopalians, and Baptists. However, it would be several years before the Methodists found their way through the

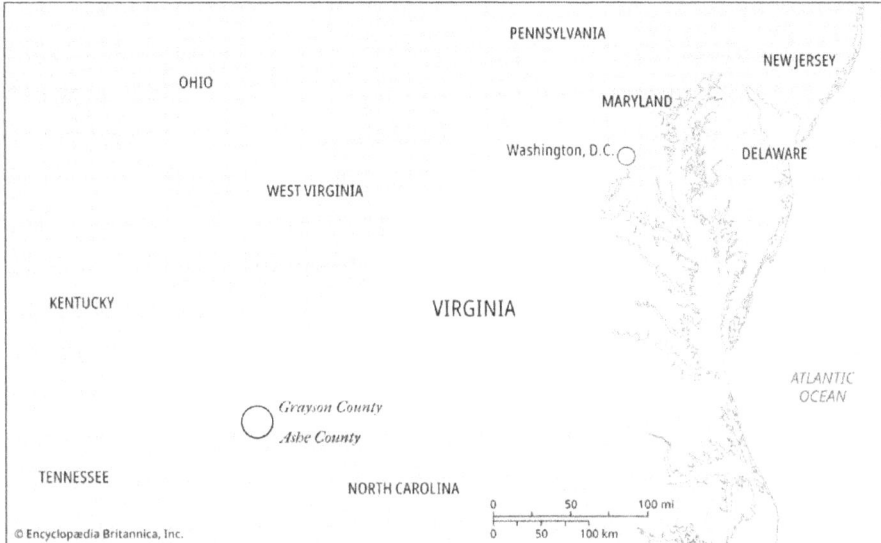

Map of Virginia and North Carolina. Grayson County, Virginia, lay across the border from Ashe County, North Carolina. Courtesy of Encyclopedia Britannica.

Alleghenies. They first arrived about 1785 in the form of old-fashioned Methodist preachers calculated to make an impression steeped in the Methodist doctrine in opposition to Calvinism, which was the prevailing doctrine of that time. One of its able leaders was one John Baldwin, who, with others, crisscrossed the frontier settlements and by 1791, raised upwards of 1,000 Methodist societies.[4]

In addition to those denominations previously named, many of the earliest settlers were of Quaker background, from such heavily Quaker areas as Chester County, Pennsylvania. A Quaker Society of Friends meetinghouse appeared on the New River border frontier about 1785. Certificates went first to Deep River Monthly Meeting in North Carolina, but then eventually to the Mount Pleasant Meeting of Grayson County, Virginia. The Mount Pleasant Meeting discontinued about

---

[4] Anderson-Green, 431n "Some Early New River Pioneers," Virginia Historical Society.

1826 because of the migration of most of its members to Ohio and other western areas. Perhaps a more significant reason for the decline in Quaker influence was the conversion of many settlers to the Methodist and Baptist churches.

Throughout the time of settlement of western North Carolina, there were among the earliest adventurers those of the Baldwin name. There is in the northeast corner of Ashe County, North Carolina, across the border from Whitetop, Virginia, a stream called Baldwin Branch, which attests to the wide presence of the Baldwin family in northwest North Carolina and southwest Virginia.[5] Many families of the Baldwin name are still present there today. On the list of early settlers was Elisha Baldwin, probable kin of John Baldwin the Methodist organizer, and the first of the Baldwin family to settle permanently in Ashe County. Elisha was in North Carolina by 1759 when he appeared in the 1759 tax list for Rowan County, North Carolina.[6] Rowan County, at that time, encompassed all of western North Carolina, including that part that later became Wilkes County, and then Ashe County. He was probably the Elisha Baldwin of Wilkes County, in the Morgan District of North Carolina, who supported the Revolutionary War with Patriotic Services, and received pay for services rendered.[7]

According to Fletcher, Elisha was "one of the big real estate men of the day."[8] At one time, he owned more than 1,600 acres, mostly on Potato Creek and Piney Creek where he lived, and on both sides of

---

[5] Baldwin Branch N.C. Ashe stream 36.5840086-81.5965012, located across the border from Whitetop, Virginia; 1790 US Census, North Carolina, Surry, Salisbury Dist., NARA Series: M637 Roll: 7, p. 516.

[6] 1754, 1759 Rowan County, North Carolina Tax Lists. This tax list was found between the walls of the old courthouse. The list was made before Rowan Co, N.C. was divided into other counties and is the oldest tax list ever found in Rowan County.

[7] From DAR application: Ancestor # A005242. Elisha Baldwin, Service: North Carolina Rank: Patriotic Service, Birth (Ante) 1755 North Carolina, Death (circa) 1820 Ashe Co., N.C., Service Source: N.C. Rev Army Accts, Vol. I, p 10, Folio 2, #1198, Service Description: Paid for Services Rendered, Residence.-Wilkes Co.-Morgan dist.–N.C.

[8] Arthur L. Fletcher, *Ashe County, a History*.

Bakers Ridge, in present-day Alleghany County.[9] From 1785 until 1795, he entered grants totaling 675 acres registered in Wilkes County, and then from 1799 until 1807 added 13 more grants for 925 acres registered in Ashe County in the same general location on Potato Creek. His sons continued to acquire land in the vicinity until the family owned, or had owned, upwards of 3,000 acres on the northern border of Ashe County.[10] Although there is no known connection between our Thomas Baldwin, Sr., of Pennsylvania and this Elisha Baldwin, it is remarkable that Thomas chose to settle next door to Elisha. By 1796, the two of them were neighbors in Ashe County. However, Thomas never enjoyed the same success in real estate, as did Elisha.

Settlers acquired frontier land through different means. For example, an act of the Virginia General Assembly passed on June 22, 1779, established the Virginia Land Office, which provided for the rewarding of lands promised as bounty for specified Revolutionary War military service. Several men of the Baldwin name, including a Thomas Baldwin of Virginia, received warrants.[11] However, this was probably not our Thomas but a descendant of the established Baldwins of Virginia, where many of the Baldwin name had ancestors dating to the beginning of the colony in the 1600s.

Meanwhile, land acquisition in North Carolina after the Revolution was different from land patents in Virginia and elsewhere. Originally, North Carolina was a proprietary colony managed by the Earl of Granville of Great Britain, who held the title for much of the land. Residents paid a quit rent to the Earl, hoping eventually to acquire title to the land they rented. In 1777, the North Carolina General Assembly confiscated the Earl's holdings and assumed title of the land for the State.

---

[9] Bureau of Land Management (BLM), General Land Office (GLO) Records.

[10] State Archives of North Carolina, Raleigh, N. C, North Carolina Land Grant Images and Data.

[11] The papers accumulated as proof of service are now part of the records of the Executive Dept. Office of the Governor (RG#3) called "Bounty Warrants" housed in the Archives at the Library of Virginia. In order to qualify for bounty land, a soldier had to serve at least three (3) years continuously in the State or Continental line. Militia service did not count. When the claim was proved, the Governor's Office issued a certificate to the register of the Land Office authorizing him to issue a warrant.

The state in turn, issued land grants to its citizens for a nominal fee. Inhabitants or land speculators could acquire the land fee simple. Consequently, North Carolina land became more affordable than land in Virginia, making North Carolina an attractive destination for migrants moving south and west.[12]

Elisha Baldwin began purchasing land in northern Wilkes County, North Carolina.[13] Wilkes County came out of what was once Rowan County in 1778. In 1799, he bought land in Ashe County in that part that was formerly Wilkes, which became Alleghany County in 1859.[14] Although the geography changed, Elisha remained in approximately the same location on Piney Creek, Potato Creek, and Bakers Ridge, in the Blue Ridge Mountains of North Carolina, directly across the border from Grayson County, Virginia. The 1790 US Census recorded Elisha in Wilkes County, enumerated as household 68 of 76 households in Company 10.[15] A decade later, the 1800 Census located him and his large family at the same place in the Morgan District of recently constituted Ashe County.[16] Unfortunately, Thomas Baldwin, Sr., does not appear in either of the North Carolina census years of 1790 or 1800. Due to the shifting nature of North Carolina and Virginia boundaries, he may have appeared in the Virginia 1800 and 1810 census records, which were burned in 1814. He first appeared in the US Census in 1820, in Grayson

---

[12] Abstracts of Upper New River Valley Land Grants from Wilkes Co., Records, 1778-1783-Wilkes County Deed Book 1.

[13] Ralph E. Baldwin, *Theophilus Baldwin 1792 - 1851 and His Descendants* "We can place the purchase of the earliest plot of land by Elisha Baldwin in 1778 in Wilkes County."

[14] Paula H. Anderson-Green, The New River Frontier Settlement on the Virginia-North Carolina Border 1760-1820, *Virginia Magazine of History and Biography*, Vol. 86: pgs. 413-431 (1978). This source records the transaction as being in Alleghany County in 1780. However, Alleghany County did not form until 1859.

[15] 1800 US Census, Morgan, Ashe, North Carolina, Series: M32, Roll: 29, p. 72. There were four Baldwin families listed in Ashe County in the 1800 census. Although believed to be members of the same family, the alphabetized census lists provide no context to the proximity of the families to each other. Thomas Baldwin was not among the Baldwin families listed.

[16] Ibid.

County, Virginia.[17] According to Grayson County tax records, he had settled in the area by 1794.[18] The previous year—1793—a Thomas Baldwine [sic] was in Wythe County, Virginia.[19] He is probably our Thomas, Sr., because Grayson County was formed in November 1792/1793 when the county of Wythe was divided. His tax on one horse and no tithables suggests a Spartan beginning for this young family in their new home away from Pennsylvania.

Meanwhile, there were other Baldwins in western North Carolina. For example, Zenas Baldwin appeared in the 1790 Surry County tax list owning 200 acres, and again in the 1790 census with a large family of 12 (and no slaves).[20] Surry County came out of Rowan County and was the parent company of Wilkes County. Further east, in Guilford County, North Carolina, we find in 1790 the Baldwins, Daniel and Uriah, and in Orange County, in central North Carolina, John Baldwin, to name a few.[21] There is no evidence that these Baldwins are linked to Elisha Baldwin of Ashe County or Thomas Baldwin, Sr. Their presence in the same geographic location at the same time, however, and having offspring named Thomas, complicates the sorting of the Baldwin line of Thomas Baldwin, Sr., of North Carolina and Grayson County.

The importance of Elisha Baldwin and others of the Baldwin name at this particular period of the present Baldwin history lies in the possible connection of Thomas Baldwin, Sr., of Pennsylvania to the Baldwins of North Carolina, whose presence preceded him in the area where he settled. There are, of course, many possible reasons why Thomas, Sr., may have left the established environment of Pennsylvania for the wilderness of the western frontier. Whether he came because of religion, cheap land, or some other probative cause, kinship of migrant families is often a root cause of families removing from one location to another.

---

[17] 1820 U S Census, Grayson, Virginia, Series M33 Roll 131, pp. 43, 54. National Archives.

[18] Grayson County, Virginia Personal Property Tax List 1794.

[19] Grayson County, Virginia Personal Property Tax List 1794.

[20] Anderson-Green, Some Early New River Pioneers, Virginia Historical Society, 431n.

[21] 1790 US Census, North Carolina, Guilford, Salisbury Dist. Series: M637 Roll: 7, p. 496; 1790 US Census, North Carolina, Orange, St. Marys Dist. Tax. Series: M637 Roll: 7, p. 30, National Archives.

To that end, there is coincidental evidence of an ancestral connection. Elisha Baldwin was born in 1742, allegedly in Chester County, Pennsylvania, to John Baldwin. John died in Wilkes County, North Carolina, in 1794 after a long illness. We find in the Wilkes County, North Carolina Will Book records of the administration of the estate of John Baldwin on November 7, 1794. Elisha Baldwin, with James Baldwin—probable sons of John—served as administrators of the estate. A week later, Elisha returned an inventory of the estate to the court, and, in the spring of the following year, he was one of the purchasers at the estate sale, along with William Baldwin. In the May 1795 Term of Court, Elisha filed a claim against the estate for expenses in taking care of his father over a period of six years. The claim read, "Administration claim of Elisha Baldwin, Admr. Estate John Baldwin, dec'd: May 20, 1789. Keeping 4 head horses 5 months; riding to Guilford County, employing hand to ride to the Doctor and riding 3 days after Dr. Means; Jun 2, 1792; taking 4 horse creatures 6 months; Nov 15, 1792: Riding 3 weeks after horses ran away, tending upon him 9 months being sick and getting necessarys [sic] such as he wanted; Dec 1793: wintering 3 horses, corn & fodder; March 3rd: He deceased and was buried at my expense; Dec 1794 & 1795; wintering 3 horses---Total amount 59 pounds, 8 shillings."[22] There was a family squabble in court over the estate settlement. Jacob Baldwin entered a Plea of Trespass against Elisha and James. The case settled, and there was no suit.[23] Numerous court appearances and land records document the presence of Elisha Baldwin in Ashe County from at least 1759 until he died in 1812.[24]

---

[22] Wilkes County, N.C., Will Book I, pp 404, 450.

[23] Court Records 104.508.11, Wilkes Estates Records, 1794. John Baldwin–"you [Sheriff of Wilkes County] are commanded to bring in body Elisha Baldwin, Exr. John Baldwin, deceased to answer to Jacob Baldwin in a plea of Trespass. Court Min. 7 Nov 1794-Letters Adm gr Elisha on est. John Baldwin Deceased." 4 May 1796 "Jacob Baldwin vs. James Baldwin and Elisha Baldwin, Administrators: No suit." Archives of North Carolina.

[24] Mrs. W. O. Absher, *Wilkes County Court Minutes 1789-1797*, Vol. 4, p. 18, 5 May 1795. "Ord. Elisha Baldwin, [et al]...view road from Zacheriah Wells road come into John Glossups road to Virginia line, crossing New River at horse ford," p. 31, 4 May 1796. Ord. Elisha Baldwin, [et al]...being on S & N side Potato Creek, work on road to top of Chestnut Ridge & Michael Bumgarner be overseer, p. 42. 1797? Ord. Elisha

There is no documented proof of a direct relationship of Elisha Baldwin to John Baldwin, earlier mentioned as the Methodist clergyman of Ashe County, although genealogists suspect Elisha and John were brothers, nor is there proof that Elisha was the son of John Baldwin of Bucks County, Pennsylvania, as others claim. Likewise, there is insufficient documentation at this time to link his family with Thomas Baldwin, Sr., of Chester County, Pennsylvania.[25] However, the birth of Thomas' grandson, Thomas Lee Baldwin, in Ashe County in 1796, lends circumstantial evidence of a family connection. Both families settled within a day's ride of each other in the same vicinity on the upper plateau of the Blue Ridge Mountains.

Neither Elisha Baldwin nor his descendants owned slaves, a quality shared by our Thomas Baldwin, Sr., and all of his descendants but not necessarily shared by others of the Baldwin name living in North Carolina and Virginia. The role of slavery in a family tree, especially in the critical period of the Baldwins' relocation from Pennsylvania to Virginia, may distinguish families of the same surname. Thomas Baldwin, Sr., and none of his descendants owned slaves. However, this

---

Baldwin, [et al]... view road from George Bargers at Praters Creek to about half mile below Samuel Robinetts; see also Ashe County Deeds [index on microfilm] Deed Books A & B, p 434 12 May 1802 Elisha Baldwin witnessed land transaction on Laurel Fork of New River; see also Ashe County, North Carolina Court of Pleas and Quarter Sessions, May Term 1808 "Ordered by the Court that Joshua Cox, the present register call on the widow or heirs of Elisha Baldwin, the former register to get the books and all papers relative to the registers office and to safely keep the same." August Term 1808 "A deed from Elisha Baldwin to Wm. Baldwin for 75 acres proven by the oath of Isaac Baldwin." August Term 1810 "A deed from Elisha Baldwin to Jos. Baldwin for 150 acres proved by Jno. McMillion;" Find a Grave Memorial ID 113202251.

[25] Names of Pensioners for Revolutionary or Military Services, including Ages and Names of Heads of Families with Whom Pensioners Resided June 1, 1840. This material was returned by the marshals of the several judicial districts under "The Act for Taking The Sixth Census," under the direction of the secretary of state. Printed in 1841 by Blair and Rives, Washington, D.C., and compiled by Mary Campbell Chappell. Listed are John Baldwin, age 79, and John Baldwin, Jr. This is part of the valuable genealogical research material of Mary Campbell Chappell, found after her death in 2003.

does not rule out the possibility that a Baldwin raised in an anti-slavery household did not succumb to the use of slavery afterwards.

10

Ashe County

The earliest confirmed evidence of Thomas Baldwin, Sr., outside of Pennsylvania comes from North Carolina. His grandson, Thomas Lee Baldwin—patriarch of the present Baldwin line—was born on 12 Mar 1796, and, according to family tradition, was born in Ashe County, North Carolina.[1] However, he must have been born in the area of Wilkes County that later became Ashe County because a county by the name of Ashe did not exist until three years after his birth, when the North Carolina General Assembly officially formed Ashe County in 1799.

An analysis of the history of the geography of the county may shed light on the claim that Thomas Lee was born in Ashe County in 1796, when the county did not form until 1799. The Morgan District Brigade was an administrative division of the North Carolina militia during the American Revolutionary War. Established by the North Carolina Provincial Congress on May 17, 1782, the unit disbanded at the end of the war, but the district name remained. Morgan District was in the Yadkin Division, one of ten representative divisions created by the US Congress in 1789 when North Carolina joined the Union. The district included Wilkes County, the parent of Ashe County. Following the first US Census in 1790, Yadkin Division dropped the name Morgan District in 1792, and included both Ashe County and Wilkes County as part of the First Congressional District, although the General Assembly did not officially separate Ashe County from Wilkes County until 1799.[2] The

---

[1] Find a Grave, Thomas Lee Baldwin, Memorial ID 5495587. Memorial page for Thomas Lee Baldwin (12 Mar 1796–26 Nov 1879), citing Gum Springs Cemetery, Stockton, Cedar County, Missouri, maintained by Richard Baldwin (contributor 46484194). Born 12 Mar 1796, a date confirmed by his gravestone that records his death 26 Nov 1879 at the age of 83 years, 8 months, and 14 days.

[2] United States. Dept. of State, *Return of the Whole Number of Persons within the Several Districts of the United States*. Philadelphia: Childs & Swaine, 1791, according to "An act providing for the enumeration of the inhabitants of the United States,"

North Carolina County Formation. Maps show approximate county divisions within present state boundaries for the years beginning in 1775, 1780, and 1800. The western portion of the state remained sparsely populated well into the 19th century. Ashe County, associated with **Thomas Baldwin,** formed in 1799. Ashe was originally part of Rowen County and then Wilkes County. Previously identified as the District of Ashe, it once extended into Surrey County. Maps by L. Polk, Denmark.

NORTH CAROLINA
AT THE BEGINNING OF
1775

NORTH CAROLINA
AT THE BEGINNING OF
1780

NORTH CAROLINA
AT THE BEGINNING OF
1800

1792 date of Ashe County as a demographic district is significant to the Baldwin family history because it implies that there was a section identified as Ashe County at the time of the birth of Thomas Lee Baldwin.[3] Therefore, notwithstanding its official creation date of 1799, officials recognized a section of North Carolina called Ashe as early as 1792 when it became part of the First District of US congressional representation from North Carolina, supplanting the old Morgan District of 1789.[4] Thus, we may conclude that Thomas Lee was born in that section of Wilkes County called Ashe.

The conundrum of the birth of Thomas Lee Baldwin, allegedly in Ashe County, is part of the formation of the county itself. Ashe County is in the far northwestern corner of the State of North Carolina, bounded on the north by Grayson County, Virginia, and on the west by

---

passed March the first, one thousand seven hundred and ninety-one [i.e. 1790] (American Imprint Collection, Library of Congress).

[3] Corbitt, D. L. Congressional Districts of North Carolina, 1789-1934. *The North Carolina Historical Review.* Vol. 12, No. 2 (April 1935), pp. 173-188, pp. 174-175.

[4] Ibid.

Tennessee. Watauga County lies to the south, and Wilkes County touches Ashe on the south and southeast. Alleghany County bounds it on the east. Originally, Ashe County, Alleghany County, and part of Watauga County were part of Wilkes County. Therefore, when investigating the locations of the movements of the Baldwin family, it is necessary to associate county records with the founding dates of the counties involved. For instance, Rowan County, North Carolina, became a county in 1753, and was divided into Surry County in 1771. Wilkes County came from Surry County in 1777, and part of Wilkes became Ashe County in 1799. Genealogical records in any of these North Carolina counties may potentially relate to the same family, although they may appear to identify different families in different locations. The rapid growth of population on the western frontier in the late 18th century caused a commensurate growth in counties, whereby a family in one county appeared to move to another county when, in fact, they did not move at all. What changed was the geography around them. County records usually remained with the original county. Thus, hypothetically, a Baldwin family that lived in Rowan County, North Carolina, before 1771, and in Surry County until 1777, may be the same Baldwin family living in Ashe County after 1799.

Ashe County borders Tennessee on the west and Virginia on the north, located entirely within the Appalachian Mountains region of North Carolina. Much of the county sits atop a rolling plateau some 3,000 feet above sea level. Mountains and hills cover the plateau, dominated by Mount Jefferson, which at an elevation of nearly 5,000 feet towers above the landscape.[5] The legislative charter that designated Ashe County identified the region as "that part of the County of Wilkes, lying west of the extreme height of the Appalachian Mountains."[6] Relatively inaccessible, the region was once one of North Carolina's

---

[5] Ashe County out of Wilkes County 1799, Wilkes out of Surry 1777. , Surry out of Rowan 1771, Rowan out of Anson 1753, Anson out of Bladen 1750, Bladen out of New Hanover County, 1734, New Hanover out of Craven 1729, Craven out of Bath 1705, Bath created 1696 precincts renamed Beaufort, Hyde, and Craven, Bath abolished in 1739.

[6] John H. Wheeler, *Historical sketches of North Carolina from 1584 to 1851*, pp. 168-169.

"Lost Provinces," so-called in the 1800s. Lowlanders joked that the only way to get there was to be born there.[7] In the mountainous northwest corner of the state, west of the Eastern Continental Divide, the high Blue Ridge Mountains isolated Ashe County from the rest of the state, where it remained underserved by roads and railroads for decades. Transportation in the county exhibited meager beginnings, relying on trails used by horses and pack animals. Enterprising pioneers constructed a few all-weather roads, several of which were private and required the payment of toll fees.[8] The first highway to connect Ashe County to points east did not arrive in the county until 1911. The area's mountainous topography caused the county to be closely connected to Grayson County, Virginia, and other destinations that shared a location on the west side of the Alleghany foothills.

Today, Ashe County is a traditional, mountain community, steeped in the traditions and values developed through experience and struggle. From its earliest days, the county enjoyed an Arcadian and idyllic setting. The main river in the county is the New River, a very old river, which, uncharacteristic of rivers in Appalachia, flows north. Many creeks and streams of the New River Basin feed the New River in Ashe County. The mountainous scenery and pleasant climate historically sustained extensive ranges for pasture and rural farmland where cattle and poultry were agricultural mainstays. Although the face of the county is mountainous, its fertile valleys have long yielded a host of grain crops and vegetables in abundance. It has extensive ranges for pasture, pure air and water, and a favorable climate. The county once boasted an abundance of iron and saltpeter.[9] Today, we know Ashe County for its Christmas tree farms, which have for several years, furnished the National Christmas tree for the White House in Washington, D.C.

The history of Ashe County adds a colorful chapter to the geography that the Thomas Baldwin family called home. Ashe County was once home to the Cherokee, Creek, and Shawnee Indian tribes. The first

---

[7] Dave Tabler, (August 30, 2016). The Lost Provinces. Appalachian History. Archived from the original on February 5, 2018. [Retrieved February 4, 2018].

[8] History-Ashe County. [www.ashecountygov.com. Retrieved Dec 31, 2022].

[9] John H. Wheeler, *Historical Sketches of North Carolina, from 1584 to 1851* (Vol. 1). Publisher Philadelphia: Lippincott, Grambo, 1851, p. 27.

surveys of western North Carolina stopped short of including this region. Because in 1746, the Commissioners said, that it was not then practicable, the country "being very thinly peopled, nor can we be supplied either with corn for the horses or provisions for ourselves and those employed by us there being no inhabitants that can assist us to the west of the Saxapahaw River."[10] The earliest Europeans to visit the area came in 1752 when a party of the Moravian Church visited from Pennsylvania to explore a location for missions of the church in the south. Wheeler's *History of North Carolina* says Ashe County was first settled about 1755.[11] However, Historian J. F. Fletcher wrote, "It is extremely doubtful if any permanent settlements were made in Ashe County as early as 1755." For many years, people spoke of the territory as "No Man's Land."[12] The region did not record its first land deed until 1773.

The western border of Ashe County, and indeed North Carolina, was the cause of much unease. Many believed among the people of North Carolina and among the people of other states as well that the North Carolina line in the northwestern section of the State followed the crest of the Blue Ridge Mountains, though neither North Carolina nor Tennessee claimed the territory. No state actually exercised authority over this territory for many years until the State of Franklin, the onetime precursor to the State of Tennessee, claimed the crest of the Blue Ridge as its eastern boundary in 1784. During this period, the territory that became Ashe County was part of the self-declared Free Republic of Franklin, which grew out of the American Revolution, and in 1784 existed within the boundaries of the Washington District, the large district that marked the beginnings of the State of Tennessee. The founders of Franklin hoped to make Franklin the 14th state of the Union. There was, for a time, two state governments—Franklin and Tennessee—issuing land grants for the same territory, which posed problems for the residents of the region. However, after bitter exchanges between officials of Franklin and North Carolina, and Indian uprisings

---

[10] J. D. Lewis, from www.carolana.com.

[11] John H. Wheeler, *Historical Sketches of North Carolina*, p. 27

[12] J. F. Fletcher, *A History of the Ashe County, North Carolina and New River, Virginia Baptist Associations*. Raleigh, N. C.: Commercial Printing, 1935.

within the new State of Franklin, the venture failed, and by 1791, governance of the region came under North Carolina. Until the year 1792, what became Ashe County was part of Franklin and considered part of the abortive, short-lived State; and then, in 1792, Ashe and the other North Carolina territory previously attached to Franklin became part of Wilkes County, North Carolina. Finally, in late 1799, the North Carolina legislature separated Ashe and Wilkes to create Ashe County. Nevertheless, long after the State of Franklin collapsed, a dispute over the border between Tennessee and North Carolina persisted until 1807. Border disputes between North Carolina counties were an annual occurrence well into the 20th century. It required 28 General Assembly acts finally to establish the current boundaries of Ashe County in 1915.

The pioneers who created homesteads and cultivated fields also built churches. Organized religion was of importance to the settlers. We do not know the religious persuasion of the Thomas Baldwin family, except that Thomas Baldwin, Sr., of Chester County, Pennsylvania, was probably Episcopalian. Based on later generations, it appears that the family leaned toward Presbyterian and Methodist Episcopalian, which for many years following the Revolution, became the protestant choice to supplant the official Anglican Church of England. However, there are among Baldwin descendants Baptists and Society of Friends of the Quaker faith, though the latter appears to be more a case of marriage into a Quaker family, rather than a practiced membership of the Baldwin family.

The establishment of religion on the western frontier was dangerous and difficult work. Charles Coale Wrote, "The country, at this time, was new and thinly settled. They [the clergy] met with many privations and sufferings and made but little progress. Most of the country through which they traveled was very mountainous and rough, and the people ignorant and uncultivated, and the greater part a frontier exposed to Indian depredations."[13]

Native Americans were part of the new frontier. Before the arrival of the whites, the region was a valued Indian hunting ground. So fruitful

---

[13] Charles B. Coale, *The Life and Adventures of Wilburn Waters, the Famous Hunter and Trapper of White Top Mountain : Embracing Early History of Southwestern Virginia, Sufferings of the Pioneers, etc.* Richmond: G. W. Gray, 1878.

was the region that it was a place of seasonal hostilities between the Shawnee tribes of the Ohio to the north and the Cherokee Indians to the south. The Cherokee lived around the Tennessee River, while the Shawnee resided north along the Ohio. The land in between the two camps was hunting ground for both. Each claimed hunting rights to the territory, a favorite part of which happened to be in northwest North Carolina and southwest Virginia, exactly where the new frontier took shape, and precisely where Thomas Baldwin, Sr., decided to make his new home. The outer frontier of the Revolutionary War became another way to define the Indian problem. Egged on by loyalist supporters, Indian depredations continued throughout the Revolutionary War and did not cease until 1794, at about the time Thomas Baldwin, Sr., settled in Grayson County, Virginia.

Consider the story of Henry Byrd, Revolutionary War soldier from Montgomery County, Virginia, the parent county of what later became Wythe County in 1790, which, in turn, spawned Grayson County in 1792, the home of the Thomas Baldwin Family. Writing in 1835 of his experiences during the war, Mr. Byrd said, "We met at the lead mines in Montgomery [near Austinville now in Wythe County] and were ordered to guard the frontier and prevent the Indians from doing mischief on the settlement. We were pretty generally on the march from place to place, as the Indians had certain places they would come in; and there were Tories lying out in the blew ridge [sic: Blue Ridge] which were also troublesome."

"We marched first and crossed New River at Harbards Ferry [*sic*: Harbert's Ferry, later Jackson Ferry] and marched for the flower Gap in the Blew ridge [*sic*: near present Austinville]. We went on from the flower Gap westwardly under the mountain until we came to the three forks of New River where we encamped and lay a while to scout. We took a few Tories as we would come up on them in camp. We ranged about there a while and marched on to a Creek called Fox creek [in present Grayson County] when we came on an old Camp of Tories which they had abandoned."

Mr. Byrd Continues, "About the first of the year 1781 there was a call for men again to march in to North Carolina. I was drafted in the service of the United States first of February 1781 as a private in Montgomery

County State of Virginia under the command of Capt. [Stephen] Saunders Colo. Crocket [*sic*: Walter Crockett]. There were part of the men left to guard the lead mines as there were a great many hands at work then for the publick [*sic*] and Indians and Tories ware troublesome… We would go some times for several miles in searching for Indian signs or waylay certain places where they were expected to pass and then would return to camp again. After [my] six months was out I received a discharge from Capt. Saunders and returned home. A short time after my return home there was a call for men again to go after the Indians. I volunteered myself again… We rendezvoused at Cripple Creek and marched on to the head of Holston River from there we marched north into Burks Guardian [*sic*], which is in Russell County [*sic*: Burkes Garden is in present Tazewell County, Virginia]."

Mr. Byrd concluded his narrative, writing, "There was always a considerable guard kept up for the purpose of protecting the workmen at the mines… I recollect there were orders received for men to be drafted and held in readiness to march when called… Owing to the danger which existed on the fronteer [*sic*]: the Tories lying out in the mountains robbing at different times the settlers, the Indians committing depredations on them that the Exigency of the times called for men to be out continually. The men which were stationed at the lead mines had continually to be in active service going out [in] the Country that no Enemy might come upon them unapprised."[14]

Henry Byrd, who narrated the above story, married into the Baldwin family. After the war, he returned to Grayson County, married Nancy Baldwin in 1798, the daughter of James Baldwin, thought to be the son or close kin of Elisha Baldwin.[15]

To understand that the American frontier was a dangerous place, one needs look no further than the story of another Thomas Baldwin—who we will call Thomas Baldwin of Kentucky—whose family died at the hands of marauding Indians. Thomas Baldwin of Kentucky came from

---

[14] Pension Application of Henry Byrd (Bird) S30307 VA, Library of Congress.

[15] Marriages Grayson County Virginia 1793-1853 compiled by John P. Alderman, 1974. "Grayson County James Baldwin surety for the marriage of Henry Byrd and Nancy Baldwin, daughter of James Baldwin dated 18 Nov 1798, alternate date married by Rev Robert Jones Feb 1799."

the same part of the country as other Baldwins, and was kin to the Baldwins who settled in the Quaker communities of North Carolina at about the same time our Thomas Baldwin, Sr., moved his family to North Carolina from Pennsylvania. Thomas of Kentucky was born in 1748, roughly the same time as Thomas, Sr., of Pennsylvania. He married early in North Carolina. He became a close friend of Daniel Boone, also a native of North Carolina. In May 1780, Boone convinced him to move west with his wife, two sons, and his 11-year-old daughter to Boone's frontier outpost at Boonesborough. On an earlier expedition, Boone's eldest son James had died when Indians attacked their party near Lexington, Kentucky, on October 9, 1773. Nevertheless, at Boone's urging, Thomas moved his family to Boonesborough, building a temporary cabin nearby. Hardly had the family settled into their new home when several Indians attacked them, burned the cabin, and instantly killed Thomas' wife and eldest son. They took Thomas captive along with his other son and daughter. The Indians subsequently tortured and burned his son at the stake while Thomas looked on helplessly. In the night, when his captors slept, Thomas managed to escape, leaving his daughter behind, abandoned. The Indians quickly pursued him. To his good fortune, a friendly Indian caught up with him and aided in his escape. He reached Boonesborough three days after the massacre. A rescue party returned with him to the scene of the crime, but did not find his daughter. He buried his wife and sons and returned to Boonesborough. In due time, a peace treaty with the Indians removed them further west. He learned from the Indian who had helped him that his daughter had died in captivity. He returned to the site of the massacre at his home place, and there constructed a hut in the far extreme of the western Kentucky frontier to repose near the graves of his family. For the next 50 years, he lived alone, secluded from human society. Daniel Boone visited him in 1818, two years before Boone died in 1820. Thomas remembered Boone once told him of the dangers in building the frontier, "when while carrying a log on one shoulder, he was obliged to carry his loaded rifle on the other." The narrator of the story of Thomas Baldwin of Kentucky wrote, "Those who at that period at the hazard of their lives, first attempted to explore and form settlements in the western wilds." Thomas Baldwin of Kentucky wrote in his journal, "Many dark and sleepless nights have I spent, separated from the cheerful society of men, scorched by the summer's sun, and pinched by the winter's cold, an instrument ordained to settle the wilderness!"[16]

---

[16] Roy C. Baldwin, *Narrative of the Massacre, by the Savages, of the Wife and Children of Thomas Baldwin.* NY: Martin & Wood, 1835, pp. 23-24.

11

Grayson County

Thomas Baldwin, Sr., and his family settled in due time in Grayson County, Virginia. It is from these southern roots that subsequent generations came to populate the Midwest. When Thomas arrived in the late 18th century, western Virginia was still an open wilderness, which only a few years earlier had constituted the homeland of Native Americans.

Western Virginia was a world apart from the Baldwin home in Pennsylvania. Everything was different: the soil, the terrain, the rivers, and most of all the inhabitants. The western frontier, while colonial in heritage, was uniquely American. This was the new breed of explorers. One observer wrote, "The backwoodsmen, whatever their blood, had already become Americans. One in speech, thought, and character. They had lost all resemblance to Europe. They were tough and supple as the hickory out of which they fashioned the handles of their long axes."[1] All that was English was set aside in favor of the comportment of a few hardy individuals who evolved a way of life in which survival trumped all social and political ambitions.

When Thomas Baldwin, Sr., and his family arrived in southwest Virginia, settlement of the wilderness had progressed noticeably from previous years. Indian troubles had diminished, and the population of white settlers had increased until homesteads dotted the frontier. Nevertheless, stories persisted of past atrocities, enough to instill in late arrivals the need to be cautious and to prepare for their safety and that of their families.

Grayson County, Virginia, features a varied landscape, ranging in elevation from 2,500 feet in the bottomlands to the highest point in the state—5,729 feet—Mt. Rogers, on the Grayson County and Smyth County border. The hills are densely forested in black walnuts, white

---

[1] Theodore Roosevelt, *The Winning of the West* (Vol. 1). New York: Current Literature Publishing, 1905, p. 141.

Blue Ridge Mountains. The Thomas Baldwin, Sr., family followed the Allegheny Mountain Range south from Pennsylvanian to North Carolina, finally settling in the New River Valley of Virginia, at the base of the Blue Ridge Mountains. Photo by William Jackson, ca. 1895. Library of Congress Prints and Photographs Division Washington, D.C.

and yellow poplars, chestnuts, oaks, hickories, and extensive pines. The dominate feature of the land is the New River and its vast watershed, which sustains the fertile plateau. The river originates in northwestern North Carolina and flows north into southwestern Virginia. Grayson County, on the Blue Ridge Plateau, occupies an enviable position in the list of Blue Ridge counties. Grayson, with its lofty mountains, picturesque high waterfalls, beautiful rivers and streams, and excellent grazing and farming lands, made it a favored settlement destination.

Most of the early settlers who came into the region came south from Pennsylvania along the Great Wagon Road through the Valley of Virginia. The stretch of the New River on the Virginia-Carolina border near where the Baldwins settled was among the later areas of the wilderness to attract settlers. Many of the earliest pioneers bypassed the area. Thomas Perkins Abernethy and Anderson-Green explained, "The reason for this is obvious. The main route through the Valley, the oft-mentioned Warrior's Trace [Great Wagon Road], did not continue westward, but crossed the Blue Ridge at the Staunton River water gap."[2] Thus, the pioneers on the Wagon Road actually crossed the Blue Ridge and detoured around the southwest corner of Virginia, where the valley narrows near New River. The Baldwins were among more than forty first-generation New River families who finally penetrated the Blue Ridge into this natural cul-de-sac in southwest Grayson County.

The eighteenth-century frontier of the New River Valley, located on the western Virginia-North Carolina border, owes its settlement to a class of individuals termed "plain folk." Historian Anderson-Green wrote, "The industry and self-sufficiency of this group is especially evident in the New River settlement, which was geographically remote from the East, at the southern end of the Valley of Virginia, on the western side of the Blue Ridge Mountains."[3]

The New River border frontier generally encompassed part of Grayson County, Virginia, as well as Ashe and Wilkes counties, North Carolina. It was in this region that the Thomas Baldwin, Sr., family settled among the first-generation settlers in the river valley adjoining Grassy Creek on Little Reed Island Creek, which flows into the New River. Their origins, motivations for migration and settlement, and their location and home site followed the general lifestyle of the "plain folk" of western Virginia. Notwithstanding their common characterization as hill people, Anderson-Green, quoting Abernethy, says, "contrary to the popular conception that those who pushed the frontier westward were uncouth, uneducated, but picturesque figures…, most of them were men of position and good education."[4] He concluded, "The majority of migrants came from the Pennsylvania-New Jersey area… The majority of settlers did not come alone, but as members of large extended families, usually those of married brothers headed by a father-patriarch, or by a widowed mother. Further, an extended family of one surname was generally linked to two or more other families by intermarriage and

---

[2] Anderson-Green, Paula Hathaway. The New River Frontier Settlement on the Virginia - North Carolina Border (1760-1820). *Virginia Magazine of History and Biography*, 1978, Vol. 86, No. 4 (Oct, 1978), pp. 413-431, p. 415.

[3] Ibid, p. 413.

[4] Ibid, p. 415.

by other associations that extended back in time over thirty or more years before the settlers arrived in the New River Valley."[5] In addition to Pennsylvania, multiple Baldwin families came to western Virginia at about the same time, some from eastern Virginia, and others from different parts of North Carolina. Like the Baldwins of the present genealogy, the majority was born in the Pennsylvania-New Jersey area. James G. Leyburn wrote, there were "many who had been born in Pennsylvania. As younger sons, ambitious men, or those dissatisfied with the crowding in a growing region, they were looking for better opportunities elsewhere."[6]

Thomas Baldwin, Sr., fit among the middle class of antebellum Virginians; that is, mostly farmers owning a few horses and between 100 and 500 acres.[7] There were, on the southern frontier, however, forces that diminished the feeling of class status that helped to create a sense of unity. For example, the rich and the poor are associated in all religious activities and in the schools, and the frequent ties of blood kinship between families. Moreover, because the population was relatively small, there was a limited choice of mates; marriages often took place without great regard for status, although certain families within the valley tended to favor each other for choice of mates.

It is impossible to trace the interrelatedness of the different Baldwin families. They all likely shared the same ancestral roots in England, which, after many generations, coalesced again in the settlements of the New River Valley. Analysis of the 1760-1820 era of the New River Valley frontier settlement shows that the first-generation settlers were often extended families of predominantly English "plain folk" background, who had a determination to form a middle-class agricultural lifestyle, all intent on becoming independent landholders.[8]

Kinship ties were important in a remote, isolated area such as the New River Valley and its surrounding mountains. Eventually, kinship through marriage included almost everyone in one vast network. Hence, by 1800, any given individual was likely to be a cousin, in one degree or

---

[5] Ibid, p. 415.
[6] Ibid, p. 424.
[7] Ibid, p. 427.
[8] Ibid, p. 431.

another, to practically everybody within a radius of thirty miles around. We are not able to include Thomas Baldwin, Sr., in such a vast network of kinship because he arrived in the neighborhood later than others did, and most members of the family moved on after barely one generation. Nevertheless, the marriages that did occur confirm the claim of status melding in the population. For instance, Rebecca, daughter of our Thomas Baldwin, Sr., married Joseph Jackson, son of a well-to-do merchant and proprietor in Pennsylvania.

The period from at least when Thomas' daughter Rebecca was born in Pennsylvania, the family's life in Ashe County, North Carolina, until the family appeared on the Wythe County, Virginia, tax list is a blank. Based on the birth of her son, Thomas Jackson, in 1798, we estimate that Rebecca was born about 1774, in Pennsylvania, a gap in the family's history of a couple of decades. This gap of time may be considerably shorter if an estimate of the birth of Rebecca's brother, Jeremiah Baldwin in 1786, is accurate, as claimed by genealogists. Jeremiah's son, born in August 1806, said in the 1880 census that his father was born in Pennsylvania. Because Jeremiah married in January 1806, the estimate of his birth in 1786 may be slightly in error. Nevertheless, based on Jeremiah's assumed birthdate of 1786, we conclude that Thomas Baldwin, Sr., left Pennsylvania sometime after 1786, and probably around 1792 when Rebecca was 18, and Jeremiah was about six years old. The earliest public record of the Baldwin family is a Thomas Baldwine [sic] who appeared on the Personal Property Tax List for Wythe County, Virginia, in 1793.[9] The following year, Thomas Baldwin, Sr., and Thomas Baldwin, Jr., were on the 1794 Grayson County Tax List.[10] Grayson County was formed in 1793 out of Wythe County, which accounts for the different tax lists. The family's existence appears to have been modest in the beginning. On the Grayson County tax list of 1794, Thomas, Sr., and his son Thomas, Jr., owned taxable property amounting to four horses between the two of them.

The part of Grayson County in which they settled—that part that became Carroll County, Virginia—was a sparsely populated place in

---

[9] Wythe Personal Property Tax List 1793– [online-New River Notes]
[10] Grayson County, Virginia, Personal Property Tax List for 1794.

1793. According to tax rolls of the region, there were 730 white adult males—less than two men per square mile—46 slaves over the age of twelve, 1,432 horses, and no coaches or other convenient conveyances.[11]

The Grayson County property tax rolls introduce a genealogical mystery in the movements of Thomas, Sr., and his family. He appeared on the rolls in 1793 and 1794 but disappeared between 1795 and 1796. Curiously, in 1796, his grandson, Thomas Lee, was born, not in Grayson County but in Ashe County, North Carolina. One may interpret this to mean that for reasons unknown, the Baldwin family returned to Ashe County for a short period before reestablishing a home in Grayson County. Such mobility was common among early settlers. Moreover, Thomas did not own land at the time and was free to move without the encumbrances of homestead chores. Thomas did not appear on the real-estate tax rolls until 1799, when he paid 15 cents on 90 acres in Grayson County valued at $30.[12]

Thomas, Sr., made his first land acquisition in 1798 when he acquired 20 acres on the "waters of Grassey Creek, a branch of Little Reed Island Creek."[13] We do not know precisely where the property was located

PENNSYLVANIA
VIRGINIA
NORTH CAROLINA
TENNESSEE
& KENTUCKY

Thomas Baldwin Locations. A modern outline map of Pennsylvania, Virginia, North Carolina, Tennessee, and Kentucky shows locations of Thomas Baldwin, Sr., in Chester County, Pennsylvania, and on the Virginia-North Carolina border, separated by a distance of more than 500 miles. Map by K. Burchett.

---

[11] Gibson Worsham. *A Survey of Historic Architecture in Grayson County, Virginia.* Richmond, Va.: Virginia Department of Historic Resources, 2002, p. 22. Citing Alderman, John P. *Carroll 1765-1815, the Settlements: a History of the First Fifty Years of Carroll County.* Virginia. Hillsville, Va.: Alderman Books, 1985.
[12] Grayson County, Virginia, Land Tax List—1799 [online–New River Notes].
[13] Thomas Baldwin [Sr?] 20 a. On the waters of Grassey Creek, a branch of Little Reed Island, 2 Oct 1798; see also Land-grant 2 October 1799. Baldwin, Thomas. grantee. Wythe County. 20 acres on the waters of Grassey Creek, a branch of Little Reed Island. Transcriptions of records disagree as to the location. However, Grayson

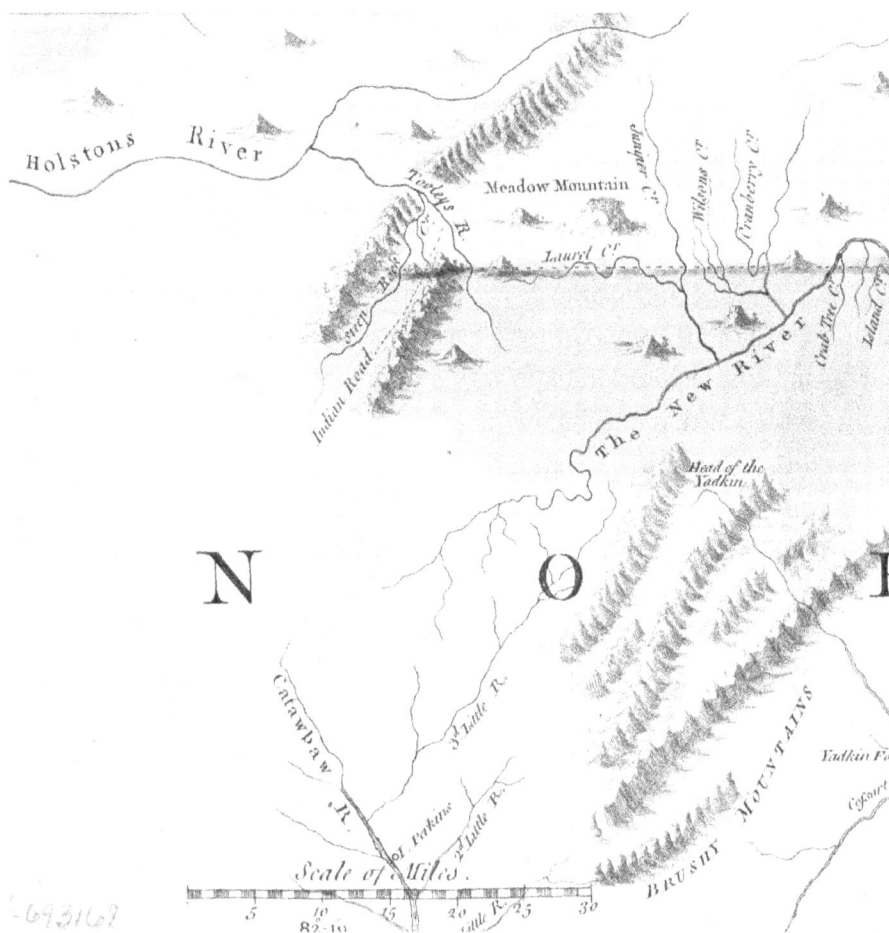

Settlement Area. Thomas Baldwin, Sr., settled in Grayson County, Virginia, near the Virginia-North Carolina border about the year 1792, at the foot of the Blue Ridge Mountains east of Indian Road and south of Meadow Mountain. Excerpt from Fry-Jefferson Map, 1754. Library of Congress Geography and Map Division Washington, D.C.

because in those days, surveys often used natural markers to define property lines, often within a relatively broad geographic area identified by the watershed in which it fell. Hence, one deed may locate a property "on the waters of Grassey Creek" while another "on the waters of Little Reed Island Creek." We conclude that he lived in Grayson County, Virginia, on the waters of Little Reed Island Creek and Grassey Creek, tributaries of the New River; near the North Carolina border in that part

---

County came out of Wythe in 1793. Therefore, the property could not have been in Wythe County unless there were two separate 20-acre tracts, which is unlikely but possible under the same date of acquisition.

of Grayson County that is today Carroll County, Virginia, in the Upper New River Valley. He may have owned more land unaccounted for in the deed records, considering he owed taxes on 60 acres in 1799.

The Baldwin homestead appears to have been a family affair. Thomas, Sr., and his son, Thomas, Jr., appeared together again in the 1800 Grayson County property tax list, still having four horses and no slaves.[14] The absence of slaves applied to almost all of his neighbors in that section of Grayson County. Slaves were expensive. The farmers of Grayson County could not afford them even if they wanted to, and there is no evidence that the Baldwins of Grayson County and subsequent generations had any interest in becoming slaveholders.

By the turn of the century, Thomas, Sr., had established his family in Grayson County enough to add substantially to his land holdings. In the spring of 1808, he acquired 296 acres on the "waters of Little Reed Creek in two tracts of 230 and 66 acres, respectively."[15] These parcel grants were part of Treasury Warrants, probably granted to Revolutionary War volunteers or real estate speculators, and then sold by the owners to buyers at a nominal price. Under this system, 100 acres cost about $5, not counting a reasonable profit at the time of the sale.

---

[14] 1800 Grayson County, Virginia, Personal Property Tax List. Since most of the 1800 Grayson County census burned in 1814, tax lists are about the only way to obtain similar data. This record, taken from information on file in the Library of Virginia does that to some degree.

[15] 1808 Land Grant, 25 March 1808, Baldwin, Thomas, grantee, Grayson [Treasury Warrant 4519 issued 1 Apr 1780] Description: 230 acres on the Waters of Little Reed Island Creek.[Other names William Chaffent, German Ballard (1820 census), Meredith Shockley (1820 census), John Wilerman, Hoser Mill Creek, John Fagin], Date 1808-03-25, Location: Grayson County; Middle Little Reed Grants & Deeds: p. 178, 185 citing Cameron & Paige] Report; 1808 Land Grant 25 March 1808, Baldwin, Thomas, grantee, Grayson County [Grayson created 1793 from part of Wythe] 66 acres adjoining Gainer Pierce &c. [Treasury Warrant 20812 issued 19 Nov 1783, same as 1812 warrant used by Thomas Baldwin Jr][Other names Gainer Pierce][Also same warrant number used by Churchill Jones to secure 100 acres in Grayson County, Eagle Bottom Creek and Stephen's Creek, Bounty No 20812 originally issued to John Harrington, Ref: Pierce, Gainer, Publication: 28 August 1805 [microfilm] Virginia State Land Office. Grants A-Z, 1 124, reels 42 190; Virginia State Land Office. Grants 125, reels 369. Location: Grayson County. Description: 100 acres on Little Reed Island Creek and adjoining Edward Bond.

Meanwhile, Thomas Baldwin, Jr., now married and with a young family, began to emerge as an independent household. For example, an early mention of him in the records is as Captain Thomas Baldwin of the Grayson County Militia from 1806 to 1807. Service as a militia officer was a high honor. Militia titles were sometimes honorary or used to gain social stature in a community, especially when travelling from one community to another.[16]

Meanwhile, word came from time to time of Elisha Baldwin's family living on the other side of Grayson County. For instance, news appeared in the Ashe County court records on June 6, 1810, that someone had accused Elisha's son, Enoch Baldwin, of stealing and carrying away one weeding hoe of the property of Moses Halsey. The court found the evidence sufficient and ordered Enoch tried in the County Court. The Grand Jury refused to indict him at the August Court 1810. It happened, also, that Elisha's son, Joseph, married Catherine Hart, an Indian woman.

The Thomas Baldwin family appears to have been relatively successful. In 1812, Thomas Baldwin, Jr., acquired 300 acres in Grayson County, "on the waters of Little Reed Island."[17] He had his own family by now. He chose to remain in Grayson County on property next to his father. Over time, he, too, became a dependable member of the pioneer community. For example, the 1813 Grayson County, Virginia Court Order Book states, "At a court begun and held for the County of Grayson on Tuesday the 23rd day of March 1813. Present Joshua Hanks, John Fielder, William Ballard, and Joseph Elliott, Gent. Justices. The Grand Jury returned into Court and made presentments in the following words, to wit: At March term 1813, We the Grand Jury impannel [sic] for the county of Grayson do present the overseer of the

---

[16] Grayson County Militia Officers 1793-1812, Antebellum Grayson County, Virginia Militia- [online-New River Notes].

[17] 1812 Land grant 13 May 1812, Boldwin, [sic] Thomas, Jr., grantee. Grayson County. Warrant 20812 issued 19 Nov 1783 same as 1808 patent, [doc image on file][Other names John Hair, Isaac Green] 300 acres on the waters of Little Reed Island adjoining Isaac Green, Related: See also the following surname(s): Greene. Location: Grayson County. Description: 119 acres on the waters of Little Reed Island Creek and Beaverdam Creek branches of New River.

road leading west of the Ward's Gap road near the Camping Spring down to the county line the same being out of repair by information of John Green, sen., and Thomas Baldwin, Jr., two of our own body. Also do present William Bobbett, Jr., surveyor of the Dug Spurr road, the same being out of repair from Big Reed Island to Little Reed Island, by information of Thomas Baldwin, Jr., and Meredith Shockley, two of our own body. Also, do present Esau Worrell, surveyor of the road from Little Reed Island to Crooked Creek, the same being out of repair by information of Thomas Baldwin, Jr., and Meredith Shockley, two of our own body." In addition to its genealogical detail, this court entry locates the Baldwin family.[18] Ward's Gap, mentioned in the court entry, is a physical feature located today in Carroll County, Virginia, an area known today for its scenic views.[19]

An 1815 county real estate assessment describes the Thomas Baldwin, Sr., homestead. "One farm on Grassey Creek, the waters of Little Reed Island containing one hundred and sixty-six Acres, more or less, having thereon one dwelling house of logs, 23 feet in length by 18 feet in width, one barn, valued at $400. One other tract of land on Little Reed Island containing two hundred and thirty acres, unimproved, valued at $40. Total: $440."[20] The 1815 list contained a record of the acreage of each farm and the type of material of each building, together with the value of the land improvements. The list identified landowners living within that part of eastern Grayson County that became Carroll County, which included the Baldwin property. In 1815, there were 211 landowners and some 290 tracts of land owned by the inhabitants, in some cases both improved and unimproved land. The first tract listed was the main farm and home place with a short description of the house. The most popular house form in Grayson County in 1815 was the "cabben." The reference to a "dwelling house of logs" for Thomas, Sr., and not a cabin identifies him as one of the more prosperous residents

---

[18] Ward's Gap is at coordinates Latitude 36.6679103 and Longitude -80.6322911.

[19] Carroll County, Virginia, came out of Grayson County in 1842.

[20] John P. Alderman, *Carroll 1765-1815 : The Settlements : A History of the First Fifty Years of Carroll County, Virginia*, Virginia. Hillsville, Va.: Alderman Books, 1985, p 387.

Old Barn. This old Virginia barn in Grayson County, Virginia, typified the log structure architecture found in the New River Valley when the Baldwin family lived and farmed there in the early 1800s. Houses and farm buildings built of logs often perched on the slopes of the mountain terrain. Sketch by Edwin Forbes, 1863.

of the area. Eighty-eight houses in the survey were log dwellings, and only twelve had an associated barn, like the Baldwin farm did. A log house usually had a shingle roof, a stone foundation, and a stone chimney. The size of the house was about the same or slightly larger than other similar homes in the area. The value of Thomas, Sr.'s, land placed him at or above most of his neighbors. Most of them lived in insubstantial dwellings of poor construction.[21] There were only 47 barns in that part of Grayson County in 1815.[22]

The three generations of Baldwins—Thomas, Sr., Thomas, Jr., and Thomas Lee appeared together for the last time on the 1825 tax roll for Grayson County.[23] Thomas Baldwin, Sr., late of Chester County,

---

[21] Gibson Worsham. *A Survey of Historic Architecture in Grayson County, Virginia.* Richmond, Va.: Virginia Department of Historic Resources, 2002. Citing Alderman, *Carroll 1765-1815, the Settlements,* Worsham, pp. 19-21.

[22] Ibid, Worsham, p. 20.

[23] Grayson County, Virginia Personal Property Tax List–Partial 1825 [online-New River Notes]. The three Baldwin generations also appeared together on the 1824 tax roll.

Pennsylvania, Ashe County, North Carolina, and Grayson County, Virginia, died in the winter of 1826.

Will of Thomas Baldwin, Sr.

"I, Thomas Baldwin, Sr., of the County of Grayson and State of Virginia being weak in body but in sound and perfect mind and considering the uncertainty of life make this my last will and testament do will and bequeath to my grandson Thomas Baldwin thirty dollars, also to my granddaughter Hannah Gallimore thirty dollars out of money on hand or first money collected, the balance of my estate personal and real I will and bequeath to my lawful heirs to be equally divided between them, my personal property to be sold on twelve months credit, my land to be sold on one, two, or three years credit, say payable in equal installments[;] be it understood that my daughters children, Rebecca Jackson, deceased, to have the same share that she would be legally entitled to provided she was living. Setting aside all wills previously made by me. I appoint my son Thomas Baldwin and my son-in-law Thomas Ward, Executors of this my last will and testament. Signed & sealed in the present of Eli Cook, John Gallimore, this 3rd day of February 1826." [Signed Thomas Baldwin, Sr.] [24]

A postscript to the Thomas Baldwin, Sr., story involves his alleged wife, Mary. There is among his descendants a theory that the Mary Baldwin, widow, who signed a consent for "Judith" to marry Thomas Fore in Grayson County, in 1827, was the widow of Thomas, Sr., who had died the previous year.[25] However, the 1820 census for Grayson County, which lists Thomas as the sole person in his household above age 45, suggests that Mary died before 1820.

---

[24] Grayson County, Virginia Wills 1793-1849, Will of Thomas Baldwin, Sr., Will Book #1, Grayson Co., Virginia 1826, p. 309. Names son, Thomas, heirs of dec. dau. Rebecca Jackson, other ch. names or numbers not given. A son-in-law, Thomas Ward, grandson Thos. Baldwin, ganddau. Hannah Gallimore. Execs.: Thomas Baldwin (son) and Thomas Ward (son-in-law), Signed: Thomas Baldwin, Sr., Witnesses: Eli Cook and John Gallimore Probated: March 1826-Eli Cook and John Gallimore witnesses with Thomas Baldwin and Thomas Ward executors came with Eli Cook, Churchwell Jones, Jeremiah Starr and Thomas Bryant their securities acknowledged. M. Dickenson County Court Minutes, p. 38.

[25] According to family historian, Minnie Baldwin.

12

Daughters of Thomas Baldwin, Sr.

Thomas Baldwin, Sr., was about 80 years old when he died. We know nothing of his personal life, except that he married and had children. Baldwin family historians have tried unsuccessfully to connect him to one "Mary Anne," last name unspecified, married around 1773, in Chester County, Pennsylvania. They had children: Rebecca, Thomas, Jr., Mary, Hannah, and Jeremiah, all born in Chester County before 1792.[1]

Rebecca (Rebekah) Baldwin was born about 1774.[2] She died about 1809. Rebecca married Joseph Jackson before 1798, in Virginia.[3] Joseph died in 1818.[4]

Rebecca was the oldest daughter of Thomas Baldwin, Sr., mentioned in his will of 1826, "be it understood that my daughter's children, Rebecca Jackson, deceased, to have the same share that she would be

---

[1] Will of Thomas Baldwin, Sr., Will Book #1, Grayson Co., Virginia, 1826, p. 309, "I, Thomas Baldwin, Sr., of the County of Grayson and State of Virginia being weak in body but in sound and perfect mind and considering the uncertainty of life make this my last will and testament do will and bequeath to my grandson Thomas Baldwin thirty dollars, also to my granddaughter Hannah Gallimore thirty dollars out of money on hand or first money collected, the balance of my estate personal and real I will and bequeath to my lawful heirs to be equally divided between them, my personal property to be sold on twelve months credit, my land to be sold on one, two, or three years credit, say payable in equal installments; be it understood that my daughters children, Rebecca Jackson, deceased, to have the same share that she would be legally entitled to provided she was living. Setting aside all wills previously made by me. I appoint my son Thomas Baldwin and my son-in-law Thomas Ward, Executors of this my last will and testament. Signed & sealed in the present of Eli Cook, John Gallimore, this 3rd day of February 1826. Signed Thomas Baldwin, Sr.

[2] Thomas B Jackson, 18 Aug 1877, Death Info Minnesota Rice Co. Deaths 1850-2001, Register of Deaths, pp. 25-26. Mother and father, Joseph and Rebecca, both born in Pennsylvania.

[3] Ibid, pp. 25-26. Thomas B. Jackson died at the age of 82, calculated birth in 1798.

[4] Alderman, John Perry. *Carroll 1765-1815, the Settlements: a History of the First Fifty Years of Carroll County.* [S. l.] : Central Virginia Newspapers, 1985.

legally entitled to provided she was living." Born in Pennsylvania, she came with the Baldwin family to Virginia when she was about 18 years old. She married Joseph Jackson, also from Pennsylvania, but there is no indication that they knew each other in Pennsylvania. The birth of their son, Thomas B. Jackson, in 1798 in Virginia, implies that the two of them met in Virginia around 1797.

Joseph Jackson was the son of Samuel Jackson and Rebecca Dixon of Jefferson Township, Fayette County, Pennsylvania, originally from London Grove, Chester County, Pennsylvania. A brief biography of the Jackson family provides insight into this well-to-do Pennsylvania family into which Rebecca Baldwin married. "One of the conspicuous figures in Fayette County's early history was Samuel Jackson, a sturdy Quaker from Chester County, and a businessman of large and liberal enterprise that made him quite famous in his day. Early in the year 1777, he settled in Fayette County, at the mouth of the Redstone Creek."[5]

Mr. Jackson selected a site for his home near the place now called Albany and built thereon a log cabin. In 1785, he erected a spacious stone mansion and resided there until he died in 1817. He was a millwright by trade. Soon after locating in Albany, he built at the mouth of Redstone Creek a gristmill, sawmill, and an oil mill. He engaged likewise to a considerable extent in the building of flatboats, for which there was a lively demand from emigrants desiring to journey to the lower country, the lower county, in this case, being mainly Virginia and North Carolina. His home in Fayette County, Pennsylvania, was in extreme southwest Pennsylvania abutting on present West Virginia. A large, athletic man, he moved with a "peculiar and accustomed step, his long arms thrown crosswise behind, and with as much thoughtfulness in his manner as if he were going to one of his own First-Day meetings." Those who knew him said, "Jackson was a man of peculiar and at times eccentric disposition, while not infrequently his Quaker blood would boil with unaccustomed heat and stir up matters rather unpleasantly to the objects of his wrath." During the Whiskey Insurrection of 1794, Mr. Jackson, who, as a member of the Society of Friends, was conscientiously

---

[5] Franklin Ellis, Ed., *Fayette County Pennsylvania*. Philadelphia: L. H. Everts, 1882, pp. 615-617.

opposed to distillation, favored the acts of the government as a means of suppression. Samuel Jackson expanded his business enterprises as time progressed and grew to be a man of distinction. He established the first paper mill west of the Alleghenies, carried on a store at Brownsville, embarked in the manufacture of iron outside of the county, had interests in various enterprises, and in 1817 founded the Albany Glass Works on the Monongahela River." The glass works had an eight-pot furnace, employed about fifty men. He built for their convenience a store and 20 or more tenement houses. The works produced common window glass, and obtained sand from the neighborhood of Perryopolis, hauled in wagons. Mr. Jackson died before the glassworks business was operational. Two of his sons took over the business.

The elder Samuel Jackson and his wife, also named Rebecca, had five sons and three daughters. His youngest son was Joseph Jackson, who eschewed the glassworks business, moved to Virginia, and married Rebecca Baldwin. Joseph and Rebecca settled in Grayson County, Virginia, in the eastern part of the county that would later be Carroll County, Virginia, in the Appalachian foothills embracing the Piedmont. Over the course of the next few years, from 1798 to 1806, Joseph and Rebecca bought and sold land on Crooked Creek and Chestnut Creek along the Iron Ridge. Jackson continued the entrepreneurial traits learned from his father. He and Rebecca bought 600 acres at Chestnut Creek that included a forge, iron-smelting "bloomery," and all the tools and "utensils" needed for ironwork. Despite their purchase and sale of several hundred acres, this was the only property the couple owned when Joseph died prematurely in 1808. We do not know if Rebecca preceded him in death.[6]

---

[6] Grayson County Deed Book 1-144, 1798, Joseph Jackson bought land from George Holland & John Ganning but sold it [in a few] years; D. B. 1-348 28 Oct. 1800 Lower Chestnut Joseph Jackson 95£ to: David Noblett both of Grayson 140 acres on Chestnut Creek, adj. John Frost & Jacob Fanning. (Ref D. B. 1-263); D. B. 1-427 23 Feb 1802 Joseph & Rebekah Jackson of Grayson $200 to: Green berry G. McKenzie 164 acres on east side of Chestnut Creek (Ref D. B. 1-77); D. B. 2-172: 26 Feb 1802 Joseph & Rebekah Jackson of Grayson to: John Graybell of Patrick 58 acres adj. Joseph Rea Johnson, McCraw and Johnson (ref: Grant 39-487); D. B. 2-173: 26 Feb 1802 Joseph & Rebecca Jackson of Grayson to: John Graybell of Patrick 57 acres on waters of Lovels Creek, at the foot of Wards Gap, at James Harrington's corner. (Ref:

In 1816, Thomas Baldwin, Jr., was surety for the marriage of Robert Green and "Polly" Jackson, believed to be his niece, Mary "Polly" Jackson, daughter of Joseph and Rebecca, born February 2, 1792.[7] Census records and documents confirm that Robert and Mary were both natives of Virginia.[8] The Green family came originally from New Jersey via Stafford County, Virginia, and then to Grayson County in the fall of 1791, where Robert Green was born on November 14, 1792. Robert and Mary "Polly" likely accompanied the Green family into Clinton County, Ohio, when the family moved there in 1816, coincidental with the first Newberry Monthly Meeting at Martinsville.[9]

D. B. 1-197); D. B. 2-26: 23 Feb 1803 Joseph Jackson of Grayson $2000 (deed of trust) to: Alexander Smyth of Wythe Conveys 600 acres at Chestnut Creek, the tract on which the forge is situated purchased by Jackson from Hugh Montgomery who bought it from Andrew Kincannon and Daniel Carlin, together with all tools and "utencils" belonging to the forge and bloomery. Also, with dwelling and outbuildings in Greensville at Grayson Courthouse. (Ref Grant 10-174 and Grant 17-614 in the name of Daniel Carlan); D. B. 2-86 14 Oct 1804 Joseph & Rebekah Jackson of Grayson to: $4000 Thomas Wester & John Cook of Philadelphia 450 acres on Crooked Creek (Ref Grant 55-492; D. B. 2-87: 24 Oct 1804 Joseph & Rebekah Jackson of Grayson to: $4000 Thomas Wester l& John Cook of Philadelphia 475 acres on waters of Chestnut Cr. And the Iron Ridge (Ref Grant 55-496); Grayson D. B. 3-234 Joseph Jackson bought 600 acres from Daniel Carlan (Grayson D. B. 2-361) This became Carroll County, Va. and was the only land he owned at his death in 1808. Foreclosed (Grayson D. B. 3-324); D. B. 2-138: 22 Nov 1806 Joseph & Rebekah Jackson of Grayson $500 to: Thomas Wester & John Cook of Philadelphia 450 acres on Crooked Creek, adj. Jeremiah Coulson (Ref Grant 55-492; see D. B. 2-86 and D. B. 2-237: 22 Nov 1806 Joseph & Rebekah Jackson of Grayson $600 to: Thomas Wester & John Cook of Philadelphia 475 acres on Chestnut Creek and the Iron Bridge, adj. Michael Farmay (Ref Grant 55-496: see D. B. 2-87).

[7] Marriages Grayson County Virginia 1793-1853, compiled by John P. Alderman, 1974.

[8] 1880 US Census for Mahlon Green, Bangor, Marshall, Iowa; Mahlon Green Death Certificate Iowa State Board of Health 64-00160 dated 13 Feb 1905 attests Mahlon Green was born in Clinton County, Ohio, to Robert Green and Nancy Jackson, of Virginia.

[9] Find a Grave Memorial ID 141813068, "The Old Folks" of Clinton County newspaper article. The Newberry Monthly Meeting records show that the first monthly meeting was held the "12 Mo. 2, 1816." The name came from Newberry County, or District, in South Carolina. Newberry Monthly Meeting was "set off"

They were a devout Quaker family. Robert and Mary settled in the village of Martinsville, Clark Township, Clinton County, Ohio.[10] Here they raised a large family of six sons and one daughter. Robert Green died April 5, 1834, at the age of 41. Mary died February 14, 1840, likewise at age 41. There is no record of the circumstances of their premature deaths. Both burials were at the Newberry Friends Quaker Burial Ground (present Martinsville Friends Cemetery), Martinsville, Clinton County, Ohio. [11]

In addition to Mary "Polly," Joseph and Rebecca Jackson had several children. Their son Thomas B. Jackson was born in 1798 in Virginia. It is through him that we are able to learn something of the lives of Joseph and Rebecca. Thomas Jackson married Nancy Brown, daughter of Samuel Brown, on July 25, 1826, in Grayson County. Thomas' uncle, Thomas Baldwin, Jr., was surety for their marriage.[12] Thomas and Nancy Jackson moved to Wayne County, Indiana, where Nancy died about 1830. Thomas married secondly Sarah Bower on September 22, 1831, in Wayne County.[13] Sarah died about 1837, and Thomas married a third time to Margaret Green on February 8, 1838, in Centerville, Wayne County, Indiana.[14] In 1840, they moved to Tipton County, Indiana, and then in 1855 to Webster County, Iowa. Finally, in May of 1857, Thomas and Margaret moved to Minnesota with their three sons, where they settled in Blooming Grove Township, Waseca County, Minnesota. They bought an 80-acre farm, later sold it, and moved to Morristown, in Rice County, Minnesota. All three of their sons served

---

(Started or Approved) from Clear Creek Monthly Meeting by Fairfield Quarterly Meeting, "11 Mo. 2, 1816."

[10] Pliny A. Durant, Ed., *The History of Clinton County Ohio* (Vol. 2). Chicago: W. H. Beers, 1882, p 795.

[11] Find a Grave Memorial IDs 187055549, 187055546.

[12] Marriage Bonds, 1793-1852 Marriages, Grayson County, Virginia, 1793-1853, compiled by John P. Alderman, 1974, transcription of marriage bonds: Marriage bonds, v. 1 1793-1808, Marriages Grayson County 677 p. 81, 25 July 1826. The record gives Thomas Baldwin as Sr.; however, Thomas, Jr.'s, father Thomas Baldwin, Sr., had died earlier in 1826.

[13] Indiana, Marriages, 1811-2019, Indiana Genealogical Society, [online Family Search Historical Records] p. 73.

[14] Ibid, p. 19.

in the Civil War in the Minnesota Infantry. Thomas B. Jackson, Jr., died of wounds received at the Battle of Altoona Pass.[15] Thomas B. Jackson, Sr., died August 18, 1877, at the age of 82. The Register of Deaths recorded him as a "Morristown farmer, born in Virginia to Joseph and Rebecca of Pennsylvania."[16] His wife, Margaret Green Jackson, died June 6, 1900. The burials of Thomas and Margaret Jackson were in Riverside Cemetery, Morristown, Minnesota.[17]

Meanwhile, Sarah Baldwin, second daughter of Thomas, Sr., was born on July 27, 1777, in Pennsylvania. Her birth in

Thomas B. Jackson. The son of Rebecca Baldwin Jackson, he was the grandson of Thomas Baldwin, Sr., of Grayson County, Virginia. A member of the Society of Friends, he was part the Quaker migration of Virginians to Indiana and the Upper Midwest that included the migration of his cousin Thomas Lee Baldwin to the same location in 1829. Photo Courtesy of Julie Hanson.

1777 located the Baldwin family at the time in Chester County, Pennsylvania. Sometime later, she moved with the Baldwin family to Virginia. In 1799, at age 22, she married Samuel McClure in Grayson County, Virginia.[18] McClure was also a native of Chester County, Pennsylvania. They had two sons and seven daughters. The family

---

[15] *History of Steele and Waseca Counties, Minnesota.* Chicago: Union, 1887, pp. 582-583.

[16] Death Information, Minnesota, Rice Co., Deaths 1850-2001, Register of Deaths, pp 25-26, Thomas B Jackson 18 Aug 1877.

[17] Find a Grave Memorial IDs 90392692, 90392693.

[18] Marriages, Grayson County, Virginia, 1793-1853, compiled by John P. Alderman, 1974, Typescript (mimeograph), Includes index, Contains transcription of marriage bonds. Marriage bonds, v. 1 1793-1808, #70, p 10. "Rev. Geo. Quesenberry certifies that he married Samuel Mick Cluer and Sary Baldin by license, Apl 3, 1799."

removed from Grayson County to Highland County, Ohio, in October 1813 and settled on the Leesburgh and Centerfield Road, Fairfield Township, Highland County, in southwestern Ohio. The following biography of the McClure family, into which Sarah Baldwin married, appeared in 1880.

"The McClures were originally either from Scotland or Ireland. The earliest authentic information concerning the family in this country is that James McClure and Martha, his wife, who was of English descent, settled, during the latter half of the eighteenth century, in Chester County, Pennsylvania. From there they are known to have moved, in 1798, to Grayson County, Virginia, where the son Samuel, the oldest of five children, followed them, a little later. Samuel was born April 13, 1777. The year after they immigrated to Virginia—March 14, 1798—Samuel married Sarah Baldwin. They lived in Virginia until 1813, when, with seven children, they removed to Ohio, arriving in Fairfield Township [Highland County] November 10th, after a long, roundabout, and tedious journey, by way of Limestone (now Maysville), Kentucky, and Hillsborough, [Ohio], which village then contained more stumps than houses. They located permanently in the eastern part of the township... Here, Samuel McClure, for many years, carried on farming and wagon making—the latter being his regular trade. He was a very ingenious artificer and a natural mechanic, being able to construct almost any article of wood or iron that was needed in the then-new country. After living for many years at the Rees place, he removed to Leesburg, where he engaged in the mercantile business, in which he was modestly successful."[19] According to those who knew him, Samuel McClure was, during his life, "one of the most influential and public-spirited men in the township, and served for many years as a justice of the peace..., and was county commissioner in 1829-30."[20]

The will of the elder James McClure, of Grayson, Virginia, written February 27, 1816, mentioned his son, Samuel McClure, to receive "a certain small horse which he borrowed from me when he moved to

[19] *History of Ross and Highland Counties Ohio*, pp. 96, 402, 414-415.
[20] Ibid.

Ohio, note of $8.00 he is to pay."[21] Meanwhile, Thomas Baldwin, Sr., did not mention his daughter, Sarah Baldwin McClure, by name in his will of 1826, in Grayson County, Virginia, except as one of his "lawful heirs" entitled to an equal share of his estate. When Sarah and Samuel McClure removed from Virginia to Ohio in 1813, they had a family of seven children.[22] Besides their own children, they brought with them several of the children of John Talbot, who was the husband of Samuel's eldest sister. These Talbot children, Sarah and Samuel reared as their own.[23] Sarah Baldwin McClure died on August 28, 1846, at age 69, in Fairfield, Highland County, Ohio.[24] Samuel married a second time, taking as his wife Helen O. Hixson in 1849, sister of Daniel Hixson, and a woman much younger than Samuel, by whom he had a son, Harvey L. McClure, who settled in Fairbury, Nebraska.[25] Samuel died on April 28, 1855, at age 78, a man "loved and respected by all." He died in Leesburg, Highland County, Ohio, with burial in Crispin Cemetery beside Sarah across the creek from Centerfield.[26]

Meanwhile, family historians have yet to research the life of Mary Baldwin, the fourth child of Thomas Baldwin, Sr. She was born about 1777 and was probably the Mary Baldwin who married Thomas Ward. He was no doubt the Thomas Ward named as a son-in-law in the 1826

---

[21] Will of James McClure, of Grayson, Virginia, written February 27, 1816, Court Records of County & State Residence of Testator.

[22] Obituary of daughter Nancy McClure Littler, *The News-Herald,* Hillsboro, Ohio, February 13, 1890.

[23] Obituary of Mrs. Rebecca J. Hixsom, Find a Grave Memorial ID 76577105.

[24] Find a Grave Memorial ID 74484468. [The Memorial ID gives the birth of Sarah Baldwin as 27 Jul 1777. Family records give a date of 13 Jul 1776]; see also the obituary of daughter Nancy McClure Littler, *The News-Herald* Hillsboro, Ohio, February 13, 1890,

[25] Ohio County Marriages, 1789-2016, p. 310 #5488 Samuel McClure and Helen Hixson, 1849, National Archives, Washington D.C., Record Group: Number: 29, Series Number: M653, Residence Date: 1860, Home in 1860: Fairfield, Highland, Ohio, Roll: M653_986, p. 142 [Family History Library Film: 803986].

[26] Find a Grave Memorial ID 74484449.

will of Thomas, Sr. The 1820 and 1830 censuses show a Thomas Ward living in Grayson County with his unnamed wife and six children.[27]

Meanwhile, of the Baldwin daughter, Hannah, we know nothing, except that the will of Thomas names a granddaughter named Hannah Gallimore, assumed to be the daughter of Hannah and John Gallimore, or Gillmore, who was a witness to Thomas, Sr.'s, will.

---

[27] 1820 US Census, Grayson, Virginia, p. 54, NARA Roll: M33_131; 1830 US Census Grayson, Virginia, Series: M19, Roll: 190, p. 285 [Family History Library Film: 0029669].

Exodus to the Midwest

13

Sons of Thomas Baldwin, Sr.

Jeremiah Baldwin, youngest child of Thomas, Sr., was born about 1786 in Pennsylvania.[1] He died November 26, 1829, in Champaign County, Ohio, at the age of 43. His burial was in Corbett Cemetery (aka Morecraft), Wayne Township, Champaign County.[2] Jeremiah married Hannah Thornbrough on January 27, 1806, in Grayson County, Virginia.[3] Hannah was born in 1788, in Kentucky. She died November 2, 1829, in Champaign County, Ohio. Her burial was in Corbett Cemetery (aka Morecraft), Wayne Township, Champaign County.[4] Thomas, Sr., did not mention Jeremiah by name in his will of 1826, except as one of his "lawful heirs" entitled to an equal share of his estate.

It is from the genealogy of Jeremiah that we learn some of the Baldwin family history. Jeremiah's son, Thomas, noted in the 1880 US Census that his father was born in Pennsylvania, probably Chester County.[5] Jeremiah came with his parents as a small child to Virginia, eventually to Grayson County, Virginia, where in January 1806 he married Hannah Thornbrough.[6] Jeremiah and Hannah had at least six

---

[1] 1880 US Census, Place: Scioto, Ross, Ohio, Roll: 1063, p. 354B, Enumeration District: 155.

[2] Find a Grave Memorial ID 46804043.

[3] Marriages, Grayson County, Virginia, 1793-1853, compiled by John P. Alderman, 1974, Typescript (mimeograph), Includes index, Contains transcription of marriage bonds, Marriage bonds, v. 1 1793-1808, p. 21. "(171) Jeremiah Baldwin and Hannah Thornbrough Bond: 1806-1: dated Jan 27, 1806, Principal: Jeremiah Baldwin, Surety: Samuel Mclure [*sic*]. For the marriage of Jeremiah Baldwin to Hannah Thornbrough, Return: 1-55: Rev. "George Quesenberry certifies that he married Jeremiah Bowdon and Hamar [*sic*] Thornberry on Oct 25, 1806."

[4] Find a Grave Memorial ID 46804066.

[5] 1850 US Census, Scioto, Ross, Ohio, Roll: 1063, p. 354B, Enumeration District: 155.

[6] Marriages Grayson County Virginia 1793-1853, compiled by John P. Alderman, 1974, Virginia Vital Records, 1715-1901, Marriages since 1793 Grayson County, Marriage of Jeremiah Baldwin and Hannah Thornbrough, Grayson, Bond: dated Jan

children, including a son, Thomas, named for his grandfather, born August 17, 1806.[7]

The Grayson County personal property tax lists for the years 1805 and 1810 listed Jeremiah along with Thomas Baldwin, Jr., and Thomas Baldwin, Sr.[8] Soon after 1810, Jeremiah moved his family to western Ohio, settling in Wayne Township, Champaign, Ohio, in the same location as his Baldwin kin, in what became known as the First Great Migration out of western Virginia.

Jeremiah took up farming and was a pioneer among those of Wayne Township, Ohio, and a respected citizen of the community. Residents used the Baldwin home to elect township officers as early as 1811. He was in the 1820 US Census for Wayne Township, Champaign County, and his name appeared yearly on the county tax lists. Of the Trustees who served the township in its early organization and before 1840, Jeremiah Baldwin was often among them. His son, Thomas, was likewise frequently on a list of township officers of various kinds.[9]

We know little about the life of Jeremiah Baldwin. The histories of Champaign County, Ohio, are mostly silent about him. There were several prominent men of the Baldwin name associated with the settlement of Ohio living in Champaign County, who, if not his immediate, kin likely shared the same Baldwin roots. Baldwins were active in writing the 1802 Ohio Constitution, signed by Michael Baldwin of Ross County, Ohio, who was also the first Ohio Speaker of the House. Meanwhile, Richard Baldwin and his wife, Eleanor Williams, came to

---

27, 1806, Surety Samuel McClure for the marriage of Jeremiah Baldwin and Hannah Thornbrough. Return 1-55: "Rev. Geo. Quesenberry certifies that he married Jeremiah Bowldon [sic] and Hanar Thornberry [sic] on Oct 25, 1806."

[7] 1820 US Census, Place: Wayne, Champaign, Ohio, p. 488, NARA Roll: M33 86, Image: 268. Thomas gave his place of birth as Ohio. However, at the time of his birth, Jeremiah was still in Virginia.

[8] 1805, 1810 Grayson County, Virginia, Personal Property Tax Lists. The 1810 Grayson County Tax List is the best substitute available for the 1810 Federal Census. Grayson County and a number of other counties lost their earliest census records when the British burned Washington in 1814, during the War of 1812. [online-New River Notes, transcribed by Jeffrey C. Weaver, May 1998].

[9] John W. Ogden, *The History of Champaign County, Ohio,* Chicago: W. H. Beers, 1881, pp. 120, 254, 522-523, 545.

Champaign County in 1824. Mr. [Richard] Baldwin engaged extensively in farming and stock dealing, and at one time was the leading livestock trader in the King's Creek Valley. Judge Samuel V. Baldwin rose from his law practice in Urbana Township to become probate judge in 1840. Ohioans remember Judge Baldwin in connection with Baldwin Mound, an ancient Ohio Woodland Indian mound that overlooks the Mad River Valley on Judge Baldwin's old farm southeast of Urbana.

Jeremiah Baldwin did not enjoy such acclaim in his lifetime, perhaps in part because he died relatively young. Jeremiah died on November 26, 1829. His wife Hannah preceded him in death by only 14 days, passing on November 12, 1829, at the age of 41. We do not know the cause of their premature deaths. However, when family members die close together, it usually implies a disease epidemic or some kind of traumatic cause. Their burial was in Wayne Township, Champaign County, Ohio, in Corbett Cemetery, also known as Morecraft Cemetery, located north of Blue Road, and west of Chatfield Road.[10] Also buried in this cemetery are Jackson Baldwin and Eliza Ann Baldwin, thought to be the children of Jeremiah and Hannah Baldwin. Both died very young, Jackson on December 1, 1847, and Eliza Ann on August 4, 1848, at the age of 23. Ironically, their deaths came but 10 months apart.[11]

Conflicting dates raise questions about the timing of Jeremiah's removal to Ohio and the date of his death. For example, in 1813, Hannah Baldwin—the name of his wife—witnessed the will of Isaac Green, longtime neighbor of Thomas Baldwin, Sr., of Grayson County, Virginia.[12] Moreover, a Jeremiah Baldwin sold land April 18, 1831, to Thomas Ward—his alleged brother-in-law—in Grayson County, probably the husband to Mary Ward mentioned in the will of Thomas Baldwin, Sr., as his son-in-law. Furthermore, when Thomas Baldwin,

---

[10] Champaign County Cemeteries Vol. 2, Compiled 1955 Urbana Chapter DAR, Copied by Mrs. Charles E Russell and Ms. Edgel Lutz.

[11] Find a Grave Memorial IDs 46803999 and 46804110.

[12] Jerimiah Baldwin' name is on the 1805 and 1810 Grayson Co., Va. Tax Lists but not on the 1813 list. A "Hannah Baldwin" witnessed Isaac Green's Will in 1813. On April 18, 1831, a "Jerimiah Baldwin" sold land to "Thomas Ward" who was probably the husband to Jerimiah Baldwin's sister, Mary Baldwin Ward [online John Fevburly forum Aug. 7, 2009].

Jr., and Thomas Ward settled the estate of Thomas Baldwin, Sr., as executors of his will, in April of 1831, Jeremiah Baldwin held a voucher against the estate.[13] The 1813 date for Hannah Baldwin's witness to Isaac Green's will suggests that Jeremiah was not in Ohio until after that date, which conflicts with the previous record of him being there before 1811. More puzzling, however, are the 1831 transactions that appear to place Jeremiah in Grayson County two years after his proven death in 1829, in Ohio. These transactions may represent someone named in the estate settlement acting on behalf of the deceased Jeremiah Baldwin. Likewise, the sale of land in April 1831, the same month as the estate settlement, suggests that Jeremiah's son, Thomas, settled matters in Grayson County on his deceased father's behalf.[14] Thomas Baldwin, the presumed eldest son of Jeremiah and Hannah Baldwin, lived a long and successful life in Ohio. He married Sarah Sharp on April 28, 1831, in Ross County, Ohio, which was coincidentally the month and year of the settlement of Thomas Baldwin, Sr.'s estate in Grayson County.[15] Sarah Sharp was born on July 11, 1811, in Ohio. Thomas and Sarah raised a large family. They owned a large farm in West Scioto Township, Ross County, Ohio, near Chillicothe. Their family, inferred from the 1850 US Census, included seven children.[16] Thomas died February 22, 1884, at

---

[13] Will Book #1, Grayson Co., Virginia, 1826, p. 387 Thomas Baldwin–Settlement, Churchwell Jones and Jonathan Cook settled with Thomas Baldwin and Thomas Ward, exec. for the estate, Vouchers against the estate held by: John Gallimore, Shadrack Collins, William Hail, Jesse Brown, Jeremiah Baldwin, Samuel Brown, Doctor's bill, James Webb, Sheriff, Thos. Ward, and Thos. Baldwin. One note on James Johnson who is insolvent, Thomas S. Baldwin, John Hill, Eli Cook, loss on S. Gallimore, John Gallimore, and Jonathan Cook. 4 March 1831-C. Jones and Jonathan Cook, Recorded: April 1831, M. Dickenson County Court, p 50, transcribed by Alderman, p. 387 [online Patty LaPlante, p 50].

[14] Ibid.

[15] Ohio, County Marriages, 1789-2016, Ross, Marriage Registers 1825-1834 Vol. C, image 152, county courthouses, Ohio. Thomas Baldwin and Sarah Sharp 28 Apr 1831 Ross County, Ohio.

[16] Records of the Bureau of the Census, Record Group Number: 29, Series Number: M432, Residence Date: 1850, Home in 1850: Scioto, Ross, Ohio, Roll: 725, p. 98a, National Archives in Washington D.C.

age 77 years, six months, and six days, of Gangrene.[17] Sarah moved to Dayton, Ohio, following the death of Thomas.[18] She died May 22, 1894, passing at the age of 82 at Chillicothe, Ross County, Ohio. Their burials were at Grandview Cemetery, Chillicothe.[19]

Meanwhile, the eldest son of Thomas Baldwin, Sr., Thomas Baldwin, Jr., eclipsed in age his younger brother Jeremiah by at least a decade. The eldest son and progenitor of our Baldwin line, Thomas, Jr., was born about 1775, probably in Pennsylvania. He died after 1830 in Grayson County, Virginia. Thomas married twice, first to Hannah Ricks, and then to Elizabeth Brizendine, both in Grayson County, Virginia.

Thomas was about 16 or 17 years old when he came south with the Baldwin family, perhaps older because the day after Christmas 1792, he married Hannah Ricks, the daughter of Jonas Ricks of North Carolina, a devout follower of the Quaker faith. Men did not usually marry until age 21. Nevertheless, we find the marriage of Thomas Baldwin to Hannah Ricks on December 26, 1792. She was born February 23, 1771, which suggests that Thomas, Jr., was likely born about 1770 or 1771, instead of 1775 as previously estimated by family historians.[20]

Their son, Thomas Lee Baldwin, was born March 12, 1796, in Ashe County, North Carolina. Thomas Lee would grow up to carry the Baldwin name into the Midwest, eventually to establish the Baldwin line in Missouri.

Hannah Ricks was a Quaker. The Ricks family attended the Springfield Monthly Meeting in Guilford County, North Carolina, which was some 50 miles from where the Baldwins lived. We do not know how Hannah met Thomas Baldwin or the circumstances of their courtship. However, we know that in 1796, the Quakers condemned Hannah for her "marriage out of unity," meaning she married a non-

---

[17] Ohio, County Death Records, 1840-2001, v 3 p 3. Thomas Baldwin d. 22 Feb 1884 77 yrs. 6 mo. 6 days gangrene W. Scioto Ross.

[18] Williams' Dayton City Directory: A Full Alphabetical Record of the Names of the Inhabitants of the City of Dayton, Ohio, a Business Directory, City Guide, United States Post Office Directory, etc., 1887-1888. Widow Sarah Baldwin from 1887 to 1888 Dayton, Montgomery, Ohio, Thomas Baldwin Residence.

[19] Find a Grave Memorial IDs 95274382 and 95274464.

[20] Ricks, Howard, Ed. History and Genealogy of the Ricks Family of America (Rev. ed.). Salt Lake City, Utah: Ricks Family Association, 1957. (Originally 1908), p. 24.

Quaker. The next year—1797—Westfield Monthly Meeting granted Hannah a certificate to transfer her membership to Westfield, which is on the Virginia-North Carolina border, immediately south of and close to the Baldwin homestead.[21] There is no record that she ever attended Westfield.[22] By the turn of the century, the Baldwin family had settled in Grayson County, Virginia. Thomas, Jr., and Hannah had a second son, James, in 1799.

The name of Thomas Baldwin, Jr., first appeared in Grayson County records on the 1805 tax roll along with his father, Thomas, Sr., and brother Jeremiah.[23] We find them together again on the 1810 tax list.[24]

---

[21] Hinshaw, Vol. 1, p. 870. "Hannah RICKS, daughter of Jonas RICKS, was b. 23 February 1771, married Thomas BALDWIN, John WALTER and Rob. JOHNSON bondsmen [Guillford County Marriage bond No. 53238]. Springfield MM abstracts record a Hannah BALDWIN (former RICKS) condemned for her marriage out of unity 2 January 1796, and with a certificate granted to Westfield MM 2 September 1797."

[22] Ricks, Howard, Ed. History and Genealogy of the Ricks Family of America (Rev. ed.). Salt Lake City, Utah: Ricks Family Association, 1957. (Originally 1908), p. 24. Hannah Ricks, born 23 February 1771, married Thomas Baldwin, John Walter and Rob. Johnson bondsmen. Springfield MM abstracts record a Hannah Baldwin (former Ricks) condemned for her marriage out of unity 2 January 1796, and with a certificate granted to Westfield MM 2 September 1797. These records are the only known clues to the movement of this Baldwin family. Several Guilford County families are found in Westfield MM records during this period, and while there is a Baldwin among them, there was no mention of a Baldwin with wife named Hannah.

[23] Grayson County, Virginia Personal Property Tax List—1805–New River Notes, transcribed by Jeffrey C. Weaver, May 1998 [online http://www.newrivernotes.com/va/gray05pp.htm].

[24] February Court. At a Court begun and held for the county of Grayson on Tuesday the 26th day of February 1811. Present Joshua Hanks, George Currin, William Ballard & William Hail} G. Justices. A deed from Isaac Green to Thomas Baldwin, Jr., was proven in court by Reuben Greer a subscribing witness. March Court. At a court begun and held for the County of Grayson on the 26th day of March 1811. Present Joshua Hanks, John Comer, Joseph Fields, Matthew Dickey & William Ballard} G. Justices. A deed from Isaac Green to Thomas Baldwin, Jr., was acknowledged in Court by the said Isaac and ordered to be recorded; November Court. At a Court begun and held for the county of Grayson Tuesday the 26th day of November, 1811. Present: Matthew Dickey, George Currin, Joshua Hanks, Joseph Fields, William Ballard, & Joseph Elliott} Gen. Justices. Thomas Baldwin, Jr., to John Albert

By that time, they had acquired nine horses between them to farm the recently acquired 300 acres of land on Little Reed Island Creek that his father bought in 1808.

We assume that Thomas, Jr., was a farmer because by 1811, he had begun to build his own land holdings with a couple of parcels deeded to him by his neighbor, Isaac Green, and another 300 acres he purchased in 1812.[25] The latter acreage lay on the watershed of the Little Reed Island Creek and Beaverdam Creek.[26] He paid property taxes in 1813— 32 cents on two horses—and we see him engaged in Grayson County Court business during the year.[27] "At March term 1813, We the Grand Jury impannel [sic] for the county of Grayson do present the overseer of the road leading west of the Ward's Gap road near the Camping Spring down to the county line, the same being out of repair by information of John Green, sen., and Thomas Baldwin, Jr., two of our own body… Also do present William Bobbett, Jr., surveyor of the Dug Spurr road, the same being out of repair from Big Reed Island to Little Reed Island by information of Thomas Baldwin, Jr., and Meredith Shockley, two of our own body.[28] As with the case of Thomas, Sr., the court's reference to Ward's Gap locates the Baldwin homestead in the New River Valley.

In 1815, a description of his homestead appeared in the 1815 county real estate assessments. "Thomas Baldwin, Jr., one farm on the Beaverdam Creek containing one hundred and ten acres, having thereon one dwelling house of timber, one kitchen, and stable, valued at

---

attachment, continued [New River Notes online. http://www.newrivernotes.com/va/gray1810tl.htm.]

[25] New River Notes [online http://www.newrivernotes.com/va/gc1811cord.htm].

[26] Land grant 13 May 1812. Boldwin, [sic] Thomas, Jr., grantee. 1812–0513 Location: Grayson County. Description: 300 acres on the waters of Little Reed Island adjoining Isaac Green. Source: Land Office Grants No. 62, 1811-1812, p. 416 (Reel 128). Available on microfilm. Virginia State Land Office. Grants A-Z, 1-124, reels 42-190, Virginia State Land Office. Grants 125, reels 369-[see Reed Island Land Owners file for adjoining properties]..

[27] The 1813 Grayson County, Virginia Court Order Book. Transcribed by Jeffrey C. Weaver, June, 1998 [New River Notes online http://www.newrivernotes.com/va/gray1813tl.htm].

[28] The 1813 Grayson County, Virginia Court Order Book [New River Notes online http://www.newrivernotes.com/va/gc1813cord.htm].

$185. One other tract on the Greenbrier Road joining John Starr, containing three hundred Acres, having thereon two cabbens [*sic*] and one barn, valued at $160. Total: $345.[29] He paid taxes on this property in 1817.[30] Thomas, Jr., appears to have improved on the living standard of his father. A dwelling house of timber mentioned in the appraisal of his property was rare in the region, not to mention one with a kitchen and stable. There were only ten timber dwellings listed in the 1815 survey, and only four of these had a stable and kitchen built apart from the house, like that of Thomas, Jr. However, from the comparatively lesser value of his property, we may assume the house was a relatively small structure. However, his estate improved with the addition of a second tract of land containing two cabins and a barn.

Thomas, Jr., served on the Virginia Superior Court held in Grayson County from 1818 to 1820, and had the unenviable duty to pronounce guilt on residents of the Baldwin name who came before him.[31] John and Enoch Baldwin of the Elisha Baldwin household, and the same who appeared in court in 1810, accused of stealing the property of Mosley Hasley, came into court a decade later, this time indicted for an assault with intent to kill. The court continued their indictments until the next term, sparing Thomas, having in the meantime left the court, from having to try the case. We do not know what happened to John and Enoch, except that it was not the last time they came before the court, usually for fighting and assault.

In 1818, the marriage of Thomas, Jr., and Hannah Ricks appears to have ended. There is a theory among family historians that Hannah Ricks married Daniel Potter in 1818 and later moved to Indiana. Others claim this was another Hannah Ricks, daughter of Thomas Ricks, and that our Hannah died about 1818.[32] In any event, on June 11, 1820,

---

[29] John Perry Alderman, *Carroll 1765-1815, the Settlements a History of the First Fifty Years of Carroll County, Virginia,* Central Va. Newspapers, Inc., ca. 1985, FHL fiche #6050973 p. 387. *Note:* Middle Little Reed Grants, p. 178.

[30] Grayson County, Virginia Personal Property Tax List – 1817 [New River Notes online http://www.newrivernotes.com/va/gray1817tl.htm].

[31] Grayson County, Virginia Superior Court Order Book 1809-1821 [New River Notes online http://www.newrivernotes.com/va/gcsupct.htm].

[32] Genealogy. com [online https://www.genealogy.com/forum/surnames/topics/ricks/176/].

Thomas married Elizabeth Brizendine. The Rev. Elisha Beller certified their marriage in Grayson County.[33]

From the year 1820 forward, US census records confirm the Baldwin family in Grayson County. Before 1820, tax records substituted for the censuses lost in the 1814 fire. The census data, although missing important information like names of household residents, give a larger picture of the population. For example, the Baldwins were farmers, according to the census. Of particular interest, too, in 1820, the unnamed spouses of both Thomas, Sr., and Thomas, Jr., appear to be living. Thomas Lee was on his own and living apart but not yet married.

Thomas, Jr., continued to work a modest farming operation, paying his taxes, doing community work as a school commissioner and as a helpmate to the indigent. Several court records tell of his service as overseer of the poor, meaning he became a legal guardian to children cast on bad times.[34] He served on the Grayson County Court regularly.[35] His name as a justice appeared 37 times in the 1826 court record alone.[36] This was not easy because any court appearance in person required him to travel to the courthouse at Galax, a good half day's ride west of where he lived.

When Thomas Baldwin, Sr., died in 1826, the job of clearing his father's estate fell to Thomas, Jr.[37] The court record states, "March 1826. The last Will and Testament of Thomas Baldwin dec'd was presented in court and proven by Eli Cook and John Gallemore [sic] subscribing witnesses and ordered to be recorded and Thomas Baldwin & Thomas Ward Executors therein named came into court and together with Eli Cook, Churchwell Jones, John Hoi;, Jeremiah Starr & Thomas Bryant their securities entered into and acknowledged their bond in the penalty

---

[33] Marriages, Grayson County, Virginia, 1793-1853, compiled by John P. Alderman, 1974, [ii], 39, 198 leaves. Typescript (mimeograph). Includes index. Contains transcription of marriage bonds. Marriage bonds, v. 1 1793-1808, p 10.

[34] Grayson County Va., Court Order Book 1811-1829, pg. 92, July 1827 [New River Notes online http://www.newrivernotes.com/va/grayorph.htm].

[35] Patrick County, Va. Wills William Moore, Estate Administration Patrick County, Virginia December 15, 1825 Transcribed by William E. Harrold.

[36] Grayson County, Virginia, 1826 Court Order Book pp. 2, 4, 8, 10,13, 37, 38,40, 41, etc.

[37] Grayson County, Virginia, 1826 Court Order Book, p. 10.

Exodus to the Midwest

of $2,000 with condition as the law directs and took the oath of
Executors whereupon a certificate is granted them in form. Ordered that
Churchwell Jones, Eli Cook, John Hill, Lewis Starr and Isaac Moore or
any three of them after being sworn for that purpose appraise the
personal estate of Thomas Baldwin [Sr.] dec'd and make report thereof
to court" [38] The court's order was carried out, and in May 1826 "an
inventory and appraisement of the personal estate of Thomas Baldwin
[Sr.] dec'd was returned to court and ordered to be recorded."[39] The next
month—in June—An Inventory of Sales of his estate was presented in
court and ordered recorded. An estate sale in September and recorded
in January 1827 was the last formal record of Thomas Baldwin, Sr. [40]

Thomas, Jr., continued to live and work his farm in Grayson County
on Beaverdam Creek. His name appeared in court records in 1827 and
1828 as Thomas Baldwin, Esq., for providing foster care for two orphan
children.[41] By 1830, many of the Baldwin family had already migrated
or were in the process of migrating to Indiana, Ohio, and other points
in the Upper Midwest, including the migration of his son Thomas Lee
Baldwin. Thomas, Jr., disappeared from the records after 1830, either by
death or having migrated himself to parts unknown. By 1835, there were
no Baldwins listed on the tax rolls of Grayson County.

---

[38] Ibid.

[39] Will Book #1, Grayson Co., Virginia 1826, Page 319 Thomas Baldwin – Inventory
Taken by C. Jones, Eli Cook, John Hill, L. Star and Isaac Moore for Thos. Baldwin
and Thomas Wood, admrs. Recorded: May 1826 - M. Dickenson CC (both from p
40); see also James I. Douthat publication: Signal Mountain, Tenn.: Mountain Press,
1988, FHL film #1750813; Alderman, p 319.

[40] Will Book #1, Grayson Co., Virginia 1826, Page 321 Thomas Baldwin - Estate Sale
27 April 1826 - Lists buyers + Notes held by the estate. Recorded: June 1826 - M.
Dickenson CC Also, Will of Thomas Baldwin, Sr., Will Book #1, Grayson Co.,
Virginia 1826, Page 338 Thomas Baldwin - Estate Sale 1 Sept 1826 - Lists buyers
Recorded: Jan 1827 - M. Dickenson CC p 42; Alderman, p 338; Patty LaPlante.

[41] Grayson County Court Orders 1826-1832, July 1827, p. 92: Aug. 20, 1828. Orphans
Delilia Hicks and James Woods, son of Sally Woods.

14

Thomas Lee Baldwin

Thomas Lee Baldwin was born on March 12, 1796, a Saturday, in Ashe County, North Carolina, the son of Thomas Baldwin, Jr., The earliest mention of Thomas Lee by name is in 1822, in Grayson County, Virginia, when he married Nancy Brizendine. It is possible that Thomas Lee is included in earlier records, but since both his father and grandfather also had the name Thomas, it is not always possible to assign a record precisely to Thomas Lee. However, it is probably Thomas Lee, who the census recorded in the summer of 1820, living alone, "engaged in agriculture." We do not know, but he likely occupied one of the cabins on his father's tract of land on Beaverdam Creek.

Marriage of Thomas Lee Baldwin and Nancy Brizendine. The Circuit Clerk of Grayson County recorded the marriage of Thomas Lee Baldwin and Nancy Brizendine on July 25, 1822. Virginia County Marriage Records, Circuit Court Clerk Offices, Grayson County, Virginia,

Nancy Jane Brizendine was born on May 2, 1801, in Charlotte County, Virginia.[1] Her marriage to Thomas Lee was recorded on July 25, 1822, the Reverend John Cocke officiating. At the time, Thomas Lee

---

[1] Grayson County, Virginia Marriages 1793-1836, "BALDWIN, Thomas, and Nancy BRIZENDINE - 25 Jul 1822."

would have been 26 years old and Nancy would have been 21. They were married on a Thursday.[2] In the small world of Grayson County, Thomas Lee's father had married Elizabeth Brizendine two years prior, a member of the same Brizendine family.[3]

Nancy was the daughter of Isaac and Mary Brizendine of Charlotte County, Virginia. The Brizendines were relatively late arrivals to Grayson County. They arrived first in Franklin County, Virginia, around 1817, and by 1820, they had settled in the Upper New River Valley near the Baldwin homestead. Isaac Brizendine was one of the few in Grayson County who owned slaves.[4] He descended from the Brizendines of Essex County, Virginia.

Thomas Lee and Nancy lived in Grayson County, Virginia, until about 1828.[5] The estimated date is based on the birth of their first two children, Sarah L. and Thomas Jackson, who were born in Virginia, and the birth of their third child, William Mattison, born on December 29, 1829, in Wayne County, Indiana. The date of Thomas Lee's departure from Virginia cannot be earlier than 1828 because he appeared on the Personal Property List for Grayson County in 1828 with property of one horse for which he paid a tax of 12 cents.[6] His grandfather had died in 1826, and, although his father was still living in Grayson County, many of his close relatives had died, either moved, or were in the process of moving to the Upper Midwest.

Thomas Lee was 32 years old when he left Grayson County, Nancy was 27, and their two small children, Sarah and Thomas Jackson, were ages three and two respectively. We imagine that he made the initial trip to Indiana alone, leaving Nancy and their small children to follow later. However, it is possible that the family made a single journey together,

---

[2] Marriages, Grayson County, Virginia, 1793-1853, compiled by John P. Alderman, 1974, [ii], 39, 198 leaves. Typescript (mimeograph). Includes index. Contains transcription of marriage bonds. Marriage bonds, v. 1 1793-1808, p 58.

[3] Ibid, p. 10.

[4] 1820 U S Census, Grayson, Virginia. 43; NARA Roll: M33_131, Image: 60.

[5] Jimmy O. Baldwin, in History of Cedar County, bet. 1991 & 1998, pp. 145-146. Greene County Archives and Records Center, 1126 Boonville, Springfield, Mo.

[6] New River Notes [online http://www.newrivernotes.com/va/gray1828tl.htm].

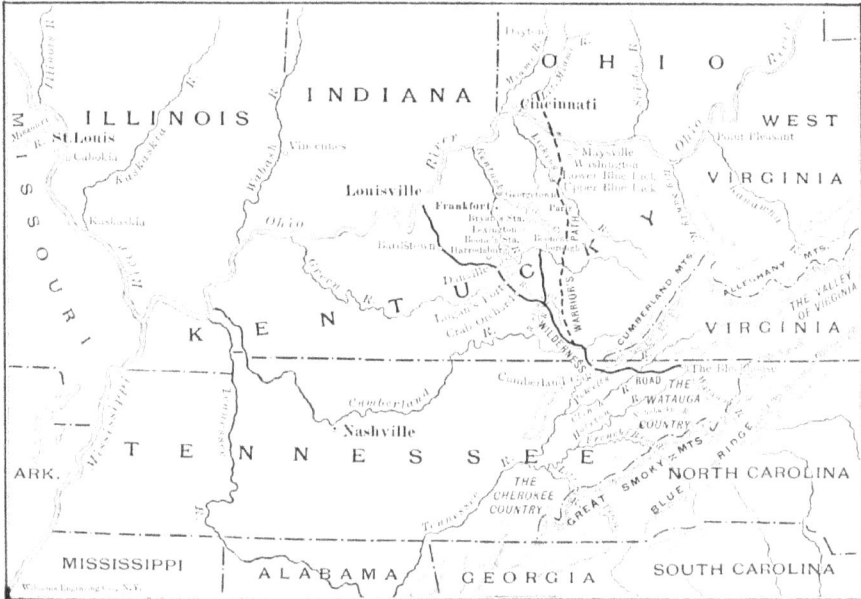

Map of the Wilderness Road. The Baldwin family lived in the Blue Ridge
Mountains of southwest Virginia, in Grayson County across the state border
from North Carolina. The Wilderness Road and Warrior's Path connected the
area with destinations in Kentucky, Tennessee, Ohio, and Indiana. Big Sandy
River and Kanawha Trace were alternate routes to the north. Bruce, *Daniel
Boone and the Wilderness Road,* 1911, p 341.

traveling in a party with other migrants. Old family lore, which
speculated that they traveled with Nancy's parents and other members
of the Brizendine family who moved west at about the same time, is
inaccurate because the Brizendines did not join the Baldwins in Indiana
until after 1830.

Thomas Lee was at the vanguard of the Second Great Migration out
of western Virginia. By 1830, the density of settlements in the Upper
New River Valley had grown to more than seven men per square mile.

Kanawha Trace. Inscribed on this 1827 map is the route Thomas Lee Baldwin
probably took from his home in Grayson County, Virginia, to Wayne County,
Indiana, in 1828. The heavily traveled Kanawha Trace began in the Quaker
communities of North Carolina. It entered Virginia at approximately the
location of the Baldwin homesteads on Grasse Creek and Little Reed Island
Creek (lower right) before crossing the Blue Ridge Mountains and proceeding
along the Kanawha River into Ohio, and then on to Indiana. The length of the
trip was about 400 miles and required two to three weeks. Map by Philippe
Vandermaelen, *Parties des Etats-Unis* (Amer. Sep. 50). Bruxelles:
Vandermaelen, 1827. David Rumsey Historical Map Collection.

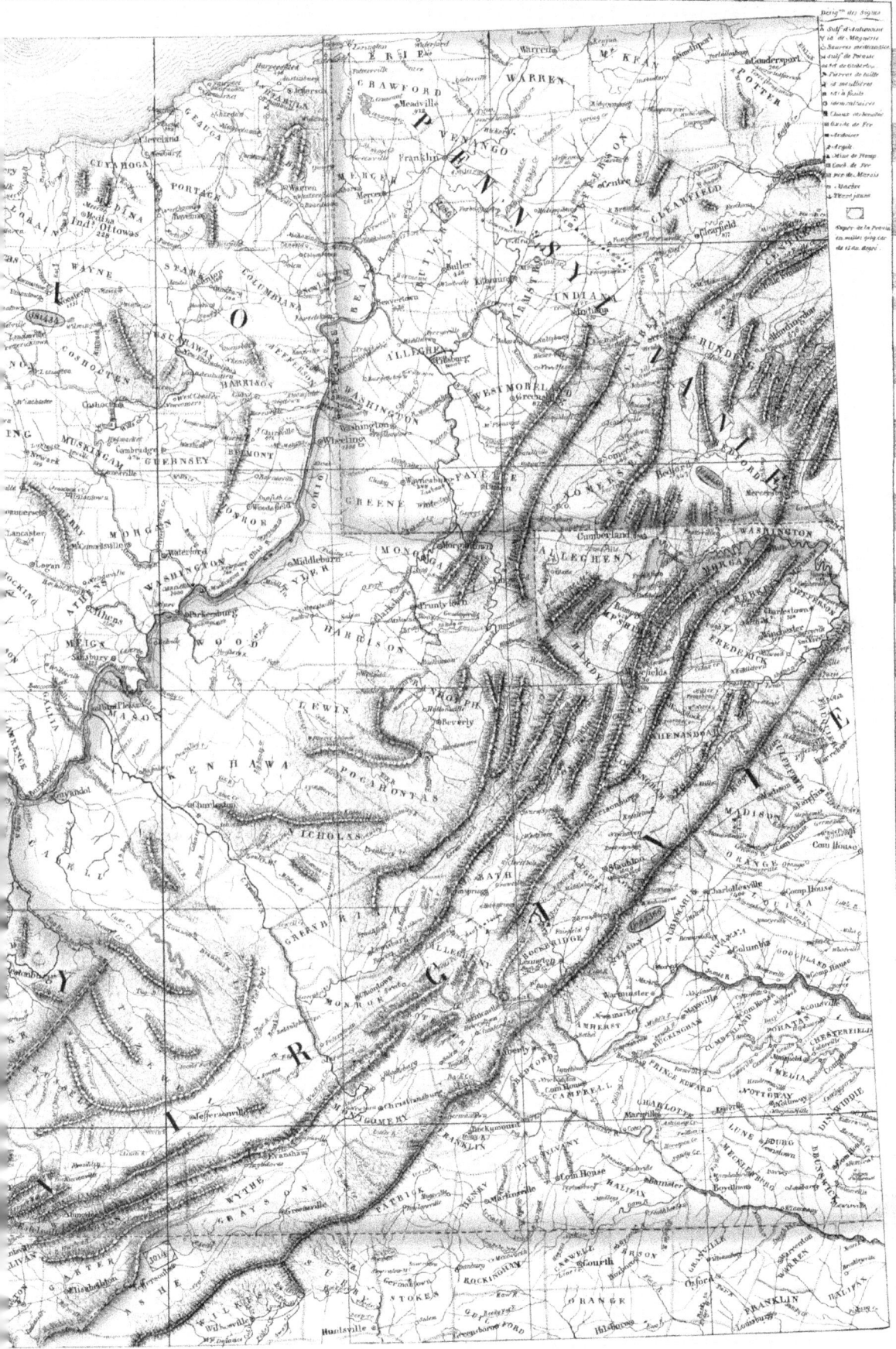

The Kanawha Trace Way Bill

New Garden, Guilford County, N. Carolina Bill of the Road to Richmond, Indiana, Crossing the Blue Ridge at Ward's Gap, and traveling the Kanawha Route

---

(facing page)

Clemmons - - - -	4	4	Peters' - - - - - -	3	142
Beesons - - - -	5	9	Mouth of Indian River-	7	149
Kerners - - - -	3	12	Pack's ferry - - -	10	159
Bitting's - - -	17	26	Blue Stone River - -	5	164
Gording's - - -	14	43	Pack's - - - - - -	6	170
Unthank's - - -	14	57	Hervey's - - - - -	17	187
Perkin's - - - -	4	61	Blake's - - - - - -	6	193
Mankins' - - - -	8	69	Road's fork - - - -	16	209
(At Wards Gap)			Cotton hill - - - - -	6	215
Cornelius' - - -	5	74	(4 m. over)		
Road's fork - - -	6	80	Falls of New River -	5	220
Reedisland River -	14	94	Benjamin Morris's - -	8	228
Fugat's Ford			Leonard Morris's - -	17	245
of New River- -	1	95	Venables' - - - - -	5	250
John Feely's - - -	5	100	Cobb's - - - - - - -	7	257
Walker's Mountain-	15	115	Coal River and Coal		
Shannon's - - -	3	118	Mountain in the way to		
Thos. Kirk's - - -	9	127	Hanley's - - - - -	18	265
Giles Court House-	2	129	M'Collister's - - - -	12	277
Peters ferry - - -	3	132	Grice's - - - - - - -	16	293
Peters town - - -	7	139			

(reverse page)

Ohio River - - - -	9	302	Leisburg, in Highland		
700 yds wide -Galliopolis			County, Ohio - - -	3	396
Woods			Joel Willis's - - - -	4	400
on Rackoon Ck-	11	313	Morgantown - - - - -	4	404
Judge Poor's - - -	15	328	Wilmington - - - - -	10	414
Town of Jackson -	8	336	Todd's fork Creek - -	3	417
Scioto Salt works.			Ceasar's creek - - -	10	427
Coonts's - - - - -	11	347	Little Miami at		
Richmond - - - - -	5	352	Waynesville - - -	3	430
Highbank-Prairies-	5	357	Springborough - - - -	8	438
Kilgore's ferry -	5	362	Franklin on the		
(Scioto)			Great Miami - - -	4	442
Chilicotho - - - -	4	366	Tapscott's - - - - -	2	444
Elijah Johnsons on			Big twin Creek - - -	4	448
Paint Creek - - -	9	375	Eaton - - - - - - -	17	465
Greenfield - - - -	12	387	White Water Meet House		
Rattlesnake creek			RICHMOND ---------	16	481
at Monroetown-	6	393			

-This Bill may not be precisely correct in every instance-

(foolscap paper - before 1820) obtained from Argus Ogborn - Quaker Historian, Richmond IN. New Garden was in Greensboro NC -- Whitewater Meeting was begun 1809)

Kanawha Trace Way Bill. A description of points along the Kanawha Trace from New Garden, North Carolina, to Richmond, Indiana. Thomas Lee Baldwin likely followed this same trail from his home near Ward's Gap (mile 69 on the waybill), over the Blue Ridge Mountains, to Indiana. The first column of numbers indicates miles between place names while the second column is the cumulative distance from the beginning of the Trace in North Carolina to Richmond, Indiana, a total of 481 miles. Whether Thomas Lee traveled this exact, same route is unknown. Nevertheless, the Way Bill covers the route Thomas Lee could have taken, beginning at about Reed Island River near the Baldwin homestead in Virginia, and ending at Richmond, Indiana, a journey of approximately 387 miles. Courtesy of Merle C. Rummel, *The Kanawha Trace Way Bill,* from an original 19th century document.

Newly opened lands in the Upper Midwest lured Virginians to pack up their possessions and migrate to Ohio, Illinois, Indiana, and Missouri. For the Baldwins, the destination meant primarily Ohio and Indiana. The young Baldwin family may or may not have followed the usual route through southwest Virginia to Pound Gap in what was then Tazewell County. Once across the gap, they could book passage on flat boats, then float down the Big Sandy River to the Ohio River, and then down the Ohio to their destination. On the other hand, there were other migration routes available besides the Big Sandy River. For example, Cumberland Gap offered an alternative. However, it is doubtful that they chose the route through Cumberland Gap up the Warrior's Path because the gap meant a detour south from where they lived. Moreover, primary destinations during the Second Migration were not the fertile valleys in Tennessee and Kentucky, reached through the Cumberland Gap, but the newly opened land in Indiana, Illinois, and Missouri.

By 1820, the extent of settled area in the eastern United States reached as far west as St. Louis, Missouri. A crude network of trails, roads, and turnpikes was in place connecting the major cities and forts throughout the region. When Thomas Lee left Grayson County, Virginia, in 1828, he began his journey near Reed Island Creek, in Virginia, and ended it in Richmond, Indiana. The trip as the crow flies was about 300 miles, but by trail closer to 400 miles. If Thomas Lee traveled by foot and not the Big Sandy River route, he could have taken one of two westward routes: either the Wilderness Road or the Kanawha Trace. He lived east of the Blue Ridge Mountains, and either path posed a formidable challenge for early pioneers from that region.

It is unlikely that Thomas Lee followed the Wilderness Road but instead took the more direct path of the Kanawha Trace. The Kanawha Trace became a well-traveled road in the early 19th century that connected Quaker settlements in North Carolina with Quaker centers in Indiana and Ohio. The Trace passed through the Baldwin homestead in Virginia. A good description of the Kanawha Trace is that of Merle C. Rummel, author and Quaker historian.[1] He provided a detailed, mile-by-mile account, taken from an old Trace Way Bill of what it was like to traverse one of these early pioneer routes.

The Kanawha Trace began at New Garden Quaker Meeting House, near Greensboro, Guilford County, North Carolina, and proceeded north to Richmond, Indiana, crossing the Blue Ridge Mountains at Ward's Gap. Richmond, Indiana, is in Wayne County, where new Quaker settlements were established, and where Thomas Lee moved his family in 1828. A Quaker would walk with a team and wagon all the way from New Garden to White Water Meeting House in Richmond. A large community of Quakers grew up in Indiana at the beginning of the 19th century, and the Kanawha Trace was a major route from the South both to Indiana and to Quaker settlements in Ohio. Early Quaker emigrants did not use Daniel Boone's Wilderness Road, according to Rummel. Only a few of the Carolina Brethren who followed the Wilderness Road into Kentucky came up into Ohio and Indiana. The Kanawha Trace was their route. While a direct connection to the Quaker faith remains unconfirmed for Thomas Lee Baldwin's branch of the Baldwin family, many Baldwins were prominent in early Quaker history. Thomas Lee appears at least to have shared their strong moral ethos against slavery. In any event, Thomas Lee would have known the Kanawha Trace to be a viable alternative to the Wilderness Road and Pound Gap.

The Kanawha Trace starts in the Yadkin River Valley of North Carolina, where there existed several Quaker Meeting Houses, and in the same general area as the beginning of the Wilderness Road. After the Trace entered Virginia from North Carolina, Thomas Lee would have picked it up going down Little Reed Island Creek through Popular

---

[1] Rummel, Merle C., *The Kanawha Trace Way Bill*. Maggie Stewart-Zimmerman, 1998, [online Rootsweb]
http://homepages.rootsweb.com/~maggieoh/Migrate/merle.htm. December 2004.

Camp Mountain. The Trace followed present-day VA 100. The Baldwins had farms on Little Reed Island Creek. Trails connected their location with the Trace along the Kanawha River. The Trace crisscrossed Reed Island and New Rivers. In those early days, the lack of bridges in the frontier areas meant that obstacles that we now ignore drastically affected travel patterns. As Rummel points out, a traveler sometimes went longer distances or took worse routes because there was no way they could cross a River.

Across present West Virginia, the Kanawha Trace followed the Shawnee Indian War Path close to the New, or Kanawha River. The trail came out at the Falls of the New River, now Kanawha Falls (where the Kanawha River Dam is). Portions of the Trace in this area are now underwater. Here, the route entered the Kanawha Valley pressed closely on either side by high, rugged mountains, and here, below the Falls, early settlers built flat boats and floated down the Kanawha River through what is today Charleston, West Virginia, to Point Pleasant, then down the Ohio River to Cincinnati. Some migrants opted to take boats down the Kanawha River, while others chose to walk the trail. Those who chose not to take the river route could choose a road overland.

Starting at Gallipolis, Ohio, the Kanawha Trace followed an Army road built to prosecute the Indian wars, now the approximate route of US Highway 35. It proceeded to Chillicothe, the first Capital of the State of Ohio. Chillicothe had been a major Shawnee Indian center and is noted today for its Hopewell Indian mounds (Mound City). Leaving Chillicothe, the Kanawha Trace followed the Zane Trace, another early pioneer road, and followed an old Indian trail that went west up a wide valley to South Salem, Ohio, keeping to the highlands into Wilmington, Ohio. The Trace went westward from Wilmington along present OH 73, coming eventually to St. Clair's Fort, which still stood, in Thomas Lee's day, from the Indian Wars. US 35 highway follows the Trace to Richmond, Indiana, the destination of Thomas Lee. By 1827, the National Road, built by the government across the upper tier of states, had entered Indiana as far as Richmond and may have made the last few miles of the journey a little easier. The total trip from where Thomas would have picked up the Kanawha Trace at Little Reed Island Creek was 387 miles to Richmond.

Some travelers could average as much as 40 miles a day, but a party traveling with women and children would progress more slowly. Such a journey to Richmond would have taken between two and three weeks. It was customary for men to band together in advance to make exploratory expeditions to frontier destinations before returning to Virginia to bring wives and other family members back to Indiana. We do not know if Thomas Lee made such an exploratory trip.

Although he and Nancy likely traveled in a party of several people, walking with two small children would have been a long and hard journey under the best of circumstances. Both the Big Sandy River and the Kanawha Trace were arduous trips. There were no railroads to Indiana in 1828, and based on Virginia tax records, Thomas Lee did not own much at the time. The Quakers invented the Conestoga wagon for such trips, canvas-covered, horse-drawn conveyances that eased the journey for its occupants. Whether the Baldwins were able to afford horse and wagon transportation, boat passage, or simply walked the nearly 400 miles is unknown.

The Second Great Migration roughly covered the period 1820-1840, making it plausible that Thomas Lee Baldwin and his family joined the migration in 1828. We do not know the reason Thomas Lee decided to leave Virginia. Perhaps it was the lure of the Indiana frontier and the opportunity to join fellow Virginians in a new adventure. It may have been, as family tradition says, a desire to get away from slavery, which he did not like, and which grew rapidly in the slave states of the South. States like Virginia and North Carolina made a trade of exporting black workers into the Deep South, where the cotton industry flourished. Because of their historic rejection of slavery, many of the Quakers from Virginia and North Carolina departed and moved north to Indiana, many of them settling in Wayne County, Indiana. Slavery in Indiana was unlawful. There are many stories of Quakers purchasing slaves from their owners to take them to Indiana and free them. It became an important stop along the Underground Railroad where Wayne County citizens worked tirelessly to aid fugitives towards freedom, helping them flee to the north.

On the other hand, Thomas may just have grown tired of Appalachia and the isolated life of farming in the upland valleys of the Blue Ridge

Mountains, seeing instead a better future for his children in the fertile plains of the Midwest. In any event, sometime in late 1828 or early 1829, he began the long trip from Virginia to Indiana that effectively reversed the journey his grandfather had taken four decades earlier down the Great Wagon Road from Pennsylvania to Virginia.

15

The National Road

Wayne County, Indiana, is located along the Ohio border in Eastern Indiana, a prosperous farming community. It is of interest that Thomas Lee Baldwin chose to settle in Wayne County, Indiana, given its history. Before becoming a state in 1816, Indiana Territory was part of the Greenville Treaty of 1795, which concluded hostilities between the United States and the Indians who occupied the region, and who recognized Ohio Territory as part of the US, but not Indiana Territory. Ohio Territory became a state in 1803, ceding at the same time a wedge of land to Indiana Territory, the part of the Greenville Treaty yet in Indian lands, on the border between Indiana and Ohio. In 1809, another treaty opened a 12-mile strip for settlement along the Ohio line. North Carolina Quakers settled in this region as early as 1806, near Elkhorn and Abington, and along the Whitewater River.[1] Elkhorn soon became a region familiar to Thomas Lee, who later settled near there about 1832. Wayne County officially formed in 1811 with the county seat at Salisbury, a town since abandoned. Salisbury was a small settlement just south and about midway between Richmond and Centerville. The county seat moved to Centerville, and then to the present county seat of Richmond. Indiana became a state in 1816.[2]

One of the provisions in the formation of Indiana, Ohio, and all territories of the original Northwest Territory Ordinance of 1787 required the total abolishment of slavery in the territories formed from it. Notwithstanding that, and because the territory was originally part of Virginia, that portion still belonging to the Indians in Indiana tolerated

---

[1] 1790 US Census, North Carolina, Randolph, p. 293, National Archives and Records Administration (NARA).

[2] Young, Andrew W., *History of Wayne County, Indiana, from Its First Settlement to the Present Time*, Cincinnati: Robert Clarke, 1872.

Indiana Map of 1831. Indiana was a state under development in 1828 when Thomas Lee Baldwin removed from Grayson County, Virginia, to settle in Wayne County, Indiana, on the Ohio border. A large portion of the state in the north was still wilderness occupied by the indigenous Indian tribes of the area. Finley, *Indiana*, 1831, p, 26, David Rumsey Historical Map Collection.

immigrants who brought slaves with them until the creation of the state in 1816. When slave owners sought to sell their slaves to the South, Governor William Henry Harrison intervened to forbid such sales, thus effectively freeing all slaves in Indiana.

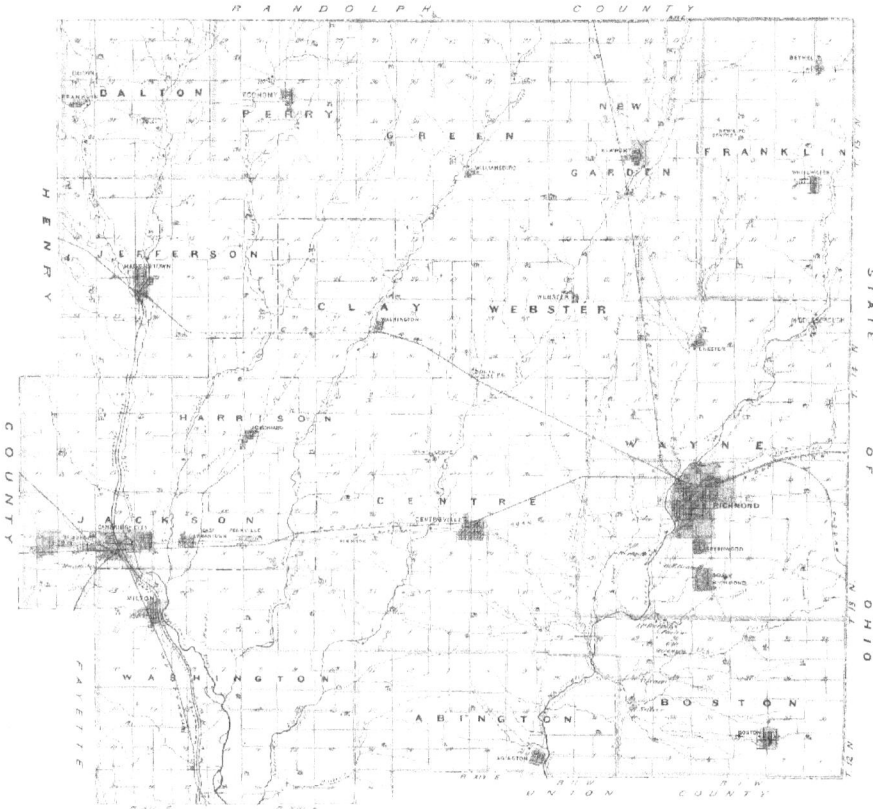

Map of Wayne County. The largest town in the county was Richmond, which became a hub of converging railroads, as shown on this 1876 map. There were no railroads in Wayne County when Thomas Lee Baldwin arrived there in 1828. The first rail line did not reach the county until 1853. Andreas, *Map of Wayne County*, 1876, p. 102, David Rumsey Historical Map Collection.

Aside from its rich farmland, Wayne County is a landscape of high tablelands cut by deep canyon-like river valleys. One of its historic features is the prehistoric earthworks scattered along the bluffs of the streams. Wayne County provides much evidence of the occupancy by the Mound Builders, part of the American Indian Mississippian culture found throughout the basins of the Ohio and Mississippi rivers.[1]

We cannot say exactly where Thomas Lee and Nancy first settled in Wayne County. Thomas Lee was not in the 1830 census for Wayne County. There were other Thomas Baldwins in Wayne County, having arrived there at an earlier date. However, none matches the family of Thomas Lee and Nancy.[2] A Thomas Baldwin appeared in the 1830 census in New Garden County, about the same age as Thomas Lee. However, the 1840 census enumerated the same family again in Wayne County at the same time that the 1840 census of Hancock County, Indiana, listed Thomas Lee. Therefore, the two Thomas Baldwins could not be the same person. It is not possible to identify either household because the US Census did not list the names of family members until 1850.

Old Wayne County Courthouse. The original log courthouse of Wayne County, Indiana, is the only such structure left in the Old Northwest Territory. Built in 1812, the courthouse originally stood in Salisbury, later moved to Centerville. This would have been the courthouse in use during the time Thomas Lee Baldwin lived in Wayne County. Photo Courtesy of Lisa Wallen Logsdon.

Sometime after 1830, Nancy's parents and brothers joined the Baldwins in Wayne County. The Baldwins and Brizendines remained closely aligned as an extended family. For many years, the Baldwin family previously believed that the elder Brizendines—Isaac and his wife—never moved to Indiana, did not leave Virginia, and Nancy never

---

[1] Observations on the Prehistoric Earthworks of Wayne County, Indiana, *Eighth Annual Report of the Geological Survey of Indiana*, 1876.
[2] Dorrell, Ruth. *Pioneer Ancestors of Members of the Society of Indiana Pioneers.* Indianapolis: Indiana Historical Society, 1983.

saw them again after 1828.[3] However, the 1840 US census shows them living with their son Isaac, Jr., in Hancock County, Indiana, near the household of the Baldwins. They doubtless made the journey with their sons from Grayson County, Virginia, to Wayne County, Indiana, shortly after the 1830 census, which had recorded them in Grayson County. They then moved with the Baldwins to Hancock County, where the 1840 census listed them.[4]

Thomas Lee almost certainly continued the Baldwin occupation of farming, although he does not appear to have owned land in Wayne County, perhaps instead renting a place or working for another family. According to family sources, he opened a farm in Wayne County where he remained until the year 1841, at which time he moved to Hancock County, Indiana.[5] However, census data indicate that he moved to Hancock County before 1841. Sometime along the way, Thomas Lee developed an interest in the horse business.[6]

In 1837, He entered and purchased 37.17 acres in Hancock County, Indiana. The odd acreage was due to the skewed survey grid that usually occurred in the northern latitudes because of the Earth's curvature. In that same year, the Brizendine brothers entered patents for parcels of land adjoining the land of Thomas Lee. The availability of land was one of the main reasons migrants left Virginia and elsewhere to resettle in the Midwest. The opening of the Northwest Territory added vast amounts of land to the US frontier, which soon became the preferred destination of a new pioneer generation pushing westward.

The availability of land in Indiana was relatively new. Before the American Revolution, the British prohibited colonists from crossing the Appalachians into the lands belonging to the native Indians. Squatters could not legally own land in Indian Territory. The land that became Indiana was part of the Northwest Territory, ceded to the United States by Great Britain at the end of the Revolution. As a result, the sale and settlement of all land came under the regulation of the US government.

---

[3] Jimmy O. Baldwin, in History of Cedar County, pp. 145-146.

[4] 1840 US Census, Union, Hancock, Indiana, Roll: 82, p. 212, Family History Library Film: 0007725.

[5] Correspondence, Letter to Minnie Cornwell from Jessie Hastins, no date.

[6] Jimmy O. Baldwin. In History of Cedar County, pp. 145-146.

Consequently, through a series of questionable treaties, the Indians reluctantly moved further west to make room for white settlement. The government instituted a method of surveying land based on a rectangular grid system, unlike the "meets-and-bounds' system employed in Virginia, for example. In Virginia, boundaries were often arbitrary, followed no particular shape, and generally relied on vague boundary markings, such as trees and other impermanent markers. Consequently, land disputes among owners often led to arguments resolved in court. In contrast, the rectangular grid system began at a fixed meridian running north and south with a baseline bisecting it east and west. Surveyors ruled off a given area into sections of 640 acres each. A section was one square mile in size. The US government then sold these parcels of public land to fund the Federal government. The rectangular survey system thereafter became the standard for settlement of the remainder of the continent. Out of this new method came the unsung heroes of the American westward development as a nation. Surveyors had to survey the land before any sale could proceed. Surveyors were often the first ones to set foot on wilderness land. Poorly paid and minimally equipped, these surveyors braved the elements, Indian attacks, and primitive living conditions to create the paper framework into which settlers established themselves.

Once surveyors completed a tract of land, the General Land Office (GLO) advertised the land for sale. Anyone who wished to purchase land in Indiana, for example, filed a purchase with the GLO in Indianapolis. To make a land purchase, the buyer had to go to Indianapolis or send a representative to the GLO office there. The minimum fixed price for government land originally was $1 per acre. However, by the time Thomas Lee purchased land in 1837, the price had increased to $1.25 per acre. The purchase had to be in cash. The minimum acreage was usually 40 acres. The procedure for purchasing land required the purchaser to examine a plat book to determine the location of an available tract. He then filled out an application indicating his choice in a tract book. The registrar certified that the land was available for purchase, after which the buyer took the certified application to the receiver and paid for the land. Following the purchase, the GLO in Washington issued a land patent, or deed, to the land.

Meanwhile, surveyors had surveyed the National Road (US 40, present I 70) to Richmond, Indiana, in 1827. By 1834, the road extended from Richmond, Indiana, across Hancock County to Indianapolis, and beyond, a convenient trip of about 70 miles connecting Richmond to Indianapolis, inestimably easier than the 400-mile previous journey the Baldwins made across the Blue Ridge Mountains from Virginia to Indiana. The National Road would become a major asset to westward migrations. Thomas Lee Baldwin would have traveled the relatively

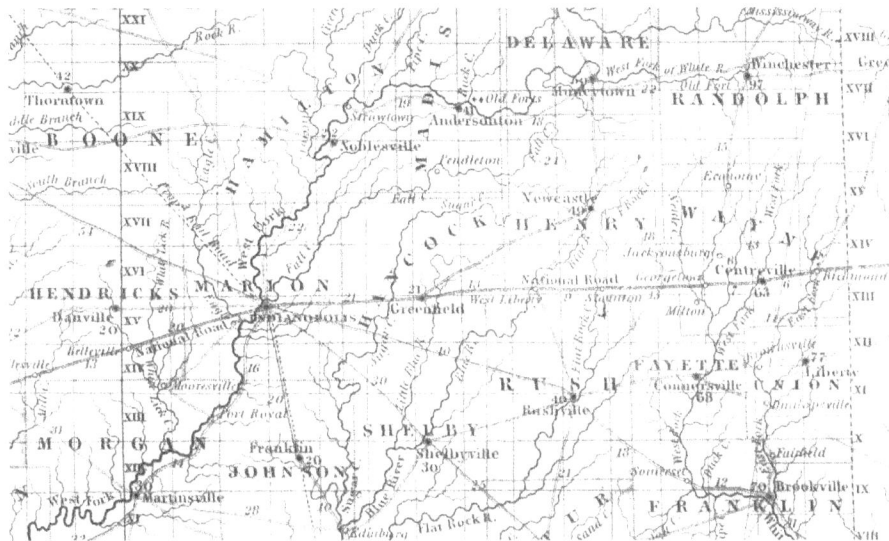

Map of the National Road. This map segment shows the location of the National Road from the Ohio border, across Wayne County and Hancock County, Indiana, passing through Greenfield, on to Indianapolis, and beyond. The proximity of the Road to the Thomas Lee Baldwin farm was about five miles north of the Road. Excerpt from a map by Mitchell & Young, *Indiana*, 1834, David Rumsey Historical Map Collection.

short distance across Henry County, Indiana, from Wayne County to Hancock County, almost certainly along the National Road, the newly constructed, main east-west transportation route.[7] The National Road that Thomas Lee traveled was the first attempt by the United States to provide a means to move people and goods across America's vast territory. The road, initiated under the Presidency of Thomas Jefferson, started in Cumberland, Maryland (it originally was called the

---

[7] *A New Map of Indiana with its Roads and Distances,* Philadelphia: S. Augustus Mitchell, 1848.

"Cumberland Road"), eventually traversing Pennsylvania, Virginia (now West Virginia), Ohio, Indiana, and Illinois, ending in Vandalia, Illinois, near St. Louis. It initially stopped short of its original plans to go to St. Louis, but in later years extended on to Jefferson City, Missouri. The general route of the old National Road is very close to US Highway 40 and Interstate 70.

Completion of the first section of the National Road in the East was in 1818, and it was soon the most heavily traveled highway in America. The grading and surfacing made it by far the most comfortable road to travel for its day. Stagecoaches and commercial wagon traffic were heavy, with teams of wagons carrying grain and produce from the interior to markets in the East, and manufactured products to the West. Many taverns and inns along the way catered to travelers, where men exchanged the latest news and politics around the roaring fireplaces. The towns along the National Road grew rapidly and became some of the most important trading centers in America. Baltimore benefitted the most as the eastern terminal of the National Road, rivaling New York, Philadelphia, and Boston as the prime seaport of the United States. Work crews completed the Road across Ohio and first moved into Indiana through Richmond, in Wayne County, in 1828, about the time Thomas Lee migrated to Wayne County from Virginia. His migration westward through Indiana and later to Illinois roughly parallels the period of construction of the National Road, which reached Hancock County in 1835. Crews built the Road through an unbroken forest. One gang of men started the work by cutting the trees and clearing the right of way. Another removed the stumps, and a third graded the roadbed. As each section opened, wagon trains going west and livestock going to Cincinnati heavily traveled it. The National Road was an added attraction to early settlers in the area because it provided a much-needed transportation system for people and goods moving in and out of the region. Like many other frontier states, Indiana suffered tremendously from an inability to move products. For example, during the pioneer days vast acres of cleared trees simply went up in smoke, burned because there was no way to move them from the abundant supply to a mill or any area where there was demand.

Indianapolis White River Covered Bridge. Completed in 1834, it introduced a long tradition of covered bridges in Indiana. This one built on the National Road has two passages to accommodate traffic going both ways. Thomas Lee would have been familiar with this bridge. The state razed the bridge in 1902-1903. Schrader, *Indianapolis remembered: Christian Schrader's Sketches of Early Indianapolis,* Indiana Historical Bureau, 1987.

Thomas Lee knew the National Road well. Originally, the National Road was a dirt road with its culverts and bridges constructed in the most substantial manner. In Hancock County, for example, stone crossings arched over small streams while bridges spanned the larger streams, such as Sugar Creek, Six Mile, and Brandywine. Enclosed wooden bridges constructed over Brandywine and Sugar Creek each had two driveways, each about twelve feet wide. History records much about the Old Plank Road, when wooden planks paved portions of the roadbed of the National Road. This work occurred in Hancock County about 1850 or 1851, beginning at Indianapolis and proceeding eastward. Thomas possibly traveled the Plank Road on return trips to Indiana and back east, but it did not exist at the time he lived in Hancock County.

From the time the National Road first opened, one of its inviting features for travelers was the tavern. This bit of Americana has a long tradition, which remains preserved today in the modern motel. The great amount of travel westward over the old Centerville state road in Indiana and, later, over the National Road, caused a great many of these taverns, or eating houses, to be established along this line. There were days in which fifty or more teams followed each other westward in one train. Many of the travelers camped along the road, while others drove into the large stable yards and slept in their wagons. In connection with the tavern, the keeper ordinarily had a stable with a large yard in which he kept the wagons and horses. In fact, this was a legal requirement. For the protection of travelers, a law, approved in 1825, required a tavern keeper to prove, among other things, that he could provide a good house with at least three apartments, and a stable convenient to said house, with at least four good stalls. The owner had to show further that he owned at least two beds and bedding over and above what his family needed. Drovers also went along the road with droves of hogs, sheep, cattle, etc., for market at Indianapolis or Cincinnati. Many tavern keepers were prepared to care for such droves and flocks by having pens and lots fenced near the tavern. Signs hung up at each establishment could always identify taverns. Ordinarily, the word "Tavern," painted on a large board, announced this fact. Others displayed a brightly polished brass plate with a design of some kind engraved upon it. The bill for a traveler to stay at a tavern included the cost of supper and breakfast, the night's lodging, and the care of his horse. Furnished meals cost 15 cents. Board, including three meals daily and bed, was $1.25 per day, coincidentally the same going rate for an acre of government land. Staying at a tavern could be expensive and viewed by some as a luxury. Many travelers elected instead to camp by the roadside.

The extension of the National Road through Indiana and Illinois encouraged westward expansion of the United States. It, along with the opening of vast new tracts of public lands in Indiana, Illinois, and Missouri, had a marked influence on many pioneer families to move westward. Indiana's population, for example, more than quadrupled between 1820 and 1840 and many came to the state upon the National Road. The Road had a similar influence, no doubt, on the Baldwin and Brizendine families who moved in the mid-1840s westward along the path of the Road to new parts of the country. The Road passed through Greenfield, Indiana, near the Baldwin and Brizendine farms. The Baldwins eventually traveled beyond the reach of the National Road to settle in southwest Missouri. Meanwhile, they first reestablished themselves in Hancock County, Indiana.

16

Fresh Start

Thomas Lee opened a farm in Union Township, Hancock County, Indiana. According to family tradition, he moved his family from Wayne County to Hancock County in 1841. However, it is likely he moved earlier than 1841. He is listed in the 1840 census for Hancock County and, therefore, his removal from Wayne County must have occurred between March 20, 1837, the date of approval of his land patent, and 1840, the date of the census, although it is possible he opened his farm in Union Township before 1837.

All of the Baldwin and Brizendine land patents were in Hancock County, Indiana, Section 6, located at Township 16-North, Range 7-East. The GLO signed the patents on behalf of President Martin Van Buren on March 20, 1837.[1] Essentially a bill of sale, the patents show that Thomas Lee and the Brizendines completed their applications for land in Hancock County while still living in Wayne County and using a Wayne County address. Some observers take this to mean that Thomas Lee lived in Wayne County from the time of his arrival there in about 1828 until 1837, when he purchased the Hancock land, or a period of around nine years before moving to Hancock County. However, the date of a patent was often only a rough guide as to when the person actually began living on the land. Due to the high demand for land, there was a significant backlog in processing claims. Several years could pass between the time a person entered and purchased land, then applied for a patent, and the date the GLO actually signed the patent. This, combined with the practice of "preemption", whereby persons assumed the right to purchase land on which they had already settled, or that they

---

[1] Bureau of Land Management, General Land Office Records, Land Patents. Thomas L. Baldwin of Wayne County, Indiana, Certificate 26110, issue date 3/20/1837, Land Office Indianapolis, sale-cash entry, Indiana, 38.17 acres, no metes and bounds, serial #IN0860, 425, SE 1/4 NE 1/4 Sec 6 Township 16-North Range 7-East 2nd Principal Meridian, Indiana, Hancock County. [/s/ President Martin Van Buren]

Indiana Land Patent. Land patent issued to Thomas L. Baldwin of Wayne County, Indiana, Certificate 26110, issue date 3/20/1837, Land Office Indianapolis, sale-cash entry, Indiana, 38.17 acres, no metes and bounds, serial #IN0860, described as "SE 1/4 NE 1/4 Sec 6 Township 16-North Range 7-East 2nd Principal Meridian," Indiana, Hancock County. [/s/ President Martin Van Buren]. Bureau of Land Management, General Land Office Records, Land Patents.

had cultivated before the completion of a sale. Therefore, we cannot determine with complete accuracy when Thomas Lee and the Brizendines left Wayne County to settle on purchased government land in Hancock County, Indiana. The government did not permit preemption until 1830. Therefore, it seems probable that they remained in Wayne County until at least 1831, and probably later. In any event, the Baldwin and Brizendine families appeared in the 1840 census in Hancock County, living next to each other on the land they had purchased.

The Baldwin family, along with members of the Brizendine families, lived next to each other in the same geographic area. Although the names of other household members besides the head of household did not appear in census records before 1850, the ages of individuals in Thomas Lee's household in 1840 correspond to known family members. Included was Thomas Lee age 44, his wife Nancy 39, and eight of their eleven children: Sarah 15, Thomas 14, William 11, John Calvin 8, Nancy

5, Joshua 4, James 2, and Lucinda 1. Not accounted for on the 1840 census of the Baldwin household was their son Caleb, who would have been age 9, and who was probably staying with a member of the Brizendine family at the time of the census. Meanwhile, Isaac Brizendine and his wife, Mary Polly, ages 72 and 67 respectively, parents of Nancy Baldwin (Thomas Lee's wife), were living nearby. Other members of the Brizendine family were also living in the same vicinity, including Nancy's younger brothers: Brooks, Edmond, Young, and LeRoy.[2] The entire Brizendine family moved to Hancock County at the time the Baldwins moved, with the apparent exception Elizabeth Brizendine, who many think married Thomas Baldwin, Jr., Thomas Lee's father, and who remained in Virginia. Meanwhile, there were no other Baldwins besides Thomas Lee and his family listed in the 1840 census in Union Township, although there were many other Baldwins in Hancock County at the time.

When Thomas Lee arrived in Hancock County from Wayne County, it was a developing region but in many ways still a wilderness. According to the Society of Indiana Pioneers, anyone who settled there before 1830 was a pioneer of the county.[3] While not prominent in the county, the Baldwins and Brizendines were, nevertheless, among the oldest families to settle there. Indiana historian George Richman, in his *History of Hancock County*, includes Thomas Baldwin, Brooks Brizendine, and Young Brizendine on a list of 122 names of the earliest settlers who entered land in the county recorder's office.[4]

The area that became Hancock County was first settled about 1818. The Methodists were the first religious society organized in the county. The first road in the region was an old Indian trail known as the "Napoleon Trace". At the time of the organization of the county, the territory was an unbroken wilderness of wild deer, bears, panthers, wild cats, wolves, and rattlesnakes. There are many stories of pioneers

---

[2] 1840 US Census, Indiana, Hancock, Union Township, Series M704 Roll 82 p. 212, National Archives.

[3] According to the Society of Indiana Pioneers, an individual was a pioneer of the county if they resided there on or before December 31, 1830.

[4] Richman, George J., *History of Hancock County, Indiana, Its People, Industries and Institutions.* Indianapolis, Ind.: Federal, 1916.

literally cutting their way through the woods to their homesteads. The entire population was about 400, not including numerous Indians who made it their home.

The Indians lived in the region for generations well before it became Hancock County. They were eventually pushed out to make way for white settlers, forced to leave behind their ancestral ties to the land and to abandon ceremonial sites that meant little to the new occupants. Nearly 50 years after Thomas Lee was there, the state of Indiana took note of the Indian past: "That there were people in the county before the first white settlers arrived is, of course, well known. Spearheads, arrow points, stone axes, etc., may still be found in all parts of the county, especially on the hills and bluffs bordering the creeks and rivers. Skeletons have been found in gravel pits in different parts of the county... There are [about five miles east of the Baldwin farm] some curious earthworks that probably belong to the age of the Mound Builders. These are located on the south side of Brandywine, at the extreme point of a very abrupt bend of that creek... From this point, a levee, three feet high and ten feet wide, has been constructed to the ancient bed of the stream. The excavation which furnished the earth for this embankment is distinctly seen in the projecting point of high ground... These works are evidently artificial and ancient, for large trees are now growing on the sides of these pits and on the embankment... When, by what people, or for what purpose these works were made, we venture no conjecture."[5] Today we recognize this statement made in 1885 as a description of a ceremonial outpost of the Woodland Indian Culture, perhaps one connected to the great Hopewell tribes of Ohio.

Hancock County separated from Madison County and was organized on March 1, 1828, about the time Thomas Lee was settling in Wayne County two counties over to the east. The name Hancock was in honor of John Hancock, president of the convention that adopted the Declaration of Independence, who signed his name to the Declaration large enough, he said, so King George III could see it without his glasses.

---

[5] Richman, George J., *History of Hancock County,* quoting the state geologist for the year of 1885.

Hancock County is flat, there being but few hills except in the immediate vicinity of the watercourses where most of the first settlements occurred. The soil is fertile, but pioneers considered the black low grounds almost worthless in the early history of the county until properly drained. The first exports of the county were ginseng, venison, hams, furs, flax, and tow linen. The land in the region where Thomas Lee settled is level, except along the creeks, where it is rolling. Its natural drainage is towards the south but much of the land was marshy and forested which settlers drained and then cleared for cultivation.

Hancock County originally consisted of three townships: Blue River, Brandywine, and Sugar Creek.[6] Today the county has nine townships instead of the original three. There have been changes in the township alignments since the county was first organized. For example, in 1838, Union Township, the home of Thomas Lee Baldwin, comprised the eastern part of Buck Creek Township, the western part of Harrison Township, and the southeast corner of Vernon Township. Then, in 1853, the county divided Union Township between Buck Creek, Vernon, and Center, thereby obliterating Union Township. The old Baldwin home place, originally in Union Township, today is located in Center Township. The northern part of Center Township was once Union Township.

Blue River is the largest stream in Hancock County and was a good millstream for the early pioneers. Sugar Creek is next in size, enters the county near the northeast corner, and runs in a southwest direction. Brandywine Creek rises in Brown Township about a mile west of Warrington and runs in a southwesterly direction through Brown and Jackson Townships, to the central portion of Center Township, and south through Brandywine Township. Other streams in Hancock County are Buck Creek, Nameless Creek, Six Mile Creek, Little Brandywine Creek, Little Sugar Creek, and Lick Creek.

---

[6] Williams, D. J., & Williams, T. E. Q., *A History of Hancock County, Indiana, in the Twentieth Century*, 1995.

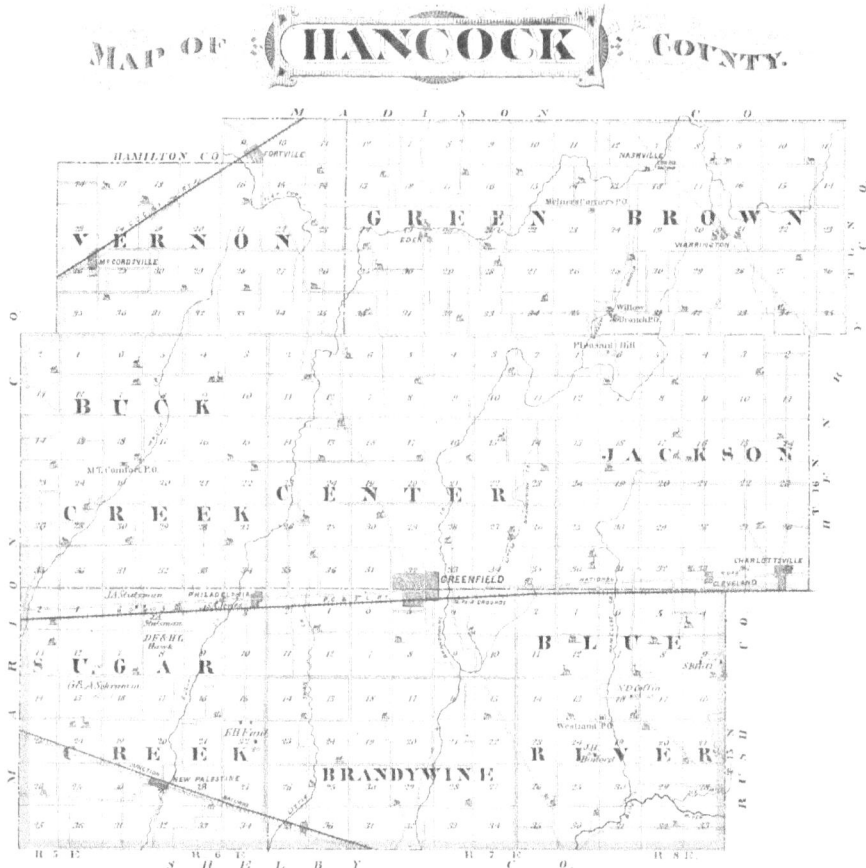

Map of Hancock County. Early settlers built along the two creeks which flow south through the region, Sugar Creek and the Brandywine. This map reveals the mosaic of surveyed sections of land that comprised the townships of Hancock County. Here, farms evolved out of the labors of the early settlers. A line of trees traced the meandering path of Sugar Creek to the west of the Baldwin property in Section 6 of Center Township. Meanwhile, Brandywine Creek is a short distance east, as it makes its way toward Greenfield at the center of the township and county. *Map of Hancock County*, 1876, David Ramsey Map Collection.

The Baldwin and Brizendine farms were located not far from the present town of Maxwell, in Section 6 of Township 16 North, Range 6 East. Thomas Lee entered 37.17 acres in 1837,[7] Young M. Brizendine entered 40 acres on the same date,[8] and along with his brother, Edmond,

---

[7] BLM, SE 1/4 NE 1/4 Sec 6, Township 16-North Range 7-East 2nd Principal Meridian, Indiana, Hancock county. 20 March 1837.
[8] BLM, Young M. Brizendine, 40 acres, NESE 6/ 16-N 7-E No 2nd PM, Hancock, Indiana. 20 March 1837.

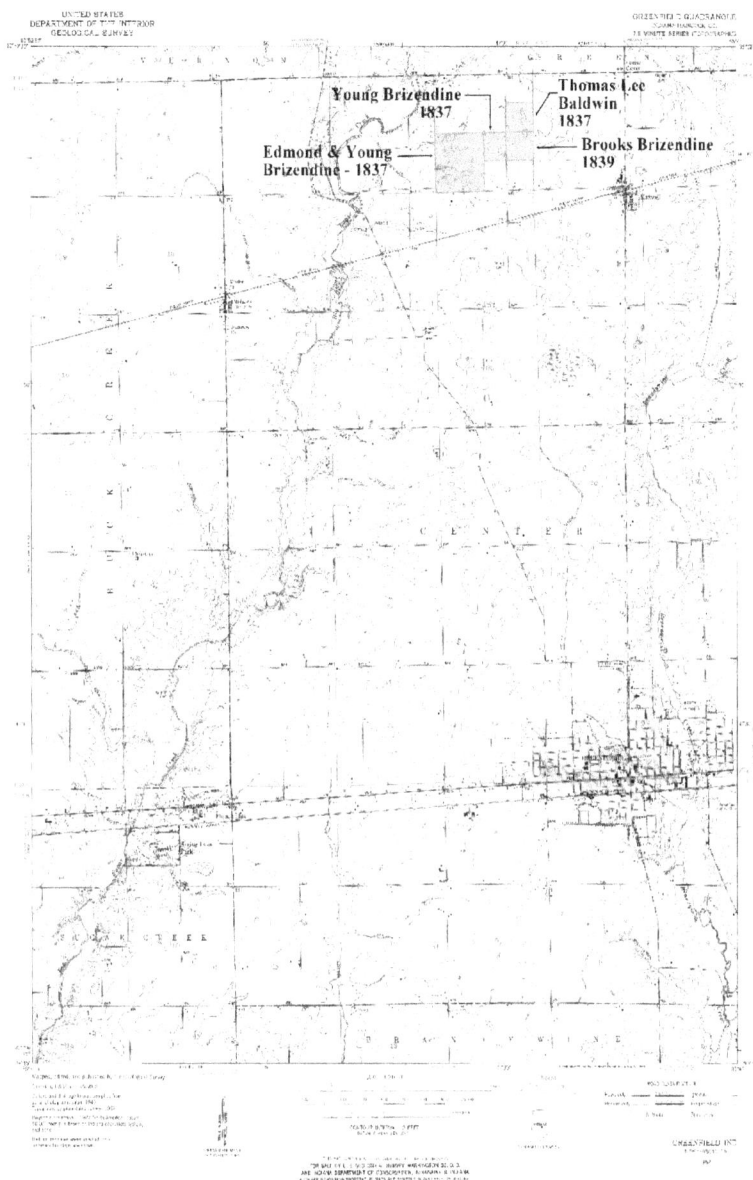

Thomas Lee Baldwin and Brizendine Brothers Farms. The Baldwin and Brizendine families owned about 250 acres in Center Township, Hancock County, Indiana, north of Greenfield, Indiana, near Indianapolis to the west. Railroads and improved highways shown on this modern topographical map did not exist in the time of Thomas Lee. Likewise, the map shows the new townships after the 1853 realignment. The new townships formed well after Thomas Lee had left Hancock County and made his way to Illinois. Many of the place names familiar to him have disappeared or changed. For example, the post office at Fortville once bore the name of Walpole. In Thomas Lee's time, he knew Cleveland by the name Portland, and Eden went by the name of Lewisburg. Lewisburg, or Eden, was very close to the Baldwin farm, which was about a mile north of the present town of Maxwell. US Department of the Interior Geological Survey, Greenfield, Indiana, Quadrangle, 1952.

purchased another 130.64 acres at the same time.[1] A little later, Brooks Brizendine added to the holdings, buying 40 acres adjoining the property of Thomas Lee and the Brizendine brothers, Edmond and Young.[2] The properties were about a quarter mile east of Sugar Creek. Years later, the railroad passed very close to their farms. The tracks have since been abandoned and torn out, but the old railroad bed is still visible. Today, a utility line traverses the properties. The towns of Mohawk and Maxwell did not exist at the time. It was in Hancock County that Thomas Lee began his business in trotting horses. He was among the first in the Midwest to breed these horses for their stamina and speed, qualities that made them good multi-purpose farm animals.

The population of Hancock County reported in 1840 was 7,525 persons; of the total, 1,494 were engaged in agriculture and nine in commerce. The Farmers' Annual Register, issued in 1845, showed that the county had four attorneys and five physicians. The principal merchants reported in the county were John Templin and Company, H. T. Hart and Company, at Greenfield, and Jonathan Evans at New Palestine. There were three post-offices: Greenfield, Philadelphia, and Charlottesville. The register also reported that the National Road passed through the county, and that the Dayton and Indianapolis stage passed east and west through Greenfield.

From the time that the first white people came into Hancock County in 1818, the county experienced rapid growth. When Thomas Lee Baldwin arrived, the population of the county was growing at a rate of about 200 per year. According to the US census reports, the population grew from 1,436 in 1830 to 7,525 in 1840, more than a fourfold increase in ten years. The first settlers faced three distinct lines of work, 1) clearing of the forests, 2) drainage of the land, and 3) construction of roads and highways for intercommunication. The first and most obvious task was to clear away the forest. To appreciate the rate at which it disappeared, the county originally contained 196,480 acres, almost all

---

[1] BLM, Edmund Brizendine, Young M. Brizendine, 130.64 acres, SW 6/ 16-N 7-E No 2nd PM, Hancock, Indiana. 20 March 1837.
[2] BLM, Brooks Brizendine, 40 acres, NWSE 6/ 16-N 7-E No 2nd PM, Hancock, Indiana. 1 August, 1839.

1840 US Census. Listed are the families of Thomas Lee Baldwin and the Brizendine brothers in Union Township, Hancock County, Indiana. Together the Baldwin and Brizendine families accounted for 42 members of the population. 1840 US Census, Series M704 Roll 82 p. 212. National Archives.

woodlands. By 1850, settlers had cleared 48,600 acres, or one-fourth, of this land. The first homes built were on knolls on small patches of ground cleared for cultivation. There were creeks and rivers in the county that carried away much of the surface water, yet there were great areas that were not reached by the streams or their tributaries. The great problem was to get drainage outlets. In the early history of the county, settlers dug outlets to drain the swampy farmland.

The first businesses in Hancock County were small gristmills built on the streams for grinding corn and wheat for settlers. These were water-powered mills, including a few located near the Baldwin farm, which figured prominently in the early history of the area. The closest one was Pierson's Mill, built in 1825, on Sugar Creek, five miles northwest of Greenfield. It is unknown if this mill was still in operation when Thomas Lee arrived in Hancock County. One newly opened mill was that of William Curry, who built his mill in 1835 on Brandywine Creek, about the middle of the north half of section 10, Township 16, Range 7. Curry's Mill was about two and one-half miles east of the Baldwin place. Meanwhile, almost as close was Willett's Mill, built in 1838, at about the time Thomas Lee arrived in the county. It was located on Sugar Creek about two miles southeast of Thomas Lee's place. Bellus' Mill, which was also located on Sugar Creek about two miles north of New Palestine, was another well-known early mill. All of these mills were small concerns. Some of them were hominy mills or "corn crackers" as commonly called; yet, they made it possible for the people of the county to obtain flour and meal without having to make a long wagon journey for it. Highways were few and went at all angles through the woods. Everywhere there were, as one anonymous writer put it, "swamps, swamps, swamps." Yet, the soil, "rich loam mixed with sand," was productive. The streams furnished waterpower for the mills, and the springs supplied pure water. Grocers and merchants, while few in the beginning, established quickly in the county. All these things added something to the comfort of the people, whose number was increasing daily. Residents could purchase the necessities of life at a number of places along the National Road, and a few stores stood along the Brookville Road in Sugar Creek Township, and at least one or two stores on the Knightstown-Pendleton state road.

In the very early history of Hancock County, the state of Indiana aided in the construction of highways connecting important points. When Thomas Lee arrived via the National Road, he found a good network of roads branching out into the county. By 1837, state roads crisscrossed Hancock County, including the Centerville state road, Brookville state road, Morristown road, Knightstown and Pendleton state road, Rushville state road, and several roads leading to and from Greenfield, including Greenfield and Noblesville road, Greenfield and Shelbyville state road, and Greenfield and Lebanon state road. The year Thomas Lee settled in Hancock County, the Indianapolis and Pendleton state road was also completed. Construction of all of these state roads occurred between 1832 and 1837.

Pioneers of the Frontier

17

Day-to-Day Life

While the state of Indiana engaged in the construction of roads connecting important points throughout the state, and the National Road was under construction westward, Hancock County also busied itself with road building within its own confines. In 1830, the population of the county was sparse, and the entire county remained mostly covered with forest. There were few farms and only a few towns and mills. The first roads connected different parts of the county with the towns or provided a way to reach mills. Practically none connected neighbor to neighbor. More roads gave access to mills built along the streams of the county than roads connected residents with the towns.

The roads in the early days did not follow section lines, but generally followed the most direct road to the mill, or to the town, or to some highway previously built to connect with a mill or a town. As soon as the forest began to disappear, and the land was put under cultivation, these roads running at various angles across the county made it inconvenient to cultivate many of the farms. As soon as fields of any size opened up, the farmers began to feel the inconvenience of the location of these highways running across their property. They began petitioning for changes in road locations. Changes in road locations came slowly, however, and it was not until after the Civil War that the relocated roads followed section lines.

Travel on the frontier was almost entirely by horse and wagon or on foot. Likewise, timber, agricultural products, livestock, and other commercial commodities went overland. Waterways and canals in the Hancock County area were generally unsuitable for moving large quantities of goods. The railroad did not reach the region until 1853, when the Indiana Central Railroad completed the first steam railroad at the south edge of Greenfield. The railroad became part of the Pennsylvania Railroad System and later the Penn-Central. These tracks, removed in the 1980s, ran very close to the old Baldwin place, but not when he lived there. In Thomas Lee's time, everything moved by horse and wagon.

Taxes have always been an issue in American history, and taxes were a general factor in westward migration. As new parts of the country were settled, the government needed more funds to build community services, often prompting pioneers to purchase cheap government land and move further westward to less populated areas. Taxation in Hancock County appears to have been one such story. The first tax levy in Hancock County was not on the value of the property; it was a specific tax, not an ad valorem tax. The amount of tax was the same regardless of the value of the property. One horse, for example, might be worth as much as two other horses, but the tax was the same on all. This changed in 1836 with an entirely different tax levy basis, one levied on the value of the property, and thus increasing potential government revenue. Under this levy, it became necessary not only to learn how many horses, oxen, wagons, etc., a man possessed, but also to assess that property at a certain value and then determine the amount of taxes from the value of the property. The method of taxation thereby changed from a specific to an ad valorem basis and was the system in effect when Thomas Lee came to Hancock County.

In 1836, taxes were twenty cents on each hundred dollars of valuation for county purposes and one cent on each 100 dollars of valuation for road purposes, as well as seventy-five cents on each poll, also for county purposes. Polls were free white males over the age of 21. As the county grew, the county required more money to transact its business. Consequently, the levy became more inclusive from year to year. For example, the levies made in 1839 and 1840 included, in addition to property taxes and road taxes, liquor license taxes, grocery taxes, a 'wooden clock' tax, and an exhibition (circus) tax for any event offered to the people and charging an admission. The county treasurer collected taxes. He did not, however, depend on people coming to his office to pay them, but rather published notice that he would be in the different townships at stated times to receive taxes. Moreover, another office, the Collector of Revenue, had the special business of collecting the taxes not already paid to the county treasurer.

The Newspaper in the area in Thomas Lee's time was the *Coon Skin*. The *Coon Skin* was a Democratic sheet published at Greenfield by Joseph Chapman, a local businessperson and politician. The paper took an active role in the political campaign of 1844, in which Democratic candidate, James K. Polk, defeated Whig candidate, Henry Clay. The publication of the *Coon Skin* was suspended when its publisher, Chapman, enlisted at the outbreak of the Mexican War. There were many other newspapers published after 1845; however, none predates Thomas Lee's departure from Hancock County. Meanwhile, neither the Baldwins nor Brizendines appear to have been politically active, nor were they among early church organizers. Although several churches were in existence in Thomas Lee's time, histories of the region do not include either name—Baldwin or Brizendine—among county officials or church leaders.

Many of the early settlers placed a high value on education. Difficult as pioneer life was, the education of their children was an important goal of even the most remote settlements. The first schoolhouse in the Thomas Lee Baldwin region was probably located within the present site of the city of Greenfield, about five miles distant from where the Baldwins lived. Over the years, one-room schoolhouses sprang up in the region. By 1840, there were seven common schools in the county, attended by 156 pupils. Out of a population of 7,525, there were but 330 persons in the county over twenty years of age, unable to read or write. The low figure belies the fact that many of the early settlers were young families made up of numerous children and young adults under the age of twenty. The low number of pupils attending school—156—attests to just how difficult it was to create accessible schools.

Most of the names of towns that are familiar to residents of Hancock County today did not exist in Thomas Lee's time. Almost all the towns on today's map came about in the 1850s or later: Charlottesville, Philadelphia, New Palestine, Nashville, and Warrington, to name some. Fortville, laid out in 1849, first had the name Walpole. For many years before the platting of the present town of Fortville, a post office and store operated about a mile north and a little west of Walpole, at a point known as Phoebe Fort's corner. The post office bore the name of Walpole. In Thomas Lee's time, he knew Cleveland by the name

Portland, and Eden went by the name of Lewisburg. Lewisburg, or Eden, was very close to the Baldwin farm, which was about a mile north of the present town of Maxwell.

One town whose name has not changed is Greenfield. Greenfield is the county Seat of Hancock County, first settled in 1828. Today, Greenfield is located on State Road 9 and US 40 just south of I-70 at the Greenfield exit. It is just 15 miles east of Indianapolis, and about five miles south of the old Baldwin home place. When officials first laid out Greenfield as a village, they immediately constructed a few essential buildings. A log jail went up in 1828. In 1829, the county erected a two-story log courthouse. Between the jail and the courthouse was a big pond in which travelers washed their horses, and which in wet weather was deep enough to swim horses. However, it did not exist in Thomas Lee's day. When the National Road opened in 1835, it was necessary to drain and fill this pond.

These first public buildings, as well as all of the first residences, were log houses built in the most primitive fashion. Then, during the thirties, Joshua Meek established a brickyard north of the little town, and for a number of years, Mr. Meek made all the brick used in the buildings at Greenfield. This included the first brick courthouse on the public square in 1833, the first brick jail in 1835, many early brick dwellings, and probably the county seminary.

The following description of the little town appeared in the *Indiana Gazetteer*, published in 1833: "Greenfield is surrounded by a body of rich, fertile land and is in a very prosperous and flourishing state of improvement. Its present population is about 200 persons. It contains two mercantile stores, two taverns, one lawyer, one physician, and craftsmen of many trades. The town is supplied with water by a very notable spring within its limits and has the advantage of mills at convenient distances on the streams which pass through the county."[1]

The first road running east and west through Greenfield was the old Centerville state road, which came into town from the east a short distance south of the National Road. All the streets in Greenfield were "dirt" streets without gravel or other material to furnish a substantial

---

[1]Op. cit., Richman, *History of Hancock County.*

Plan of Greenfield. Greenfield is the county seat of Hancock County, Indiana, situated in the middle of Center Township five miles south of the old Thomas Lee Baldwin homestead. This 1876 map is an updated version of the town from when Thomas Lee frequented Greenfield in the 1840s. Main Street is the National Road. The railroad that parallels the National Road through Greenfield did not exist in Thomas Lee's time. Greenfield was the home of the poet James Whitcomb Riley whose poems made famous the Brandywine River seen in the upper right of the map. Excerpt from *Map of Hancock County*, Chicago: Baskin, Forster, 1876, David Ramsey Map Collection.

roadbed. Not until 1853 did the Indiana Central Railroad introduce rail service to the area. Before the completion of the railroad, the Dayton and Indianapolis Express brought the mail two or three times per week from each direction. Caring for the mail was not very arduous. Local folklore says that the postmaster frequently carried the mail under his hat and delivered it to people as he met them.

The famous Indiana poet, James Whitcomb Riley, known as the Hoosier Poet, was born in Greenfield in 1849. Greenfield was his inspiration for "The Brandywine," "The Old Swimmin' Hole," and other poems that came from this local area. Riley once described Greenfield

185

as "My home and your home and your parents' home and the best home outside of heaven."[2] The Greenfield of Riley's youth was a community of simple people living a quiet, peaceful life in which the spirit of neighborliness predominated. The Greenfield of today and the larger Hancock County community retain its small town, close-knit friendliness while providing an abundance of diverse opportunities for its citizens. Located a short drive from Indianapolis, one of its attractions is the James Whitcomb Riley boyhood home, a site now listed on the National Register of Historic Places. One of Riley's most famous poems, *The Brandywine*, written and inspired by the landscape of his boyhood home, captured the essence of Greenfield and Hancock County:

The Brandywine

Sweet Brandywine!
Let's drift back to the 'olden days'
The pace 'twar slow, the livin' fine-
Kick off yer shoes, roll up yer pants
Wiggle yer toes in Brandywine! Pickin' wild berries in the bresh
In itchy, dirty, torn ol' clothes-
Gnats, 'skeeters, crawlin up yer nose!

The bobbin' cork's atwitchin' hard
Fightin' mad, 'twar thet ol' catfish-
Mama fried 'em, juicy n' sweet
My, warn't thet a lip smackin' dish!

O'er the Old Covered Bridge, we'd run
Skim stones 'crost the clear, ripplin' stream-
Take a dip near the noisy Dam
Lie down to rest- dream on, sweet dream!

---

[2] Binford, J. H., *History of Hancock County, Indiana*, Greenfield, Ind.: King & Binford, 1882.

Stumblin' round in thick bramble stand
Scratches 'long our hot, sweaty face-
Thorns snagged in our arms, legs, and tush
Not sure we'd e'er leave thet dern place!

Such joys we had in youngster ways
Fishin', swimmin', life 'twar sublime-
Songs n' laughter, soft carefree days
All up n' down Sweet Brandywine!

James Whitcomb Riley

Brandywine Creek in Greenfield, Indiana, recalls the ancestral seat of the Baldwin family in Pennsylvania. The Brandywine River of Revolutionary War history flowed near the Thomas Baldwin, Sr., home in Chester County, Pennsylvania.

In 1837, a financial crisis griped the United States and touched off a major depression that lasted until the mid-1840s. Thomas Lee most certainly felt the distress of the severe economic downturn caused by the panic of 1837. In the beginning of the crisis, the West did not feel as much hardship as the East. Indiana, Ohio, and Illinois were agricultural states. Good crops in 1837 were a relief to farmers like Thomas Lee. However, in 1839, agricultural prices fell, and the financial troubles reached Indiana. Westward expansion stalled, and pessimism set in amid a period of political uncertainty. Indiana Governor William Henry Harrison became President in 1840, and infamously served but 31 days before dying in office. For five years, the country struggled. By 1842, the economy rebounded somewhat, but full recovery did not occur until 1844. Somehow, Thomas Lee and the Brizendine brothers farmed their way through the depression. The California gold rush started in 1848, which significantly boosted the money supply in the US; by 1850, the economy was on the upswing.[3]

When Indiana historian George Richman in 1916 included the

---

[3] Reginald McGrane, *The Panic of 1837: Some Financial Problems of the Jacksonian Era*, New York: Russell & Russell, 1965, pp. 106–126.

Baldwin and Brizendine names on his list of the earliest settlers of Hancock County, he added that they were individuals whose names "are still familiar in the county."[4] This would have been partly true. Some of the Brizendine descendants remained in Hancock County. William M. Brizendine, for example, is on a 1915 tax list.[5] However, Thomas Lee and other members of the Brizendine family eventually moved on. None of Thomas Lee's children remained in Hancock County after 1844.

---

[4] Richman, *History of Hancock County,* pp. 577-594.
[5] Ibid

18

Macoupin County

The financial depression of 1837 did not deter Thomas Lee Baldwin. He had a knack for overcoming hardship, and a pioneer spirit that caused him to seek out new opportunities on the edge of the rapidly growing American frontier. Thomas Lee lived in Hancock County, Indiana, for several years. At about age 47, he left Indiana and, according to family tradition, moved further west between 1841 and 1844, settling this time first in Sangamon County, Illinois, and then Macoupin County, Illinois. They lived but a short time in Sangamon County before moving across the county line to Macoupin County. By this time, Thomas Lee had improved his farming profession in the trotting horse business. The Baldwin Horse Ranch flourished, leading to the purchase of several tracts of land in the rich agricultural region of northern Macoupin County, Illinois.[1]

Thomas Lee's youngest son, Henry, was born in Illinois about 1844. Henry was age six in the 1850 census, confirming that Thomas Lee and Nancy were in Illinois by 1844.[2] Mary Baldwin, age 20, lived by herself nearby, according to the census. It is unknown if Mary was related to Thomas Lee. Also living in the vicinity were members of the Brizendine family, some of whom apparently moved to Illinois at the same time as Thomas Lee and Nancy. The name of the census township did not appear in the 1850 census. Therefore, the location of the family in Macoupin County at that time cannot be exactly determined from the census. However, there is a family tradition that the Baldwins initially settled near what became the town of Virden, a town built after they arrived.

---

[1] Jimmy O. Baldwin, *in* History of Cedar County.
[2] 1850 US Census, Illinois, Macoupin, Unknown Township, Series M432 Roll 118, National Archives, p. 231B, [Baldwin, Mary A. 20 b. Ill living by herself at separate location, p. 237A.

In 1850, Thomas Lee recorded real estate valued at $2,240. His occupation was farming, an occupation shared by three of his sons listed on the census. For the first time in census history, enumerators of the 1850 census recorded the names of every person in the household. Thomas Lee was age 54, and Nancy was 49.[3] The census listed eight of their 11 children. Not accounted for on the 1850 census were three of their children: Sarah, age 25, Thomas Jackson, 24, and Jeremiah, 9. Jeremiah appears later in the 1860 census and apparently was not at home when the census was taken in 1850. Sarah Baldwin married in 1847, and left home. Also in the Baldwin household in 1850 were six Brizentines [sic]: Isaac, 15, James, 13, Leroy, 11, Joseph, 9, Benjamin, 6, and Malissa, age 5. All were born in Indiana, and all were probably the children of the Brizendine brothers.

Macoupin County became a county in 1829, created out of part of Madison County and the eastern part of Greene County, Illinois. The county was 36 miles long from north to south and 24 miles wide east to west. The name Macoupin is of Indian origin, abbreviated from *Macoupina*, which means "white potato," a name the Indians gave to a wild artichoke that grew abundantly along the network of streams crossing the county.[4] The largest of these waterways is Macoupin Creek. The county is also the site of several mounds from the Woodland Mississippi Indian Culture. The county seat—Carlinville—took the name of Thomas Carlin, who proposed the new county and who became governor of Illinois in 1838.

The county grew rapidly between 1850 and 1860 when many German families settled in the area as part of the great European migration of the 1850s, a time that saw large numbers of Irish and German settlements

---

[3] 1850 US Federal Census , Illinois, Macoupin County, 2 Oct 1850, National Archives and Records Administration, Washington, DC 20408. "T. L. Baldwin, 54, $2240 (value in Real Estate) b. North Carolina; Nancy, 49, b. Virginia; William, 20, b. Ind. (all children were born in Indiana); Caleb, 19; John C. 17; Nancy, 16; Joshua, 14; James, 12; Lucinda, 10; Jeremiah, 8; Henry 6; Isaac Brizendine, 15; James Brizendine, 13; Leroy Brizendine, 11; Joseph Brizendine, 9; Benjamin Brizendine, 6; Malissa A. Brizendine, 5."

[4] 1979. *History of Macoupin County, Illinois.*

SCHEDULE I.—Free Inhabitants in _____ in the County of _____ State of _Illinois_ enumerated by me, on the _3d_ day of _Oct_ 1850. _____ Ass't Marshal

		The Name of every Person whose usual place of abode on the first day of June, 1850, was in this family.	Age	Sex	Color	Profession, Occupation, or Trade of each Male Person over 15 years of age.	Value of Real Estate owned.	Place of Birth. Naming the State, Territory, or Country.				
1	2	3	4	5	6	7	8	9	10	11	12	13
		Franklin Gatlin	8	m				Ill	1			
		Perry Gatlin	3	m				Ill				
		Vicinda Gatlin	7/12	f				Ill				
1	1	Samuel Davidson	38	m		Farmer	1800	Ohio				
		Margaret Davidson	37	f				Ky				
		Sylvester Davidson	14	m				Ill			1	
		Winchester Davidson	12	m				Ill			1	
		Amanda Davidson	9	f				Ill			1	
		Emily E Davidson	7	f				Ill			1	
		Margaret A Davidson	5	f				Ill			1	
		Sarah J Davidson	2	f				Ill				
2	2	William Gibson	31	m		Farmer	2400	Tenn				
		Zillah Gibson	26	f				Tenn				
		Charlton Gibson	9	m				Ill			1	
		Leann Gibson	7	f				Ill			1	
		Merryman Gibson	5	m				Ill				
		Ellen Gibson	2	f				Ill				
		Hannah Gibson	7/12	f				Ill				
		Chancy M Moffatt	23	m		Physician		Ohio				
3	3	James Clack	38	m		Farmer	10.000	Tenn				
		Mary A Clack	26	f				Ky				
		Lydia P Clack	6	f				Ills				
		Sarah A Clack	4	f				Ill				
		William Clack	1	m				Ill				
4	4	William Clack	62	m		Farmer	150	Tenn				
		Sarah Clack	59	f				SC				1
		Frances Mercer	15	m		Farmer		Miss				
5	5	T L Baldwin	54	m		do	2240	NC				
		Nancy Baldwin	49	f				Va				
		William Baldwin	20	m		do		Ind				
		Caleb Baldwin	19	m		do		Ind			1	
		John C Baldwin	17	m		do		Ind				
		Nancy Baldwin	16	f				Ind				
		Joshua Baldwin	14	m				Ind				
		James Baldwin	12	m				Ind				
		Lucinda Baldwin	10	m				Ind				
		Jeremiah Baldwin	8	m				Ill				
		Henry Baldwin	6	m				Ill				
		Isaac Brizentine	18	m				Ind				
		James Brizentine	13	m				Ind				
		Loisy Brizentine	11	m				Ind				

J A C Howell

1850 US Census. The names of the Thomas Lee Baldwin family first appeared in Macoupin County, Illinois, on the 1850 census. The census information included the profession of the head of household and working occupants, their ages and genders, and places of birth. 1850 US Census, Illinois, Macoupin, Unknown Township, Series M432 Roll 118, National Archives, p. 231B.

established throughout the United States, but especially in the Midwest.[5] The area is famous, among other things, for Route 66, which passes through the heart of Carlinville. Meanwhile, Thomas Lee may well have been in the audience in Carlinville when Abraham Lincoln made a speech on August 31, 1858, in his unsuccessful bid for a US Senate seat against Stephen A. Douglas. Two years later, Lincoln became president.

Illinois. Arrows show the settlement of Thomas Lee Baldwin first in Sangamon County and then Macoupin County. David Rumsey Map Collection at Stanford University Libraries.

The Northwest Ordinance of 1787 charted the Illinois region. Initially, the Illinois Territory was a county of Virginia, ceded by Virginia to the Northwest Territory in 1784, and then was part of the Indiana Territory created in 1809. The Illinois Territory became a state in 1818. Organizers retained the name Illinois, an Algonquin name meaning "tribe of superior men," From two original counties in 1809, the state grew to 102 counties by 1859. During the early years of settlement by fur trappers, southern Illinois became the main focus of migration to the area, especially along the Mississippi River valley and the Wabash and Ohio rivers.

The granting of statehood to Illinois in 1818 was controversial. The population numbered fewer than the 60,000 residents the law required to become a state. Moreover, in order to include the Chicago port area, territorial representatives induced the US Congress to draw the Illinois border 51

---

[5]Macoupin County Sesquicentennial Historic Committee, *The Story of Macoupin County*, 1979.

miles to the north of the original boundary as delimited by the Northwest Ordinance.

The first capital was Kaskaskia, followed by Vandalia, along the Kaskaskia River, which held the position for 20 years. After strong pressure from Abraham Lincoln, the capital moved to Springfield by a 1837 legislative vote. Lincoln, who was born in Kentucky in the same

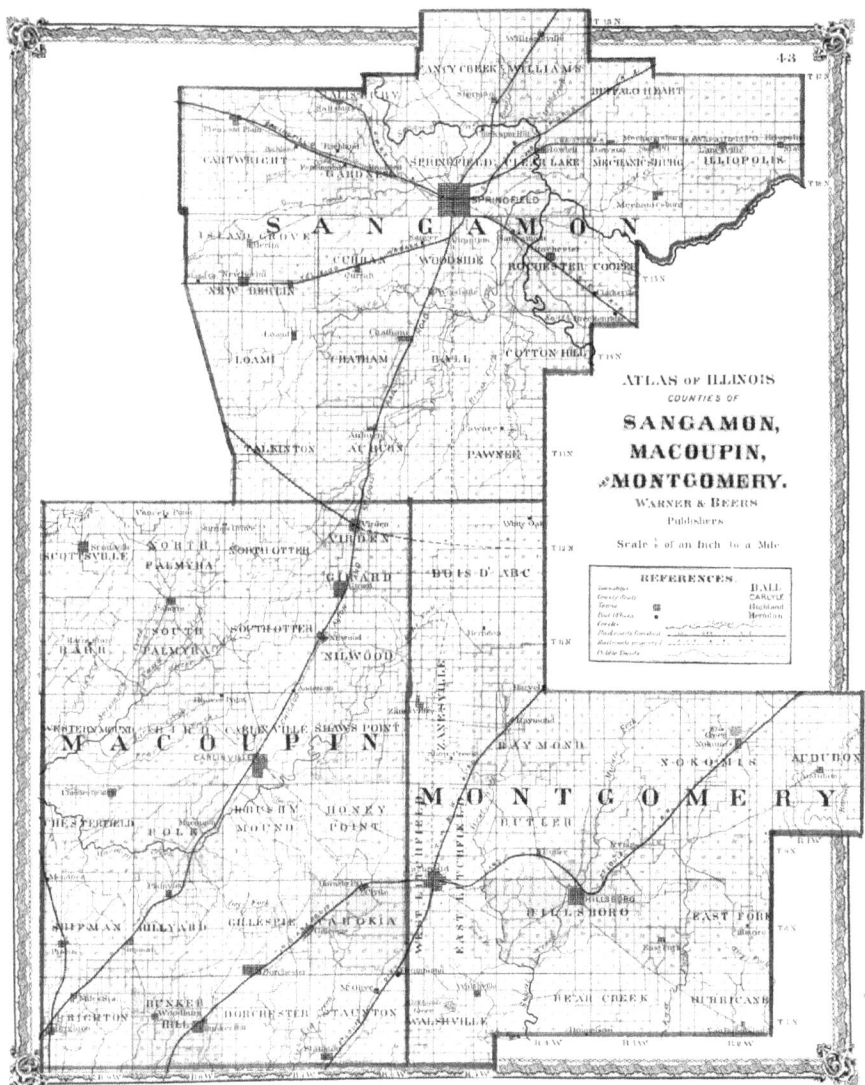

Illinois Counties. Thomas Lee moved his family from Hancock County, Indiana, first to Sangamon County, Illinois, and then to Macoupin County in west central Illinois. They settled near Virden, in Virden Township of Macoupin, in the upper northeast corner of the county. The family arrived there after 1844, *Atlas of Illinois, Counties of Sangamon, Macoupin, and Montgomery,* Chicago: Warner & Beers, 1872.

year the Illinois Territory was created, moved first to Indiana and then to Illinois, gaining what education he could along the way. In 1834, he was elected to the Illinois legislature as a Whig and became the party's floor leader. For the next 20 years, he practiced law in Springfield, except for a single term (1847–1849) in the US Congress. It was at this time that Thomas Lee moved his family to Illinois and settled in Macoupin County on a farm about 20 miles south of Springfield, where Lincoln lived in 1855.[6] Lincoln was a little younger than Thomas Lee was, and there is no proof that they knew each other, but they had much in common with regard to geography and the conditions of their childhoods, not to mention the trail of their migrations through Indiana to Illinois.

In 1855, Lincoln was a candidate for senator but withdrew his candidacy, and the next year he joined the new Republican Party. He gained national attention in 1858 when, as a Republican candidate for senator from Illinois, he engaged in a series of debates with Stephen A. Douglas, the Democratic candidate. He lost that election but continued to prepare the way for the 1860 Republican convention, where he received the nomination for President of the US on the third ballot. He won the election over three opponents.

Portrait of Abraham Lincoln. In a portrait taken at the time of his nomination for the US Senate in 1857, Lincoln was at the beginning of his ascendency to the presidency. He lost the senate election but became popular for his position on slavery and his opposition to the Kansas-Nebraska Act that ignited the border wars between Missouri and the Territory of Kansas. Library of Congress.

---

[6] *Atlas of Henry Co. Illinois to Which is Added an Atlas of the United States,* Chicago: Warner & Beers, 1875.

Meanwhile, early statehood problems engulfed Illinois. In the 1830s, the state had been near bankruptcy because of government financing of canals and railroad construction. The Black Hawk War in 1832, fought between the Indians and newly arrived settlers over possession of

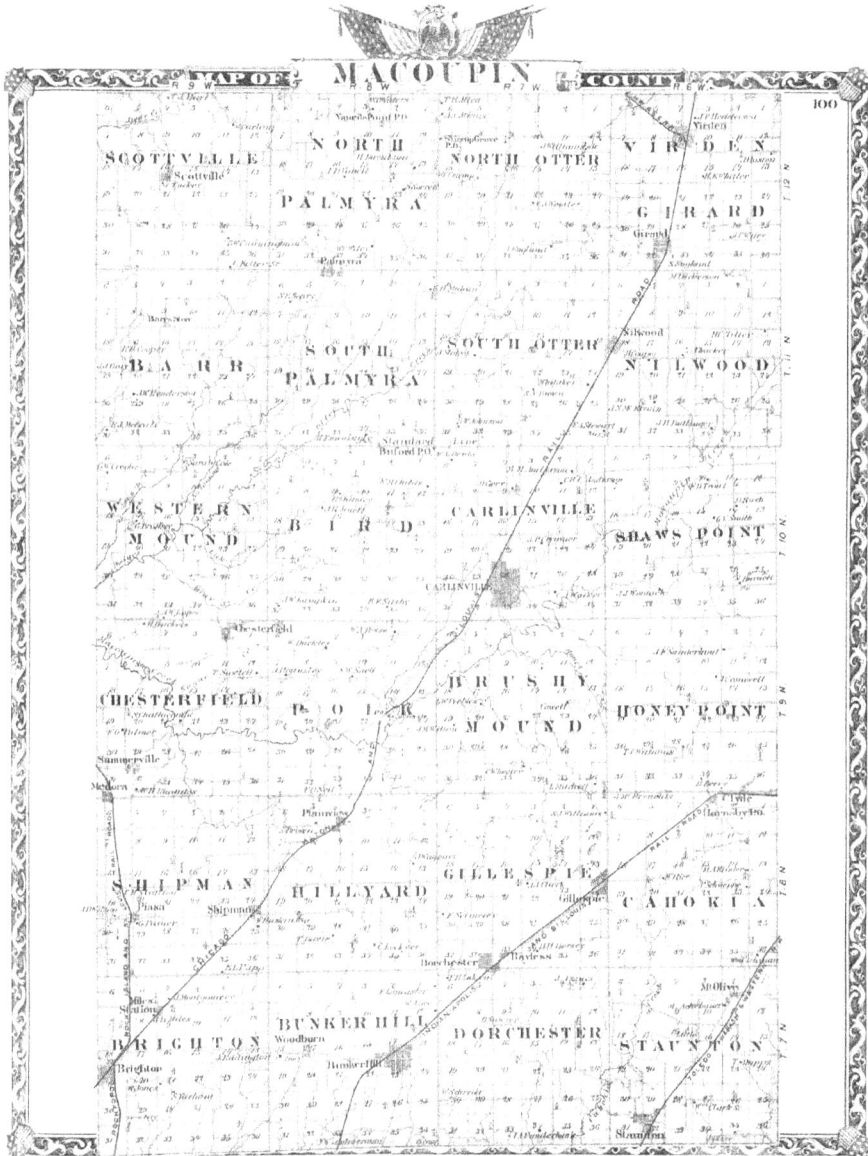

Map of Macoupin County. The Baldwin Horse Ranch was in the northeast corner of Macoupin County. Recorded references to the Baldwin family include North Otter, Virden, and Gerard Townships. Thomas Lee owned multiple farms where both he and his sons lived. *Atlas of Illinois,* Chicago: Warner & Beers, 1876.

Illinois land, became a national scandal. Disease was rampant and death common. Adherents to Mormonism, who migrated from Missouri in 1839, were the target of many charges of illegalities, and finally driven from the state in 1846 after the murder of their leader, Joseph Smith, in 1844. It was against this background that Thomas Lee came to Macoupin County to begin a life that would keep him in Illinois for the next 23 years.

Thomas Lee's farm in Illinois was located in Township 12, Range 7. Other members of the Baldwin family were in Township 12, Range 6 and Township 13, Range 7, all in the Edwardsville Land District. Township 12, Range 6 became North Otter Township. No records of government land purchases for Thomas Lee are available. We know approximately where he lived in the county based on census records. Land in his vicinity was part of the Government Land Sale Program, and it is likely that Thomas participated. On the other hand, it is possible that he purchased his land from an individual, but those deeds have not yet been located. There are records of land sales in 1850 and 1851 to two of his sons, Thomas Jackson and William Mattison, which occurred in nearby Sangamon County across the county line north of Macoupin County.[7]

Largely because of generous government land policies, Illinois quickly became a prosperous agricultural state. Government land offices either sold sections of land to settlers for $1.25 per acre or provided them with certificates of preemption. "Preemption" was the process through which a settler could stake a claim to a piece of land for up to four years without paying for it as long as he (or she) cultivated it, built on it, or otherwise "improved" it. The government's goal was to encourage settlement of the wilderness. Many businesspeople bought up government land for speculation and later sold it. A buyer could buy up to 640 acres, but most entered tracts of about 40 acres.

The 1860 US Census listed Thomas Lee's post office as Virden. When Thomas Lee settled in the region around 1844, the town of Virden did not exist. Virden sprang up just to the northeast of him in Range, 6 in

---

[7] BLM, Thomas J. Baldwin, No. 25227, Illinois, 1 July 1851, Edwardsville Land Office, 40 acres, Twp 13N Range 7W, SW1/4SW1/4 Section 33, Sangamon County.

the far northeast corner of the county. He lived nearby and doubtless did business in Virden and Gerard Townships. His farm was located in Township 12 North, Range 7 West. Meanwhile, his daughter Nancy and her husband James Walters also lived in Township 12, Range 7, but their post office was Gerard.

Old Macoupin County Courthouse. The second courthouse built of brick and costing $15,000 replaced the old log structure in 1838. This brick building was the courthouse in use during the time of Thomas Lee in Macoupin County. Abraham Lincoln famously tried cases in this courthouse. Owners demolished the courthouse in 1869. Photograph Courtesy of Annette Miner.

Virden was an example of the rapid growth that took place during westward expansion. Because of its importance to Thomas Lee's region of the county, a brief account of its history follows. "In the year of our Lord 1852, Messrs. A. McKim Dubois, E. Keating, V. Hickox, John A. Chestnut, and C. P. Heaton purchased Section 9, on Range 6, in Township 12, Macoupin County, Ill., and surveyed it for village lots. Four acres in the center of the section were allotted for a public square, which is now fenced, sown down with blue grass, and beautified with locust trees," so wrote the *Carlinville Free Democrat* in 1859.[8] The embryo village took the name Virden after John Virden, who erected the first hotel there in 1853. The *Free Democrat* continued its description, "In September of 1852, the St. Louis, Alton, and Chicago Railroad was completed to this point, and the depot was erected the following winter. In December of 1852, the first house was built on the

---

[8] *Carlinville Free Democrat.* October 27, 1859. History of Virden, Virden, Macoupin County, Ill.: Author.

north-west corner of Green and Springfield streets, by Alexander Hord. It had to serve the purpose of a hotel until February, when Virden built his hotel on Matteson Street, which he named the Virden House, later called the Silloway House under various proprietors. The patronage at Hord's house was such that the table was seldom free, with farmers arriving with their produce at all hours of the night. Lodgers had to sleep on the floor because there weren't enough beds. On November 1, 1852, C. P. Henton sold the first goods in a building on Jackson Street. The nearest house was two miles off. A week later, Henry Fishback of Carlinville opened another store on Jackson Street, in the building next to the present [1859] post office, on the west. In Jan 1855, John Evans and George Fortune entered into partnership with Henton, and in September 1858, the name was changed to Evans and Fortune. Meanwhile, John Beattie and Thomas R. McKee carried on the business for Fishback. In one year, it was sold to Beattie, and in the fall of 1856, it was bought by William West. Between 1853 and 1859, there were over 50 business owners in Virden. The post office was established in 1853."

The *Carlinville Free Democrat* article concluded, "By 1859, there were 124 buildings. The buildings were of various colors, with white, blue, pink, brown, and green window-shutters. One of the buildings was a district schoolhouse, erected in 1854 on the corner of Jackson and Church streets; its size was twenty by twenty-four; cost, $500. In 1858, an addition was built, twenty-five by thirty-three feet; cost, $1,000. Scholars in attendance in the winter of 1858 were 170; two female teachers and one male teacher; a circulating library of 122 volumes in the district. A select school for women was taught by Miss Elizabeth Davis in 1857, and, in 1858, Mrs. Mary Chandler taught at the school… Physicians in 1854 were F. Fuller, C. P. French, and C. H. Holliday. Dr. Henry practiced some in 1854. Dr. Helm a few months in 1857 and died. Dr. A. Shutt came here in 1858 and went away in 1859. Dr. C. Teal settled here in January 1859, and Dr. W. A. Knox in May following. Lawyers were Mahlon, Ross, and John Rodgers."

Thus was the history of Virden in the year 1859. Within little more than a decade from their arrival about 1843, the Baldwins saw a town built from scratch on the rich farmland of Macoupin County, Illinois.

Macoupin County Farm Scenes. These views sketched in 1879 in South Otter Township were typical of the homesteads in Macoupin County, Illinois, where Thomas Lee Baldwin lived.

North Otter. Thomas Lee kept a successful horse ranch in North Otter Township and owned multiple pieces of property along with his sons in both Macoupin and Sangamon County, Illinois. *History of Macoupin County, Illinois*, 1879, pp. 201, 205.

19

John Calvin Baldwin

he fifth child and fourth oldest son of Thomas Lee Baldwin and Nancy Brizendine Baldwin was John Calvin Baldwin. He was born September 29, 1832, and, according to family tradition, was born in Hancock County, Indiana.[1] Other evidence suggests his birth was in Wayne County, Indiana, because the Baldwin family does not appear to have moved to Hancock County until after 1832.[2]

John Calvin Baldwin. Son of Thomas Lee Baldwin and ancestor of the Cedar County branch of the Baldwin family, John Calvin lived in Macoupin County, Illinois, before removing to Kansas and then to Missouri. He posed for this picture about 1850. K. Burchett Photo File.

John Calvin spent his childhood on the Baldwin horse farm near Greenfield, Indiana, going to school and roaming the countryside along Sugar Creek and the

---

[1] Find a Grave Memorial ID 5495647.

[2] Michelle Fisher, *Fisher Family Tree* (Aug 2001) [online Genealogy of the Baldwin family back to Thomas Baldwin, Sr.] The source includes the life dates of the children of John Calvin and Frances Pherby Baldwin. The source does not list his children with Cordelia O'Connor; see also Jimmy O. Baldwin, in History of Cedar County, pp. 145-146.

Brandywine. A verse from James Whitcomb Riley's poem about the Brandywine paints an inviting picture of what it was like to grow up in rural Hancock County.

O'er the Old Covered Bridge, we'd run
Skim stones 'crost the clear, ripplin' stream-
Take a dip near the noisy Dam
Lie down to rest- dream on, sweet dream!

About 1841, John Calvin moved with his parents to Sangamon County, Illinois, and then to Macoupin County, Illinois. There, he grew to adulthood working on the family farm and learning the agricultural trade. Soon he met Frances Pherby Jackson, a neighbor girl and the daughter of Brice Bradley Jackson and Mary Jane Haggard.

Frances was born on October 5, 1840, near Diamond, in Newton County, Missouri.[3] Her ancestral family originated from the Yellow Creek area of Montgomery County, Tennessee, having moved there originally from North Carolina.[4] Her grandfather was Brice Jackson [Sr.]. He died in 1832 in a steamboat accident on the Mississippi River. The story of that accident recounts how, on April 3, 1832, the steamboat *Brandywine* left New Orleans bound for Louisville, Kentucky. On the evening of the 9th, 30 miles above Memphis, the boat caught fire. Efforts to extinguish the flames were unsuccessful, and within minutes, the entire boat was engulfed in flames. Some 230 passengers, who were crowded onto the *Brandywine,* desperately tried to escape the burning inferno by the only means available, which was the boat's yawl. In their haste to launch it, the conveyance flipped over and sank. People threw themselves into the water in a frantic attempt to escape the heat and smoke. Seventy-five people either drowned or burned to death, including women and children. One of those who perished was Brice B. Jackson, grandfather of Frances Pherby Jackson.[5]

---

[3] Jimmy O. Baldwin, in History of Cedar County, p. 145.
[4] 1830 US Census, Place: Montgomery, Tennessee, Series: M19, Roll: 179, p. 29 [online Family History Library Film: 0024537].
[5] Find a Grave Memorial ID 151546589.

Meanwhile, Brice Jackson [Jr.], future father of Frances, entered land patents in Morgan County, Illinois, and moved there with his wife Mary sometime about 1831, around the time of his father's death. Their first child was born in Morgan County.[6] Mr. Jackson entered two additional patents in 1837 and 1844, and he acquired about 200 acres in Morgan County.[7] However, for unspecified reasons, he removed from Morgan County, Illinois, to Newton County, Missouri, near Diamond in 1839, where Frances was born, the only member of the Jackson family born in Missouri, because soon thereafter, Mr. Jackson returned to Illinois, this time settling in Macoupin County around the year 1844.[8] Two more Jackson children were born in Macoupin County.[9] He entered additional patents for another 95 acres in Macoupin County for tracts of land near the tracts of the Baldwin and Brizendine families.[10] Mr. Jackson died September 5, 1861, in Douglas County, Kansas, where he was living with his children. He survived his wife, Mary, who died on October 5, 1854, when Frances was age 14.[11]

John Calvin and Frances married on Christmas Eve, December 24, 1856, in Carlinville, the county seat of Macoupin County, Illinois.[12]

---

[6] Find a Grave Memorial ID 34615470; .1850 US Census, Macoupin, Illinois, Records of the Bureau of the Census, Record Group Number: 29, Series Number: M432, Roll: 118, p. 231a. The National Archives in Washington D.C.

[7] Land Patents in Morgan County, Illinois, Brice B. Jackson, 9/16/1831 #4842 Ill. 014N-008W,W½SE¼ Sec 33; 8/1/1844 #12227 IL 013N-008W, W½NW¼ Sec 4, 3/18/1837 #9313 IL 014N-008W, NW¼SW¼ Sec 34, Bureau of Land Management (BLM), General Land Office (GLO) Records.

[8] 1840 US Census, Place: Marin, Newton, Missouri, Roll: 227, p. 257 [online Family History Library Film: 0014856].

[9] 1850 US Census, Macoupin, Illinois, Records of the Bureau of the Census, Record Group Number: 29, Series Number: M432, Roll: 118, p. 231a, National Archives in Washington D.C.

[10] Land Patents in Macoupin County, Illinois, Brice B. Jackson, 1/1/1849 #24136 Ill. 012N-006W, SE¼SW¼ Sec. 6, 5/1/1850 #24622 Ill. 012N-006W,NW¼NE¼ Sec. 7, 6/1/1852 #25484 Ill. 12N-006W, SW¼NE¼ Sec. 7, Bureau of Land Management (BLM), General Land Office (GLO) Records.

[11] Find a Grave Memorial IDs 28885692 & 28885710.

[12] Illinois Statewide Marriage Index, 1763–1900, Baldwin, John C., and Jackson, Francis P., 12/22/1856, License #2736 Macoupin County.

Frances was 17, and John was 24. Their first child, a daughter, Mary Frances, was born June 30, 1858.[13]

Shortly after the birth of Mary, John Calvin and his older brother William Mattison Baldwin removed from Illinois with their families to Kansas Territory, in part to establish the Baldwin horse business in Kansas. According to family historian, Jimmy Baldwin, Thomas Lee sold part of his Illinois land, bought land in Ottawa, Kansas, and sent John Calvin to Kansas to set up a branch of the horse business. Two other sons remained in Illinois to take over the operation of the Illinois branch of the trotting horse business. Thomas Jackson managed the ranch in northern Macoupin County, recognized by the Illinois Stockman's Association as the "Baldwin Horse Ranch." Caleb J. oversaw the ranch south of Carlinville.[14]

John Calvin settled first in Breckenridge County, Kansas, while William Mattison found a home in Douglas County. The genealogical record in Kansas is challenging because there were Baldwins already in Kansas by the time John Calvin and William arrived there, including Baldwins with first names of John and William. One source claimed that the other John and William were also from Illinois, the same as the Baldwin brothers.[15] Several geographic sites in Kansas have place names of the earlier Baldwins, who were in Kansas at least by 1854, places like Baldwin City and Baldwin Creek in the northeast part of the state, to name two. The Baldwin brothers and the earlier John and William Baldwin may be the same in some genealogical records. However, our John Calvin and William did not arrive in Kansas until after 1854. Moreover, marriage records and births of their children place them in Illinois at the same time as events associated with the other Baldwins in Kansas. It is possible but unlikely that John Calvin and William traveled back and forth from Illinois to Kansas. This was common in the early history of the Kansas Territory. However, it is more likely that Kansas was a destination of multiple pioneers of the Baldwin name and not

---

[13] Fisher, *Fisher Family Tree.*
[14] Jimmy O. Baldwin, in History of Cedar County, pp. 145-146.
[15] Willard C. Heiss, *The Census of the Territory of Kansas, February 1855, w/Index & Map of Kansas Election Districts in 1854.* Indianapolis, Ind.: Author, 1967.

necessarily related. There is no proof that the earlier Kansas Baldwin immigrants were of Thomas Lee Baldwin's line.

Kansas Territory represented the new western frontier of America, isolated and dangerous. To determine the future statehood of the Kansas Territory, emigrants from all parts of the nation came to Kansas, trying to influence elections contested by pro- and anti-slavery factions under the new Kansas-Nebraska Act. Under the Act, the government allowed territories to vote to decide the future of a state. The local population of Kansas was a mix of anti- and pro-slavery sentiments, which manifested itself in a deeply contentious rivalry. The Kansas troubles constituted a potentially hostile welcome for new settlers to the area, sometimes erupting into violent confrontations.

Voting in Kansas. This sketch done in 1855 illustrates pro-slavery Missourians voting in one of the many elections that occurred in Kansas Territory between Free State and pro-slavery groups to determine Kansas statehood. Richardson, *Beyond the Mississippi; from the Great River to the Great Ocean*, 1867, p. 101.

Kansas was in the middle of significant political turmoil when the Baldwin brothers arrived, deeply divided between Free State and pro-slavery factions. As early as 1854, territorial elections held in Kansas tried to elect representatives to the US Congress and to adopt a constitution in preparation for the territory's admission to the Union. These hotly contested elections made it impossible to determine who was a resident of the territory and who was not. Groups of men, organized as far to the east as New York, traveled to Kansas to vote in these elections. These emigrant societies were organizations against slavery. One such group, the Massachusetts Emigrant Aid Society, pushed Kansas residents off their claims to take control of the newly formed town of Lawrence, Kansas. Two of the early Baldwins testified at one inquiry at Westport, Missouri, in the summer of 1856 to having had such treatment by this society. So aggressive was the Massachusetts Society that people knew it locally as the Lawrence Association. Many Emigrant Aid Society members lived in Kansas City, traveling to voting places in Kansas on election days. Citizens referred to them as being seen going back and forth with carpetbags in hand. Nearly every one of these eastern emigrants carried a gun.

Kansas Territory Pioneers. Six unidentified armed men posed for a picture near Lawrence, Kansas, in 1856 during the Kansas statehood troubles. Kansas State Historical Society.

The Kansas-Nebraska Act declared that any new states added out of the western territories could determine their own status as a free or slave state. So confusing were the first Kansas elections, and so corrupt, that the US Congress investigated in 1856 to try to determine what the true will of the Kansas people was. It is in this report of the troubles in Kansas that the Baldwin name appears on 33 different pages, beginning as early as 29 November 1854, and suggesting that Baldwins were active in early

Kansas politics.[16] Based on information contained in the report, the Baldwins were probably settlers and not of the Emigrant Aid Society crowd. The names of John Baldwin and William N. Baldwin are most frequently listed, mostly in poll-books from the 1st District of Lawrence covering the various elections of 1854, 1855, and 1856.[17] The western half of this district became a substantial part of Douglas County when it formed in 1855, where William Mattison Baldwin of the line of Thomas Lee settled in 1859. Meanwhile, other Baldwin names appearing in the 1856 Congressional Report include Benjamin, Henry, Andrew, David, and S. R. Baldwin. Henry was an election clerk for the 2nd District in the constitutional election of December 1855. David was an election judge serving the Pottawatomie Precinct of the 5th District in the election of January 1856, and S. R. Baldwin was a candidate for State Representative from the Tenth District in 1856, all of which predate the period of John Calvin and William of Thomas Lee's line in Kansas.

John Calvin Baldwin moved to the Kansas Territory around 1859 based on the birth of his daughter. Mary Frances was born June 30, 1858, according to family tradition, in Illinois. Her birth in Illinois is an anchor point used to place John Calvin in Kansas after her birth in 1858, and his arrival in Kansas around 1859. The first birth recorded in Breckenridge County was in 1856; had Mary been born in Kansas, it would have made her among the earliest native residents of the State of Kansas.

John Calvin settled further west, in what became Breckenridge (present Lyon) County, than his brother William Mattison did in Douglas County. John Calvin went there when the territory was still

---

[16] United States Congress, House Committee to Investigate the Troubles in Kansas. 1856. *Report of the Special Committee Appointed to Investigate the Troubles in Kansas, with the Views of the Minority of Said Committee.* Washington, D.C.: Author, 1856.

[17] Heiss, Willard C., Description of election districts, First District. "Commencing in the Kansas river, at the mouth of Cedar creek; thence up said river to the first tributary above the town of Lawrence; thence up said tributary to its source; thence by a direct line to the west side of F. Rolf's house; thence by a due south line to the Santa Fe road, and along the middle of said road to a point due south of the source of Cedar creek; thence due north to the source of said Cedar creek, and down the same to the place of beginning."

wild and in the grip of conflicting ideologies over slavery and the politics of the admission of Kansas to the Union. While the Baldwin brothers avoided some of the earliest troubles in Kansas, they came at a time when tensions were very high and, while we do not know their political and social viewpoints, the Baldwin name was already prevalent in the politics of the Territory.

John Calvin Baldwin settled in Breckenridge County, in east central Kansas Territory. White settlers were in the area by 1846, but the first store did not open there until 1854, which was not only the first one in the county, but also the only one in southern Kansas outside of the regular Indian posts. This store, called Worthingtons, was a hotel as well as a supply station, and played an important role in the settlement of Breckenridge County. With few exceptions, early immigrants to Kansas settled along the creeks in the northern half of the county. John Calvin settled in Kanzas [*sic*] Township (present Waterloo Township) in the northeast corner of the county. We do not have a precise address for him. Kansas was a federal land state, which officially opened for white settlement in 1854, but no records indicate, any government land purchases by John Calvin or the Baldwin family, notwithstanding family tradition that Thomas Lee bought land in Ottawa, Kansas.

Breckenridge County was one of 33 counties established in the Territory of Kansas by the first territorial legislature held in 1855. At the same time, the legislature created Douglas, Franklin, Madison, and Riley counties, all of them other counties connected to the Baldwins. At first, Breckenridge, being one of the least populated counties, remained attached to Madison County for civil and military purposes. A system of attaching thinly inhabited counties to those able to maintain an organization substituted for county government when the county population was not large enough to justify an organization. A wave of new settlers came into the county in 1856 and a much larger number in 1857, causing the legislature to officially recognize Breckenridge County in 1857. John Calvin arrived shortly after these earliest waves of settlement in the area.

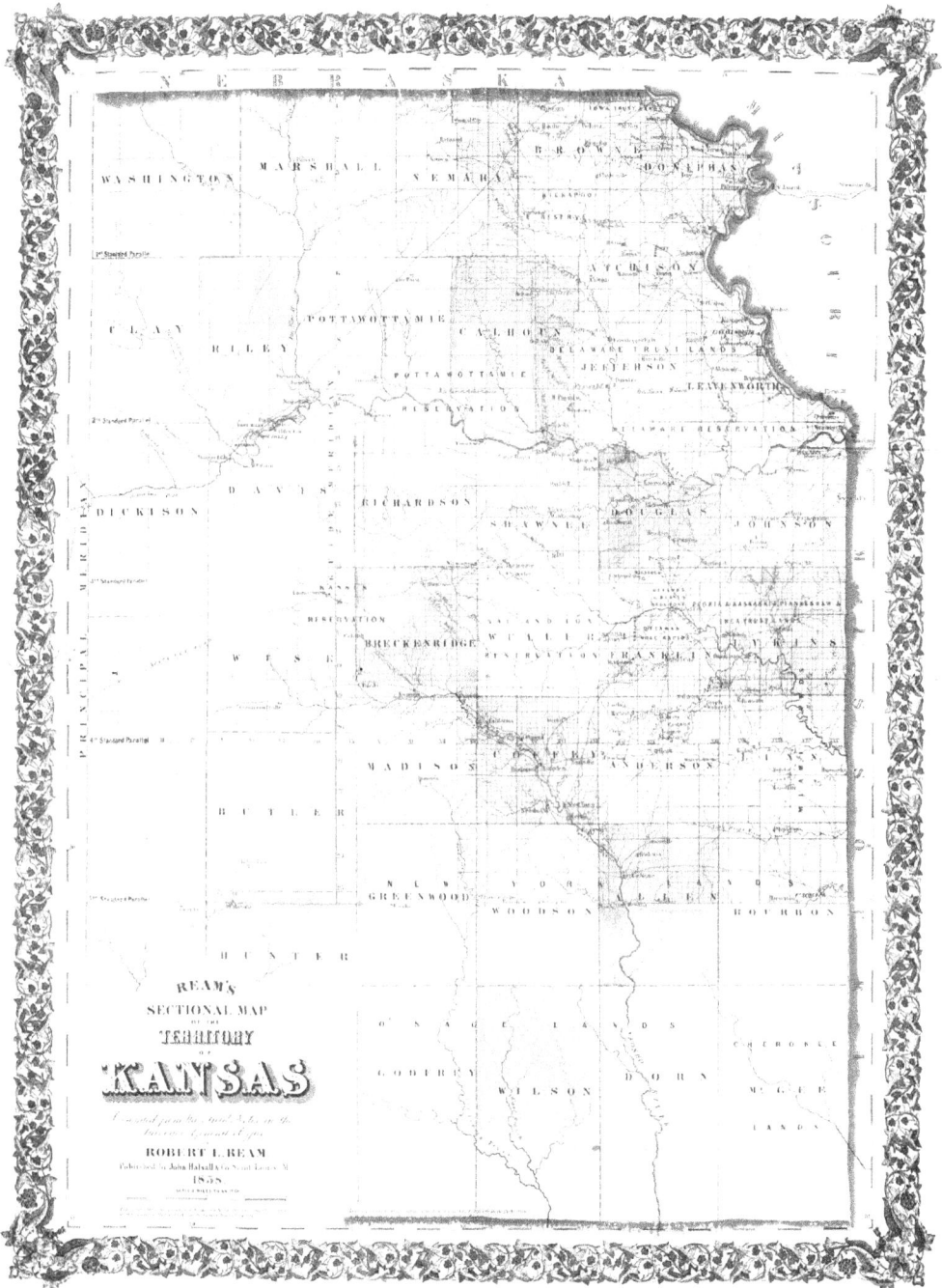

Kansas Territory in 1858. John Calvin Baldwin moved from Macoupin County, Illinois, to Breckenridge, Kansas Territory, about 1859 at the height of bitter fighting over Kansas statehood. Breckenridge County (center of the map) was on the frontier of western settlement and a hotbed of tensions between Free State and pro-slavery factions. Ream, *Sectional Map of the Territory of Kansas*, 1858. David Rumsey Historical Map Collection.

From its beginning, Breckenridge County was a raucous place. The first county seat was Agnes City. However, in 1858-59, a bitter fight occurred between Americus and Emporia over the location of a new county seat; Americus won by 14 votes. The county never erected a courthouse in Americus, but people continued to regard it as the county seat up until the general election of 1860 when Emporia was given the permanent honor. John Calvin was in Breckenridge County in 1860, and no doubt witnessed the political rancor in Americus and Emporia. Among the other early towns that figured in the county seat contest, was the town of Waterloo, a town laid off in 1858 close to where John Calvin lived on what was then the State Road located 15 miles north of Emporia.

John Calvin Baldwin and his young bride, Frances, and infant daughter, Mary, arrived in Waterloo Township about the time Breckenridge County established its own county government. The first assessment of property in Breckenridge County occurred in 1858, but it appears to have been of little value because people accused the assessor of being prejudiced. The Kansas Territory and Breckenridge County was a troubled frontier at the time, and a dangerous place for the young Baldwin family.

20

Trouble in Kansas

John Calvin Baldwin, like his father, was in the horse business. According to family historian Jimmy Baldwin, he went to Kansas for the expressed purpose of opening a branch of the Baldwin Horse Ranch. Horses were the mode of transportation and power by which the nation moved and developed its agricultural economy. Anyone engaged in farming needed horses. Moreover, as pioneers moved westward, cattle- and oxen-driven wagons soon gave way to mules and horses as the preferred methods of travel. Just as horse businesses had grown up in Illinois and elsewhere along the National Road and other trails, so were such businesses invited by the opening of trails further west. John Calvin likely took a branch of the family horse business west to meet the growing demand of an expanding nation because the first record of him in Kansas is on the famous Santa Fe Trail.

Many of the storied tales of the Old West took place along the Santa

Pioneer Caravan. Horse-drawn and oxen-yoked transportation was a common sight along the trails across Kansas Territory, as adventurous settlers moved further west. This caravan, on its way to Santa Fe, New Mexico, dates to ca. 1844. Courtesy of New Mexico History Museum.

Fe Trail. It was the major avenue of travel for many years. From it branched many historical roads like the Chisolm Trail, Oregon Trail, and Mormon Road, to name a few. The Pony Express rode the Santa Fe Trail, and many of the incidents of the Indian Wars were set along these trails in both the Territory of Kansas and further west. In 1820, the country beyond the State of Missouri was a vast uncharted land where only the bravest and hardiest of white men ventured. Great herds of buffalo roamed the plains. Indians, war-like and protective against the encroachment of settlers into their land, moved in bands, inflicting serious casualties on any hapless adventurers. As if that were not enough, streams crisscrossed the land, treacherous for their bottoms of quick sand. Beyond the plains lay the desert, and after that, the advance outposts of Spain in the New World, who were equally unsupportive of new settlements of white men. Nevertheless, the opportunity for trade with these distant lands was inviting, particularly in the southwest, where goods of Mexico pushed northward toward new markets in the US. When Mexico overpowered the Spanish, Santa Fe, New Mexico, quickly became one of the terminal points of western trade and a destination of the Santa Fe Trail.

Narrow Escape from the Buffaloes. Immense herds of buffalo populated the Kansas plains during their "running season" on their way north. The buffalo hunt supplied many of the wants of the Plains Indians. When pressed, buffalo sometimes turned on predators and stampeded into parties of migrants. Richardson, *Beyond the Mississippi*, 1867, p. 168.

The first trip west along what would become the Santa Fe Trail left Arrow Rock, Missouri, on September 1, 1821, led by Captain William Becknell, a successful Missouri trader and businessperson. It was a small party of men. They returned from New Mexico four months later with saddlebags bulging with the silver dollars of Mexico and stories about the desire of the Mexicans to trade. In 1825, the US Government signed a treaty with the Osage Indians, thus obtaining the right of way for a public highway known as the Santa Fe Trail. Notwithstanding, the friendliness of the Osage, other tribes like the Kiowa, Cheyenne, and the Sioux Indians took a toll on life on the Trail, trying to stop the westward movement of the white man. Eventually, the departure point for the Santa Fe Trail moved westward from Arrow Rock to Independence, Missouri, a town that owes its beginning in 1827 to the Santa Fe Trail. Virtually the entire population of early westward settlement funneled through Independence, Missouri, and the Kansas City-Westport region. Years later, the Baldwin brothers likely followed this route from Illinois, across Missouri, and into Kansas. The slow travel of the first oxen-driven wagons on the trail soon gave way to the faster, more maneuverable horse- and mule-pulled conveyances, and the need for horses to pull them. John Calvin Baldwin did not move to the Kansas Territory until many years after the establishment of the Santa Fe Trail, taking up his initial residence near the main line of the trail in Breckenridge County. Nevertheless, the hardships of pioneer life persisted, not to mention the growing prospects of Civil War.

The Santa Fe Trail passed through Waterloo Township of Breckenridge County. where John Calvin settled. From its several Missouri River branches, the Trail consolidated as one road in Johnson County, Kansas. It entered Douglas County near the southeast corner of the county, proceeding through the storied towns of Willow Springs and Palmyra, Kansas, the latter becoming part of the town of Baldwin, Kansas. John Calvin's older brother, William Mattison Baldwin, settled in Douglas County. However, the name Baldwin, in this case, honors John Baldwin, a native of New York and local mill operator who pre-dated the arrival of our William by a few years. The people of Baldwin City unwittingly found themselves surrounded by the events that led up to the American Civil War. Three miles east of Baldwin was the town

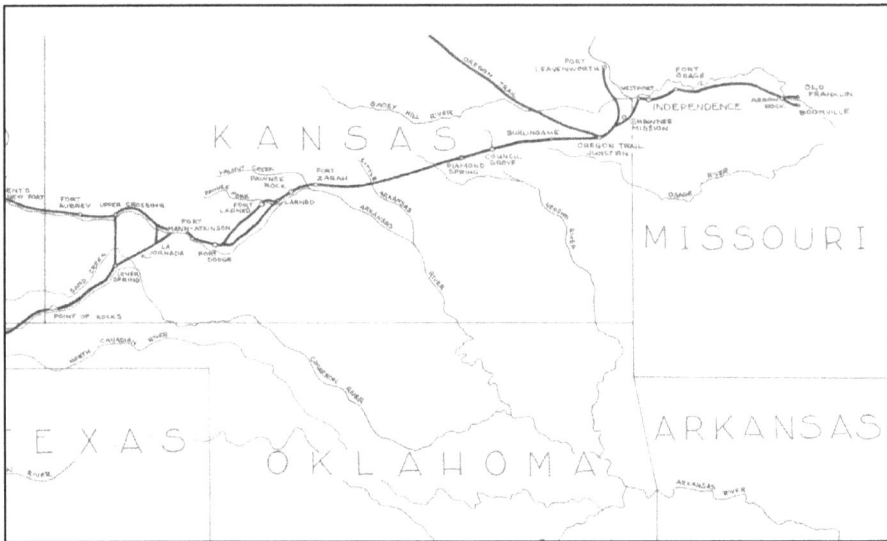

Santa Fe Trail. The Trail passed through Breckenridge County, Kansas, where John Calvin lived. Travelers along the tail required large numbers of horses, some of which the Baldwin horse business was able to furnish. The trail opened in 1821 and eventually reached from Arrow Rock, Missouri, to Santa Fe, New Mexico. Map excerpt Courtesy of Kansas Historical Society.

site of Black Jack, where the Battle of Black Jack took place on June 2, 1856. The night before that battle, John Brown, the leader of the Free State forces, stayed in Prairie City near the Santa Fe Trail.

The Santa Fe Trail crossed Osage County before coming into Breckenridge County near the northeast corner of the county, and crossed the northern part of the county in a southwesterly direction. Waushara on Chicken Creek, Elm Creek, the crossing of 142 Creek, and Agnes City on Bluff Creek were stopping places of more or less importance to the trail at different times, and all place names associated with John Calvin Baldwin.[1] Not far west of Waushara and Agnes City was the town of Council Grove, the site of the signing of the original Osage treaty that allowed the trail. For many years after the Santa Fe Trail opened, Council Grove was the only trading post between Independence, Missouri, and Santa Fe, New Mexico. Council Grove was the rendezvous point of westward-bound travelers and traders who

---

[1] Osage County began as Weller County in 1855 and formally organized in 1859 from Weller and the southern part of Shawnee County.

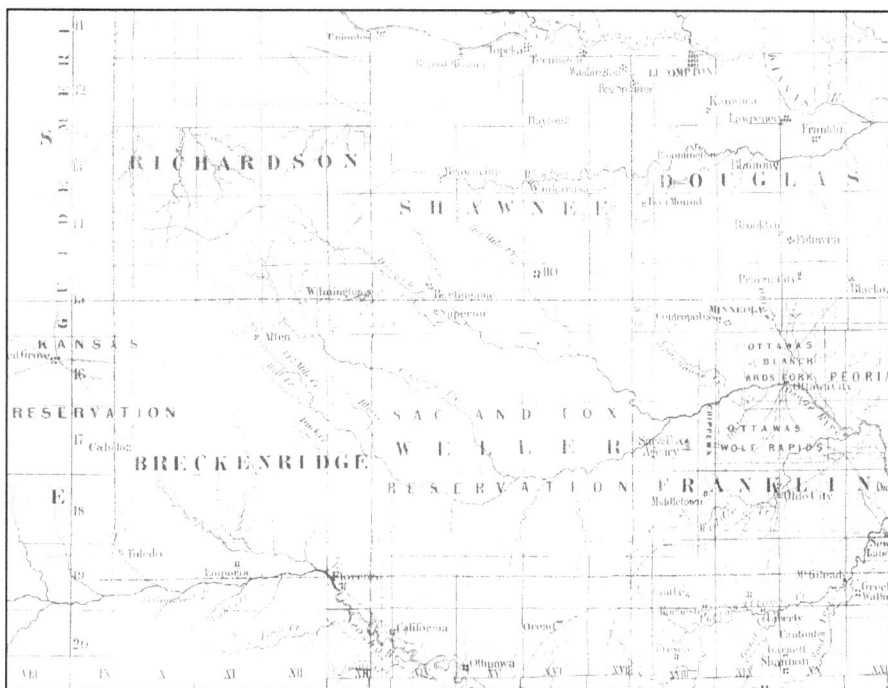

Breckenridge County. The Santa Fe Trail crossed the Kansas River on its way across Douglas and Osage counties (formerly Weller and part of Shawnee) through the northern part of Breckenridge County. John Calvin lived south of the trail in the Elk Creek vicinity. His brother, William Mattison, lived in Douglas County. Ream, *Sectional Map of the Territory of Kansas*, 1858. David Rumsey Historical Map Collection.

were crossing the plains. For years, the region from Council Grove, Kansas, to near Santa Fe, New Mexico, was the most hazardous part of the trail, which was 897 miles long from beginning to end.

So rapid were the new settlements in Kansas, the problem of securing mail became a serious one. Before this time, Santa Fe coaches dropped the mail at the Worthington Store and Hotel, where riders distributed it to the settlements at private expense. Worthington's was the first and for many years, the only store in southern Kansas outside regular Indian posts. It stood on the Santa Fe Trail in Breckenridge County. Transport of the mail was through pro-Southern towns in the growing sectional strife between North and South. As the prospects of war grew closer, there was a great deal of dissatisfaction with mail delivery. The settlers did not wish to trust the pro-slavery men who handled the mail. Finally, they agreed on a mailbox at Lawrence, to which all mail came, and thence brought by private conveyance to Emporia. A great deal of the mail was lost, and communication with friends and family was difficult. John Calvin received his mail at Waterloo. Meanwhile, travel was equally difficult. There were no railroads in the county in John Calvin's time. The first efforts to secure a railroad were in 1859, but it was not until 1864 that workers built the first railroad.

Coincidental with the move of John Calvin to Kansas, the Republican Party rose to national prominence because of the adoption of the Kansas-Nebraska Act, and with its rise ascended the political fortunes of Abraham Lincoln.[2] He bore a hard message on slavery. He told a Kansas audience, in 1858, "The further spread of slavery should be arrested, and it should be placed where the public mind shall rest in the belief of its ultimate extinction."[3] He spoke against popular sovereignty, the core of the Kansas-Nebraska Act, because it opened, in his view, the possibility of legalized slavery everywhere.[4] "To admit slavery in one place was to admit it in many places," he reasoned. "It is only traveling to the same place by different roads."[5]

Lincoln spoke many times in Kansas, both before and after he had secured the Republican Party nomination for the presidency. Many consider these some of the best speeches he ever made on the subject of slavery.[6] The opposition press lampooned him frequently for his appearance. "He is made up of head, hands, feet, and length," said one reporter, "a spectacle of long, swinging arms, and a general hirsute appearance." Nevertheless, his ideas on slavery resonated with the Free State voters who often came as much to see the man as to hear his words.[7] As residents of Lincoln's home state of Illinois, the Baldwins would have known about him both in Illinois and in Kansas.

---

[2] Frank H. Hodder, *The Genesis of the Kansas-Nebraska Act*, 69.

[3] Lincoln, *Abraham Lincoln: Complete Works*, 252; Herndon and Weik, *Herndon's Lincoln*, 3:465.

[4] Lincoln in Kansas, in *Transactions of the Kansas State Historical Society, 1901-1902.* Vol. 7, 544.

[5] Lincoln, *Abraham Lincoln: Complete Works*, 531.

[6] Lincoln in Kansas, in *Transactions of the Kansas State Historical Society, 1901-1902.* Vol. 7, 552.

[7] Edward A. Pollard, *Southern History of the War: The First Year of the War*, 42, 44.

Lincoln the Politician. Abraham Lincoln as he appeared about 1858. The photograph shows him in an image widely reproduced on presidential campaign ribbons. Lincoln reportedly liked the photograph and often signed prints of it for admirers. Library of Congress.

Those who saw Lincoln speak said he always stood squarely on his feet, toe even with toe, and one foot never before the other. He never touched or leaned on anything for support and made few changes in position or attitude once he began to speak. He never ranted or walked backward or forward on the platform, as was the custom of many orators. To ease his arms, he would grasp the lapel of his coat with his left hand, keeping his thumb upright and his right hand free to punctuate a point, the ever-familiar Lincoln posture.[8] As he spoke, his voice changed. It lost its acute and shrilling pitch at the beginning of a speech and mellowed into a harmonious and pleasant sound rising to impassioned eloquence. His speeches seemed to improve as he went along and gained steam.[9] Notwithstanding his sunken chest, he rose a splendid and imposing figure. His little grey eyes flashed in a face aglow with the fire of his profound thoughts. No one who ever heard him

---

[8] Francis Grierson, *The Valley of Shadows*, 201.
[9] Eugene F. Ware, *The Lyon Campaign in Missouri*, 40.

speak of the Declaration of Independence, for example, came away doubting the patriotic sincerity of this Illinois lawyer.[10]

A great comet appeared in the sky in the summer of 1858. Evenings found people sitting on their porches and watching it, as the heat of the day abated amid pleasant surroundings of crêpe myrtle bushes, their rose-colored blossoms flanking the steps. Voices drifted through the night in the warm, languid air of a summer night, filled with the sweet fragrance of white jasmine and honeysuckle, while the great comet hung majestically in the heavens. It generated great excitement around the world. Lincoln commented on it during the Lincoln-Douglas debates. He admired this strange visitor and sat for hours in front of his Kansas hotel looking at it. He could be seen sitting there in his rocking chair, his lanky posture curled in one of his favorite attitudes, one leg thrown over the arm of the chair, sometimes bending forward and clasping his hands over his knee, as if to get a closer look.[11] The comet stayed in the sky for some ten months before fading from view. It first appeared to the naked eye in late June 1858, reached its brightest magnitude in September, and disappeared in March 1859, appearing as it did at a time as if to warn of worse things yet to come in the discordant mood of the country. It seemed to verify old terrors of superstition. It signified in the minds of many the specter of dissolution of the Union that threatened the nation, coming nearer and nearer. Everyone said the comet was a sign of war.[12]

---

[10] This description of Lincoln as orator is excerpted from Herndon and Weik, *Herndon's Lincoln*, 2:408.

[11] Walter B. Stevens, *Lincoln and Missouri*, 81-82; Stevens, *Centennial History of Missouri*, 677.

[12] Gasperini, Galli, and Nenzi, The Worldwide Impact of Donati's Comet, 340-345; Herndon and Weik, *Herndon's Lincoln*, 2:405.

Turning Point

21

Bad Times and Worse Times

By June 1858, the avid abolitionist, John Brown, who was at the heart of the Kansas troubles and a strong proponent of violence to achieve his abolitionist goals, regained his stride in Kansas after spending most of 1857 raising financing among Eastern abolitionists to fund his planned slave uprising at Harpers' Ferry, Virginia. He had long intended as his purpose to strike a blow at slavery in its own stronghold in the South.[1] Brown left Kansas and spent most of the year of 1857 in the East making plans and begging for financing to support his plan; unbeknownst to his enemies, who thought that he was still hiding somewhere in the Territory of Kansas.[2] In the wake of the Supreme Court's opinion in the Dred Scott case, that slavery was an unstoppable universal right, Brown burst on the public scene, urging Eastern abolitionists to act. He made speeches that inflamed antislavery activists.[3] By 1858, he was back in Kansas.

News of Brown's presence in Kansas reignited the atrocities on both sides.[4] The fight against slavery took a grave turn. On December 20, 1858, Brown led two armed guerrilla bands out of Kansas down the Little Osage River into Vernon County, Missouri, across the Missouri border.[5] They raided two proslavery homesteads.[6] They killed one elderly slave owner, a well-liked local farmer, and pillaged property and livestock.[7] Already abhorred by proslavery forces for a previous massacre at Pottawatomie, Brown's incursion into Missouri drew

---

[1] Sanborn, *The Life and Letters of John Brown*, 167.

[2] Ibid., 437.

[3] Ibid., 467.

[4] Brown, *Reminiscences of Old John Brown*, 54.

[5] Ibid., 68.

[6] Sanborn, *The Life and Letters of John Brown*, 482.

[7] Brown, *Reminiscences of Old John Brown*, 68.

Portrait of John Brown. Extremist among anti-slavery leaders, Brown willingly used violence in support of his abolitionist views. He was active in Kansas about the time John Calvin Baldwin moved there. Library of Congress.

further widespread condemnation of him as both a murderer and a thief.[8]

In February of 1859, Missouri state military forces officially entered the Kansas dispute to suppress the troubles in western Missouri. Missouri Governor Robert M. Stewart sent Brigadier General D. M. Frost with Lieutenant Colonel John S. Bowen and six hundred and thirty armed state militia out of St. Louis to southwest Missouri to protect the citizens along the border.[9] It was the first deployment of a Missouri military force in the Kansas troubles. The elite force bearing, the name the Southwest Battalion, patrolled and protected the Missouri frontier.[10] Southwest Missouri had become the stronghold of the rebellion. The battalion's show of force had a powerful morale effect on the border, inspiring confidence against Free State marauders.[11]

Meanwhile, two hundred US Dragoons stationed at Fort Scott, Kansas, kept an uneasy peace on the Kansas side of the border. Their job was not to take a political side in the conflict but to protect the functions of the government and to prevent John Brown's ally, James

---

[8] Ibid., 68.

[9] C. R. Barns, *The Commonwealth of Missouri, a Centennial Record*, St. Louis: Bryan, Brand, 1877, p. 284; Missouri, *Journal of the House of the State of Missouri*, pp. 26-28. Robert M. Stewart was elected governor by a majority of only 334 votes, attesting to the split of the Missouri electorate on the slavery question.

[10] Herklotz, "Jayhawkers in Missouri," 17:510.

[11] Ibid., 17:512.

Montgomery, and his Jayhawkers from disrupting the process.[12] Nevertheless, although not in confrontation with each other, it was a time when Union soldiers occupied the same contested sectional grounds as a slave state militia, namely the Southwest Battalion of

Marais Des Cygnes Massacre. A band of proslavery men crossed the Missouri border into Kansas and on May 19, 1858, captured eleven antislavery men killing five and wounding five in one of the bloodiest raids of the Kansas-Missouri fight. Richardson, *Beyond the Mississippi*, 1867.

Missouri.

Under this uneasy military supervision, the political future of Kansas' statehood reached a settlement with the ratification of its antislavery constitution in October 1859. Free State men in Kansas chased the last proslavery advocates back into Missouri. Nevertheless, Kansans were loath to take their foot off the throats of their political enemies. The press kept up a steady drumbeat of vitriolic diatribe against Missouri slavery.

It is unlikely that John Calvin knew John Brown, but he certainly knew of him. John Brown left Kansas in January 1859 to lead his infamous raid on Harper's Ferry in October 1859. John Calvin arrived in Breckenridge County, Kansas at about this time. Whether he arrived before John Brown left the state and before the constitutional election, we do not know.

---

[12] Ibid., 17:508.

In 1860, there were 3,500 inhabitants in Breckenridge County, but the drought of that year so discouraged the settlers that many returned east and those who stayed saw actual want and suffering. John Calvin was among those who stayed. In the summer of 1860, the census located him and his family—Frances and two-year-old Mary—in Waterloo Township, living on 160 acres of unimproved land in the Waterloo Post Office district.[13] The census identified him as an owner, agent, or manager. His 160 acres had a cash value of $500. He owned $75 in farming implements and machinery, and had $300 worth of livestock exclusively in the form of eight working oxen. These details, taken from the 1860 agricultural census, cast doubt on whether John Calvin was in the horse business, at least in the beginning. However, his identity as "agent or manager" raises the possibility that he was engaged in a business of some sort. According to family tradition, John Calvin established part of the Baldwin Horse Ranch in Kansas, for which he would have been the manager and proprietor. The theory of the horse business becomes complicated because (1) he appears to have settled in Waterloo, Breckenridge County, and not Ottawa, Franklin County, and (2) his only reported livestock in 1860 were eight working oxen. On the other hand, another possible scenario has him working as an agent of a way station. His knowledge of horses and his likely management of his father's interest in horses is a plausible explanation. Thomas Lee would have owned the horse business, and not John Calvin. The plausibility of this theory has credence when one considers that the Pony Express had multiple way stations along the Santa Fe Trail where riders changed horses every 15 miles. The Baldwin specialty in trotting horses ideally fitted the Pony Express for the breed's particular quality of speed and stamina.

In any event, the census of 1860 suggests that John Calvin arrived in Kansas in late 1859, and settled on a tract of rough land in need of clearing for farming purposes because the census recorded zero farm produce for the year 1860. Compared to other farmers in the region, his

---

[13] 1860 US Census, Kansas, Waterloo, Breckenridge, taken 20 Jul 1860, Dwelling #56 Family #38 John C. Baldwin, 27, Farmer, $500 real estate /$200 property, b. Indiana; Frances P., 18, b. Missouri; Mary F., 2, b. Illinois." Waterloo P.O., National Archives and Records Administration, p. 6.

personal holdings were modest, except for his eight oxen. Oxen were the common work animals in the Waterloo farming community, outnumbering horses and mules by a ratio of almost 2 to 1. These sturdy draft animals were ideal for clearing land and, in John Calvin's case, possibly pulling the wagon that brought him, Frances, and baby Mary from Illinois to Kansas.

On May 18, 1860, Abraham Lincoln became the Republican Party's nominee for President. The fight for Kansas had unified the Republican Party and divided the Democrats.[14] The Democratic Party blew up at the convention of 1860, practically handing the election to Lincoln and the Republicans.[15]

Meanwhile, on October 27, 1860, John Calvin and Frances had their second child, a daughter Nancy Jane, named for her grandmother and born in Waterloo Township, Breckenridge County, in a nation on the brink of Civil War.

As the presidential campaign of 1860 progressed, excitement reached a fever pitch in Kansas. Those who were not interested in politics before and who were not even voters suddenly took more than a passing interest in events.[16] Crowds gathered in towns every day to get the latest news.[17] Kansas politics mattered.[18] The new Free State of Kansas bordered Missouri, which had the largest voting population of any of the slave states. The two states found themselves caught up in the hottest political battle the country had ever seen.[19]

The election of 1860 triggered widespread panic in western Missouri in the border counties along the Kansas line. The people in that part of the state were the core of Southern sympathizers. Their Southern roots and bitter exchanges with Free State Northerners in the border war with Kansas left little doubt as to their allegiance. The region was

---

[14] Gerteis, *Civil War St. Louis*, 38.

[15] Switzler, et al, *Switzler's Illustrated History of Missouri*, 300.

[16] Stevens, *Lincoln and Missouri*, 73.

[17] Anderson, *Memoirs: Historical and Personal*, 12.

[18] Switzler, et al, *Switzler's Illustrated History of Missouri*, 297-298; Herndon and Weik, *Herndon's Lincoln*, 2:466-468.

[19] Snead, *The Fight for Missouri*, 15; McElroy, *The Struggle for Missouri*, 21.

unanimously proslavery.[20] Proslavery men saw Lincoln's candidacy as a national referendum on the Kansas troubles. He did not receive a single vote in Vernon County, Missouri, the same being true for almost all the counties in southwest Missouri. He got one vote in another county, cast on a bet that no one would vote for him. A fellow bet five dollars that someone would, and then voted for Lincoln to win the bet.[21] Bates County cast eleven votes for Lincoln; proslavery men wrote the names of the eleven voters on large placards and posted them at every crossroads in the county.[22]

Secessionist fever ran high in the South. Even before Lincoln took office, southern states began to secede from the Union. Civil war was imminent. The Confederate army attacked Fort Sumter, in Charleston Harbor, South Carolina, on April 12, 1861, beginning what would be a long and bloody civil war.

The name of Breckenridge County was for John C. Breckenridge, a congressional representative from Kentucky, subsequently vice-president of the United States under James Buchanan, and a staunch pro-slave advocate. Congress expelled him from the US Senate in 1861 for supporting the rebellion. Consequently, on February 6, 1862, the anti-slavery Kansas Legislature changed the name of Breckenridge County to Lyon County in honor of Nathaniel Lyon, the Union general killed while leading the Union Army at the battle of Wilson's Creek, Missouri, August 10, 1861. Thereafter, county records refer to John Calvin as living in Lyon County, Kansas. Consequently, Breckenridge County, Kansas, appears on only one US Census, that being the census of 1860, which recorded John Calvin Baldwin living in Breckenridge with his family in Waterloo Township, in the extreme northeast corner of the county.

The first military company to leave Kansas for the seat of war was the Emporia Guards, in May 1861. In 1862, Lincoln called for additional troops, and Lyon County (aka Breckenridge) responded with about 150

---

[20] Herklotz, Jayhawkers in Missouri, 17:507. Missouri, General Assembly, *Journal of the House of the State of Missouri*, 566; Missouri, General Assembly, *Journal of the House of the State of Missouri*, 26-28.

[21] Schrader, Reminiscences, 26.

[22] Blankenbecker, Pioneer Life in Bates County, 139-141.

Lyon County. The boundaries of Kansas counties changed many times in their early histories. Madison County disappeared in 1861, its territory being divided between Breckenridge (present Lyon) and Greenwood counties. All north of the line between Townships 21 and 22 became Lyon County in 1864. The Baldwin home was in Waterloo Township, upper right section. They lived near Admire, the location of the grave of their infant daughter Nancy Jane. *Lyon County*, Philadelphia: L. H. Everts, 1887, p. 156.

volunteers. However, John Calvin was not among them. His part in the Civil War barely receives mention, unlike his brothers, some of whom served in the Union Army for the duration of the war. The war in Kansas and Missouri did not reach the level of battle intensity seen in other parts of the country. Early on, the Union forces secured Missouri despite the pro-slavery sentiments of many Missouri residents, and Kansas lay generally beyond the reach of the most intense fighting, but not beyond the atrocities of guerrilla bands that roamed about inflicting death and destruction on the civilian population. Several tragedies occurred in connection with the guerrilla activities between pro-slavery and anti-slavery bands. In 1862, a band of Free State men killed a woman in Topeka. Shortly thereafter, the notorious Confederate guerrilla Bill Anderson raided a Kansas home and killed two men, robbed several homesteads, and destroyed property at Elk Creek. It was an ominous warning to John Calvin because Anderson trafficked in stolen horses along the Santa Fe Trail, robbing and looting.

John Calvin left Breckenridge (Lyon) County temporarily and moved to Douglas County near the Free State enclave of Lawrence, Kansas, and closer to his brother William Mattison, who lived at Clinton, Kansas, in Douglas County. We do not know his reason for relocating, perhaps to gain a better sense of security for his family or some other unknown reason during the unsettled national turmoil. His father-in-law, Brice Jackson, lived at Willow Springs, in Douglas County, near Marion Township, where William Mattison Baldwin lived.[1] Mr. Jackson lived with his son James and Frances Baldwin's other siblings, which provided a good reason to move to Douglas County.[2] There may have been another reason, too. To add to the distress of the political climate, the year 1862 marked a low point in the personal lives of John Calvin and Frances Baldwin. Their infant daughter, Mary Frances, died on November 20, 1862, at the age of four. Her burial was at Ulrich Cemetery, at Pleasant Grove, in Douglas County, near Lawrence, Kansas.[3] Soon after her death, John Calvin, Frances, and their baby

---

[1] 1860 US Census, Willow Springs, Douglas, Kansas Territory, Group Number: 29, Series Number: M653, Roll: M653, 349, p. 134.
[2] Find a Grave Memorial ID 28885692.
[3] Find a Grave Memorial ID 86295386.

daughter Nancy Jane returned to their farm at Waterloo, in Lyon County, near the Santa Fe Trail. Here, a third daughter was born on January 15, 1863, at Ottawa, Kansas, in Waterloo Township, Lyon (former Breckenridge) County. They named her Anna Eliza. The family remained in Waterloo Township for the duration of the war.

The movements of John Calvin during this time lack documentation. Some think he moved his horse-breeding farm to Ottawa, in Franklin County, Kansas, because that is where his daughter Anna Eliza was born. Various claims place him at other times in Lyon (Breckenridge) County, Osage County, Franklin, and Douglas counties, all within a relatively small geographic area of eastern Kansas. His older brother, William Mattison, had a farm in Douglas County, Marion Township, not far from Waterloo, and the two brothers would likely have remained in close contact with each other. Whatever John Calvin's role in the horse breeding business was, the business had a presence in Kansas. The Kansas Breeding Association listed it as the "Baldwin Horse Ranch."

22

Civil War and Beyond

ivil War descended on the nation. Thomas Lee Baldwin remained in Illinois. The 1860 census enumerated on June 1, 1860, showed him, Nancy, and four of their children living in Macoupin County, Illinois, Township 12 Range 7. Their Post Office was Virden, Illinois. Thomas Lee, age 65, was a farmer with real estate valued at $4,235 and personal property worth $529. Three of his sons were also working on the farm. In the household, too, at the time of the census was 15-year-old Melissa Brittendine [*sic*: Brizendine], probably a niece of Nancy Brizendine Baldwin. Officials instructed enumerators of the census of 1860 to record the names of every person in the household. However, the census listed no relationships between members of a household.[1] Thomas Lee and his sons were successful farmers with a range of agricultural pursuits, including horse breeding. The 1860 agricultural schedule for Macoupin County recorded him with 200 acres under cultivation and another 47 acres of unimproved land. He had 27 head of livestock from horses, mules, and cattle to sheep and swine. That year he harvested 1,200 pounds of Indian corn, some tobacco, and a little hay. The sheep and cows produced enough wool and dairy products to meet family needs.[2] The relatively high values of his real estate and personal property placed Thomas Lee among the more elite of Macoupin County farmers.

Despite his success in agriculture, national political unrest did not bypass Illinois. It was inevitable that the Baldwin family would take the

---

[1] 1860 US Federal Census, Twp. 12 Range 7, Macoupin, Illinois M653 206 p. 203, P.O. Virden, 30 Aug 1860, National Archives and Records Administration, Dwelling #1460 Family #1399 Thomas L. Baldwin, 65, Farmer, $2235/$529, b. N.C.; Nancy, 56, b. Va.; Lucinda, 20, b. Ind.; Jeremiah, 19, Farmer, b. Ind., attended school; Joshua, 23, Farmer, b. Ind.; Henry, 16, Farmer, b. Ill., attended school; Malissa A. Brittendine(sic), 15, b. Ind., Virden P.O.

[2] 1860 US Census Agriculture Schedule, Place: Township 12 Range 7, Macoupin, Illinois, Archive Collection Number: T1133, Roll: 8, p. 37.

side of the Union in the sectional strife descending on the nation. The Civil War was ultimately about slavery. We do not know the political persuasion of Thomas Lee; that is, how deeply he personally felt about the moral issue of slavery, except that he appears to have moved from North Carolina, apparently in part to avoid slavery in the South. Neither Thomas Lee nor his ancestors owned slaves. None of the Baldwin family did. There were those of the Baldwin name who were slaveholders, but none was of Thomas Lee's lineage. In any event, we know that six of the Baldwin and Brizendine sons fought for the Union.

The slavery question in Illinois was a problem of lasting political importance. The French brought slaves into Illinois Territory very early, but the ordinance of 1787, which was to govern the new Northwest Territory of which Illinois was a part, forbade slavery. Some tried to interpret this as a prohibition of the introduction of "new slaves" into the territory, so as not to interfere with existing slaveholding conditions. The idea arose to identify black slaves as indentured servants and such servitude became part of the Indiana code of 1803. In 1823, the Illinois legislature sent a resolution to the people of Illinois asking for a constitutional convention to amend the constitution with the unexpressed aim of legalizing slavery.[3] A majority of the men of the state, and probably a majority of the entire population, were either born in the southern states or descended from southern people. Nevertheless, Illinois voters rejected the resolution and upheld slavery to be illegal in Illinois. Interestingly, the leader of the opposition to slavery was Governor Edward Coles, a Virginia slaveholder who had freed his slaves upon coming to Illinois.

When Thomas Lee Baldwin arrived in Illinois, the issue was still unsettled. There was continuing economic interest among some to bring slavery into the state. By 1842, the moral issue had become political, and the Liberty party organized, uniting in 1848 with the Free Soil party on a platform to resist the extension of slavery. In 1854, these parties broadened their coalition to secure a majority in the state legislature. Two years later, these elements formally organized as the

---

[3] Grace Humphrey, *Illinois: The Story of the Prairie State* (Centennial Edition). Indianapolis, Ind.: Bobbs-Merrill, 1917.

Republican Party and elected their candidates for state offices. This was the first time that the Democratic Party had been defeated in Illinois, its organization having been in control since the admission of Illinois to the union.

An important influence in this political revolution was a change in the character of the population. Until 1848, the southern element predominated in the population, but after that year, the immigration from the northern states was greater than that from the South, and the foreign element increased, not to mention the influx of anti-slavery migrants from the Quaker centers of the South. The influence of immigration and sectionalism upon Illinois politics is evident in the fact that the first six governors—from 1818 to 1838—were born in southern states. After that, few were of southern origin.

The Illinois Constitution of 1848 abolished slavery and forbade the immigration of slaves into the state. However, slavery remained a central political and economic issue. In 1858, the famous contest for the office of US senator occurred between Stephen A. Douglas, a Democrat, and Abraham Lincoln, a Republican. Douglas won the election, but the vote showed that Illinois was becoming more northern in sympathy. Two years later, in 1860, Lincoln, then a candidate for the presidency, carried the state.

The policy of Illinois in the early period of the Rebellion was one of marked loyalty to the Union; even in the southern part of the state, the majority of the people had no sympathy with the proslavery men in their efforts to dissolve the Union. The Illinois Legislature of 1861 provided for a war fund of $2,000,000. There was, however, opposition to a continuance of the war. In 1862, Illinois Democrats regained control of the legislature and adopted resolutions against further conflict, recommending an armistice and a national convention to conclude peace. Lawmakers ratified pro-slavery clauses, and by 1863, more pronounced opposition to the policy of the national government developed. A mass meeting was held at Springfield in July at the insistence of the Democratic Party, and adopted resolutions that condemned the suspension of the writ of habeas corpus, endorsed the doctrine of state sovereignty, demanded a national assembly to determine the terms of peace, and asked President Lincoln to withdraw the proclamation that emancipated the slaves. The Knights of the Golden Circle and other secret societies, whose aims were the promulgation of state sovereignty and the extension of aid to the Confederate states, began to flourish. In 1864, there were 50,000 members of the Sons of Liberty in Illinois.[4] Then, in the elections of 1864, the Republicans and Union Democrats united. After an intense campaign, they were successful in regaining power. The new Illinois legislature was the first among the legislatures of all the states to ratify the 13th Amendment to abolish slavery.

Amid the backdrop of political turmoil, the state of Illinois contributed 255,092 men to the federal army of the Civil War. Thomas Lee sent four of his seven sons to fight for the Union: John Calvin, age 28, Joshua, 26, James, 23, and Jeremiah, 21, along with two cousins, Joseph and LeRoy Brizendine, nephews of Nancy, Thomas Lee's wife. John Calvin Baldwin lived in Kansas at the time and joined the Kansas Militia. All three of the Baldwin boys from Illinois joined the 122nd Illinois Infantry at the same time and fought side by side in some of the toughest campaigns of the war. The Union Army mustered them in together with Company E on September 4, 1862, at Carlinville, Illinois, and mustered them out together on a Saturday, July 15, 1865, at Springfield, Illinois. All served at the rank of private except Joshua, who received a promotion to Corporal. Three of the older Baldwin brothers—Thomas Jackson, William Mattison, and Caleb J.—remained out of the war ostensibly to look after the Baldwin horse ranches.[5]

The 122nd Illinois Regiment organized at Camp Palmer, Carlinville, Illinois, in August 1862, and mustered into service on September 4, 1862, with 960 enlisted men. In the fall of 1862, the regiment saw duty at various defensive and guard posts in Kentucky and Tennessee. In December 1862, they marched from Trenton, Tennessee, to Jackson, Tennessee, to protect the Ohio and Mobile Railroad and guard supplies stored at that place. During the regiment's absence, rebels captured the hospital at Trenton, killed three officers, and took 60 prisoners. Elements of the 122nd joined in pursuit of the rebels, and on December

[4] E. B. Greene, E. B., *Sectional Forces in the History of Illinois* (No. 8). Indianapolis, Ind.: Publications of the Historical Library of Illinois, 1903.

[5] Jimmy O. Baldwin, in History of Cedar County, pp. 145-146.

27, 1862, about 11 a.m., a Union force of 1,540 men met the rebels in battle, numbering some 6,000 men and 18 pieces of artillery. For three hours, the smaller Union force fought until the rebels pulled back and left the field in possession of the little force. The 122nd Regiment lost 22 enlisted men and 1 officer. No casualty figures list losses for the rebels, except that the Union men captured half of the rebel artillery and 500 rebel prisoners. The battle-tested 122nd marched into the Deep South, taking up positions in Corinth, Mississippi, and Town Creek, Alabama.

Throughout most of the year of 1863, the assigned duty of the 122nd was to protect the Memphis and Charleston Railroad, and to aid General Ulysses S. Grant in operations against Vicksburg, Mississippi, which surrendered to Union forces on July 4, 1863.[6] The 122nd engaged in numerous skirmishes in the South until December 1863, when the unit moved to Paducah, Kentucky, to resist rebel forces active in that area. A considerable force of the rebel army attacked Paducah, and three companies of the 122nd, E, H, and K, took part in the defense, and aided in repelling the rebels in three separate assaults. In the summer of 1864, the 122nd returned to Mississippi and remained there for some time. Skirmishes took place almost every day. Marches were long, grueling, and the weather was hot; cases of sunstroke often occurred. The regiment moved to the defense of Tupelo, Mississippi, then under impending attack from the Confederates. On July 14, 1864, the Union met them at around 9 a.m. To reach the Union position, the rebels had to pass through an open field. The 122nd held the ground on the right, covering the road leading into Tupelo. One observer described the action. "As the enemy advanced across the open plain, covered by a heavy artillery fire, the One Hundred and Twenty-second and the rest of the Brigade moved forward from the opposite side, and met the enemy just at the crest of the ridge, and opened a destructive fire upon them with such effect that their ranks were shattered and the whole force driven back with heavy loss in men and officers. Three times the assault was repeated and repulsed with equally disastrous results to the rebel force. At about 2 p.m., the enemy discomfited, withdrew, leaving the Union forces masters of the field and in possession of the rebel dead.

---

[6] Official Records of the War of the Rebellion; Dyer's Compendium.

The loss of the One Hundred and Twenty-second was 10 killed and 33 wounded." Among the casualties of the 122nd were officers from companies A and K, but not Company E of the Baldwin brothers.

The 122nd Regiment command returned to Tennessee, and in the fall and winter, the command engaged in skirmishes around St. Louis, Missouri, and along the Missouri River as far west as Kansas City and

John Calvin Baldwin. Pictured about the time of the Civil War, John Calvin lived in Kansas at the time and served in the Kansas State Militia on the Union side. Three of his brothers joined the Union 122nd Illinois Regiment. All four brothers survived the war. K. Burchett Baldwin Photograph File.

back. Ordered to Nashville, Tennessee, the 122nd fought in the Battle of Nashville on December 15 and 16, 1864, in which the 122nd lost 26 men killed and wounded. The battle occurred after a massive snow and ice storm stalled the rebel offensive. Union forces attacked and overwhelmed the Confederate Army, pursued them into Alabama, and effectively destroyed the retreating Army of the Tennessee. The commanding general of Union forces specifically commended the 122nd for its conduct in the battle.

In the spring of 1865, with the war winding down, Union forces pushed the rebels into defensive positions around Blakely and Spanish Fort, which constituted the eastern defenses of Mobile, Alabama. The 122nd Regiment materially aided in the capture of Blakely, losing 20 men killed and wounded in battle. The war ended in April, and on June

5, 1865, the 122nd Regiment marched to Mobile where on July 15 it mustered out, and proceeded thence to Springfield, Illinois. At Springfield, the 122nd troops received their pay and officially received discharge on August 4, 1865.[7]

Meanwhile, in Kansas, John Calvin joined the Kansas State Militia. In 1864, when Missouri Confederate General Sterling Price threatened Kansas, 300 Kansans answered the call to repel his invasion. They were in active duty for only about a month, but effectively dissuaded Confederate designs on Kansas. On October 13, 1864, at Paola, Kansas, John Calvin enrolled in Company D of the Santa Fe Road Battalion, also known as the Osage County Battalion Regiment. The campaign lasted only a week and ended on October 28, 1864, with the defeat of Price's army in Arkansas. The action marked the end of the Confederate crusade for the border region, despite continued guerrilla warfare that threatened citizens on both sides of the border. John Calvin does not appear to have engaged the Confederates in battle. This was common for state militia soldiers. The men of Kansas played a key part in protecting their homes, driving out hostile Indians in the west and southwest, and keeping in check the bushwhackers in the south.[8] Another of the name, John C. Baldwin, participated in the same containment action against General Price. He belonged to Company O of the Third Regiment Kansas State Militia operating out of Lawrence, Kansas. This unit was the Silver Grays, comprised of men over the age of 45. Unless his service was an exception to the age limit, this could not have been our John Calvin because in 1864, he age was 32.[9]

---

[7] Illinois, 122nd Illinois Infantry Regiment History, Adjutant General's Report, Illinois [online-USGenWeb Project, transcribed by Susan Tortorellit, 1997].

[8] 1890 Special Schedules of the Eleventh Census Enumerating Union Veterans and Widows of Union Veterans of the Civil War, Series Number: M123, Records of the Department of Veterans Affairs, Record Group Number: 15, p. 3, NARA. Missouri, Cedar, no town given] Township: Linn Twp. South, District 62, Baldwin, John C., Soldier Company KSM [Kansas State Militia], no service data given.

[9] Muster Rolls, Kansas State Militia, Kansas. Adjutant General's Office (Vol. 9, 1864, p. 59. Muster Roll of Captain E. H. Sanford, Company D of the Santa Fe Road Battalion [aka Osage County Battalion Regiment], Kansas State Militia, Lt. Colonel M. M Murdock, from 13 Oct 1864 to 28 Oct 1864. J. C. Baldwin Priv. joined and

---

sworn in May 16 at Waterloo by T. F. Burns, ordered into active service Oct 13 at Paola by Gen. Curtis, relieved from duty Oct 28 by Gen Curtis.

23

A Personal Story

The next certain date and location for John Calvin in Kansas is February 10, 1864. On that date, three-year-old Nancy Jane died. Her burial was at Pleasant Ridge Cemetery, near the village of Admire, in northern Lyon County, and near the Baldwin farm.[1] John Calvin and Frances lost two daughters within in the space of 15 months, leaving only Anna Eliza, barely a year old when her sister died.

We can only imagine the grief John Calvin and Frances felt for the loss of their daughter, to bury her in a distant wilderness, especially coming so soon after the death and burial of Mary on the same perilous frontier. The following fictional narrative may capture some of their painful experience.

John Calvin blew out the lamp and crawled into bed. A nearly full moon lit up the prairie and reflected a pallid light into the small dark Kansas sod house. Better-than-expected fall weather had postponed the need for a fire in the fireplace. He lay for a long time, his eyes open, staring at the ceiling, but seeing nothing. After a long silence, his voice softly breaking, he asked, "You alright?"

"Yes," Frances replied.

There are no words to wash away sorrow for the death of a child. Little Nancy seemed so healthy just a few days ago. The fever came on suddenly; she was gone within hours. The young couple experienced that helpless feeling that comes from being alone in the middle of nowhere. No doctors, no close neighbors came to help.

The Baldwins' story is a story like that of so many others who went west to claim the promise of a new land, only to have their youthful adventure turn to tragedy. John Calvin had taken the family horse-trading business to the furthest frontier of the West. The Oregon, Santa

---

[1] Find a Grave Memorial ID 53018137.

Fe, and Overland trails all crossed Kansas. The demand for good horses could only go up. Politics played no part in John Calvin's decision. The Baldwin family never owned slaves and could not afford them even if they wanted to. Guilt swept over John Calvin. Coming to Kansas was a bad idea. He should have known better. After all, he was older: 31 on his last birthday. Frances seemed to read his mind in the darkness.

"I belong here with you, John." She said. "Kansas is our home. Mary and Nancy are gone, but we have Anna Eliza."

John Calvin's mind drifted out to Nancy's grave, a small grave in a makeshift cemetery that amounted to no more than a dot on the endless prairie. They called it Pleasant Ridge. He had scraped together enough money to buy a small, hard headstone, one that could stand the erosion of the harsh prairie wind. He wanted to do that for her.

"Kansas is hard," he said. "Maybe we should go back home."

"Maybe," Frances whispered, "Maybe someday."

Unexpected discoveries reward the research work of a genealogist. For many years, family historians knew of the deaths of the Baldwin sisters, but no one knew under what circumstances the two children died, nor did anyone know where their burials were in Kansas. The first discovery was the gravesite of Nancy Baldwin, at Pleasant Ridge, Kansas. The Flint Hills Genealogical Society of Kansas released a survey of old gravestones in a forgotten section of Pleasant Ridge Cemetery. In the 1940s, the Daughters of the American Revolution took headstone readings at Pleasant Ridge and put together the earliest known readings. Members of the Flint Hills Genealogical Society read the stones again in the 1980s. Some of the stones originally read by the D.A.R. had disappeared in the intervening years. Vandalism and natural forces through the years had also taken a toll.

Fortunately, on the new Flint Hills list was the name of a child, Nancy L. [sic] Baldwin, along with her life dates. Correspondence sent to the Flint Hills Society raised a few discrepancies about Nancy's gravestone—Nancy J. instead of Nancy L., for example—and a follow-up inquiry asked for information regarding Mary Frances Baldwin, her sister and the first daughter of John Calvin and Frances, known from family records to have died in 1862—perhaps also in Waterloo Township. Like her younger sister, Mary was about four years old when she died. The inquiry asked if additional records for Pleasant Ridge might indicate a possible burial for Mary Frances.[2] A representative of the Flint Hills Society responded, "This cemetery does have old stones which are hard to read due to weather and aging. Many burials do not have stones—whether they once did or not, we do not know. We have been working on identifying who is buried in the cemetery and have discovered that there are many individuals in the cemetery that do not have stones nor are they listed on the sexton records… There is also the possibility that both girls are listed on one stone and the reader only read one side of it."[3]

Pleasant Ridge Cemetery was new at the time of Nancy's burial in 1864. Her stone is the sixth-oldest in the cemetery. The oldest readable stone in the cemetery is that of Benjamin Dunmire, a landowner in the area, who died in 1857. Other prominent names found in the cemetery are Bush, Plumb, Burns, and O'Dell. Leonard W. Bush was part of a group of people active in the Wisconsin Aid Society of 1857, one of many non-Kansas organizations that came to Kansas to influence the territorial organization in the struggle between free and pro-slavery forces.[4] Among the other names in the cemetery, P. B. Plumb was one of the founders of Emporia, Kansas, in 1857, and later a United States Senator from Kansas. George W. Burns came to Breckenridge County (present Lyon) from Kenebe County, Maine, in 1858, and B. M. O'Dell was one of the earliest landowners in the Waterloo, Kansas, neighborhood. These and others were the neighbors of John Calvin. J. G. W. Stinson, for example, lived just a mile to the south of the cemetery.

As it turned out, the burial of Mary Frances was not at Pleasant Ridge Cemetery but instead at Ulrich Cemetery, near Pleasant Grove, Kansas, in Douglas County. Nevertheless, the location of the gravesites of Mary and Nancy confirmed the locations of John Calvin and Frances for the years 1862 and 1864. The discoveries of the graves put them at specific locations in Lyon and Douglas counties at particular times. Pleasant

---

[2] Flint Hills Genealogical Society [online
Http://www.rootsweb.com/~ksfhgslc/pleasantcemr.htm. 2001.
[3] Email correspondence Regina Falcetto [online falcetto@yahoo.com 02/04/05.
[4] Biography of L. W. Bush, files of Lyon County Historical Society, Stories of the Santa Fe Trail.

Ridge Cemetery is on the west side of Section 27, Township 15, Range 12, just a stone's throw south of the old Santa Fe Trail, and not far from the early Post Office of Waushara, Breckenridge County (now Lyon County), Kansas. The old Trail was divided into two trails beginning just east of Waushara and ran some four miles before coming together again, the division never being apart more than three-quarters of a mile. The south branch of the divided trail passed the cemetery. Southeast of the cemetery is a State D.A.R. Marker on the site of the Old Mail Station. John Calvin was here by 1859 and in 1860 listed Waushara as his Post Office. Meanwhile, Ulrich Cemetery, the burial place of Mary, sits in the middle of a small geographic area that includes Baldwin City, Lawrence, Pleasant Grove, and Willow Springs, Kansas, the latter being the home of the Brice Jackson family, the family of Frances Pherby Baldwin. William Mattison Baldwin, brother of John Calvin, lived in this same area near Clinton, Kansas.

Meanwhile, we do not know the circumstances of the children's deaths. No one knows how or under what circumstances either of the two Baldwin sisters died. Infant mortality ran high on the frontier. If John Calvin was away during the war, Frances cared for the children alone. No other known family members lived in Breckenridge County at the time. Frances was only 18 when Mary died, which may account for the Baldwins' move to Douglas County to be nearer family members.

Meanwhile, the experience of John Calvin and his horse business is probably a story of missed opportunity. By the time he arrived in Kansas, the Santa Fe Trail was fading in popularity and not used as much. Alternative routes sprang up over the years and use dropped off considerably with the coming of the Santa Fe Railroad. Wagon caravans picked up goods at the railhead, and the length of the trail decreased as the railroad increased. With the change, the greater need for the horse business diminished, too.

The activities of John Calvin while in Kansas have sparse documentation. He seems to have been at one time or another in various parts of eastern Kansas. His older brother William's farm was in Douglas County, Marion Township, and not far from Waterloo, in Lyon County, and the two brothers would likely have remained in contact with each other. Some think John Calvin moved his horse-breeding farm to Ottawa, in nearby Franklin County, Kansas. The fourth Baldwin child, Sarah Almina (Mina), was born in October 1864, allegedly in Ottawa. The Baldwin family also claims that a fifth daughter, Emma Callie, was born November 13, 1866, in Kansas, and died September 22, 1869, in Missouri, but no confirmation of her is available outside family recollection.[5] In any event, in 1867, John Calvin, Frances, and their two surviving daughters—Anna Eliza and Sarah Almina—left Kansas and moved the horse ranch to Missouri. William Mattison remained in Kansas, where he lived out the rest of his life.

Meanwhile, in Illinois, in the 1860s, it was a practice of entrepreneurs in Illinois to sponsor excursions to Missouri to try to interest clients in migrating to the state in hopes of selling them land. One such company, the Missouri Immigration Associates, organized several groups of people from the Macoupin County, Illinois, area to come to Barton County, Missouri. Visitors lodged in nearby farmhouses, ate good meals, and toured around county properties for sale. Southwest Missouri was attractive for its small grains and prairie hay production. Excursion managers from Illinois brought people to the state by various routes. Some people came down the rivers part of the way, others followed trails, and still others took nearby rail lines. Whether such excursions included Cedar County, Missouri, is unknown, nor is there evidence that Thomas Lee or a member of his family participated in any of these visits. Nevertheless, Thomas Lee sold his Illinois property and moved to Cedar County, Missouri. By 1867, Thomas Lee, Nancy, and six of their seven sons were in or near Linn Township of Cedar County. Henry was the only son who remained in Illinois near his sister, Sarah Baldwin Worth. Lucinda Baldwin died at the age of 21 in Illinois, and the other daughter, Nancy J., married J. B. Walters and likely remained in Illinois, too. The remainder of the Thomas Lee Baldwin family, except William Mattison, moved to Missouri.

---

[5] Jimmy O. Baldwin, in History of Cedar County.

24

Illinois and Kansas Kin

Of the children of Thomas Lee who did not move to Cedar County, Sarah, Nancy, and Henry, remained in Illinois, William Mattison continued to live in Kansas, and Lucinda died in Illinois before the Baldwin exodus to Missouri occurred. These Illinois and Kansas Baldwins were the aunts and uncles of the Cedar County Baldwins who preserved the legacy of the Baldwin heritage in places and ways apart from their Missouri kin, each one with family stories of their own.

Sarah L. Baldwin was the firstborn of Thomas Lee and Nancy Brizendine Baldwin. She was born on Friday, September 16, 1825, in Grayson County, Virginia. She was about three years old when her parents carried her to Wayne County, Indiana. We have no firsthand accounts of that trip, but one may imagine the adventure that such a journey would be for a young child. Sarah moved next to Hancock County, Indiana, and then, as a teenager, to Illinois. At the age of 21, she married William Worth of Morgan County, Illinois. The couple moved several times in west central Illinois before settling in Sangamon County, Illinois.

William Worth was of a pioneer Virginia family, son of a veteran of the Black Hawk War and a justice of the peace in Illinois.[1] Born in Adair County, Kentucky, on August 4, 1825, near Columbia, on a farm, his father moved with him to Morgan County, near Jacksonville, Illinois, in the fall of 1829.[2] He spent his youth in Morgan County, living in Jacksonville from 1829 to 1846. After William and Sarah married in

---

[1] *History of Sangamon County, Illinois*, Chicago: Inter-state Publishing, 1881, p. 1039.

[2] Find a Grave Memorial ID 34797440 & 53060178. John Worth died 25 Apr 1852 (aged 69–70). His burial was in Lebanon Cemetery, Petersburg, Menard County, Illinois, and not Morgan County as the *History of Sangamon County* stated in 1881. Elizabeth Hopkins Worth died 16 Mar 1863 (aged 76–77). Her burial was in Roaches Chapel Cemetery, Atlanta, Logan County, Illinois.

Morgan County, they moved first to Sangamon County, Illinois, and then to Macoupin County, Illinois.[3] In the fall of 1850, the US Census located them on a farm in Macoupin County with sons, James, age two, and John, age eight months.[4] The Worths eventually chose to return to Sangamon County to make their family home and settled on a farm near Auburn, Illinois. Except for three years at the beginning of their marriage, Sarah and William lived their entire lives on a farm in Talkington Township, in Sangamon County, which lies east of Morgan County and due north of Macoupin County, where the Baldwin family lived. For several years, Sarah's brothers, Thomas Jackson Baldwin and William Mattison Baldwin, and her sister, Nancy J. Baldwin Walters, all lived near each other in Sangamon and Macoupin Counties.[5]

William and Sarah Worth were successful in farming, owning substantial assets in real estate and property by the time they were in their forties.[6]

It was an early farming tradition for sons and daughters to work on the family farm until of age to start their own families. Records indicate that both the Worth and Baldwin families followed this tradition. It was also common in early days for family members to exchange labor, and for relatives to work for each other. For example, William Worth hired his brother-in-law, Henry Baldwin, Sarah's youngest brother, to work on the Talkington Farm. Henry chose to remain in Illinois when other members of the Baldwin family moved to Missouri around 1867.[7] Meanwhile, at other times, members of the Brizendine family, Sarah's cousins, worked on the Worth farm.[8]

---

[3] Illinois Statewide Marriage Index, 1763–1900, Vol. B, Page 56, License No. 1712, Morgan County.

[4] 1850 US Census, Macoupin, Illinois, M432, p 465, National Archives and Records Administration (NARA).

[5] 1860 US Census, Illinois, Sangamon, Subdivision 17, Auburn Post Office, p. 233, NARA. W. Worth age 32, S. Worth age 30 [*sic*].

[6] 1870 US Census, Illinois, Sangamon, Talkington, p. 20, NARA. William age 45 & Sarah age 40 [*sic*], Talkington Post Office.

[7] *Ibid*, 1870 US Census.

[8] 1860 US Census, Illinois, Sangamon, Subdivision 17, Auburn Post Office, p. 233, NARA.

After 1881, William and Sarah continued to live and work their farm in Section 33 along the south line of Talkington, near the village of Lowder, Illinois, and near the Chicago-Burlington-Quincy Railroad that passed through Lowder. We know that in addition to farming, William served as Sangamon County road commissioner during this period. William died in 1900, and Sarah passed in 1909. Their burials were in West Cemetery, located about a mile west of the village of Thayer, between Auburn and Virden, in Auburn Township, Sangamon County, Illinois. Thayer is south of Springfield, Illinois.[9] The children of William and Sarah Worth were James S., John T., William H., Nancy E., Charles J., and Ella. Five of their ten children died in childhood, four in infancy, and John T. died sometime after his tenth birthday between 1860 and 1870.[10] William H. later joined the Baldwin family in Missouri, where he lived at Cane Hill, in Madison Township.[11]

Meanwhile, Nancy Jane Baldwin, the sixth child of Thomas Lee and Nancy Baldwin, stayed in Illinois, too. She was born in 1834 in Hancock County, Indiana. She married James Walters in 1857. James was one of nine children born to Lydia Donner Walters and James Walters [Sr.] in Kentucky. In 1829, the Walters family moved to Decatur County, Indiana. The senior Mr. Walters died there in June 1830, when young James was 12. In 1839, widow Mrs. Walters moved her family to Sangamon County, Illinois, and settled in Auburn Township.

We know little about Nancy Jane Baldwin Walters except for the information contained in census records. By 1870, James and Nancy Jane were in Township 12 Range 6, living in Virden, Illinois.[12] Nancy's father, Thomas Lee, and others of the Baldwin family had also lived in the same township until 1867, when they removed to Missouri. In 1870, James Walters was working as a carpenter, with real estate holdings of $2,000. Their two children, James J. and William B., ages 14 and 12, were attending school. Ten years later, in the spring of 1880, the boys were

---

[9] Find a Grave Memorial IDs 28939860 & 28939875.

[10] 1880 US Census, Talkington Township, Sangamon, Illinois, E.D. 206, sheet 11-E.D. 230, sheet 33, Series T9, Roll 249, NARA.

[11] 1880 US Census, Missouri, Cedar, Cane Hill, 253, p. 35, NARA.

[12] 1870 US Census, Illinois: Macoupin County (NARA Series M593, Roll 250), p. 30.

gone but James and Nancy were still living in Virden.[13] James, also known as J. B. Walters, was age 62 in 1880, several years older than Nancy was at age 45. The 1880 census listed James as a laborer. Curiously, throughout all the 1880 census records covering the Baldwin family, almost all of Thomas Lee's children listed their father as being born in Virginia, except Nancy Jane, who remembered he was born in North Carolina.

We know little about Lucinda Baldwin, the ninth child of Thomas Lee and Nancy Baldwin. She was born in 1839 in Hancock County, Indiana, and died on Christmas Eve, 1860, at the age of 21, in Macoupin County, Illinois. At the end of August 1860, less than four months before her death, she was alive and living with Thomas Lee and Nancy, and her brothers, Jeremiah, Joshua, and Henry, at the family place in North Otter Township, Macoupin County, Illinois. She never married, and no one knows what caused her death.[14]

The final Baldwin child to remain in Illinois was Henry. Henry Baldwin was the youngest of Thomas Lee and Nancy Baldwin's 11 children, and the only child to be born in Illinois. In 1860, at the age of 16, he lived with his parents and worked on the family farm in Macoupin County.[15] He and his older brother, Jeremiah, attended school that year. Lucinda, 20, and Joshua, 23, were also still living with their parents at home. When Thomas Lee moved his family to Missouri about 1867, Henry remained in Macoupin County, the only Baldwin son who remained in Illinois.[16] In the summer of 1870, he was staying with his older sister, Sarah, and her family in Talkington, Sangamon County, Illinois.[17] In the 1880 census, he was back in Macoupin County living with the John Carey family in Girard Township. He was 36 and single, working as a farm hand.[18] Henry apparently did not marry. We know nothing of him after 1880.

---

[13] 1880 US Census, Illinois: Macoupin County, NARA Series T9, Roll 232, p. 27.

[14] Jimmy O. Baldwin, in History of Cedar County, pp. 145-146.

[15] 1860 US Census, Illinois, Macoupin, Town 12 Range 7, p. 203, NARA.

[16] Jimmy O. Baldwin, in History of Cedar County, pp. 145-146.

[17] 1870 US Census, Illinois, Sangamon, Talkington, p. 20 NARA.

[18] 1880 US Census, Illinois: Girard Township, Macoupin County, NARA Series T9, Roll 232, p. 3.

Meanwhile in Kansas, Baldwin descendants of Thomas Lee's line owe their presence to William Mattison Baldwin, who, when most of the Thomas Lee Baldwin family descended on Cedar County, Missouri, he elected to remain in Kansas, where he enjoyed a long and productive life. He was the third child of Thomas Lee and Nancy Baldwin, born in 1829, and the first of their children to be born outside of Virginia. He was born in Wayne County, Indiana, and was later brought to Hancock County, Indiana, by his parents. The phonetic spelling of Madison as 'Mattison' was no doubt intended to celebrate a popular 19th-century trend of naming children after presidents and important religious and biblical figures. Other middle names of Thomas Lee's sons included Washington, and Jackson, not to mention John Calvin Baldwin, namesake of the famous 16th-century Protestant theologian. It is apparent, too, that Baldwin first names were a continuation of names given to relatives of previous generations.

William Mattison was about nine years old when the Baldwins moved to Hancock County, where he spent his early youth on the family farm near Greenfield. He doubtless spent many hours on Sugar Creek, and on Brandywine Creek that flows near Greenfield, on its way to the Blue River. William moved next at the age of 14 to Illinois. He remained at home with his parents into his early twenties, helping his siblings to operate the family farm in Macoupin County, Illinois.[19] On August 6, 1851, at the age of 21, he purchased 40 acres of government land in section 32 of Sangamon County, not far from where his brother, Thomas Jackson Baldwin, had opened his farm the year before.[20] The Baldwin brothers' farms in Sangamon County were located just across the county line from Macoupin County, where Thomas Lee lived. Thomas' daughters, Sarah Baldwin Worth and Nancy Jane Baldwin Walters, and their families also lived in the same part of Sangamon County.

---

[19] 1850 US Census, Illinois: Macon and Macoupin Counties, NARA Series M432, Roll 118.

[20] US Bureau of Land Management (BLM), SESW Sect 32, Township 13N, Range 07W, Meridian 3, 6 August 1851, Vol. 340, p. 079.

In 1854, William married Susan Collins, and they set up housekeeping not far from the other Baldwins.[21] Here, their first two children, Riley T. and Mary M., were born. Sometime after 1858 but before 1863, William sold his farm in Sangamon County and moved his family from Illinois to Kansas.[22] His younger brother, John Calvin Baldwin, moved to Kansas at about the same time, and it is probable that they went there together, although they appear to have ended up in different parts of Kansas. William settled first in Marion Township, Douglas County, where he opened a farm. In 1870, at the age of 40, He had a personal estate value of about $5,000, a tidy sum for the Kansas frontier.[23] He later moved to Elk Township in Osage County, Kansas, near

William Mattison Baldwin. The family posed for this portrait at Ottawa, Kansas, about 1866. Pictured are William, his wife Susan, and three of their seven children: James, Riley, and Mary. K. Burchett Photo File.

---

[21] Genealogists sometimes confuse William Mattison with another William Baldwin living in Sangamon County at the same time who married Mary J. Parkinson. That William was the son of Johnson Baldwin from Kentucky. William Mattison, Thomas Lee's son, married Susan Collins Worth on 27 July 1854. She was from Tennessee, born on 3 December 1830.

[22] 1870 US Census, Kansas, Douglas, Marion Township, image 18 of 24, citing NARA microfilm publication M593 433, p. 412B; *History of Macoupin County, Illinois.* Brink, McDonough, 1879, p. 254, lists a William M. Baldwin elected in 1875 to Supervisor of Cahokia Township, Macoupin County, Illinois. However, there are no contemporaneous records to indicate that he left Kansas after 1870.

[23] Ibid., p. 254.

the town of Overbrook.[24] John Calvin, meanwhile, settled his family in Breckenridge County (present Lyon County) before moving to Missouri. William Mattison and Susan remained in Osage County, Kansas, for the rest of their lives.

The old Santa Fe Trail ran across northern Osage County, passing through the towns of Overbrook, Scranton, and Burlingame.[25] Overbrook, where William Mattison and Susan Baldwin spent their last years, was a relatively new town, founded in 1886 when the Kansas, Nebraska, and Dakota Railroad built through the area. Its location in Elk Township on a ridge, separating the waters of the Wakarusa and the Marais des Cygnes rivers, makes it the highest-elevation town in Osage County. The earliest description of Overbrook was in the *Burlingame Independent* newspaper on November 11, 1886. "Upon either side [of the railroad] are the stakes marking the lots and blocks of the new town, among which the carpenters were busy erecting a handsome store building and at another point a residence… Another new frame building is owned by a blacksmith. The railroad track as graded crosses the town site from east to west, and ample provisions have been made for side tracks, depot grounds, stock yards, etc. Overbrook was named by a construction engineer for the railroad, who named it after his hometown of Overbrook, Pennsylvania."[26] The first business in Overbrook was a grocery store. There was no other railroad station or trading point for miles around, so Overbrook attracted a good business from the start. Residents moved in from the surrounding area. By 1888, the town had two general stores, a grange store, a depot, a druggist, a hardware store, two blacksmiths, two carpenters, a confectioner, and a barber. The community was once a center for the mining of bituminous coal.[27] Today, still a small town, Overbrook had a population of about 1,000 people in 2025. It lies in northern Osage County on highway US

---

[24] 1880 US Census, Kansas: Douglas, Edwards, and Elk Townships, NARA Series T9, Roll 380) Today, the Clinton Reservoir covers old Clinton, the Kansas post office where William Mattison Baldwin received his mail.

[25] William G. Cutler, *History of Kansas*, 1883.

[26] Noble Prentis, *History of Kansas,* Winfield: E. P. Greer, 1899.

[27] Roger Carswell, *The Early Years of Osage County,* North Newton: Mennonite, 1982.

56 just east of US 75 between three federal reservoirs: Clinton, Pomona, and Melvern reservoirs, none of which existed in William Mattison's time.

William Mattison was a farmer his entire life, and in the Baldwin tradition, made farming a family enterprise. William and Susan Baldwin had seven children: Riley Thomas., Mary M., James William, John H., Ida Ann, Emma J., and Charles M. The older children—Riley and Mary—were born in Illinois; the other five children were born in Kansas. His sons, particularly James and John, worked on William's farm or on nearby farms of their own.[28] Riley, meanwhile, according to the 1880 census, at age 24 was in college. This would make Riley the first of the Baldwins to attend college. The name, Riley, suggests a connection to the Riley family of Hancock County, Indiana, and James Whitcomb Riley, the famous Indiana poet who grew up as neighbors of the Baldwins in Hancock County. James Whitcomb's parents, Reuben and Elizabeth Riley, were contemporaries of William and Susan Baldwin. The elder Mr. Riley was prominent in county and state politics.

Riley Thomas Baldwin graduated from college, became a Methodist Episcopal preacher, married Emma Anna Cralk in 1883, and had several children. He died in Pasadena, California, on August 6, 1903, at the age of 47. Both he and Emma are buried at Oketo, Kansas.

William Mattison Baldwin and Susan Collins Baldwin were married for 58 years. They retired to a comfortable life in Overbrook, Kansas, where they were cared for in their old age by family members, in particular their granddaughter, Nellie Finch, who stayed with them while working as a telephone operator in Overbrook.[29] They raised Nellie and their grandson George Finch after their daughter Ida Ann Baldwin Finch died in 1891.[30] The elderly couple—William Mattison and Susan—lived long enough to see the advent of the telephone, the automobile, and the airplane. They lived to a ripe old age, surviving all

---

[28] Find a Grave Memorial ID 21067722.

[29] 1910 US Census Elk, Osage, Kansas, Roll: T624 451, p. 12A, Enumeration District: 0097, FHL microfilm: 1374464.

[30] 1900 US Census Elk, Osage, Kansas, Roll: 494, p. 6, Enumeration District: 0116, FHL microfilm: 1240494.

but three of their seven kids. Emma Baldwin died in infancy, Ida Ann Baldwin Finch died in 1891, and Charles Baldwin died in 1903.[31]

William Mattison Baldwin died on a Monday, April 14, 1913, at the age of 83. Susan died two years later, shortly before Christmas, on December 16, 1915, having just turned 85 a few days before. Their burials were in Overbrook City Cemetery, Osage County, Kansas, along with their son, Charles, and other Baldwin family members. Many have come and gone since the founding of Overbrook in 1886. The Overbrook City Cemetery is a relatively small 5-acre plot of land dedicated to the memory of those who lived and worked in this little Kansas community. The Baldwin descendants of William Mattison and Sarah Baldwin continue to live in and around Osage County, Kansas.

---

[31] Find a Grave Memorial ID 26531803.

New Ground

25

Family Reunion

One of the main reasons for moving the Baldwin Ranch to Cedar County, Missouri, besides reasonable land prices, was the region's well-established reputation for trotting horses. Beginning in the early 1800s, horse breeding in southwest Missouri developed a reputation for excellence. The Missouri Fox Trotter is a product of the Ozark Mountains. Combining the stamina and agility of the Morgan horse breed with other trotter breeds out of Kentucky, Tennessee, and Virginia, the Missouri Fox Trotter was an international sensation, certainly well known by the Baldwins when they decided to move to Cedar County. Today, the national headquarters of the Missouri Fox Trotting Horse Breed Association is in Ava, Missouri.

When Missouri became a state, an area in the southwest part bordering on the northwestern edge of the Ozarks became what is now Cedar County. This area was once the home of the Osage Indians and was an important part of the great, unsettled territory of a largely undeveloped wilderness. The Osage tribes ceded their claim to the land in 1808. The US Government gave the territory to the Kickapoo Indian tribe, who relinquished their claim to the land and returned it to the Government in 1832.[1] Historian F. M. Williams described the land and its pioneers. "The first settlers here beheld a fair country, finely diversified with hill and valley, woodland and prairie, pleasing and inviting. There were clear, running streams with fine fish and spread around were rich bottomlands, timber, and prairie, ornamented here and there by occasional majestic, towering cliffs, grand and imposing. Undulating prairies, natural meadows, covered perhaps half the entire county, and more than half, westward. Woods bordered these prairies usually in well-defined lines, while only a few feet away on the prairie side, hardly a shrub would be, to mar the lovely smoothness… Nearly

---

[1] Clayton Abbott, *Historical Sketches of Cedar County Missouri*. Greenfield, Mo.: Vedette, 1967, p. 1.

every new settler was a hunter, and from the abundance of wild game, choice delicacies were on every table. Often, when all had gathered around the fireside at the close of the day, there was an animated recital of the day's doings. Of which the shooting of deer and turkeys might be a part, or finding a bee tree or seeing some fine, new tracts of country. If in the breaking season, it might be when hunting the oxen, for the oxen, after being worked all day breaking prairie, must be turned loose at night to get their living."[2]

Cedar County was formed in 1845 out of parts of Polk, St. Clair, and Dade counties. Before its formation, all of Dade County and the larger part of present Cedar County were within the territorial limits of Green County.[3] The first group of municipal townships set up in 1845 in Cedar County included Madison, Jefferson, Cedar, Benton, and Linn townships, the latter destined to be the home of the Baldwin family.[4] The first county seat was on land purchased and donated to the county by six leading citizens of the community, among them Thomas English, a prominent name later associated with the Baldwin family. On these 50 acres of land, surveyors laid out the town of Lancaster (later Stockton), and the sale of lots began in the spring of 1846.[5]

County officials soon discovered that a town named Lancaster already existed in northern Missouri. Consequently, the name changed in 1847 to Fremont in honor of John Charles Fremont, the prominent explorer, Army General, and son-in-law of US Senator Thomas Hart Benton of Missouri. Thereafter, the county court conducted business at Fremont, although the county did not have a courthouse until 1855.[6] The Missouri Legislature grew disenchanted with the political positions of General Fremont and changed the name of the county seat from Fremont to Stockton in 1859, allegedly without the consent of the people of Cedar County, and ostensibly named for Robert F. Stockton, a US

---

[2] F. Marion Williams, *Early Days in Cedar County*, Kansas City: Punton-Clark, 1908, pp. 7, 11.

[3] Ibid., p. 49.

[4] Ibid., p. 51.

[5] F. Marion Williams, *Early Days in Cedar County*, pp. 55-56; H. C. Adamson, *Rebellion in Missouri in 1861*, p. 110.

[6] F. Marion Williams, *Early Days in Cedar County*, p 59.

Navy commodore with a distinguished military record in the Mexican War.[7]

Southwest Missouri played a pivotal role in the Civil War, beginning with the border hostilities in Kansas, the US Supreme Court decision regarding Missouri slave Dred Scott, and the armed collision of US and rebel forces in St. Louis in 1861. Stockton was a thriving town of about 300 people when the War began, and the only town of importance in the county.[8] The people of Stockton divided in their political beliefs. Nevertheless, the town was one of the only towns in southwest Missouri to advocate for a strong Union presence.[9] Confederate General Sterling Price, in his bid to retake Missouri from the Union, advanced north to the Osage River before retreating through Cedar County back to the southwest corner of the state after the Battle of Wilsons Creek in 1861. He stopped for a time at White Hare, a few miles southeast of the site where Jerico Springs now exists. Meanwhile, guerrilla warfare continued in the area throughout the War. On one occasion in the summer of 1863, after a short skirmish, Confederate guerrillas fell back from a fight at Gum Springs, retreating to the corner of southwest Missouri. They paused at the village of White Hare. Fearing pursuit from Union troops, they left their wounded in the care of the people of White Hare, some of whose residents were sympathetic to the Southern cause. Both sides considered White Hare of importance as a supply station. White Hare figured prominently in the Baldwin family story. In later years, the town went by the name of Omer.[10]

The courthouse at Stockton burned during the Civil War when Confederates raided Stockton on October 5, 1863. One of J. O. Shelby's men who saw it during the raid described it as a "fine brick structure which was given to the flames." During the War, the building was an armory used by the Union Enrolled Militia and considered a legitimate target, burned in retribution for the burning of Nevada, a Confederate

---

[7] Adamson, *Rebellion in Missouri in 1861*, p. 244.

[8] Ibid., p. 99.

[9] Williams, *Early Days in Cedar County*, p. 81.

[10] Adamson, *Rebellion in Missouri in 1861*, pp. 105, 258. The village site is on the SW corner of SW 1/4, SW 1/4, S. 16, T. 33, R. 27, about 1 miles south and west from Stockton and some 7 miles east of Jerico Springs.

town, by Union soldiers. Consequently, Cedar County was without a courthouse for four years until a new one went up in 1867 in the middle of the town square at a cost of $10,000. This building served the county for the next 72 years, and was the courthouse at which succeeding Baldwin generations did business. The present poured concrete structure replaced it in 1939.[11]

Cedar County Courthouse. The Baldwins arrived in Cedar County in 1867, the same year workers completed construction of the courthouse on the Stockton Public Square, at a cost of $10,000. The building replaced one burned by Confederate troops in 1863. It served as the courthouse until 1939 when a new concrete building replaced it. Abbott, *Historical Sketches of Cedar County Missouri.*

After the Missouri Compromise and the admission of Missouri to the Union in 1821, the US Government surveyed the vast territory covering the southwestern part of the State. Upon completion of the survey, the government offered the land for sale, available to all comers at $1.25 per acre.[12] To encourage more people from the East to move west, the Homestead Act of 1862 urged people to settle up to a quarter section of 160 acres of public land. If they lived on it for five years and grew crops or made improvements, this land did not cost anything per acre, but the

---

[11] Ibid., p. 64.
[12] Abbott, *Historical Sketches of Cedar County Missouri*, p. 1.

settler did pay a filing fee. The land belonged to the settler at the end of five years if he or she built a house on it, dug a well, plowed 10 acres, fenced a specified amount, and actually lived there. Additionally, one could claim a quarter section of land by timber culture, commonly called a 'tree claim'. Tree claims required the settler to plant and successfully cultivate 10 acres of timber. Only about ten percent of the public land after 1850 went to homesteaders. Speculators or the government itself owned much of the land, and sold it or held it off the market. The railroad companies made large profits reselling it to homesteaders. The Baldwins apparently purchased their land outright from the sale of their land in Illinois and Kansas because government records show no patents for the Baldwins of Cedar County, Missouri.

We do not know exactly what route Thomas Lee and the Baldwin family followed from Macoupin County, Illinois. However, it was most likely through St. Louis. The principal westward route of immigrants through Missouri was up the Missouri River from St. Louis. Historian Marion Williams describes the typical route. "Many traveled by boat, others drove their covered wagons along trails following the river. Jefferson City and Boonville were two points where Cedar County immigrants departed from the main route and took a course to the southwest. Some went by boat up the Osage to Osceola, or even to Roscoe, when the water was high. From Roscoe, the trek by wagon on into Cedar County was short… Another immigrant route went directly southwest from Jefferson City through Hermitage, by the site where Humansville was later built, and on into Cedar County territory. Practically all supplies of manufactured goods came into the new settlements over these two routes, and continued to do so until well after the time of the Civil War."[13] Railroads began to grow across Missouri after the Civil War. However, the line did not reach southwest Missouri until 1870.

Meanwhile, John Calvin, who was in Kansas at the time of the Baldwin migration from Illinois, would have traveled overland from eastern Kansas, the roughly 150-mile distance into Cedar County.

---

[13] Williams, *Early Days in Cedar County*, p. 69.

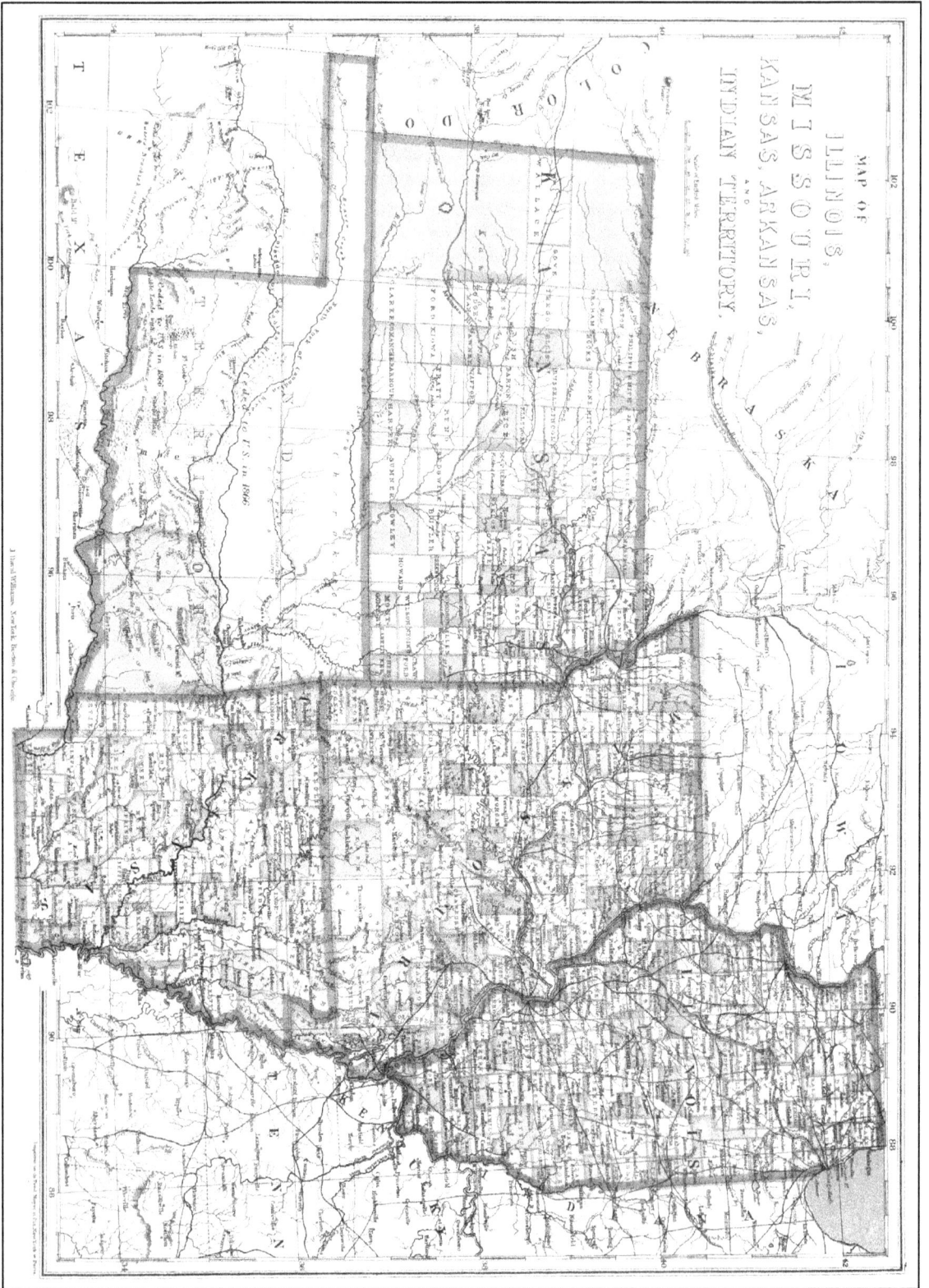

MAP OF
ILLINOIS,
MISSOURI,
KANSAS, ARKANSAS,
AND
INDIAN TERRITORY.

When John Calvin, Frances, and their daughters left Kansas in 1867, Anna Eliza was age 4, Sarah was 3, and Emma Callie was a year old. Their daughters, Mary and Nancy, had died in Kansas, and on September 22, 1869, Emma Callie died at the age of 2, in Missouri. The location of her burial is unknown. Of the first five children born to John Calvin and Frances Baldwin, all were daughters. Only two of the five survived.

Map of Illinois, Missouri, Kansas, Arkansas, and Indian Territory. Thomas Lee Baldwin came to Missouri from Macoupin County, Illinois, in 1867, at the same time John Calvin Baldwin left Lyon County, Kansas. The two families met in southwest Missouri. This map incorrectly showed Fremont as the county seat of Cedar County. The name changed from Fremont to Stockton in 1859, 14 years before publication of the map in 1873. Jones & Hamilton, *The Peoples' Pictorial Atlas*, David Rumsey Historical Map Collection.

26

Cedar County

People of the Baldwin name were in southwest Missouri before Thomas Lee and his family arrived. Philip Baldwin came from Ohio to Missouri in 1840, settling in Section 6, Township 28, Range 26, of Lawrence County.[1] He made a number of government land purchases in subsequent years.[2] He married Elizabeth A. Estill in 1847, and the couple had seven children.[3] Their daughter, Delia Baldwin, married Henry Norton, and the couple raised nine children on their Lawrence County farm. Mention of other members of this Baldwin family is in early county records. Philip's sister Nancy Baldwin and her husband Hardin Houston Davis died in Lawrence County, murdered by the bushwhackers in the Civil War; the marauders killed Nancy in the fall of 1861 and Hardin the following spring, leaving seven orphans. The burials of Nancy and Hardin were in Davis Cemetery, at Miller, Missouri. Hardin Davis was a Union soldier in the Ozark Home Guard.

Other siblings of Philip and Nancy Baldwin were Mary, John, William, Thomas, Henry, and Joshua, all born in Fayette County, Ohio. All were the children of William Baldwin and Catherine Berkheimer. Like their brother Philip, Thomas and Joshua were farmers in Lawrence County, where they purchased several tracts of government land beginning as early as 1852. Meanwhile, John Baldwin, also a native of Ohio, lived north of Cedar County in the abutting county of St. Clair. This John of St. Clair lived from 1843 until 1934, and served as a Democrat in the Missouri Senate from 1911 to 1917. He was a wealthy

---

[1] *Goodspeed's 1888 History of Lawrence County* (1973 reprint Lawrence County section of *Goodspeed's Newton, Lawrence, Barry and McDonald Counties History*, Goodspeed). Cassville, Mo.: Litho Printers. (Original work published 1888).
[2] US Bureau of Land Management (BLM) Records.
[3] Gary R. Hawpe, [online Rootsweb.com, Lawrence County, 1997].

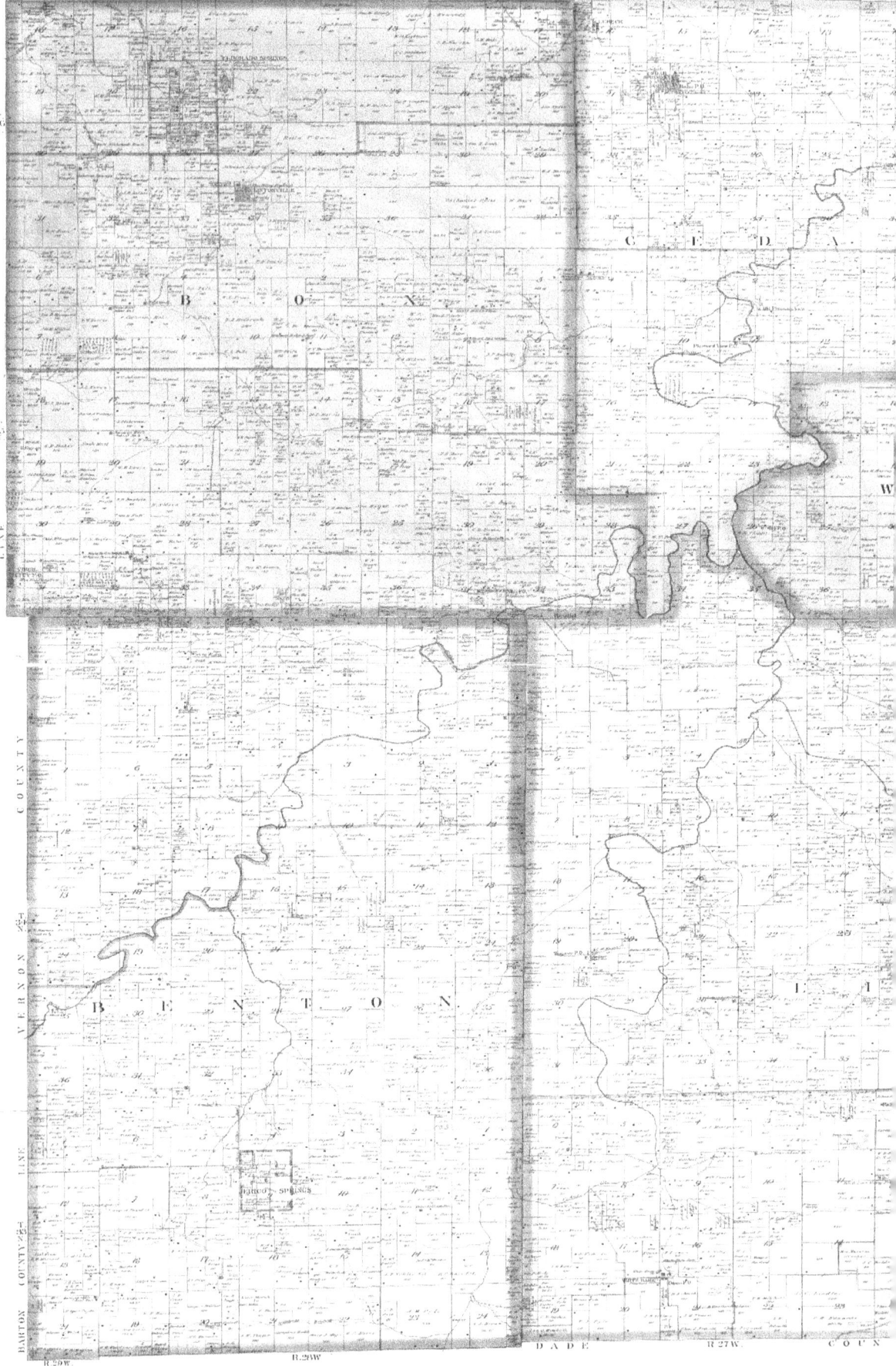

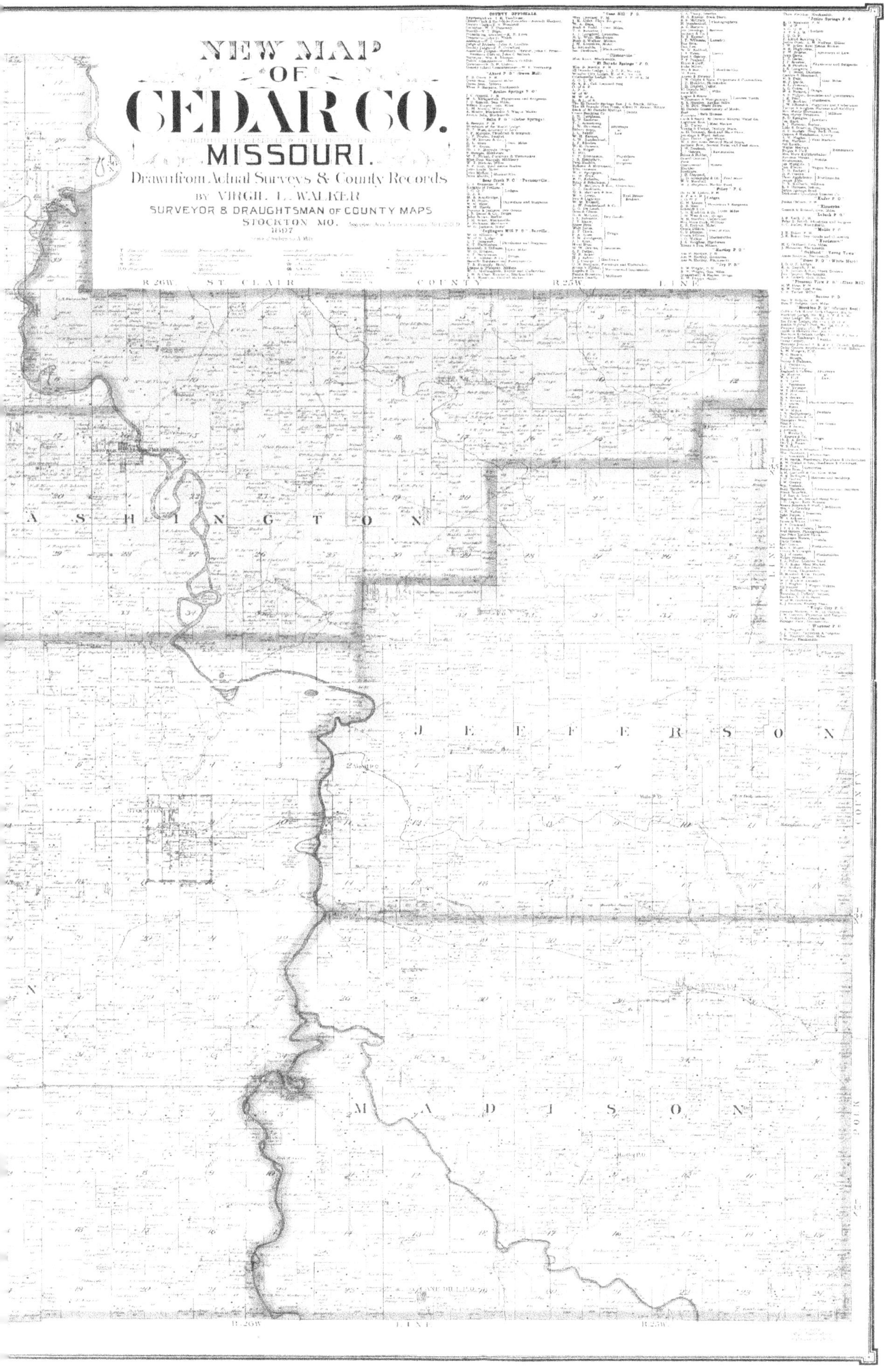

NEW MAP

OF

CEDAR CO.

MISSOURI.

Drawn from Actual Surveys & County Records

BY VIRGIL L. WALKER

SURVEYOR & DRAUGHTSMAN of COUNTY MAPS

STOCKTON MO.

1897

R 26 W.   ST. CLAIR   COUNTY   R 25 W.   LINE

W A S H I N G T O N

J E F F E R S O N

M A D I S O N

R 26 W.   LINE   R 25 W.

farmer and ranch owner with properties both in Missouri and in New Mexico.[1]

The ancestry line of Thomas Lee Baldwin is sometimes confused with these other Baldwin neighbors because Thomas Lee also had children named Nancy, John, William, Thomas, Henry, and Joshua. In fact, his sons, Thomas and Joshua, were farming in Cedar County, Missouri, about the same time that the other Baldwin brothers, Thomas and Joshua, were doing the same in Lawrence County. Furthermore, these were not the only Baldwins in Lawrence County. The names of James and Jacomyer Baldwin appear as early as 1841, adding to the confusion because this James Baldwin went by the initials J. C., the same as John Calvin Baldwin.[2] The origin of these Baldwins is unknown, but they apparently were not related to the others of Lawrence County, St. Clair County, or Cedar County. Meanwhile, yet another of the Baldwin name, Elizabeth Baldwin who married Jackson Box of Lawrence County, appears to have come from Tennessee, the daughter of William Baldwin, originally of Virginia, and Elizabeth Luttrell.[3]

Most of the Lawrence County Baldwins, as well as those in St. Clair County, came to Missouri by way of Pennsylvania, West Virginia, and Ohio or Tennessee. Our Thomas Lee, meanwhile, came from North Carolina and Virginia through Indiana and Illinois. Although there is no known connection between these families, nevertheless Delia Baldwin Norton, daughter of Philip of Lawrence County claimed an ancestral line of Philip (1), William (2), John (3), William (4), John (5), Francis (6), and William (7), the latter two generations (6 and 7) being

Map of Cedar County. Linn Township is at center bottom of the map. Stockton is in Linn Township upper right. The property of John Calvin Baldwin is at the bottom of Linn Township in Sections 13 and 14 just to the left of the crease on this 1897 map. Walker, *New Map of Cedar Co. Missouri*, 1897. Library of Congress Geography and Map Division Washington, D.C.

---

[1] Find a Grave Memorial ID 34969969.

[2] Mrs. Howard W. Woodruff, *Marriage Records, Dade County, Missouri: Books A and B, 1863-1872, and Abstracts of Wills and Admins. A, 1841-1867*, Kansas City, Mo., 1971. J. C. Baldwin witness to John Gambill will, dated 14 Mar 1859, proved 2 Mar 1861. Will Book A, 205-206.

[3] *Goodspeed's 1888 History of Lawrence County.*

from Oxfordshire, England. Francis (6) was the original immigrant to America. He allegedly came with two brothers, Thomas and John, who settled in Pennsylvania, and from whom the Baldwin line of Thomas Lee possibly descended. Thus, the Baldwins of Cedar County and the Baldwins of Lawrence County, although not immediately kin, probably shared the same ancestor. Thomas Lee's line traces to his grandfather, Thomas Sr., of Grayson County, Virginia, via Pennsylvania and North Carolina, who would have been contemporary with John (3) in the Lawrence County Baldwin lineage. That John of Lawrence County had a brother named Thomas, but that Thomas is unproven as Thomas Lee's grandfather, Thomas, Sr. Meanwhile, William Baldwin of Lawrence County, born in 1779 and father of Elizabeth Baldwin Fox, is of interest because of his Virginia roots. He would have been contemporary with Thomas, Jr., Thomas Lee's father. There is an enticing possibility that all southwest Missouri Baldwin lines are of the same English ancestry.

Thomas Lee Baldwin was age 71 in the year 1867 when he sold his horse ranch in Illinois and moved to Cedar County, Missouri. He and Nancy, then age 69, bought land on O'Connor Prairie in Linn Township, where they settled into old age, living near their children.[4] In the summer of 1870, the census showed them living on the Baldwin farm with their son Joshua in dwelling #397 in the rural Stockton Post Office district. Thomas Lee worked the farm; Joshua provided additional farm labor. The census recorded real estate valued at $4,720, and personal property worth $1,000.[5] In their later years, family members, including numerous grandchildren, surrounded Thomas Lee and Nancy. Several lived nearby. Their oldest son, T. J. [Thomas Jackson] Baldwin, age 43, a farmer, born in Virginia, was listed in the 1870 census with his wife, Sarah Wood Baldwin, age 31, who was born in Illinois. They lived next door to Thomas Lee with their 8 children as Family #395. Thomas Jackson and Sarah went on to have four more children, bringing the total to 12, and continuing the Baldwin tradition of large families. Furthermore, Jeremiah Baldwin—youngest son of Thomas Lee—and

---

[4] Jessie Hastins Letter to Minnie Cornwell.
[5] 1870 US Census, Census, Missouri, Cedar, Lynn [sic] Township, Post Office Stockton, 28 June 1870, Series M593, Roll 768, p. 84, National Archives.

his young bride Nancy lived with T. J. for a time adding to his family until they acquired their own place.[6]

The West Side of the Square in Stockton. The courthouse (left) stood at the center of the town's businesses clustered around it, atop sloping terrain that descended north to Stockton Branch and the mouth of Stockton Cave, which ran beneath the town. Photo from about 1890. Abbott, *Historical Sketches of Cedar County Missouri,* 1967.

The Baldwins settled in a relatively undeveloped but rapidly growing part of Cedar County. In 1870, the population in Stockton was about 500 inhabitants; there were two shoemaker shops, one saddle and harness shop, one tailor shop, one cooper shop, two blacksmith shops, and one wool-carding machine. In addition to these industries, there were at that time three hotels, six general merchandise stores, two drug stores, one hardware store, and one bookstore.[7] Every day industry in Cedar County comprised largely saw mills and grist mills. Small grist mills sprang up in all parts of the county; every stream had its mill.

One of the nearby villages close to the Baldwins was Cane Hill, named in part for its role in molasses making. Cedar County historian Clayton Abbott wrote, "Making of sorghum molasses has been an industry of Cedar County since the area was first settled. The climate and much of the soil are such that the product here is of a very high quality. In the early days, there was usually one molasses maker in each community. His neighbors grew the cane, stripped and topped the stalks, and hauled it to the cane mill, where it went through the roller press. The juice was put in an evaporator-type pan and cooked to the proper viscosity by the molasses maker, who continually screened the

---

[6] 1870 US Census, Linn, Cedar, Missouri, Roll: M593_768, p. 83B, NARA.
[7] Abbott, *Historical Sketches of Cedar County Missouri*, p. 184.

scum and foam from the top of the boiling juice during the entire cooking process."[8]

With the Civil War over and in the recent past, the citizens of Cedar County each year celebrated Independence Day. Abbot described a typical celebration. He wrote, "Early in the morning on the Fourth of July, wagons, buggies, hacks, and even horseback riders, headed in the direction of Stockton. The vehicles were loaded to capacity with men, women, and children, dressed in their best Sunday clothes. Typical of the group was the man who rode at the front of his wagon holding the driving lines, which he jerked now and then as he urged the team to a brisker walk, as the wagon rumbled over rocky roads, stirring up a cloud

Making Molasses in the Ozarks. The making of molasses began early in Cedar County and proceeded well into the twentieth century. Roller presses were coveted property passed from generation to generation. The mule hitched to the lever that turned the press seen in this photograph was the embodiment of rural life and the family farm in Missouri. Abbott, *Historical Sketches of Cedar County Missouri,* 1967.

of dust. He sat on the right side of the spring seat, and as often as necessary, he applied the brake lever to keep the wagon from pushing the horses into a run as it descended the hills. Beside the man was his wife, wearing a duster to protect her fine dress, decked out with a large brimmed hat, or sunbonnet, to protect her delicate features from the hot sun. In the back of the wagon were the children sitting on blankets or quilts thrown over a layer of hay. The little girls wore braids or pigtails and stockings, while the boys usually had on knee britches. The grown girls sat in chairs, which slid hither and yon with each bounce of the wagon, unless there happened to be an extra spring seat available. Some drove the typical covered wagon, with the bows and wagon sheets; on

---

[8] Ibid., p. 264.

hot, sultry days, the sheets were kept rolled up on the sides to allow the occupants the benefit of the cool summer breeze… A cavalcade such as this converged upon the City of Stockton each Fourth of July. They came from all directions and arrived in the middle of the forenoon. Those from the north, east, and west drove through the square, around the old brick courthouse, and up South Street to the picnic grounds, which were

Public Water Pump. Merchants of Stockton filled their drinking water buckets from a well in the center of the town square. A pipe connected the well to the cave below and the spring-fed stream that ran through the cave. On the corner is one of two drug stores in town. Abbott, *Historical Sketches of Cedar County Missouri,* 1967, photo about 1890.

located seven or eight blocks up, on the west side of the street. Each driver found a spot of his choosing in the south part of the grove, where he unhitched his horses, tethered them to a tree, or to the wagon, and gave them a supply of hay to eat… The concession stands at the picnic grounds closed late in the afternoon, but many people remained at the square until after dusk to see the fireworks display, which was the climax of a long, eventful day; then all headed for home. One by one, the wagons pulled out of town, with hardly a noise except the knocking of the wheels of the wagons on the axletrees. The heads of the families sat silently in the front seats, and the small boys and girls curled up in the back of the wagons and fell asleep."[9] The town elders left little to chance when it came to the safety of the community. On July 28, 1868, an ordinance was passed that prohibited the use of firearms within the city of Stockton.[10]

The family of John Calvin and Frances Baldwin continued to grow in Cedar County with the births of Maggie Ellen on October 5, 1868, and Lillie Christina, born on July 12, 1870. The 1870 census found John

---

[9] Ibid., pp. 272, 275.
[10] Ibid., p. 144.

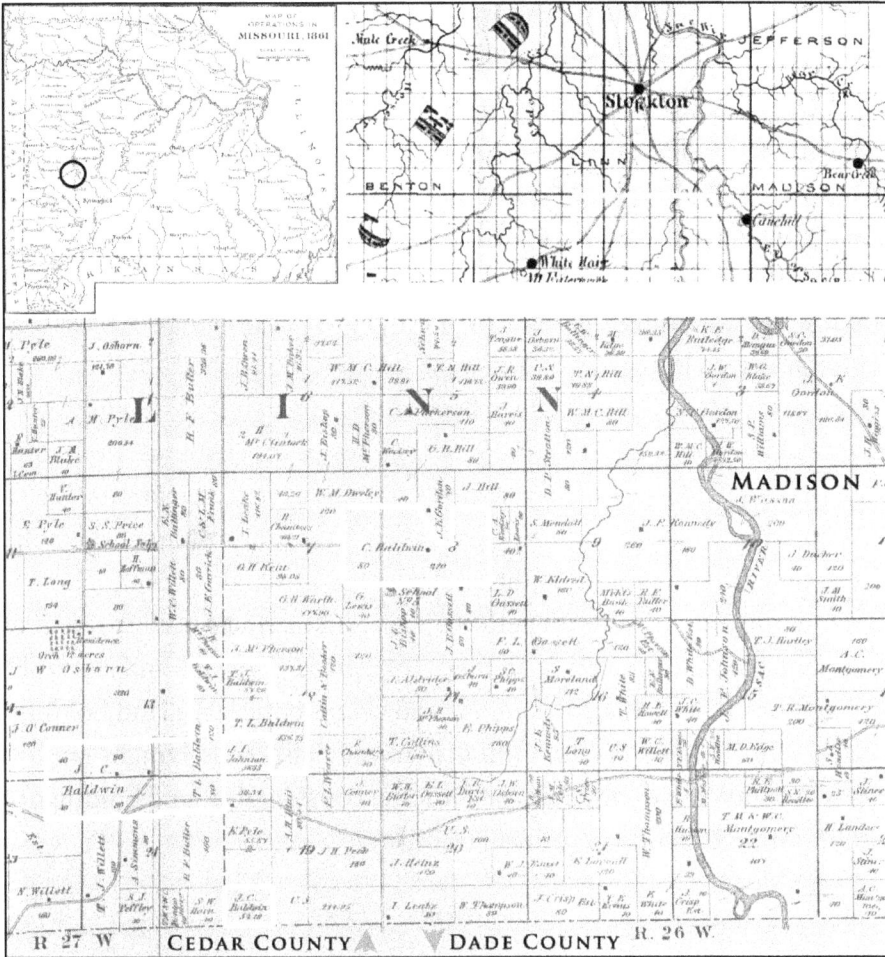

Baldwin Land in Linn Township in 1879. The Baldwin family owned more than 1,000 acres of land west of Sac River in the south part of Cedar County. Town names on the perimeter of the map show the distance from the edge of the map to other locations in Cedar County. Snead, *The Fight for Missouri*, 1860; *Campbell's New Atlas of Missouri*, 1874; & Reily, *Map of Cedar County, Missouri*, 1879. Library of Congress.

Calvin and his family living as Family #287 in Linn Township of Cedar County, with Anna E., age 7, Sarah 5, and Maggie E., age 1. John Calvin owned real estate valued at $3,000 and a personal estate of $1,000.[11]

By 1879, the Baldwin family owned more than 1,000 acres of land in South Linn Township. Thomas Lee owned 393.03 acres total: 200 acres in Sections 13 and 24, Township 33, Range 27, and an adjoining 136.75

---

[11] 1870 US Census, Missouri, Cedar County, Linn Township, Series M593, Roll 768 p. 41, National Archives.

acres in Section 18, plus 56.34 acres in Section 19, Township 33, Range 26. His son Thomas Jackson bought tracts of 40 acres in Section 13 and 57.2 acres in Sections 18, Township 33, Range 27. Caleb had 290 acres in Sections 7 and 8, next door to Bishop Grove School in Township 33 Range 26; and Jeremiah Washington owned 100 acres—a 60-acre tract cornering on his 40 in Sections 4 and 5, Township 34 Range 27. Meanwhile, John Calvin owned 240 acres east of White Hare in Sections 13 and 14, adjoining the land of John D. O'Connor on the west and Thomas Lee on the east in Township 33, Range 27. He had another 54.19 acres on the Dade County line in Section 19, Township 33, Range 26, for a total land holdings of 294.19 acres. Together, Thomas Lee, John Calvin, and Thomas Jackson owned contiguous acreage amounting to 784.48 acres, a sizeable farming operation in southern Linn Township. Over time, they acquired additional acreage until, altogether, Thomas Lee and three of his sons owned 1,077 acres. The tracts occupy much of the same land originally patented by Alfred Hocker and John D. O'Connor in the 1850s. Most of it lay adjacent to the large land holdings of the John Lindley Estate. John Calvin may also have bought land in Dade County, not to be confused with the considerable land holdings of other unrelated Baldwins of Dade County.

27

A Ranch of His Own

One of the first orders of business for the Baldwins was to locate a suitable school for the Baldwin children. Several schools existed in Linn Township. The movement to establish public schools in Cedar County began in 1847, well before the Baldwins arrived. The Federal Government gave the 16th section of each congressional township for school purposes. Money from the sale of these lands went into a loan fund lent to individuals and firms at a substantial rate of interest. The interest from the school funds provided for the establishment and maintenance of public schools. The first school district in Cedar County was organized in the Caplinger Mills area. The second district was organized the same year in the area of Cedar Creek, west of Stockton, and at the same time, a third was organize at White Hare. Late in the year 1849, a majority of the voters of Linn Township petitioned the County Court for a school district in the area of Fremont (present Stockton). The Fremont Academy, founded in 1850, became the first school in Stockton, a school touted in the county as a very progressive institution.[1] By 1913, there were 85 rural schools in Cedar County, not counting many other schools located in the towns and villages of the county.[2]

One of the last schools to form was Concord District No. 75, located about 6.5 miles south of Stockton, near the former town of Rowland and Bishop Grove School, and close to the Baldwin farms. According to historian Jean Nipps Swaim, "The Baldwins were one of three large early families in the district; namely, John Calvin Baldwin, James Osburn, and John D. O'Connor, each of whom had children of school age in the 1860s and 1870s. All three were likely involved with getting the school started, although there are no records for those school years. John Calvin Baldwin sent 16 children to Concord through the years; the

---

[1] Adamson, *Rebellion in Missouri in 1861*, pp. 204-205.
[2] Ibid., p. 206.

James Osburns sent 11, and the John D. O'Connors, 14. Some of the older children may have gone to subscription schools for a few months or gone without school for a while. Minnie Baldwin Cornwell's mother was an O'Connor, born in 1862, and could remember that her older brother Patrick walked to a Hunter or Hocker School just south of the Dade County line and in the evening would throw armfuls of sumac brush in the fireplace to make light for his studying. Indications are that by the time young Patrick O'Connor, born in 1856, was 13 or 14 years old, Concord School was ready for him." [3]

Education was of prime interest in Cedar County from the beginning of the founding of the county. A. R. Nichols, Principal of the Fremont Academy in Stockton, delivered remarks at Stockton on May 28, 1869, that illustrate the value placed on the well-educated citizen. Nichols said, in part, "Communities, States, and individual minds of all ages have poured their currents into the stream of the world's history… The teachings of Pythagoras, Socrates, and Plato shine like so many lights through the vista of centuries. The songs of Homer and Virgil still enchant. The researches of Copernicus, Kepler, Galileo, and Newton will bless the world through all coming time."[4] Whether such lofty remarks resonated with the local population, we do not know.

Shortly after the Baldwins settled in Cedar County, the first newspapers appeared. According to Mr. Abbott, "The first newspaper printed in Cedar County was the *Southwest Tribune*, which was established shortly after the Civil War. After one or two years of publication, the name changed to the *Stockton Tribune*." The tribune was politically Republican. Meanwhile, the *Stockton Journal* was first published about 1870 and was from the beginning editorially Democratic. Both the *Stockton Journal* and the *Stockton Tribune* was sold in 1876 and merged into one paper, retaining the name of the *Stockton Journal,* and adhering to its support of the Democratic Party. In 1887, the *Journal* sold and merged with another newspaper, the *Cedar County Republican,* which first appeared in 1886. As the name implies, this paper was a supporter of the Republican Party from its beginning…

------

[3] Jean Nipps Swaim, *The Era of the One-Room Rural Schools of Cedar County, Missouri,* [s. n.]: 1988, pp. 131-137.

[4] Abbott, *Historical Sketches of Cedar County Missouri,* pp. 208-209.

Meanwhile, the *Optic* newspaper began publication in Jerico Springs in March 1888, and continued as the leading paper in the region.[5] We know not the professed political persuasion of the Baldwins, except that they apparently supported Lincoln for president in 1860, considering that the sons of Thomas Lee all fought on the Union Side in the Civil War. Moreover, in those days, the Republican Party was the party of the anti-slavery movement, while the Democratic Party generally favored the expansion of slavery.

Thomas Lee Baldwin died at home on Tuesday, November 25, 1879, of paralysis. He was 83 years, 8 months, and 13 days old. Nancy survived Thomas for three years. She went to live with her son, Jeremiah Washington Baldwin and his wife.[6] Living in the same household was her son, James, brother to Jeremiah. Nancy Brizendine Baldwin died in the winter of 1881, on February 14, a Monday. She was not quite 80 years old. Her burial was at Gum Springs Cemetery, Cedar County, Missouri, in the Baldwin plot beside her husband of more than 57 years. Their son James died just four months and 4 days later, at the age of 42. His burial was near his parents at Gum Springs. Thomas Lee and Nancy had nine children: three daughters and six sons, five of the sons to carry on the Baldwin name. James W., the youngest, did not marry.[7]

Meanwhile, John Calvin continued the Baldwin farming operation of the breeding of trotting horses south of Stockton. The ranch took the name of the "John Calvin Baldwin Horse Ranch."[8] As time went by, he and Frances had more children; namely, their first son, John Calvin Jr., born March 21, 1872; and then Thomas Jackson, born August 22, 1874; Sammie J., born September 9, 1876; Lizzie Alice, born May 12, 1879; Martha Maranda, born October 3, 1881; and Jessie Lee, born March 22, 1884. Regrettably, tragedy struck the family again when little Sammie Baldwin died on April 10, 1883, at the age of 6. He was the youngest son

---

[5] Ibid., pp. 95, 198.

[6] 1880 US Census, Missouri, Cedar, Linn Township, Enumeration District: 251, T9-0680, p. 336D, NARA.

[7] Jimmy O. Baldwin, in History of Cedar County, pp. 145-146.

[8] Ibid., pp. 145-146.

of John Calvin and Frances. Of the 13 children born to John Calvin and Frances, seven daughters and two sons survived to adulthood.[9]

In 1890, a special census was taken of veterans of the Civil War still living. The census included John Calvin for his service as a soldier in the Kansas State Militia, and his brother Joshua, a veteran of the 5th Calvary, Company E, 122nd Illinois Infantry. For whatever reason, the survey did not list Jeremiah Washington Baldwin, who was living in Cedar County at the time, and who served with Joshua in the 122nd. Nor did it list their brother James, who died in 1881 before the veterans' census.[10]

Frances Pherby Jackson Baldwin died of cancer on Christmas Day, December 25, 1891.[11] She was 51 years and 20 days old. Her burial was in the southwest corner of Gum Springs Cemetery, in the Baldwin plot. An elegant stone marks her grave, carved with the recurring symbol of Baldwin deceased, the parting handshake. Her epitaph reads:

"Gone to rest
A precious one from us has gone
A voice we loved is silent
A place is vacant in our home
Which never can be filled."[12]

---

[9] Ibid., pp. 145-146. Greene County Archives and Records Center.

[10] 1890 Special Census (Veterans of the Civil War still living in 1890), District 62, Linn Township, Cedar County, Missouri, Enumerating Union Veterans and Widows of Union Veterans of the Civil War, Series Number: M123, Records of the Department of Veterans Affairs, Record Group Number: 15, NARA, p. 3.

[11] Find a Grave Memorial ID 5495651; Correspondence with Minnie Baldwin Cornwell.

[12] Cemetery, Gum Springs, Cedar County, Missouri, personally viewed and recorded by Sharron Burchett O'Connor.

Frances Pherby Jackson Baldwin
K. Burchett Photo Collection.

The death of Frances left John Calvin to raise their three small children still at home, the youngest being Jessie Lee, who was age seven when her mother died. John Calvin was approaching 60, and still operating a large farm and the business of breeding trotting horses in Linn Township.

A year after the passing of Frances, John Calvin married Sarah Cordelia O'Connor, a native of Cedar County, born in Stockton, and a neighbor girl nearly thirty years his junior.[13] They married on December 29, 1892. Cordelia was the daughter of John Dennis O'Connor, one of

---

[13] Missouri Standard Certificate of Death. Missouri State Board of Health Standard Certificate of Death #20223.

the original settlers of Cedar County, and his wife, Rachel Minerva Long, of Kentucky. Cordelia was one of 16 children born into the O'Connor family.

John Calvin Baldwin and Sarah Cordelia O'Conner Family. Identified in this photograph taken about 1905 at Stockton are Orpha May, Hugh G. John Calvin, Roy Carl, Minnie Casey, William Byron, Cordelia, and Harry Howard. Photo Courtesy of Doris Mae Waterman.

Cordelia had only a fourth-grade education.[14] Nevertheless, education was an important part of the Baldwin family. John Calvin took an active interest in the education of his children. Excerpts from the early records of the 1894 Directors' Proceedings shows, "Ordered J. C. Baldwin buys 60 fence posts for schoolhouse yard, and put them in the ground." In 1895, the Tax Enumeration List showed 47 children of school age at Concord and the family names included Baldwin and O'Connor. At the Annual Meeting of Concord School for the election of school officers [1895], J. C. Baldwin received the most votes for chairperson.[15] He owned land in both the Concord District No. 75 and

---

[14] 1940 US Census, Linn, Cedar, Missouri, Roll: m-t0627-02095, p. 12A, Enumeration District: 20-11, NARA.

[15] Swaim, *The Era of the One-Room Rural Schools of Cedar County, Missouri,* 1988, pp. 131-137.

Prairie View District No. 76. Prairie View was south of the Baldwin farm. His youngest daughter Minnie Cassie attended Concord No. 75, but changed to Prairie View when it was ready, because it was closer to the Baldwin home. In later years, she often attended at Concord again, as Prairie View was often too short of funds to offer the full eight months of school.[16] At the same time, Bishop Grove School was about three miles north of the Baldwin farm. William Byron and Roy Carl Baldwin sometimes walked to Bishop Grove for the spring term.

Cordelia and John Calvin went on to have seven children of their own, six of whom survived to adulthood. A son, Alvin Henry died in infancy. Their children were William Byron born October 16, 1893, Hugh G. born February 24, 1895, Roy Carl born June 20, 1898, Orpha May born December 1, 1900, Minnie Cassie born August 30, 1902, and Harry Howard born March 15, 1904.[17] John Calvin had 19 children altogether, the last born in 1904 when he was 71 years old. Fifteen of his children lived to maturity, 10 daughters, and 5 sons to carry on the Baldwin name.

John Calvin retired to the family farm. He died at Stockton on February 28, 1908, at the age of 75. His burial was in Gum Springs Cemetery.[18] His gravestone beside the stone of Frances says simply, "J. C. Baldwin - Sept. 29, 1832 - Feb. 28, 1908. The quote, "He giveth his belovethness," carved across the predella of the stone's base honors his memory.[19]

Cordelia lived on for many years, on the Baldwin farm. She never remarried and lived out her life as part of the extended Baldwin family. Cordelia's son Hugh, who never married, cared for her in her old age. When Hugh died in 1944, Cordelia passed shortly thereafter in 1945, in the early afternoon of May 22, at the age of 83, of bronchial pneumonia, at home in rural North Township of Dade County. Doctors cared for her for three weeks, but the disease and complications of senility took

---

[16] Ibid., p. 407.

[17] 1900 US Census, Place: Linn, Cedar, Missouri, Roll: 847, p. 4, Enumeration District: 0051, FHL microfilm: 1240847.

[18] Find a Grave Memorial ID 5495647.

[19] Ibid., ID 5495647.

her life.[20] Her burial was in Gum Springs Cemetery beside her son Hugh. The two of them share a common tombstone. Cordelia survived John Calvin by more than 37 years. One of the ironies of the John Calvin story is that Cordelia, his second wife, outlived his oldest daughter Anna Eliza who was the same age as her stepmother. The record on the last years of Cordelia's life is contradictory. In 1940, she was living in Linn Township, Cedar County, according to the 1940 census, and had lived there in 1935.[21] Yet, her death certificate recorded her residence as rural Dade County. The informant of her death was her son Roy Carl Baldwin who was at the time living in Greenfield, Missouri. There are several references to the Baldwin family associated with Arcola and Greenfield, in Dade County. However, the Baldwin home place was in Cedar County north of the Dade County line, ½ mile south of Omer, Missouri, in the Jerico Springs postal district

The Baldwin farm was kept running by the Baldwin family until Sarah Cordelia died in 1945. Her youngest daughter Minnie Cassie Baldwin married Lewis Cornwell in 1933, and after Cordelia died, she and Lewis took over the operation of the farm until their retirement.[22] When Lewis and Minnie retired, they moved into Stockton. Lewis died April 22, 1992. Minnie passed on March 24, 1998, at the age of 95, the last surviving child of John Calvin Baldwin.[23]

The record is relatively quiet on the religious affiliation of John Calvin Baldwin and the Baldwin family. His father Thomas Lee came from western North Carolina and Virginia, both of which saw the early establishment of a host of denominations on the western frontier. Among them were Presbyterian, Methodist, Baptist, and the Society of Friends, to name a few. In later years, Baldwins associated with the Methodist Episcopalian Church.

John Calvin appears to have been a Presbyterian. The Baldwin family burial site located at Gum Springs Cemetery, in Cedar County, offers

---

[20] Missouri Standard Certificate of Death, Missouri State Board of Health Standard Certificate of Death #20223.

[21] 1940 US Census, Cordia Baldwin, Linn Township, Cedar, Cedar, Missouri, Sheet 12, T627, National Archives and Records Administration.

[22] Jimmy O. Baldwin, in History of Cedar County.

[23] Find a Grave Memorial 5495563.

some insight into the Baldwin religious preference. Gum Springs was the choice of Baldwin burials from an early date, although later interments were at Omer Cemetery, in Cedar County, and at Greenfield and Hickory Grove cemeteries, in Dade County. Lydia Alice Baldwin, daughter of Jeremiah Washington Baldwin, and granddaughter of Thomas Lee, died in infancy in 1871, making her the first Baldwin interred at Gum Springs, and one of the earliest burials in the cemetery. The burial of Thomas Lee Baldwin in Gum Springs was in 1879, a few months after the death and burial of his granddaughter Ella, the three-year-old daughter of Jeremiah Washington.[24] Gum Springs was the name of an old Cumberland Presbyterian Campground west of Stockton, named for the local Gum family who owned land there. In addition to the cemetery next to the church, at one time the community had a small store, a schoolhouse, and a church (which still stood in 2025).[25] The Cumberland Presbyterians came into the upper Midwest from Kentucky in the early part of the 19th century, more or less concurrently with the move of Thomas Lee Baldwin from Virginia to Indiana. The denomination was prominent throughout Missouri beginning in 1819 when the first Presbytery appeared near Glasgow, Missouri, on the Missouri River. The influence of the church spread across Indiana, Illinois, and Missouri, all early locations of Thomas Lee and the Baldwin family. In 1829, the Cumberland Presbyterians organized the First Missouri Synod, which included Sangamon, Illinois—once home to Thomas Lee—and was a guiding force of church governance for many years. The church General Assembly met at Greenfield, Missouri, as late as 1921.[26] The Gum Springs Cemetery connection to the Cumberland Presbyterians and the strong presence of the church in southwest Missouri make the Cumberland Presbyterians or associated denomination the likely choice of the Baldwin family, to the extent that religion was a part of their daily lives. They were of

---

[24] Find a Grave Memorial ID 5495629.

[25] Arthur Paul Moser, *A Directory of Towns, Villages, and Hamlets Past and Present of Cedar County, Missouri.*

[26] Thomas C. Hardesty, Milton L. Baughn, and Ben M. Barrus, *A People Called Cumberland Presbyterian.* Memphis: Tenn.: Frontier, 1972, pp. 107, 116, 122, 131, 138, 409.

independent mind when it came to religious affiliation. Baldwin connections to the Society of Friends trace at least to the 18th century in Pennsylvania, and yet there is no evidentiary proof that the line of Thomas Lee Baldwin collectively embraced the Quaker faith, although the Baldwins did share the Quaker abhorrence of slavery. Marriage records of Baldwin offspring and obituaries suggest that choices of ministers and churches varied widely depending on availability, and not necessarily religious dogma.

Children of John Calvin Baldwin

28

First Marriage

John Calvin BALDWIN was born on 29 Sep 1832 in Hancock County, Indiana. He died on 28 Feb 1908 in Cedar County, Missouri, from Pneumonia. His burial was in Gum Springs Cemetery, near Stockton, Linn Township, Cedar County, Missouri.[1] John married **Frances P. (Pherby or Pherba) JACKSON**, daughter of Brice B. Jackson, of Illinois and North Carolina roots, and Mary Jane Haggard, originally of Tennessee, on 24 Dec 1856 in Carlinville, Macoupin County, Illinois.[2] Frances was born on 5 Dec 1840 in Newton County, Missouri. She died on 25 Dec 1891 in Cedar County, Missouri, from Cancer. Her burial was beside John Calvin in Gum Springs Cemetery, Cedar County, Missouri, four miles southwest of Stockton.[3]

They had the following children.

1 F   **Mary Frances Baldwin** was born on 30 Jun 1858 in Macoupin County, Illinois. She died on 20 Nov 1862 in Kansas.[4] Her burial was in Ulrich Cemetery, Pleasant Grove, Douglas County, Kansas.[5]

MARY FRANCES BALDWIN died in 1862 at the age of four. Her parents carried her as an infant from Macoupin County, Illinois, to Breckenridge County, Kansas, shortly after her birth. Her father, John

---

[1] Find a Grave Memorial ID 5495647.

[2] Illinois, County Marriages, 1810-1940, John C Baldwin and Francis P. Jackson, 24 Dec 1856, citing Macoupin, Illinois, United States, county offices, Illinois.

[3] Find a Grave Memorial ID 5495651 & 151546589. The birthdate of Frances J. Baldwin calculates to 5 Dec 1840 based on her lifespan of 51 years 20 days inscribed on her gravestone.

[4] 1860 US Census, Waterloo, Breckenridge, Kansas Territory, Record Group Number: 29, Series Number: M653, 346, p. 507, NARA. The 1860 census records Mary Frances Baldwin as age 2, born in Illinois.

[5] Find a Grave Memorial ID 86295386.

Calvin Baldwin, moved his family to Kansas to establish the Baldwin horse farm on land purchased by the elder Thomas Lee Baldwin. John Calvin and Frances came into Kansas Territory at the height of the Territory's bloody struggle to attain statehood, whether to join the Union as a slave state or a Free State. In 1860, the census located the family in Waterloo Township, Breckenridge County (later Lyon County), Kansas. Sometime between 1860 and 1862, John Calvin apparently moved upstate to Douglas County, Kansas, near Lawrence,

Baldwin Children's Gravestones. The infant daughters of John Calvin and Frances Baldwin rest in Kansas cemeteries. The burial of Mary Frances in 1862 was at Ulrich Cemetery, Pleasant Grove, in Douglas County, near Lawrence, Kansas. The grave of Nancy Jane, who died in 1864, is at Pleasant Ridge Cemetery, near the village of Admire, in northern Lyon County. Find A Grave Memorial ID 86295386; Find A Grave Memorial ID 53018137.

because the burial of Mary Frances was in Ulrich Cemetery in Douglas County, two miles southeast of Pleasant Grove, Kansas. Lawrence, Kansas, and the surrounding area was a hotbed of Union resistance to slave state advocates and a center of Union organization. John Calvin's brother, William Mattison Baldwin, had relocated from Illinois to

Douglas County about the same time that John Calvin first settled in Breckenridge County.

We do not know the cause of baby Mary Frances Baldwin's death. The family came to Kansas at a dangerous time. The country was on the brink of Civil War, and the newlywed couple faced difficult times. Frances was a young bride of 18, in unfamiliar territory far from home and family.

> 2 F   **Nancy Jane Baldwin** was born on 21 Oct 1860 in Breckenridge (later Lyon) County, Kansas. She died on 10 Feb 1864 in Waterloo, Breckenridge County, Kansas. She was buried in Pleasant Ridge Cemetery, Admire, Lyon County, Kansas.[6]

NANCY JANE BALDWIN died in 1864 at the age of three. Neither of the firstborn children of John Calvin and Frances Baldwin survived. Sometime between July 20, 1860, and her birth on October 21, 1860, John Calvin and Frances returned to Breckenridge County. While Nancy Jane could have been born in Douglas County, Kansas, her birth likely occurred instead after the family moved back to Breckenridge (later Lyon County). Nancy Jane's burial was in Pleasant Ridge Cemetery, about six miles north of Admire, Kansas, in Breckenridge County.[7]

Shortly after her birth, Kansas entered the Union as a Free State. In 1861, the Civil War ensued, and John Calvin joined the Kansas militia on the side of the Union. We do not know the cause of death of Nancy Jane. Like her sister before her, Nancy Jane faced difficult times in a dangerous place with no certainty of how things would turn out. She died in 1864, the year before the war ended.

> 3 F   **Anna Eliza BALDWIN** was born on 15 Jan 1863 in Ottawa, Waterloo, Breckenridge County, Kansas. She died on 10 Apr 1942, in Jerico Springs, Cedar County, Missouri, from Tuberculosis or Consumption. Her

---

[6] Find a Grave Memorial ID 53018137.

[7] Sources of information are the D.A.R. gravestone readings in the 1940s and the Flint Hills Genealogical Society readings in the 1980s. This information is by the members of the Flint Hills Genealogical Society and Emporia D.A.R.

burial was in Gum Springs Cemetery, Linn Township, Cedar County, Missouri.

Anna Eliza married **Edward CARDWELL**, son of Reuben Granville Cardwell and Elizabeth Stegall, on 20 Oct 1878 in Madison Township, Cedar County, Missouri. Edward was born on 15 Aug 1856 in Missouri. He died on 8 Apr 1884, in Cedar County, Missouri. His burial was in in Gum Springs Cemetery, Linn Township, Cedar County, Missouri.

Anna Eliza also married **Jesse M. Biddey**, son of Tolbert Biddey and Martha Ann Lovelady, on 8 Feb 1885. Jesse was born on 11 Apr 1860 in Georgia. He died on 8 Mar 1910 in Missouri from pneumonia & heart failure. He was buried in Gum Springs Cemetery, Linn Township, Cedar County, Missouri.

Anna also married **Austen Andrew "Ott" McCollom,** before 1920. Ott was born in 1864 in Illinois. He died in 1956 in Cedar County, Missouri. His burial was in Hall Cemetery, Jerico Springs, Missouri.

ANNA ELIZA BALDWIN was born on January 15, 1863, in Ottawa, Kansas, Waterloo Township, in Breckenridge County. She was four years old when she came with her parents to Cedar County, Missouri. She attended rural schools in Linn Township, where she settled for a fourth-grade education, and set about learning other skills on the farm in rural southwest Missouri.[8] By the time she was a teenager, there were seven siblings in her family, all vying for attention.

She married very young to Edward Cardwell, a Missouri lad lately returned to Cedar County from living with relatives in Schuyler County, Missouri. He was the son of Reuben Granville Cardwell and Elizabeth Stegall, both originally from Tennessee. Edward Cardwell and Anna

---

[8] 1940 US Census, Jerico Springs, Cedar, Missouri, Roll: m-t0627-02095, p. 1B, Enumeration District: 20-1, NARA.

Eliza Baldwin married on October 20, 1878, in Madison Township, Cedar County.

Edward Cardwell and Anna Eliza Baldwin. This unidentified and undated photograph came from a collection of Baldwin family pictures. They were identified through facial recognition technology, which identified Anna Eliza at a significant validation level compared with known later photos of her and of family members. Edward's association with Anna Eliza, and facial recognition at a high degree of similarity between him and his children, suggests that this was probably Edward and Anna Eliza's wedding portrait. They married October 20, 1878, when Eliza was age 15. K. Burchett Photo File.

Very little documentation exists on the life of Edward Cardwell. He was born on August 15, 1856. The earliest record of his presence in Cedar County is the 1860 census, enumerated on September 19. At that time, living in Madison Township, near Bearcreek (aka Paynterville), was Elizabeth Cordell [*sic*] and her three children: Thomas P., age nine, Edward, age six, and Juliany, age eight months.[9] In addition, living in the household was an infant named John Stegall, age two months. All the children were born in Missouri, according to the census; Elizabeth was born in Virginia, and the census reported her as a widow. She was,

---

[9] 1860 US Census, Madison, Cedar, Missouri, p. 127, Family History Library Film 803613. "Elizabeth Cordell."

in fact, not a widow. Her husband, Reuben Granville Cardwell, abandoned his family in Missouri in 1858 and settled in California, where he died in 1901. Elizabeth married Peter Minick in 1866 and then dropped from sight in genealogical records. Genealogists speculate that Peter Minick and George Minix (Minick) of Schuyler County were kin; thus, a reason for Edward to be in Schuyler County in 1870.

When Edward Cardwell reappeared in Cedar County in 1878 and married Anna Eliza Baldwin, Anna Eliza was age 15.[10] It was a private ceremony at the home of Edward's Uncle Samuel Stegall, in Madison Township, Cedar County.[11] The 1880 census confirmed the union of the couple, listing Edward, age 24, "Ann E." [Anna Eliza] age 17, and their infant daughter, "Laura F." [Laura Frances], living in South Linn Township, Cedar County, the location of the extended Baldwin family. Edward listed an occupation of farmer in 1880, which likely meant a connection to John Calvin Baldwin—father of Anna Eliza—who lived nearby with his large family, and who, along with others of the Baldwin clan, maintained a considerable presence in the agricultural life of southwest Missouri.[12] Anna Eliza had two children, both by Edward Cardwell; namely, Laura Frances Cardwell and Thomas Edward Cardwell. An analysis of the 1880 census placed the young couple living near Bishop Grove.

The 1880 census recorded Edward and Anna Eliza Cardwell in the voting precinct of White Hare. It was also the location of the Omer Post

---

[10] 1880 US Census, Linn, Cedar, Missouri, Roll 680, p. 337A, Enumeration District 251. "Edward Cardwell." In the 1870 census Anna E. Baldwin, Age 7, listed at home as the daughter of John C. Baldwin. She was born in Kansas. On 28 June 1870, she was living in Linn Township, Cedar County, Missouri. Anna E. not listed at the Baldwin home in the 1880 census, but rather with Edward Cardwell, her husband, and daughter, Laura F. They, too, were living in Linn Township, Cedar County Missouri, in 1880. She was 17 in 1880. Meanwhile, marriage records show she married 20 October 1878, meaning she was 15 or 16 years old when she married. Thomas Edward Cardwell, their son, was not born until 1881. Therefore, he did not appear in the 1880 census.

[11] *Missouri Marriage Records* (microfilm), Missouri State Archives, Jefferson City, Mo. "Edward Cardwell to Ann E. Baldwin."

[12] 1880 US Census, Linn, Cedar, Missouri, Roll 680, p. 337A, Enumeration District 251. "Edward Cardwell."

Office.[13] Consequently, White Hare and Omer became interchangeable names for the same place. White Hare dated to the 1830s, and the establishment of the post office at White Hare dated to December 11, 1840. The name White Hare officially changed to Omer in 1883. During its lifetime, Omer had a store, church, schoolhouse, post office, and lodge hall. During the Civil War, White Hare played an important role in local guerrilla activities.

Edward died on April 8, 1884, at the age of 27, of tuberculosis.[14] Edward Cardwell's grave stands alone in Gum Springs Cemetery without the companionship of any family members. The grave plot probably came from John Calvin Baldwin, placed adjacent to the Baldwin family section at Gum Springs, perhaps as a gift in response to the premature death of his young son-in-law.[15]

When Edward Cardwell died in the spring of 1884, he left his young widow, Anna Eliza, and their two infant children, the oldest five years old. Less than a year passed before Eliza married her neighbor, farmer, and sometimes preacher, Jesse Maries Biddey, on February 8, 1885.[16] They both lived at Stockton at the time but chose to be married at Bishop Grove Church, about six miles south of Stockton, past Gum Springs, and five miles east of White Hare and the Omer Post Office. White Hare was

---

[13] The location of Omer-White Hare was off Highway Y in Cedar County. Take Highway 39 south to Y, then right on Y 2.5 miles.

[14] Jimmy O. Baldwin, in History of Cedar County.

[15] Find a Grave Memorial ID 28958811. Cemetery, Gum Springs, Cedar County, Missouri (personally viewed and recorded). Gum Springs Cemetery is located in Linn Township, Cedar County, Missouri, 3.5 miles south of Stockton on Highway 39, just south of the 39 and 215 junction. The cemetery is on the west side of the highway. The old church was still standing in 2025. "Edward Cardwell-Aug. 15, 1856-July 8, 1884." Find-a-Grave transcription shows this as "15 Aug 1856-8 Apr 1884." The Edward Cardwell grave is located in the far southwest corner of the cemetery, the last grave in row two, counting from the west. He is buried in the Baldwin cemetery plot, near the graves of John C. and Frances Baldwin, parents of Edward's wife, Anna Eliza Baldwin. There is no proof that this is Edward's grave; however, given that the dates match dates recorded for him in census records and the fact that he is buried with the family of his wife makes a strong circumstantial case for this being his final resting place.

[16] US Marriage Records, 1805-2002 for Anna E. Cordwell [sic], Cedar County 1845-1893, p. 259.

once a thriving community destination for residents of Linn Township. Reverend S. E. O'Dell married them at Bishop Grove, a small community west of Sac River built around a church and a school, and close to the Cardwell residence and the farm where Jesse lived. The closest trading villages were at Cane Hill, 5.5 miles east across the Sac River, and Omer, four miles northwest. The young couple—Jesse was age 24; Eliza was 22—set up housekeeping in Linn Township and shouldered the task of raising the Cardwell children.[17]

Anna Eliza and Jesse did not have children. Upon their marriage, Jesse became the stepfather of the Edward Cardwell children and raised Laura and Tom Cardwell from infancy. The three of them— Jesse, Laura, and Tom—shared a common bond because they came from similar family stories. Jesse lost his father at a very early age and grew up himself a stepson, never knowing his actual father. Born April 11, 1860, in Georgia, Jesse was the son of Tolbert Biddey and Martha Ann Lovelady of Cherokee County, Georgia. Martha Lovelady had her own story to tell.[18] She was born in 1840 in Cherokee County; she married first Tolbert Biddy of Cherokee County in March of 1859, in Pickens County, Georgia, and then married Francis M. Weaver, a previously married Civil War veteran from Illinois.[19] Martha had two children from her first husband, her son, Jesse Biddey, being the older of the two.

The circumstances of the Lovelady-Biddey marriage are uncertain. Martha appeared in the 1860 census living alone, with two-month-old

---

[17] Missouri Marriage Records, 1805-2002, Missouri State Archives, Jefferson City, Mo. "Anna E. Cordwell[sic]."

[18] Lovelady Obituary, *Cedar County Republican*, 30 Jul 1931, Stockton, Missouri.

[19] Georgia Marriage Records from Select Counties, 1828-1978 for Tolbert Biddy, Pickens County, Record of Marriages, 1854-1878, p. 107; 1850 US Census, Division 15, Cherokee, Georgia, Roll 65, p. 539a; Civil War Pension Index: General Index to Pension Files, 1861-1934 for Francis M. Weaver, National Archives; *Special Schedules of the Eleventh Census* Enumerating Union Veterans and Widows of Union Veterans of the Civil War, Series No. M123, Record Group No. 15 Records of the Department of Veterans Affairs, Census Year: 1890, p. 6. Tolbert Biddy served briefly in the Civil War with the Company A of the 131st Illinois Infantry.

Jesse Biddey and Family. Tom Cardwell and his sister Laura stand behind their mother Anna Eliza (Baldwin) Cardwell and her husband Jesse Biddey. Following the death of Edward Cardwell in 1884, Eliza married Jesse Biddey in 1885. He raised the Cardwell children as his own until his death in 1910. K. Burchett Photo File.

Jesse, and working as a domestic in Pickens County, Georgia.[20] Tolbert did not appear listed; instead, Martha lived with another young mother whose husband was likewise missing. Family tradition said that Tolbert suffered a wound in a battle of the Civil War and died, leaving Martha with two children. The tradition further said that her infant daughter died in Nashville, Tennessee, during the war. Martha and her

---

[20] 1860 US Census, Dug Road, Pickens, Georgia, p. 887, Family History Library Film 803133. "Martha Biddy."

son, Jesse, next appeared in Illinois, where she married Francis Weaver in 1866.[21] Martha and Francis subsequently had four sons, all stepbrothers of Jesse Biddey. Moreover, Francis Weaver already had a son from his previous marriage, rounding out the Weaver-Biddey blended family. By 1878, the Weaver family and Jesse Biddey settled into South Linn Township, in Cedar County, Missouri.[22] Mr. Weaver acquired property adjacent to the Baldwin property, and by association, near Edward and Anna Eliza (Baldwin) Cardwell. Members of the Baldwin family owned several parcels of land in Cedar and Dade Counties. The 1880 census for Linn Township, Cedar County, listed "Jessey Bailey [sic]," age 20, stepson of Francis M. Weaver, working on the Weaver farm with his stepsiblings who were in school and could read and write; Jesse could not. The Weaver farm sat amid a trio of the Baldwin brothers, between Jeremiah Washington Baldwin on one side, Thomas Jackson Baldwin on the other, and near John Calvin Baldwin and the Baldwin Horse Ranch. Widow Nancy (Brizendine) Baldwin, matriarch of the Baldwin family, lived with her son Jeremiah following the recent death of her husband, Thomas Lee, who had died in November of 1879.[23] Nancy died in 1881.

Family relationships evolved. Anna Eliza's mother died in 1891, and in December of 1892, her father married Sarah Cordelia O'Connor, a woman of 30, nearly 30 years younger than he was, and only a year older than Anna Eliza was. Together, John Calvin Baldwin and Cordelia had seven more children, bringing to 20 the number of children fathered by John Calvin Baldwin. Their offspring resulted in an awkward family relationship in which the grandchildren of John Calvin—Laura and

---

[21] US Marriage Index, 1860-1920. "Martha Bidda [sic]."

[22] They removed to Missouri between 1867 and 1870 between the birth of their first child in Illinois in 1867 and the second in Missouri in 1870. The estimate of 1878 as the time of their arrival in Cedar County, Missouri, comes from an 1879 plat map of Linn Township showing a tract of land for F. M. Weaver.

[23] 1880 US Census for Francis M. Weever [sic], Missouri, Cedar, Linn, District 251, NARA, p. 16.

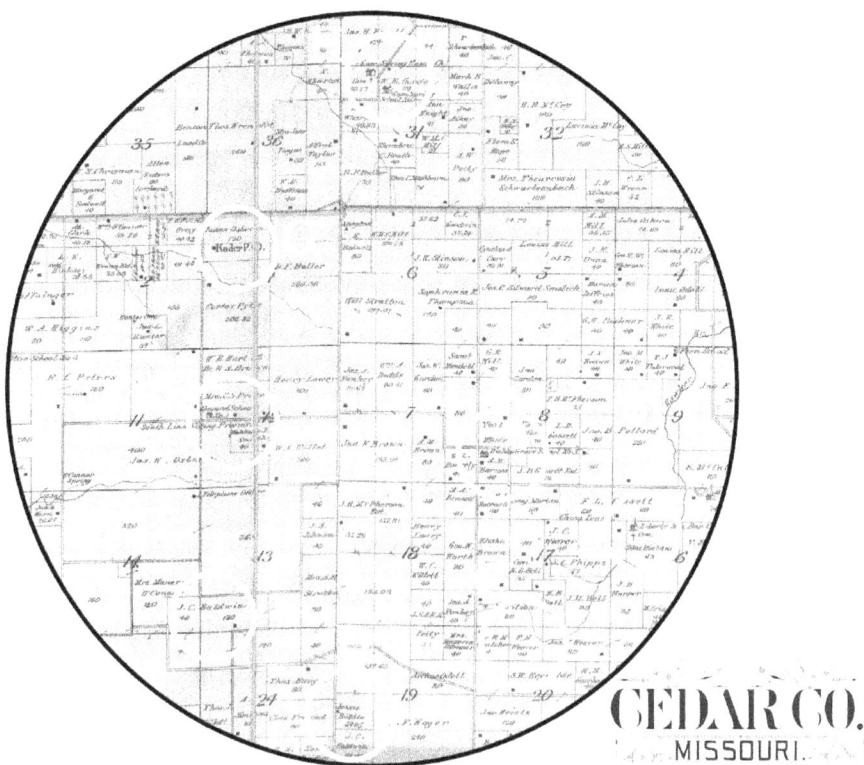

Places of Family Interest. Sites associated with Cardwell, Baldwin, Biddey, and Weaver families in 1897 were within an approximate 5-mile diameter area of South Linn Township, in Cedar County, Missouri. A. Bishop Grove was where Eliza (Baldwin) Cardwell married Jesse Biddey. B. Liberty Cemetery was the burial place of Francis M. Weaver, stepfather of Jesse Biddey. C. This was the home of Mr. Weaver. D. Jesse Biddey patented 55 acres of land adjacent to J. C. Baldwin on the Dade County line. E. The Baldwin Horse Ranch operated here. F. South Linn Voting Precinct at Concord School No. 1 was at this location. G. Kader Post Office was a country store that dated to about the time of the Civil War. H. Gum Springs Church and Cemetery served as the burial site of Edward Cardwell, the Baldwin family, Jesse and Anna Eliza (Baldwin) Cardwell-Biddey-McCollom, and Thomas Edward Cardwell. Map adapted from *New Map of Cedar Co. Missouri*, E. P. Noll, 1897. Library of Congress.

Thomas Cardwell—by his daughter, Anna Eliza, were considerably older than his children by Cordelia were.

Jesse Biddey and Anna Eliza homesteaded a piece of government land immediately north of the Dade County line and adjacent to property owned by Anna Eliza's father, and purchased sometime before 1879. This was likely the Biddey home in the early years of their marriage because on November 9, 1896, Jesse Biddey received a government land patent for approximately 55 acres next to the Baldwin property.[24] The property was north and adjacent to a similar plot owned by John Calvin Baldwin. The Biddey tract was some of the last remaining government land in that part of the county.

The Cardwell children grew to adulthood in the Biddey household. In the summer of 1900, Tom Cardwell was age 19, worked on the Biddey farm, and lived in the home of his parents in Linn Township. Laura Cardwell was in the household as well.[25] That fall, they sold the farm to Thomas Simmons; Laura married in December; and Tom, Jesse, and Eliza moved to Osiris, Missouri. Osiris was a country store on present Highway 97, 4.5 miles north and slightly west of Jerico Springs in Benton Township of Cedar County, 12 miles from White Hare, and 17 miles from the Baldwin Horse Farm and the seat of the Cardwell, Weaver, and Biddey families. The year 1900 was the year Jesse Biddey established a post office at Osiris. He opened a store there and petitioned the postal service to call the post office Osiris, which the postal service approved in 1902, naming him its first postmaster retroactive to 1901.[26] In Egyptian mythology, Osiris was the god of the afterlife and symbol of fertility, agriculture, and the religious gateway to life, death, and resurrection, all fitting choices for Jesse's religious nature.[27] Jesse became postmaster at Osiris on May 7, 1901. The pay was $37.25 a year, compared with a salary of $694.60 that John W. Jones made as the

---

[24] General Land Office Records, 1776-2015, Bureau of Land Management Certificate No. 10617, Application 17481, 9 Nov 1896, Accession Nr: MO6020-157, p. 157. "North half of the Lot numbered two of the South West quarter of Section 19 in Township thirty-three North, of Range twenty-six West of the Fifth Principal Meridian, containing fifty-four acres and ninety-five hundredths of an acre, for Jesse M. Biddey, Missouri, Cedar."

[25] 1900 US Census, Missouri, Cedar, Linn, District 51, p. 6B, NARA. "Jesse M Biddey." Birthdate for Biddy differs in the census from his death certificate. Likewise, the 1900 census recorded Tom Cardwell's birthdate as Feb 1880. His gravestone recorded 1881. Similarly, the birthdate of Anna Eliza appeared as Nov 1859, a substantial difference from the birthdate on her death certificate of November 1863.

[26] Williams, *State of Missouri in 1904.*

[27] Meyers, *Place Names of the Southwest Counties of Missouri.* Osiris store was still open and operated by Mr. Arch Walker in 1974. Located at Section 20, Township 34, Range 28.

postmaster at Jerico Springs.[28] Family tradition said that Jesse Biddey and Tom Cardwell farmed while Eliza ran the post office and operated the Osiris store. A specialty of Osiris was an elaborate display of soap that Eliza kept. It was at Osiris on November 20, 1903, that Jesse united in marriage William Wesley Stivers and Julia Ann Cardwell. Julia was the sister of the deceased Edward Cardwell. The wedding circumstantially reaffirmed the sibling relationship of Edward and Julia Ann. Her marriage was one of Jesse's last deeds at Osiris because on August 9, 1904, Dona A. Snow replaced him as postmaster.[29] It turned out that Jesse was the first of only two postmasters of Osiris. In 1906, the post office at Osiris closed after only five years of operation and mail service was moved to Jerico Springs.[30] When Eliza left the Osiris store, she took "enough soap to last ten years," according to her granddaughter.[31]

Jesse Maries Biddey died on March 8, 1910, from Pneumonia and heart failure. He was 49.[32] He contracted Pneumonia and within less than a week, the disease took his life. His burial was at Gum Springs Cemetery near the Baldwin plot, a few paces from the grave of Edward Cardwell whose son he raised to continue the Cardwell name another generation.[33]

Anna Eliza (Baldwin) Cardwell-Biddey married thirdly to Austen Andrew McCollom, a Cedar County farmer originally from Scottville, Macoupin County, Illinois, born there January 11, 1864, in the same Illinois county that was the original seat of the Baldwin family, and the origin of the Baldwin Horse Ranch. Austen McCollum—Ott, as people knew him—was a colorful character. He kept 17 goats and churned

---

[28] *US Register of Civil, Military, and Naval Service, 1863-1959* for Jesse M. Biddey, 1903, Vol. 2, pp. 210, 213.

[29] *Appointments of US Postmasters, 1832-1971*, Missouri, Cedar, p. 118.

[30] Clifford, *Historical Tours of Cedar County, Missouri.*

[31] Beatrice Interview 17 Oct 2004. Shortly before her death in 2005, Beatrice Richardson accompanied her son to various places that she had lived, and spoke of her life growing up. Two of these interviews date from 17 Oct 2004 and 19 Feb 2005.

[32] Death Certificate 4608, Missouri State Board of Health Bureau of Vital Statistics. "Jesse Maries Biddey b. 22 Apr 1860, d. 8 Mar 1910, age 49 when he died, farmer, died of Pneumonia b. Pickens County, Geo[rgia], son of Tolbert Biddey."

[33] Find a Grave Memorial ID 85106508. "11 Apr 1860-3 Mar 1910."

butter made from their milk.[34] Eliza and Ott lived in Jerico Springs, 'off school house road' (present Golden Street), in a house northwest of the

Mr. and Mrs. Austin Andrew "Ott" McCollom. This photograph pictured Ott McCollom and Anna Eliza (Baldwin) Cardwell/Biddey taken shortly after their marriage at their home in Jerico Springs. K. Burchett Photo File.

school and just west of the road (present East Harwood Street). Their place cornered on the road.

Anna Eliza died on April 10, 1942, at her home in Jerico Springs, where she had lived as a homemaker for many years. She died at the age of 79 years, 3 months, and 25 days of Lobar Pneumonia caused by chronic Tuberculosis, an ailment that plagued her for much of her life.[35] For years, she carried a Prince Albert Tobacco can to contain the

---

[34] Beatrice Interview 17 Oct 2004.

[35] Death Certificate 13998, Standard Certificate of Death, Missouri State Board of Health. "Anna Eliza McCollum."

discharge of mucus to avoid spreading the disease.[36] Her husband Edward Cardwell had died of Tuberculosis, and so had their daughter, Laura. Funeral services for Anna Eliza were at Gum Springs Church at 2 p.m. on Sunday, April 12, 1942, with Rev. Tom Scoggin officiating. Burial followed behind the church, near the grave of her husband Jesse Biddey, and a few paces up the hill from the burial site of her parents and the gravesite of Edward Cardwell. Her headstone memorialized her third marriage as the "Wife of A. A. McCollom."[37] After her death, Mr. McCollom moved to El Dorado Springs, Missouri, and died at a hospital there on April 7, 1956, at the age of 92. His burial was in Hall Cemetery, Jerico Springs, Missouri.[38]

> 4 F **Sarah Almina (Mina) Baldwin** was born on 18 Oct 1864 in Waterloo, Breckenridge, Kansas. She died 17 Dec 1932, in Arkansas. Her burial was in Gill Cemetery, Van Buren, Crawford County, Arkansas.[39]
>
> Sarah married **Quinn Morton Hill**, son of Timothy Norwood Hill, originally of Tennessee, and Louisa Loy, formerly of Kentucky, on 6 Dec 1885 in Cedar County, Missouri.[40] Quinn was born 28 May 1857, in Missouri. He died 29 Nov 1918 in Crawford County, Arkansas.[41] His burial was in Gill Cemetery, Van Buren, Crawford County, Arkansas.[42]

SARAH ALMINA BALDWIN was born in Breckenridge County (later Lyon County), Kansas. A family tradition places her birth in Ottawa, Kansas. However, based on the location of the Baldwin family in Breckenridge County, it is likely that she was born there in 1864,

---

[36] Beatrice Interview 17 Oct 2004.

[37] Memorial Services Announcement for Anna Eliza McCollom. Anna Eliza's funeral announcement carelessly listed her date of birth as 1883 instead of 1863.

[38] Find a Grave Memorial ID 5481942; Death Certificate 12641 Standard Certificate of Death, Division of Health of Missouri. "Austin A. McCollom."

[39] Find a Grave Memorial ID 37752434.

[40] Missouri Registration, Cedar, Mina Baldwin Marriage Date: 6 Dec 1885 Marriage to Q. M. Hill.

[41] Arkansas Death Index, 1914-1950, Crawford, Arkansas, Certificate Number 303, Volume Number 62.

[42] Find a Grave Memorial ID 37752447.

coincidentally eight months after the death of her sister, Nancy Jane, in Breckenridge County. The Baldwins left Kansas after the Civil War ended and moved to Missouri, where the family settled with family members from Illinois. The 1870 census located them in Linn Township, Cedar County, Missouri.[43] Sarah was five years old at the time and part of the growing John Calvin Baldwin family. She received her education in Cedar County, in Linn Township, according to the 1880 census.[44] In 1885, at the age of 21, she married Quinn Morton Hill, a Cedar County boy whose parents had moved west to settle in Missouri. The couple soon located in Jasper County, Missouri, in Galena Township, west of Joplin and south of Turkey Creek. Here, Quinn worked in the lead and zinc mines, and the couple began their family.[45] Quinn and Sarah had nine children, but only five survived, three sons and two daughters.

Quinn quit the mines and moved his family to Arkansas. In 1910, he and his sons worked as farm laborers in Oliver Springs Township, Crawford County, Arkansas, where he and Sarah died in 1918 and 1932 respectively.[46] Throughout the genealogical record, Sarah recorded her middle name variously. In earlier census records, she was Sarah A. Baldwin; later her name appeared as Sarah E. Family tradition remembers her as Sarah Almina Baldwin. The inscription on her gravestone reads simply "Mina Baldwin Hill."[47]

> 5 F **Emma Callie Baldwin** was born on 13 Nov 1866, in Kansas. She died on 22 Sep 1869, in Missouri.

EMMA CALLIE BALDWIN was the fifth child of John Calvin and Frances Baldwin, and the fourth child born in Kansas. She was their third child to die in infancy. Between her birth in 1866 and death in 1869

---

[43] 1870 US Census, Linn Township, Cedar, Missouri, Page Number 41, Record Number 6101, NARA.

[44] 1880 US Census, ED 251, Cedar, Missouri, Sheet Number and Letter, 336D, Vol. 1, T9, NARA.

[45] 1900 US Census, Missouri, Jasper. ED 31, Galena Township (west of city & south of Turkey Creek excl. Joplin city), Sheet Number and Letter 1A, T623, NARA.

[46] 1910 US Census, Oliver Springs, Crawford, Arkansas, citing enumeration district (ED) 4, sheet 14A, NARA microfilm publication T624, roll 48.

[47] Find a Grave Memorial ID 37752434.

at age two, the family removed from Kansas to Missouri in 1867.[48] Her gravesite remains unknown.

> 6 F **Maggie Ellen Baldwin** was born on 5 Oct 1868 in Cedar County, Missouri. She died on 26 Jun 1908 in Centralia, Craig County, Oklahoma, from Tuberculosis. Her burial was in Fairview Cemetery, Vinita, Craig County, Oklahoma.[49]
>
> Maggie married **Otis Edward O'Dell**, son of Rev. Simon Eli O'Dell and Martha Patsy O'Dell, on 27 Sep 1888.[50] Otis was born on 14 Jul 1867 in Ray County, Missouri. Otis married second Lizzie S. Winfrey, on 19 Oct 1911.[51] He died on 15 Apr 1950 in Vinita, Craig County, Oklahoma.[52] His burial was beside his wife, Maggie Ellen, in Fairview Cemetery, Vinita, Craig County, Oklahoma.

MAGGIE ELLEN BALDWIN was one year old and living with her parents and two sisters in 1870, in Linn Township, Cedar County, Missouri. John Calvin, Frances, and their three girls had recently returned from Kansas to resettle near the extended Baldwin family on the Baldwin horse ranch in Cedar County.[53] A decade later, the number of Maggie's siblings in the family of John Calvin and Frances had grown to seven.[54] Maggie received her schooling in Cedar and Dade counties and grew up amid the rural landscape of southwest Missouri. The nearest town of any size was Stockton. In 1888, at the age of 18, she married Otis Edward O'Dell, the son of a preacher, and lately of Gerard, Crawford County, Kansas. At the time, Maggie lived at Arcola, in Dade County, Missouri.

---

[48] Jimmy O. Baldwin, in History of Cedar County,

[49] Find a Grave Memorial ID 148172141, Plot Fairview Section, Block 02, Lot 009, Space 005.

[50] Missouri, County Marriage, Naturalization, and Court Records, 1800-1991, Otis O'Dell and Maggie Baldwin, 27 Sep 1888, citing Marriage, Cedar, Missouri, United States, Missouri State Archives, Jefferson City, FHL microfilm 007282656.

[51] Oklahoma, County Marriages, 1890-1995.

[52] Find a Grave Memorial ID 153654820.

[53] 1870 US Census, Missouri, Cedar, Linn, image 41 of 68, citing NARA microfilm publication M593.

[54] 1880 US Census, ED 251, Cedar, Missouri, Sheet Number and Letter, 336D, Vol. 1, T9, NARA.

About 1899, the couple removed to Oklahoma and settled in what was at that time Cherokee County, Indian Territory.[55] Otis worked on a horse farm at Centralia, Oklahoma. Maggie contracted cancer and died in 1908 at the age of 39. The census for 1910 found Otis living as a widower with four of their five children in Craig County, Oklahoma.[56] Otis married Widow Lizzie S. Winfrey, of Bluejacket, Oklahoma, in 1911, and continued to live and work on the farm in Craig County.[57] He became an elder in the church and followed his father's footsteps as a minister. He married at least twice more—Sarah E. O'Dell, who died before 1930, and Belle O'Dell, who died in 1945.[58] Otis died in Craig County in 1950 at the age of 82.

> 7 F **Lillie Christina Baldwin** was born on 12 Jul 1870 in Stockton, Cedar County, Missouri. She died on 2 Dec 1957 near Spokane, Spokane County, Washington. Her burial was in Riverside Memorial Park, Spokane, Spokane County, Washington.[59]
>
> Lillie married **Walter P. Davidson,** son of James T. Davidson and Christina O'Neil, of Kentucky, on 10 Oct 1894, in Arcola, Dade County, Missouri.[60] Walter was born on 12 May 1875 in Eldorado Springs, Cedar County, Missouri. He died on 28 Aug 1924 in Spokane, Spokane County, Washington. His burial was in

---

[55] 1900 US Census Indian Territory, Cherokee Nation, ED 8 Township 27 N. Range 19 E., image 9 of 59, citing NARA microfilm publication T623.

[56] 1910 US Census, Oklahoma, Craig, Township 5, ED 31, image 11 of 28, citing NARA microfilm publication T624.

[57] 1920 US Census, Oklahoma, Craig, Township 4, ED 7, image 8 of 20, citing NARA microfilm publication T625.

[58] 1930 US Census, Oklahoma, Craig, Centralia, ED 23, image 1 of 4, citing NARA microfilm publication T62; Find a Grave Memorial ID 21095109; 1940 US Census, Oklahoma, Craig, Centralia Town, Centralia, 18-23 Centralia Town, image 2 of 13, citing Sixteenth Census of the United States, 1940, NARA T627.

[59] Find a Grave Memorial ID 12656150.

[60] Washington Death Certificates, 1907-1960, Lilly C Davidson in entry for Walter P. Davidson, 28 Aug 1924, citing Spokane, Washington, reference 867, Bureau of Vital Statistics, Olympia, FHL microfilm 2,022,251.

Riverside Memorial Park, Spokane, Spokane County, Washington.[61]

Lillie married second **Richard Ewing**, son of William Ewing and Mary Anne Mayer, on 17 Nov 1936.[62] He died on 26 April 1942. His burial was in Pines Cemetery, Spokane Valley, Spokane County, Washington.[63]

LILLIE CHRISTINA BALDWIN was the seventh daughter born to John Calvin and Frances Baldwin. There were no sons in their family in the

Lillie Christina Baldwin. She married in 1894 and moved to Spokane, Washington, where she lived until her death in 1957. K. Burchett Photo File.

---

[61] Find a Grave Memorial ID 222194994.
[62] Washington, County Marriages, 1855-2008, Richard Ewing and Lillie Davidson, 1936.
[63] Find a Grave Memorial 86388432.

first 14 years of their marriage. Lillie was born July 12, 1870. She grew up on the family farm in southwest Missouri as one of a growing family of siblings in a very large extended family. Jean Nipps Swaim tells this story about Lillie and the celebration of Arbor Day at Concord School. "Three large shade trees and an iron pump mark the former site of Concord School's playground. They stand on the east side of Highway 39, six and one-half miles south of Stockton, relatively unnoticed next to the electric power transformers nearby. The dirt road that turns off the highway there leads east to where the former town of Rowland and Bishop Grove School were. Concord sat well back from the corner. Concord may have been the first school in Cedar County to celebrate Arbor Day in about 1886. The nation inaugurated the plan of making Arbor Day a school festival nationwide in 1882. At least one tree planted in 1886 is still living [as of 2025], though not on the school grounds. Minnie Cornwell heard the story from her mother, Sarah Cordelia O'Connor. At the end of the tree-planting day, there were two extra trees left over, and two of the girls took them home to plant. One of the girls was Lillie Baldwin, Minnie Baldwin Cornwell's older half-sister. Lillie Baldwin's tree thrived and grew to be a huge tree. She had her picture taken with it many times, as it grew larger and larger through the year."[64]

In 1894, Lillie married Walter P. Davidson, a native Missourian who had recently returned to his home state after living in Vacaville, Solano County, California. The Davidsons had a large presence in southwest Missouri. According to the marriage license of Lillie and Walter, Lillie was from Arcola, Dade County, Missouri, and Walter was from Vacaville, California.[65] They married when Lillie was age 24, somewhat older than her sisters had been at the time of their marriages.

Walter and Lillie made their home initially in Missouri, where their daughter, Esta, was born in 1897. The next year they removed to Vacaville, California, where their second daughter, Ruby, was born in 1899. The census of 1900 located the family in Solano County where

---

[64] Swaim, *The Era of the One-Room Rural Schools of Cedar County, Missouri*, pp. 131-137.

[65] Missouri, County Marriage, Naturalization, and Court Records, 1800-1991, Lilly Baldwin in entry for W P Davidson, 10 Oct 1894, citing Marriage, Cedar, Missouri, United States, Missouri State Archives, Jefferson City, FHL microfilm 007424387.

Walter had lived before, and where he now engaged in farming.[66] Farming in Solano County apparently proved unsatisfactory, and Walter moved his family to Washington State sometime before 1910. The 1910 census recorded them at Ephrata, Grant County, Washington.[67] Grant County was recently formed in 1909 and became a hub of three major railway systems. The Columbia River that flowed through the area was navigable. However, the land was not amenable to farming. One government official described the area in 1879 as, "…a desolation where even the most hopeful can find nothing in its future prospects to cheer."[68] Walter gave up dryland farming and sometime before 1916 moved east to Spokane County, Washington, at the foothills of the Rocky Mountains. Their daughter, Esta, married James Leroy Cook, a pharmacist in Spokane, in 1916.[69] In 1920, their daughter, Ruby, married E. H. Whitehead, a postal clerk in Spokane. Originally from England, he came to Spokane by way of Vancouver, Canada.[70]

Walter Davidson built a successful grocery business in Spokane where he lived out the remainder of his life. In 1920, he and Lillie lived in an apartment on Broadway Street.[71] Walter died in 1924. Many years later, Widow Lillie married the widower Richard Ewing, a Spokane County farmer born in Ireland.[72] Richard Ewing died in 1942. Lillie lived to be 82 years old. In her last years, she lived with her

---

[66] 1900 US Census, California, Solano, Vacaville Township, image 7 of 41, citing NARA microfilm publication T623.

[67] 1910 US Census, Washington, Grant, Ephrata, ED 74, image 14 of 15, citing NARA microfilm publication T624.

[68] Symons, *Report of an Examination of the Upper Columbia River*, p. 121.

[69] Washington, County Marriages, 1855-2008; Find a Grave Memorial ID 179560222; Find a Grave Memorial ID 190568219. Esta and J. L. Cook had a daughter, Mary Jane Cook Stussi, who lived and died in Spokane County, Washington; Mary Jane Stussi Obituary published by *Spokesman-Review* on Dec. 14, 2014. Mary Jane wrote a book on Spokane County: "Mini biographies from" *History of Spokane County, State of Washington USA of Canadian Persons Who Settled There*, 1986.

[70] Washington, County Marriages, 1855-2008, W. P. Davidson in entry for E. H. Whitehead and Ruby Davidson, 1920.

[71] 1920 US Census, Washington, Spokane, Spokane, ED 238, image 1 of 18, citing NARA microfilm publication T625.

[72] Washington, County Marriages, 1855-2008, Richard Ewing and Lillie Davidson, 1936.

daughter, Esta Cook, on a farm on Route 4, near Spokane.[73] She died on December 2, 1957, in Jane O'Brien Hospital, of heart failure.[74] Her burial was in Riverside Park Cemetery beside her first husband, Walter Davidson.[75] They share a gravestone. Attempts by genealogists to place Lillie's burial in Pines Cemetery with her second husband, Richard Ewing, are in error.[76] Burial of Richard was in Pines beside his first wife, but Lillie rests at Riverside Park, on the west bank of the Spokane River, peacefully located apart from the city amid gently rolling lawns. Meanwhile, back home in Missouri, relatives of Lillie Baldwin remembered only that she "lived away from here."[77]

8 M **John Calvin Baldwin, Jr.,** was born on 21 Mar 1872 in Cedar County, Missouri. He died on 1 Feb 1941 in Springfield, Greene County, Missouri. He was buried in Gum Springs Cemetery, Linn Township, Cedar County, Missouri.[78]

John married **Margaret "Mamie" Henry Leonard**, daughter of Joseph S. Leonard, of Massachusetts, and Ester M. Henry, of Kentucky, on 24 Sep 1893, in the home of Sanford and Ester Gillen, Dade County, Missouri. Mamie was born on 8 Sep 1876 in Cedar County, Missouri. She died on 31 May 1952. She was buried in Gum Springs Cemetery, Linn Township, Cedar County, Missouri. John Calvin, Jr., and Mamie Baldwin had six children.

JOHN CALVIN BALDWIN JR., was born on March 21, 1872, in Cedar County, Missouri, the first son born of John Calvin and Frances Baldwin. He grew up and received his schooling in Cedar County,

---

[73] 1930 US Census, Washington, Spokane, Five Mile, ED 129, image 6 of 16, citing NARA microfilm publication T626.

[74] Washington Death Certificates, 1907-1960, Lille C. Ewing, 02 Dec 1957, citing Spokane, Spokane, Washington, reference cn24761, Bureau of Vital Statistics, Olympia, FHL microfilm 2,033,771.

[75] Find a Grave Memorial ID 12656150.

[76] Find a Grave Memorial ID 86388471. Pines Cemetery, Spokane Valley, Spokane County, Washington. 86388471

[77] K. E. Burchett, Researcher's Notes, Dec 2004. Bea Richardson Interview.

[78] Find a Grave Memorial IDs 5495483 & 5495491.

Missouri. At the age of 21, he married Margaret "Mamie" H. Leonard, the daughter of Joseph and Ester M. (Henry) Leonard. They were married in Dade County, Missouri, at the home of Sanford and Ester

John Calvin Baldwin, Jr., and "Mamie". They lived and farmed their entire lives in Cedar County, Missouri, until their deaths in 1941 and 1952, respectively. K. Burchett Photo File.

Gillen, Mamie's mother and stepfather, on September 24, 1893. They were farmers in Linn Township of Cedar County, near Jerico Springs.[79] Their children were Clarence Alvin Baldwin, born on September 6, 1894, in Cedar County; Leonard J., born on September 30, 1895; Reggie Allen, born on April 25, 1898; Julie Ethel, born on September 13, 1899; Rosa Mable, born on May 10, 1902; and Harvie [sic] Calvin, born on September 22, 1905.[80]

---

[79] 1900 US Census, Linn, Cedar, Missouri, Roll: 847, p. 4, Enumeration District: 0051, FHL microfilm: 1240847.
[80] 1910 US Census, Linn, Cedar, Missouri; Roll: T624 768, p. 1A, Enumeration District: 0057, FHL microfilm: 1374781.

Their eldest son, Clarence Alvin Baldwin, married Bertha Etta Metcalf on July 25, 1914.[81] Clarence died on February 8, 1930, at the age of 35. Clarence and Bertha lost three of their seven children at an early age, an infant, and then two daughters who died the same year in 1933, less than 3 years after the death of Clarence, in 1930. A son of Clarence and Bertha, Leroy Alvin Baldwin, also died prematurely at age 38. He served in World War II.

Meanwhile, the second son of John Calvin, Jr., and Mamie, Leonard J. Baldwin, never married. Drafted in the first draft of Cedar County for the Army in World War I, Leonard J. joined Company F, 356th Infantry. Shortly after entering the service, he contracted the flu and died on February 5, 1920 at the age of 24. His burial was in Gum Springs Cemetery.[82]

Surviving descendants of John Calvin, Jr., and Mamie Baldwin largely settled in Springfield, Missouri. Reggie Allen married Virgie Tisher and lived in several places before settling permanently in Springfield. Julie Ethel married Rev. E. G. "Ira" Wyrick and lived in Cedar County before moving to Tarkio, in northwest Missouri. Rosa "Rosie" Mable married Frank S. Whistance of Cedar County.[83] Harvie Calvin married Mary Ann Brookshire and lived in Springfield.[84]

John Calvin, Jr., died in 1941 at the age of 68. Mamie died in 1952, at age 75. Their burials were in Gum Springs Cemetery, Cedar County, near Stockton, Missouri.

> 9 M **Thomas Jackson Baldwin** was born on 22 Aug 1874 in Cedar County, Missouri.
>
> Thomas married **Catherine (Kate) Martin** about 1891. Catherine was born in Feb 1876 in Kansas. [Betty Asche gives Kate's name as Sarah based on the census]

THOMAS JACKSON BALDWIN left few traces of his presence in the Baldwin family. Named for his Uncle Thomas Jackson, he was with his parents, John Calvin and Frances Baldwin, when age five at the time of

---

[81] Find a Grave Memorial ID 38742310.

[82] Correspondence with Vickie Baldwin, Email 2 Jan 2005.

[83] Find a Grave Memorial ID 96553405.

[84] Jimmy O. Baldwin, in History of Cedar County, p. 145. Jimmy O. Baldwin was the great great grandson of John Calvin Baldwin.

the 1880 census taken in Linn Township of Cedar County, Missouri, in the summer of 1880.[85] He had started school at the precocious age of five, and was doubtless a happy child growing up amid the many siblings and cousins that made up the Baldwin clan in Cedar County. Sadness, too, would have been part of his youth. His namesake and grandfather, Thomas Lee Baldwin, died when Thomas Jackson was age four, and his little brother Samma [*sic*] died soon thereafter.

He married Catherine (Kate) Martin about 1891, a Kansas girl with two small children from a previous marriage. The 1900 census found the couple living in Linn Township next door to Thomas Jackson's sister, Anna Eliza Cardwell Biddey, and her two children. A few details of his life come from the 1900 census, in addition to his location with the Baldwin family in Cedar County. First, the census confirms his birthdate as August 1874; Catherine was born in February 1876. The couple had been married for three years in 1900. Their children—listed in the census as Martin and Dorie M. Baldwin, ages seven and five, born August 1892 and January 1895 respectively—suggest the children were from a previous marriage, likely by Catherine, since all were born in Kansas. According to the census, Thomas Jackson rented land in Linn Township and engaged in farming.[86]

> 10 M **Samuel J. T. (Samma) Baldwin** was born on 9 Sep 1876 in Cedar County, Missouri. He died on 10 Apr 1883 in Cedar County, Missouri. His Burial was in Gum Springs Cemetery, Linn Township, Cedar County, Missouri.[87]

Samuel J. T. Baldwin died at the age of six years, seven months, and one day. The tenth child born to John Calvin and Frances Baldwin, he was their fourth child to die in childhood. His gravestone includes an engraving of his nickname "Samma" and the image of a child holding a

---

[85] 1880 US Census, Missouri, Cedar, Linn, ED 251, image 16 of 21, citing NARA microfilm publication T9.

[86] 1900 US Census, Missouri, Cedar, ED 51 Linn Township (twp. 33 of R. 26-27), image 12 of 17, citing NARA microfilm publication T623; 1910 US Census, Kansas, Mitchell, Solomon Rapids, ED 103, image 8 of 9, citing NARA microfilm publication T624; Find a Grave Memorial IDs 190568219 & 21128426; Mary Jane Stussi Obituary published by *Spokesman-Review* on Dec. 14, 2014.

[87] 1880 US Census, Linn Township, Cedar, Missouri, United States, citing enumeration district, sheet, NARA microfilm publication T9.

lamb.[88] His grave is in the southwest corner of Gum Springs Cemetery. Gum Springs is one of the oldest cemeteries in Cedar County, located near Stockton, Missouri, and the final resting place of five generations of the Baldwins of southwest Missouri.

> 11 F **Lizzie Alice Baldwin** was born on 12 May 1879 in Stockton, Cedar County, Missouri. She died on 28 Oct 1955, in Stanislaus County, California. Her burial was in Stockton City Cemetery, Stockton, Cedar County, Missouri.[89]
>
> Lizzie married **Lonnie "Lon" Sortor**, son of James Redford Sortor and Emerine Hornbeck, on 13 Dec 1896 in Stockton, Cedar County, Missouri. Lon was born on 29 Nov 1875. He died on 21 Jun 1941, in Tulare, Tulare County, California. His burial was in Stockton City Cemetery, Stockton, Cedar County, Missouri.[90]

LIZZIE ALICE BALDWIN married Lon Sortor of Stockton in 1896, at the age of 18. Lizzie grew up on the Baldwin horse ranch in Cedar County, but, at the time of her marriage to Lon Sortor, she recorded that she was from Arcola, in Dade County, across the county line from Cedar County. Because Lizzie was underage, John Calvin, her father, gave his written consent for the marriage to proceed. The couple married in the Baldwin home in Cedar County, Rev. J. T. Williams officiating.[91] Lon was a handsome catch for Lizzie. He was a tall boy, slender, with blue eyes and light hair.

The following year, the couple had a son, Chester Olin, born in October 1897, and by 1900 had rented a farm in Linn Township and taken up the family occupation of farming in Cedar County.[92] A decade passed and by the spring of 1910, the family had grown to four children

---

[88] Find a Grave Memorial ID 5495659.

[89] Find a Grave Memorial ID 103685121.

[90] Find a Grave Memorial ID 103685055.

[91] Missouri, County Marriage, Naturalization, and Court Records, 1800-1991, Lou Sartor and Lizzie Baldwin, 13 Dec 1896, citing Marriage, Cedar, Missouri, United States, Missouri State Archives, Jefferson City, FHL microfilm 007255167.

[92] 1900 US Census, Missouri, Cedar, ED 53 Lynn Township (twp. 34 of R. 26), Stockton city, image 5 of 31, citing NARA microfilm publication T623.

with the addition of another son, Harley Ezra, and two daughters, Zula and Opel. By then, Lizzie and Lon owned their own farm in Cedar County.[93]

Anna Eliza and Lizzie Alice Baldwin. Lizzie married and moved to Tulare, County California. Upon her death in 1955, her family returned her remains to her birthplace in Cedar County, Missouri. K. Burchett Photo File.

Little Opal Sortor died in 1913, at age four of unknown causes, and almost coincidental with the birth of a third son, Kenneth Raymond Sortor, who came along in 1913.

For the next few years, World War I occupied the nation's attention. On April 6, 1917, the United States officially entered the War. Lon Sortor registered for the draft in 1918, in Cedar County, at the age of 43, giving his occupation as farmer.[94]

From 1920 forward, Lizzie and Lon encountered interesting times. Their daughter, Zula, married Samuel W. Chapman in 1922 and removed to California sometime between 1925 and 1927. They had a son born in 1925 in Missouri, and a daughter born in December 1926 in California. However, by 1930, Zula and Samuel were back in Missouri and living on a farm in Madison Township, in southeast

---

[93] 1910 US Census, Missouri, Cedar, Linn, ED 56, image 29 of 30, citing NARA microfilm publication T624.

[94] United States World War I Draft Registration Cards, 1917-1918, Missouri, Cedar County, L-Z, image 808 of 1212, citing NARA microfilm publication M1509; Missouri, County Marriage, Naturalization, and Court Records, 1800-1991, Chester Sortor and Esta Simmons, 2 Jun 1917, citing Marriage, Cedar, Missouri, United States, Missouri State Archives, Jefferson City, FHL microfilm 007211705.

Cedar County.[95] That did not last long. In 1935, the couple was back in California, in Tulare County, where Samuel worked as a garbage collector.[96]

Meanwhile, something happened in the lives of Lizzie and Lon between 1930 and 1940, which involved their son Kenneth Raymond Sortor and the State of California. In 1930, he was age 16 and the only Sortor child still at home, living on Route 4, next door to Chester Sortor and his family, and not far from Zula Sortor Chapman.[97] Harley Sortor, his wife, Gladys, and their daughter also lived in the same neighborhood of Linn Township, all and all a happy nuclear family of Baldwin descendants.

Kenneth Raymond Sortor may have gone to prison. In the 1940 census, a Kenneth Sorter [sic], age 26 and born in Missouri, was inmate 62585 in San Quentin, California, State Prison. Five years before, he had been in Jefferson City, Missouri, according to the 1940 census. Jefferson City is the location of the Missouri State Penitentiary. If Kenneth Raymond served a term in prison, we know not why, or if, for some reason, authorities moved him from Jefferson City to San Quentin. However, the circumstantial connection may explain the movement of the Sortor family to California beginning about 1935. Lizzie and Lon Sortor moved from Missouri to California. Lon died in California in the summer of 1941, in Tulare County, probably at or near the home of his daughter Zula Sortor Chapman, who lived in Tulare County.

In the year 1942, Kenneth Raymond Sortor married Cora Ellen Thornton, daughter of Thomas E. and Belle C. Thornton, of Cedar County. A Missouri girl, Kenneth doubtless knew her from Cedar

---

[95] 1930 US Census, Missouri, Cedar, Madison, ED 12, image 20 of 24, citing NARA microfilm publication T626.

[96] 1940 US Census California, Tulare, Lindsay Judicial Township, Lindsay, 54-32 Lindsay Judicial Township, Lindsay City bounded by (N) city limits, (E) Gale Hill Av. (S) Honolulu; (W) Southern Pacific Railroad; see also Lindsay Hospital, image 29 of 40, citing Sixteenth Census of the United States, 1940, NARA digital publication T627.

[97] 1930 US Census, Missouri, Cedar, Linn, ED 11, image 15 of 16, citing NARA microfilm publication T626.

County.[98] The county had many Thornton families living around the Stockton area. It is likely they married in California and, according to the timeline, probably after Raymond got out of prison. The 1950 census found the couple living on Sweetbriar Avenue, Lindsay Township, Tulare County, California, coincidentally the location of Zula Sortor Chapman, their mother, Lizzie, and the late Lon Sortor. Kenneth and Cora Ellen had three children: twins Carol J. and Kenneth R., ages seven in 1950, and a son, Leroy, age five, all born in California. Kenneth had a job as a truck driver with a trucking company.[99]

Lizzie Baldwin Sortor died on October 28, 1955, at the age of 76, in Stanislaus County, California.[100] Harley Ezra Sortor passed in 1980 in Sonoma County, California.[101] Zula Sortor Chapman died in 1984 in Turlock, Stanislaus County, California. Her burial was in Turlock Memorial Park, Stanislaus County.[102] Relatives returned the remains of Lon, Lizzie, and Harley Ezra to Cedar County, Missouri, where their graves lie in Stockton City Cemetery alongside their son Chester Olin, who died in 1961, and among many members of the Sortor family.[103]

Kenneth Raymond and Cora Ellen apparently divorced because in 1964, Cora Thornton Sortor married Louis Quinn in Las Vegas, Clark County, Nevada.[104] Cora Ellen died in 1988. Her obituary confirmed several details of her relationship with Kenneth Raymond. "Cora Ellen Quinn, 76, of Visalia, died Sunday. She was born & educated in Missouri. She had been a Lindsay [Tulare] resident for many years before coming to Visalia in 1963. She married Louis Guinn in Las Vegas,

---

[98] 1920 US Census, Missouri, Cedar, Linn, ED 60, image 10 of 14, citing NARA microfilm publication T625.

[99] 1950 United States Census, Lindsay, Tulare, California.

[100] California Death Index, 1940-1997, Lizzie Alice Sorter, 28 Oct 1955, Department of Public Health Services, Sacramento.

[101] California Death Index, 1940-1997, Harley Ezra Sortor, 22 Dec 1980, Department of Public Health Services, Sacramento; United States Social Security Death Index, Harley Sortor, Dec 1980, citing US Social Security Administration, Sonoma, California Age 79 Birth Date 03 Jul 1901 Death Date Dec 1980.

[102] Find a Grave Memorial ID 55759569.

[103] Find a Grave Memorial ID 103685121.

[104] Nevada Marriage Index, 1956-2005, Louis Guinn and Cora Ellen Sorters, 9 Aug 1964, p. A12, Clark County, Nevada.

Nev., in 1964. In addition to her husband, she is survived by a son, Kenneth Sorters [*sic*] of Colorado Springs, Colo.; a daughter, Carol Hayes of Arroyo Grande; six grandchildren and two great grandchildren." Her burial was in Woodlake District Cemetery, Woodlake, Tulare County, California.[105] Her obituary makes no mention of Kenneth Raymond except to identify his children: Kenneth Sortors [*sic*] and Carol Sortors Hayes.

Over the years, the Sortor family added the letter "s" to Sortor. Accordingly, Kenneth Raymond Sortors died March 23, 1996 at the age of 81. His burial was in Traver Cemetery, Tulare County, California.[106] The California Death Record gave his mother's name as "Burton," perhaps a name vaguely remembered by a friend who did not know that his mother was Lizzie Baldwin Sortor.

> 12 F **Martha Maranda (Mattie) Baldwin** was born on 3 Oct 1881 in Cedar County, Missouri. She died on 31 Aug 1950 in Moundville, Vernon County, Missouri. Her burial was in Welborn Cemetery, west of Moundville, Missouri.[107]
>
> Martha married **Parker Bismark Thompson**, son of Oliver Thompson and Sephronia Eliza Thompson, on 23 Jun 1901, in Cedar County, Missouri. Parker was born on 22 Jul 1881 in Mound City, Linn County, Kansas. He died on 28 Nov 1949 in Moundville, Vernon County, Missouri. His burial was in Welborn Cemetery, west of Moundville, Vernon County, Missouri.[108]

MARTHA MARANDA (MATTIE) BALDWIN was 11 years old when her mother died in 1891. Her father, John Calvin Baldwin, soon married Cordelia O'Connor, a neighbor girl and a woman half his age. The differences in age produced a household in which Mattie was ten years younger than her stepmother, who was about the same age as Mattie's older sisters. Mattie remained in the home of John Calvin in Linn

---

[105] Find a Grave Memorial ID 76799439. Obituary of Cora Ellen Thornton Sortor Quinn.

[106] Find a Grave Memorial ID 127503358.

[107] Find a Grave Memorial ID 32241646.

[108] Find a Grave Memorial ID 32301031.

Township until she turned 18 in October 1899, living with her younger sister Jesse Baldwin and the three small sons of John Calvin and

Baldwin Sisters. .Jessie (left) lived in Vernon County, Missouri. Martha Maranda (Mattie) Baldwin married and moved to Vernon County where she died in 1950. Lizzie (right) moved to California. K. Burchett Photo File.

Cordelia.[109] In 1901, Mattie married Parker B. Thompson, originally from Kansas. He was the son of Oliver Thompson, a second-generation immigrant from England by way of Ohio, and Sephronia Eliza Thompson, a native Missourian.[110] The Thompson family settled in Mound City, Linn County, Kansas, around 1870, where Parker was born before coming to Missouri sometime after 1888.[111]

---

[109] 1900 US Census, Missouri, Cedar, ED 51 Linn Township (twp. 33 of R. 26-27), image 8 of 17, citing NARA microfilm publication T623.
[110] 1870 US Census, Kansas, Linn, Mound City, image 23 of 36, citing NARA microfilm publication M593.
[111] 1880 US Census, Kansas, Linn, Mound City, ED 128, image 25 of 30, citing NARA microfilm publication T9.

Parker Thompson and Mattie Baldwin were the same age, both age 19, when they married, which led to the odd necessity of Parker having to obtain permission to marry Mattie. The gender inequality toward women in the early 20th century required men to be age 21 to marry, while women needed to be only 18 to marry without permission. Often, women married much younger than 18, and required the written consent of a parent or guardian. In Parker and Mattie's case, she was 19 and free to marry as she pleased; Parker was also 19 but needed the approval of his father Oliver because Parker was under age 21. Oliver gave his permission. The couple entered on their marriage license that they were from Rowland, Cedar County, Missouri, which at the time was a small store and community between Arcola and Stockton.[112]

The couple first made their home in Missouri, where their oldest son, Winfred, was born. They moved to Kansas about 1903 where three more sons were born before coming back to Missouri. They resided in Rich Hill, in southern Bates County, Missouri, for a while. Soon, the 1910 census found them living in rural Blue Mound Township, on a small farm in Vernon County, Missouri, located on Papenville Road.[113]

Parker farmed and worked as a self-employed teamster. He was a physically fit man of medium height, stout build, and had blue eyes and auburn hair. When the United States entered World War I, he offered his services, registering for the draft in September of 1918 in Vernon County at the age of 37. However, there is no indication that the military accepted his offer; the War ended in November 1918.[114]

For many years, Mattie and Parker made their home in Vernon County where they owned a house in the village of Moundville. Here,

---

[112] Missouri, County Marriage, Naturalization, and Court Records, 1800-1991, Cedar, Marriage records 1897-1903 Vol. G, image 216 of 385, Missouri State Archives, Jefferson City.

[113] 1910 US Census, Missouri, Vernon, Blue Mound, ED 137, image 14 of 14, citing NARA microfilm publication T624.

[114] United States World War I Draft Registration Cards, 1917-1918, Missouri, Vernon County, M-Z, image 1556 of 2115, citing NARA microfilm publication M1509.

Parker worked the coal mines located in Vernon County, and here, he and Mattie raised five children.[115]

Moundville is a small village in southwest Vernon County. Moundville originated in 1869, so named because of a natural mound near the original town site. A post office, called Mounds, was established there in 1870, and the name was changed to Moundville in 1886.[116] Curiously, the name recalls Parker's birthplace in Kansas, named Mound City. Moundville is located along Missouri Route 43, approximately 4.5 miles north of Bronaugh, and six miles southwest of Nevada, the county seat of Vernon County. When Mattie and Parker moved there, the village had a population of about 250, but it steadily declined thereafter until today, fewer than 75 people live there.

Mattie and Parker enjoyed a comfortable lifestyle. Down-to-earth people, both had eighth-grade educations—the going level of schooling in those days, and they owned a modest home in Moundville. Parker worked the mines, and their children grew to adulthood. Sometime between 1930 and 1935, during the Great Depression, the mines ceased to be viable, and in 1935, Parker did roadwork for the WPA (Works Progress Administration). The children were out of the house and on their own, but lived nearby.[117]

Mattie Baldwin and Parker Thompson had six children. The oldest, Winfred Greely Thompson, born on December 25, 1901, in Missouri, married Ina Lois Fish. Winfred died on October 27, 1967, at the age of 65, in Gallup, McKinley County, New Mexico[118] Ira Lee Thompson, born on March 22, 1903, in Allen County, Kansas, married Blanche Gertrude Friel. Ira operated a steam shovel for fifteen years.[119] He died on February 20, 1938, at age 34, near Rich Hill, in southern Bates

---

[115] 1920 US Census, Missouri, Vernon, Moundville, ED 176, image 8 of 30, citing NARA microfilm publication T625.

[116] *The Nevada Herald,* 16 Aug 1970.

[117] 1940 US Census, Missouri, Vernon, Moundville Township, Moundville, 109-30 Moundville Township, Moundville Town (part), image 2 of 9, citing Sixteenth Census of the United States, 1940, NARA.

[118] Find a Grave Memorial ID 77803646.

[119] Death Certificate 5989, Missouri State Board of Health Bureau of Vital Statistics.

County, Missouri.[120] Joe Carl, born on January 20, 1905, died in June 1974, at Moundville. His wife was Bertha Faye Martin. Arthur H., born on November 15, 1906, in Rich Hill, Bates County, Missouri, died on April 21, 1995, in Princeton, Bureau County, Illinois. His wife was Beulah Sheridan. They married in Stanton, North Dakota. Everett Albert Thompson, born on September 30, 1912, was a deputy sheriff for 15 years in Los Angeles, California. He married Noel Fern Weaver. Everett died at Broadway Hospital, Los Angeles, on April 8, 1961, of heart disease caused by hypertension. His burial was in Rose Hills Cemetery, Los Angeles.[121] Myrtle Lorene Thompson, born on November 21, 1915, in Vernon County, the youngest child and only daughter of Mattie and Parker Thompson, married Lyle Lewis Lent, a construction worker in Moundville. He died in 1983, and she married secondly [William I.] Dunham. Myrtle died on February 10, 1998, in Nevada, Vernon County, Missouri[122]

Parker Bismark Thompson died on November 28, 1949, at age 68.[123] Mattie continued to live at their home in Moundville, in the south part of town along Maple Street, two blocks west of Hwy 43. She was unable to work now, and on August 31, 1950, nine months after the passing of Parker, she died at Moundville, at age 68. Mattie Baldwin and Parker Thompson share a grave marker in Welborn Cemetery, Vernon County, Missouri.[124]

13 F **Jessie Lee Baldwin** was born on 22 Mar 1884, in Stockton, Cedar County, Missouri. She died on 15 Aug 1964 in Nevada, Vernon County, Missouri. Her burial

---

[120] 1930 US Census, Missouri, Vernon, Moundville, ED 32, image 2 of 6, citing NARA microfilm publication T626.

[121] California, County Birth and Death Records, 1800-1994, Los Angeles, Death certificates 1961 no 6400-9070, image 896 of 3148, California State Archives, Sacramento.

[122] Find a Grave Memorial ID 71757865.

[123] Find a Grave Memorial ID 32301031.

[124] 1950 US Census, Moundville, Vernon, Missouri, Roll: 5383, Sheet Number: 5, Enumeration District: 109-22, NARA Record Group Number: *29*.

was in Newton Burial Park, Nevada, Vernon County, Missouri.[125]

Jessie married **Ernest (Ernie) Byron Hastin**, son of Samuel Dothard Hastin and Sarah A. Long, on 3 Oct 1901, in Greenfield, Dade County, Missouri. Ernest was born 29 Jan 1876, in Cedar County, Missouri. He died 3 Nov 1914, in North Township, Dade County, Missouri. His burial was in Pleasant Grove Cemetery, Greenfield, Dade County, Missouri.[126]

JESSIE LEE BALDWIN was the youngest child of John Calvin and Frances Baldwin, named, in part, for her grandfather, Thomas Lee Baldwin. After her mother died when Jessie was age seven, she grew up in Cedar County in the household of her father, along with his new wife, Cordelia O'Connor, and the second Baldwin family of half-siblings. When she was 19, Jessie married Ernie Hastin, a young man of 27, yet several years her senior. The couple listed on their marriage license that they were from Arcola, Dade County, Missouri. Ernie was the youngest son of Samuel and Sarah Hastin.[127] The Baldwin–Hastin marriage took place on October 3, 1903, in Greenfield, at the Delmonico Hotel, Rev. T. S. Brown officiating.[128] The Delmonico Hotel was one of three boarding houses located on the Greenfield Square, each establishment competing as a haven for overnight visitors to Dade County. The Delmonico Hotel predated the construction of the Washington Hotel in 1892, which became the largest hotel in Dade County and a destination for travelers and businesses in southwest Missouri. The Delmonico Hotel was a large two-story building on the

---

[125] Find a Grave Memorial ID 131738106.

[126] Find a Grave Memorial ID 82835756.

[127] 1880 US Census, Missouri, Cedar, Linn, ED 251, image 7 of 21, citing NARA microfilm publication T9.

[128] Missouri, County Marriage, Naturalization, and Court Records, 1800-1991, Dade, Marriage records 1892-1908 Vol. D-F, image 595 of 775, Missouri State Archives, Jefferson City.

southwest corner of Main and Water Streets. Sometime around 1920, the owners renamed it the Greenfield Hotel.

Jessie and Ernie bought a small farm in Linn Township, Cedar County, and started a family. By 1910, three children had been born, but only two survived.[129]

Jessie Lee Baldwin. She lived and worked in Greenfield, Missouri, before moving to Tulare, California, and then back to Vernon County, Missouri, were she died in 1964. K. Burchett Photo File.

Ernie Hastin died in 1914, of tuberculosis, at the age of 38, leaving Jessie and three small children, three because a third had been born in the summer of 1910.[130]

Jessie did not remain on the farm. The 1920 census found her as a 35-year-old widow and three small children living on Allison Street in Greenfield, Missouri. The kids: Audress, age 14, Beulah, 12, and Wilbur, 8, were attending school. Jessie worked as the proprietor of a rooming

---

[129] 1910 US Census, Missouri, Cedar, Linn, ED 57, image 10 of 18, citing NARA microfilm publication T624.

[130] Death Certificate 38387, Missouri State Board of Health Bureau of Vital Statistics.

house. We do not know if her business was related to the hotel business that prospered in Greenfield.[131]

Meanwhile, her daughter, Audress Hastin, born on October 14, 1904, married D. E. Smith. She died very young on July 11, 1926, at the age of 20. Her burial in Newton Burial Park, Nevada, Missouri, suggests that Jessie may have quit her rooming house business in Greenfield and moved to Vernon County. In 1930, Jessie and her two surviving children were living on Pine Street, Ward 2, in Nevada. Jessie was 45, Beulah 22, and Wilbur 19. Curiously, in the census record asking occupation, none of the three listed an occupation.[132] According to family lore, Jessie Baldwin Hastin operated a brothel in Nevada, but the public genealogical record is silent on that aspect of family history.[133]

About 1935, Jessie and her daughter, Beulah, removed to Visalia, Tulare County, California. Tulare County was the destination of several members of the Baldwin family over the years. The 1940 census, taken in Tulare County on June 18, 1940, listed Widow Jessie Hastin, age 56, and her daughter, Beulah, age 32, single, and living in Visalia, California. Jessie gave her occupation as a laundress at the State Hospital, where she drew an annual salary of $235.[134] Shortly after the enumeration of the census, Jessie and Beulah moved back to Missouri.

On June 9, 1943, Jessie's daughter and lifelong companion, Beulah Nadine Hastin, died. Born on October 17, 1907, Beulah was age 35 when

---

[131] 1920 US Census, Missouri, Dade. Center, ED 68, image 19 of 30, citing NARA microfilm publication T625.

[132] 1930 US Census, Missouri, Vernon, Nevada, ED 9, image 22 of 30, citing NARA microfilm publication T626.

[133] K. E. Burchett, Researcher's Notes, 6 Feb 2005. According to Bea Richardson, Jessie Baldwin Hastin operated a brothel in Nevada, Mo. Bea also said that one of her [Jessie's] sons lived toward Kansas City. [Wilbur settled in Butler, Missouri, toward Kansas City].

[134] 1940 US Census, California, Tulare, Visalia Judicial Township, Visalia , 54-78 Visalia Judicial Township, Visalia City bounded by (N) E Main, (E) Atchison, Topeka & Santa Fe Railway, (S) city limits, (W) S Court, image 34 of 35, citing Sixteenth Census of the United States, 1940, NARA digital publication T627.

she died. Her burial was in Newton Burial Park, Nevada, in Vernon County.[135]

Jessie Baldwin Hastin never remarried after Ernie died. She spent the last years of her life unable to work, living first in the William Miller Pensioners Home, in Vernon County, and then the Percifield Nursing Home, in Nevada.[136] She died on August 15, 1964, at the Percifield Home, at the age of 80 of a cerebral hemorrhage caused by the infirmities of old age. Her burial was in Newton Burial Park, Nevada, beside her two daughters.[137]

The informant of Jessie's death was her son, Wilbur H. Wayne Hastin, the youngest of her three children, born on July 24, 1910, and the lone survivor of the Jessie Baldwin and Ernie Hastin union.[138] Wilbur married Velma Katherine Collins on October 19, 1935.[139] They had three children.

Wilbur and Velma lived in Butler, Missouri, where Wilber owned the Hastins Motor Company. Wilbur died on May 21, 1990. His burial was in Oak Hill Cemetery, in Butler. Velma died on February 19, 1997. She shares a headstone at Oak Hill with her husband of 54 years.[140]

In the course of time, the name Hastin changed. Today, the name frequently appears as Hastins, Hasting, and Hastings, all issuing from the same Hastin family roots of southwest Missouri.

---

[135] Find a Grave Memorial ID 131738181.

[136] 1950 US Census, Butler, Bates, Missouri, Roll: 6087. Sheet Number: 21, Enumeration District: 7-20, Record Group Number: 29, NARA.

[137] Death Certificate 0033997, Missouri State Board of Health Bureau of Vital Statistics.

[138] Find a Grave Memorial ID 14162603.

[139] Find a Grave Memorial ID 82835756.

[140] 1950 US Census, Butler, Bates, Missouri, Roll: 6087, Sheet Number: 21, Enumeration District: 7-20, Record Group Number: 29, NARA.

29

Second Marriage

John Calvin also married **Sarah Cordelia O'Connor**, daughter of John Dennis O'Connor and Rachel Minerva Long, on 29 Dec 1892.[1] Sarah Cordelia was born on 11 Feb 1862 in Linn Township, Cedar County, Missouri. She died on 22 May 1945. She was buried in Gum Springs Cemetery, Linn Township, Cedar County, Missouri.

They had the following children.

14 M **William Byron Baldwin** was born on 16 Oct 1893 in Stockton, Cedar County, Missouri. He died on 30 Mar 1972.[2] His burial was in Sunset Lawn Chapel of the Chimes Memorial Park, Sacramento, Sacramento County, California.

William married **Lottie Mae Reynolds Heaton,** daughter of Adolphus Fernando Reynolds and Emely Saphire Rowland, on 25 Oct 1925, at Bolivar, Polk County, Missouri.[3] She was born in 1898. She was previously married to Ben Earl Heaton, of Dade County. She died in 1982. Her burial was in Sunset Lawn Chapel of the Chimes Memorial Park, Sacramento, Sacramento County, California.[4]

WILLIAM BYRON BALDWIN—who went by his middle name Byron— was the 14th child of John Calvin Baldwin, and the first child of John Calvin's second family with Sarah Cordelia O'Connor. Byron's birth was

[1] Missouri, County Marriage, Naturalization, and Court Records, 1800-1991, Cedar, Marriage applications and licenses 1892-1895, image 251, Missouri State Archives, Jefferson City.

[2] California Death Index, 1940-1997, William B. Baldwin, 30 Mar 1972, Department of Public Health Services, Sacramento.

[3] Missouri, Polk County, probate and marriage records, Images 1–249, Marriage licenses, v. N, Oct 1921-Sep 1927.

[4] Find a Grave Memorial IDs 211392277 & 211392190.

nine months and 17 days after John Calvin and Cordelia married. Byron grew up on the Baldwin farm in Linn Township, got a fifth-grade education, and set about following his father's footsteps on the family farm.[5]

John Calvin died in 1908 when Byron was age 14. The 1910 census listed Byron living with his mother Cordelia and his brothers, Hugh and Roy, on the home place next door to his older half-sister, Anna Eliza Baldwin, and her son, Tom Cardwell, and his wife Belle. Anna Eliza had recently lost her second husband, Jesse M. Biddey, in March of 1910 after a long illness. Her first husband, Edward Cardwell, died in 1878.[6]

Byron moved briefly to Iowa. When he was 24, he registered for the WW I draft on June 4, 1917. He registered in Plymouth County, Iowa, where he worked on the farm of W. S. Kanzig, at Trenton, Iowa, but gave his permanent address as RFD 1, Stockton, Missouri, representing the draft board in Linn Township, Cedar County. On the draft notice, he indicated that his mother and one brother were dependent on him.[7] He entered military service as a private on September 17, 1918, but did not see combat. The War ended in November 1918, and he joined a Casual Detachment Demobilization Group awaiting discharge, which came on June 18, 1919, well after the war ended.[8] WW I demobilization units caused a national furor because of the long delay in returning soldiers to civilian life once hostilities were over. Nevertheless, by the end of January 1920, he was back home in Cedar County, living with his mother and working the farm.[9]

[5] 1900 US Census, Linn, Cedar, Missouri, Roll: 847, Page: 4, Enumeration District: 0051, FHL microfilm: 1240847.

[6] 1910 US Census, Linn, Cedar, Missouri, United States, citing enumeration district (ED) ED 57, sheet 4B, family 76, NARA microfilm publication T624, roll 768, FHL microfilm 1,374,781.

[7] United States World War I Draft Registration Cards, 1917-1918, Missouri, Cedar County, A-K, image 81 of 1370, citing NARA microfilm publication M1509.

[8] United States, Veterans Administration Master Index, 1917-1940, image 1 of 1, citing NARA microfilm publication 76193916, St. Louis: National Archives and Records Administration, 1985.

[9] 1920 US Census, Missouri, Cedar, Linn, ED 60, image 13 of 14, citing NARA microfilm publication T625.

Byron was a good-looking lad at age 26; in the mold of Baldwin offspring, of medium height and build, blue eyes, and light hair.[10] On 25 October 1925, he married Lottie Mae Reynolds Heaton, a 26-year-old Cedar County girl from Stockton. They married at Bolivar, Polk County, Missouri, Justice of the Peace, Harry T. West, officiating.[11] It was Lottie's second marriage after her union with Ben Heaton. Ben may have had difficulty with the law. A Ben Heaton who fits his description was in Tulare County, California, about this time, according to Tulare County Sheriff's Office and Jail Records.[12] Tulare County, California, was the destination of several young adventurers from Cedar County, Missouri, including but not limited to Baldwins.

By 1930, Byron and Lottie had a four-year-old son, Lester R. Baldwin, adding to their blended family that included Alfred Stevens Heaton, age 14, from Lottie's previous marriage. The family lived next door to Cordelia Baldwin and siblings Hugh, Minnie, and Harry Baldwin, in Cedar County. Next door on the other side lived Adolphus and Emily Reynolds, parents of Lottie.

For many years, Byron engaged in farming and worked in road construction in Cedar County.[13] He and Lottie raised four sons and a daughter: Lester Leroy, Harold Thomas, Wilbur Carles [sic], Doris [Waterman], and Carl John, all born in Cedar County, Missouri[14]

Sometime before 1950, Byron and Lottie left Missouri and moved to California. The 1950 census located them and four of their five children living on Lindsay Avenue on the north side of Sacramento, in American Township, Sacramento County, California. Byron was age 56 and unable to work. Eighteen-year-old Harold helped to support the family

---

[10] United States World War I Draft Registration Cards, 1917-1918, Missouri, Cedar County, A-K, image 81 of 1370, citing NARA microfilm publication M1509.

[11] Missouri, Polk County, probate and marriage records, Images 1–249, Marriage licenses, v. N, Oct 1921-Sep 1927.

[12] Tulare County, Sheriff's Office and Jail Records, 1874-1963.

[13] 1930 US Census, Missouri, Cedar, Linn, ED 10, image 1 of 22, citing NARA microfilm publication T626.

[14] 1940 US Census, Missouri, Cedar, Linn Township, 20-11 Linn Township in Townships 33, 34, and 35, Range 27, image 16 of 29, citing Sixteenth Census of the United States, 1940, NARA digital publication T627, Records of the Bureau of the Census, 1790 - 2007, RG 29, National Archives and Records Administration, 2012.

by working as a busboy in a restaurant.[15] The oldest son, Lester, and his wife lived nearby in the same township. Lester worked in a government job as a mechanic for the U. S. Air Force at McClellan Air Force Base.

William Byron Baldwin died in 1972, at the age of 78, in Sacramento, California.[16] The informant of his death was his daughter, Doris Mae Baldwin Waterman, of Roseville, California.[17] Lottie died in 1982 and shared a gravestone with Byron in Sunset Lawn Chapel of the Chimes Memorial Park, in Sacramento, joined there by son Lester, who also died in 1982. Lester was a World War II veteran who made his home at Roseville, California. Lottie's son, Alfred Stevens Heaton, died in Yolo County, California, near Sacramento, in 1983.[18] Carl John Baldwin died on June 28, 2006, in Sacramento, at age 67.[19] His older brother Wilbur Carles died the following year, on May 19, 2007, in Sacramento, at the age of 74.[20] Harold Thomas Baldwin lived until 2019 when he died at age 87, in Fair Oaks, California. His burial was in Fair Oaks Cemetery, Sacramento County.[21] Of the five children born to William Byron and Lottie Baldwin in Cedar County, Missouri, each lived out their final years in the Sacramento Valley of California. Doris Mae Baldwin Waterman was still living at Roseville, Placer County, California, when Harold Baldwin died in 2019.[22]

15 M **Hugh G. Baldwin** was born on 24 Feb 1895 in Cedar County, Missouri. He died in North Township, Dade County, Missouri, on 16 Feb 1944. His burial was in

---

[15] 1950 US Census, American Township, Sacramento, California; Record Group Number: 29 Roll: 1465, Sheet Number: 16, Enumeration District: 34-20, NARA.

[16] Find a Grave Memorial ID 211392190.

[17] Death Certificate of William Byron Baldwin, State of California.

[18] California Death Index, 1940-1997, Reynolds in entry for Alfred Stevens Heaton, 26 Aug 1983, Department of Public Health Services, Sacramento.

[19] United States Social Security Death Index.

[20] United States Social Security Death Index.

[21] Find a Grave Memorial ID 237783377.

[22] Obituary of Harold Thomas Baldwin; United States Public Records, 1970-2009, Doris Mae Waterman, 2004-2008. [No subject of public record entered.]

Gum Springs Cemetery, Linn Township, Cedar County, Missouri.[23]

HUGH G. BALDWIN never left the family farm in Cedar County. The 15th child of John Calvin Baldwin and the second child of Cordelia, Hugh was age 10 when his father died in 1908.[24] The family record of his life suggests that he was never able to work, except possibly for a brief time in his early teens doing light farm chores. We do not know whether his disability occurred at birth or later in life. In 1910, at the age of 15, the census indicated that he worked on the farm but did not attend school. The other school-age Baldwin children that year all attended school while also working on the family farm.[25] Later census years give additional circumstantial details of his life. In 1920, for example, he was still living at home at age 24. The census indicated this time that he was unable to read and write and had no occupation.[26] It was likely Hugh who his brother, Byron Baldwin, on his WW I draft registration in 1917, noted that his mother and one brother were dependent on him.[27]

Hugh never married. In 1930, the census showed he lived with his mother, Cordelia, and younger siblings Minnie and Harry. Cordelia and Harry gave occupations of farming; Hugh gave no occupation, never served in the military, and apparently could not read and write, according to the census. A decade later, the 1940 census confirmed his condition—he was unable to work.[28] Meanwhile, his brother, Harry,

---

[23] Find a Grave Memorial ID 5495554.

[24] 1900 US Census, Linn, Cedar, Missouri, Roll: 847, p. 4, Enumeration District: 0051, FHL microfilm: 1240847. Calvin Baldwin & Cordelia.

[25] 1910 US Census, Linn, Cedar, Missouri, United States, citing enumeration district (ED) ED 57, sheet 4B, family 76, NARA microfilm publication T624, roll 768, FHL microfilm 1,374,781.

[26] 1920 US Census, Missouri, Cedar, Linn, ED 60, image 13 of 14, citing NARA microfilm publication T625.

[27] United States World War I Draft Registration Cards, 1917-1918, Missouri, Cedar County, A-K, image 81 of 1370, citing NARA microfilm publication M1509.

[28] 1940 US Census, Linn, Cedar, Missouri, Roll: m-t0627-02095, p. 12A, Enumeration District: 20-11.

Cordelia Baldwin and Family. These unidentified members of the Baldwin family surround Cordelia Baldwin seated center. The photograph, probably taken after the death of John Calvin, appears to show a blend of his older and younger children from his marriages to Frances Pherby Jackson Baldwin and Sarah Cordelia O'Connor Baldwin, including grandchildren. K. Burchett Photo File.

had married and was working 45 hours a week to keep the family farm going.[29] Henry and his family took care of Cordelia, who was in her late 70s in 1940, and Hugh, who turned 45 in February of that year.

Hugh Baldwin died suddenly on February 16, 1944, within 8 days of his 49th birthday, of coronary thrombosis. He died in rural North Township, Dade County, Missouri.[30] His sister, Minnie, informed officials of his passing.[31] The next year, Cordelia died on May 22, 1945, at the age of 83. The lifelong companionship of Cordelia and Hugh continued in death. Mother and son share a double grave marker in Gum Springs Cemetery, Cedar County, Missouri. When John Calvin Baldwin died in 1908, his burial was next to his first wife, Frances. Upon

---

[29] 1930 US Census, Missouri, Cedar, Linn, ED 10 , image 1 of 22, citing NARA microfilm publication T626.

[30] Missouri State Board of Health Standard Certificate of Death #10819.

[31] Death Certificate 10819, Missouri State Board of Health.

Cordelia's death, the family laid her to rest beside her beloved son, Hugh.

16   M   **Alvin Henry Baldwin** was born on 27 Nov 1896 in Cedar County, Missouri. He died on 22 Jan 1897 in Stockton, Cedar County, Missouri. His burial was in Gum Springs Cemetery, Linn Township, Cedar, Missouri.[32]

ALVIN HENRY BALDWIN died in infancy when he was one month old. His burial was in Gum Springs Cemetery in the Baldwin family plot. Gum Springs Cemetery is located in Linn Township, Cedar County, Missouri, 3.5 miles south of Stockton on Highway 39, just south of the 39 and 215 junction. The cemetery is on the west side of the highway. The Baldwin plot is in the southwest corner of the cemetery behind the church that stands on the property. Gum Springs is the name of an old Cumberland Presbyterian Campground named for the family of Gums who were local landowners. It had at one time a small store, but no settlement. An abandoned school stood nearby for several years before being demolished.[33] The church still stands. The well-kept cemetery next to the church is the final resting place for many Baldwins and their descendants. The inscription on the grave of infant Alvin Baldwin reads, "Alvin H. son of J. C. and Cordelia Nov 27, 1896-June 22, 1897."[34]

17   M   **Roy Carl Baldwin** was born on 20 Jun 1898 in Stockton, Cedar County, Missouri. He died on 19 Sep 1972, in St. Vincent Hospital, Sioux City, Woodbury County, Iowa. His burial was in Hillside Cemetery, Merrill, Plymouth County, Iowa.[35]

Roy married **Martha Gladys Golden**, daughter of Clarence A. Golden and Edith Beeler, on 16 Sep 1918, in Le Mars, Plymouth County, Iowa.[36] Gladys was born on

---

[32] Find a Grave Memorial ID 5495632.

[33] Moser, *A Directory of Towns, Villages, and Hamlets Past and Present of Cedar County, Missouri.*

[34] K. E. Burchett, Cemetery, Gum Springs, Cedar County, Missouri (personally viewed and recorded).

[35] Find a Grave Memorial ID 121820893.

[36] Iowa, County Marriages, 1838-1934 Gladys Golden & Roy Baldwin.

21 Aug 1901, in South Dakota.[37] She died 6 Jun 1926, in Sioux City, Iowa.[38] Her burial was in Graceland Park Cemetery, Sioux City, Woodbury County, Iowa.[39]

Roy also married **Laura E. Betsworth Fletcher**, daughter of James Edgar Betsworth and Eva Hoover, on 22 Jul 1932, in Dakota City, Dakota County, Nebraska. She previously married Earl George Fletcher, on 24 Aug 1912.[40] Laura was born on 2 May 1895, in Plymouth County, Iowa.[41] She died on 9 Feb 1963, in Sioux City, Iowa. Her burial was in Hillside Cemetery, Merrill, Plymouth County, Iowa.[42]

ROY CARL BALDWIN grew up in rural Cedar County, Missouri, received a seventh-grade education, and worked on the Baldwin family farm from an early age.[43] Roy's father, John Calvin, died in 1908, leaving Roy and his older brothers with the responsibility of caring for their mother, Cordelia, and three younger siblings, ages four to eight. At age 11, Roy had a full-time job working on the farm.[44]

---

[37] Canada, Northwest Provinces Census, 1906, Gladys Golden in entry for Clarence A Golden, 1906.

[38] Iowa, Death Records, 1904-1951, image 689 of 4428, State Historical Society of Iowa, Des Moines. An error on the death certificate gives the birth of Gladys Golden as 20 Aug 1891. However, her age at death was 24 yrs. 9 mos. and 16 days, which calculates to a birthdate of 21 Aug 1901. This corresponds closely with census birthdate estimates of 1902 and gravestone inscription of 1902. It also corresponds with her age at marriage of 18 on 16 Sep 1918.

[39] Find a Grave Memorial 8413043.

[40] Iowa, County Marriages, 1838-1934, Earl G. Fletcher and Laura E. Betsworth, 24 Aug 1912, Le Mars, Plymouth, Iowa, United States, citing reference 404, county courthouses, Iowa, FHL microfilm 1,404,989.

[41] Iowa, County Births, 1880-1935, Cora [sic] Ellen Betsworth, 2 May 1895, citing Iowa county district courts, Iowa, FHL microfilm 1,412,087.

[42] Find a Grave Memorial ID 121820879.

[43] 1900 US Census, Linn, Cedar, Missouri, Roll: 847, p. 4, Enumeration District: 0051, FHL microfilm: 1240847.

[44] 1910 US Census, Linn, Cedar, Missouri, United States, citing enumeration district (ED) ED 57, sheet 4B, family 76, NARA microfilm publication T624, roll 768, FHL microfilm 1,374,781.

For unspecified reasons, Roy left home when he was a teenager and made his way to Iowa, where he found work as a farm helper for Carl Johnson in rural Akron, Iowa. On September 10, 1918, at the onset of the nation's entry into World War I, Roy registered for the draft at LeMars, Plymouth County, Iowa, at the age of 20. LeMars is the county seat of Plymouth County, located about 20 miles east of Akron. Again for reasons unknown, on the registration form, Roy listed as his nearest relative Lon Sortors, husband of Roy's older half-sister, Lizzie Baldwin Sortors. He gave a permanent address of RFD 1, Stockton, Missouri, but did not include the names of anyone in the immediate Baldwin household.[45]

Roy grew to be a tall young man of medium build, brown hair, and brown eyes. At age 21, he married Gladys Golden on September 16, 1918, coincidentally less than a week after he registered for the draft. The couple married at LeMars, Iowa, the Plymouth County seat.[46] Gladys was the 17-year-old daughter of Clarence and Edith Golden, born in South Dakota, and a widely traveled young woman of an itinerant family. Her father was born in Missouri. He moved his family to South Dakota—where Gladys was born—and then to Manitoba, Canada, before finally settling for a while in Iowa.[47]

Roy Baldwin did not enter World War I. He and Gladys settled in Sioux City, Iowa, rented a room on West 19th Street, and found jobs working in the city. Roy worked as a laborer for an ice company and Gladys as a laundress. Clarence and Edith Golden and the Golden family had, meanwhile, left Iowa again and moved back to South Dakota.[48]

On the 1920 census enumeration for Sioux City, Woodbury County, Iowa, Roy apparently had a memory lapse regarding his Baldwin family roots. On his marriage license, he gave his parents' names as Calvin Baldwin and A. C. Connor [sic]; on the census, he claimed they were

---

[45] United States World War I Draft Registration Cards, 1917-1918, Missouri, Cedar County, A-K, image 80 of 1370, citing NARA microfilm publication M1509.

[46] Iowa, County Marriages, 1838-1934 Gladys Golden & Roy Baldwin.

[47] Canada, Northwest Provinces Census, 1906, Clarence A Golden, 1906.

[48] 1920 US Census, Spink, Union, South Dakota, Roll: T625_1724, p. 5A, Enumeration District: 252.

both born in "Nebraska."[49] Meanwhile, in the 1925 Iowa census, he said John Calvin was born in "England." Incidentally, in 1925, Clarence and Edith Golden were back in Iowa once more, and living near Roy and Gladys on Court Street, in Sioux City.[50]

On June 6, 1926, Gladys Golden Baldwin died in Sioux City, Iowa, of heart disease from complications of scarlet fever. She was 24.[51] Gladys did not have children.

Roy married secondly, Laura Betsworth Fletcher of Plymouth County, Iowa. Her first marriage to Earl Fletcher ended in divorce. In 1930, Roy and Laura were living as husband and wife and renting a $30 a month apartment on South Curry Street, in Big Spring, Howard County, Texas.[52] However, it turns out that in 1930 they were not married, at least not officially. Two years later, they wed on July 22, 1932, in Dakota City, Dakota County, Nebraska. Dakota City is on the Iowa-Nebraska border across from Sioux City, Iowa.[53]

Roy was in the construction trade. He followed seasonal work wherever the jobs took him; thus, his presence in 1930 in Big Spring, Texas, and then back to Sioux City, Iowa, in 1932, where he resided at least until 1935. In 1940, he and Laura moved again, this time to Brooklyn Avenue, in Kansas City, Kaw Township, Jackson County, Missouri, where Roy was a construction supervisor, but at the time looking for work.[54] A decade later, in 1950, he was back in Texas on a

---

[49] 1920 US Census, Sioux City Precinct 5, Woodbury, Iowa, Roll, T625_520, p. 1A, Enumeration District: 208.

[50] Iowa State Census, 1925, Clarence A. Golden, Woodbury, Iowa, United States, citing Woodbury, Iowa, United States, Iowa State Historical Department, Des Moines, FHL microfilm.

[51] Iowa, Death Records, 1904-1951, image 689 of 4428, State Historical Society of Iowa, Des Moines. Gladys died at 409 West 14th, Sioux City, Iowa. Her death certificate incorrectly gave her birthdate as 20 Aug 1891.

[52] 1930 US Census, Texas, Howard, Big Spring, ED 4, image 10 of 28, citing NARA microfilm publication T626. Roy age 31 with wife Laura age 34, age at first marriage 20 and 18 working occupation cement, construction, not a veteran.

[53] Nebraska Marriages, 1855-1995, Roy C. Baldwin, 1932. 22 Jul 1932 marriage Dakota City, Dakota, Nebraska Roy age 34 her Laura age 37.

[54] 1940 US Census, Kansas City, Jackson, Missouri, Roll: m-t0627-02173, p. 4A, Enumeration District: 116-192. 1940 Brooklyn Ave, Kaw Township, Jackson, Kansas

construction job as a carpenter and living with Laura on Ayre Street Oyster Creek, Clute, Brazoria County, Texas. Clute was a small town of about 750 people located in the greater Houston area.[55] In time, the couple settled in Laura's hometown of LeMars, Iowa. For many years, Roy worked as a supervisor doing concrete construction work for F. Leader Construction Company.

Roy and Laura had no children. They lived out the last years of their lives at LeMars. Laura died February 9, 1963. Roy died September 19, 1972, at St. Vincent Hospital, in Sioux City, Iowa, after a short illness. He was age 74. The graves of Laura and Roy Baldwin are in Hillside Cemetery, Merrill, Plymouth County, Iowa. The *LeMars Daily Sentinel* noted that his survivors included a brother, Harry of Stockton, Missouri, and two sisters, Mrs. Lewis (Minnie) Cornwell of Stockton, Missouri, and Mrs. Lloyd (Orpha) White of Fresno, California. They were the last of the 20 children of John Calvin Baldwin.[56]

> 18 F **Orpha May Baldwin** was born on 1 Dec 1900 in Cedar County, Missouri. She died on 18 Nov 1985, in Fresno, Fresno County, California. Her burial was in Belmont Memorial Park, Fresno, Fresno County, California. [57]

City, Roy C. 41, Laura 43, both grade 7 Laura b. Iowa, construction foreman, seeking work, lived in Iowa in 1935.

[55] 1950 US Census, Brazoria, Texas, Roll: 1234, Sheet Number: 39, Enumeration District: 20. Roy age 51, Laura 54.

[56] Obituary of Roy C. Baldwin, *LeMars Daily Sentinel*, September 20, 1972. "Roy C. Baldwin, 74, Sioux City, formerly of LeMars, died Tuesday (Sept. 19, 1972) at Sioux City St. Vincent hospital after a short illness. Mr. Baldwin was a longtime foreman for F. Leader Construction Co. He was born June 20, 1898, at Stockton, Mo., the son of the late John C. and Sarah (O'Connor) Baldwin. He and Laura Betsworth were married in 1932 at Dakota City, Neb. Mrs. Baldwin died Feb. 9, 1963, at Sioux City. Graveside services will be held Thursday at 10 a.m. at Hillside Cemetery, Merrill, with Rev. Donald Deines officiating. Luken-Johnson Funeral Home, LeMars, is in charge of arrangements. Survivors are a brother, Harry of Stockton, Mo., and two sisters, Mrs. Lewis (Minnie) Cornwell of Stockton, Mo., and Mrs. Lloyd (Orpha) White of Fresno, Calif. Mr. Baldwin was preceded in death by his wife, parents, and three brothers."

[57] Billion Graves record for Orpha M White (1900-1985), Belmont Memorial Park, Fresno, Fresno, California; Billion Graves record for Lloyd L White (1901-1963), Belmont Memorial Park, Fresno, Fresno, California.

Orpha married **Lloyd Lester White**, son of John Lester White and Mary Ellendar Long, on 24 Jan 1922, in Stockton, Cedar County, Missouri. Lloyd was born 22 Dec 1901, in Stockton, Cedar County, Missouri. He died on 3 Apr 1963 in Fresno, California. His burial was in Belmont Memorial Park, Fresno, Fresno County, California.[58]

ORPHA MAY BALDWIN was the first of the family born in the twentieth century. She had a distinctive first name. Her name does not appear to be in remembrance of a particular Baldwin ancestor or kin. Her parents perhaps chose the name for its biblical association. Orpha was a woman briefly mentioned in the Book of Ruth in the Hebrew Bible. However, Orpha is also a large part of the word orphan. Certainly, Orpha was not an orphan, although her father died when she was seven years old.[59] She grew up in a large family of siblings, half-siblings, aunts, uncles, and cousins who made up a substantial part of the populations of Cedar and Dade counties.

Her early education was in the rural schools that dotted the southwest Missouri landscape. In 1920, at age 19, she was living at Stockton, in Linn Township, Cedar County, with her mother, sister, and three brothers. The 1920 census indicated she and her sister, Minnie, age 17, were in school, suggesting they either pursued a high school education or attended college. However, in later records, Orpha indicated she had but an eighth-grade education. Her mother, Cordelia, and older brother, William Byron, still worked a tract of the Baldwin farm but without much help from the rest of the family.[60]

On January 24, 1922, at age 21, Orpha married Lloyd White, a 20-year-old neighbor boy from Cedar County. Their age difference meant that Lloyd's father, John White, had to give permission for his son to

---

[58] Ibid.

[59] 1910 US Census, Linn, Cedar, Missouri, United States, citing enumeration district (ED) ED 57, sheet 4B, family 2

[60] 1920 US Census, Missouri, Cedar, Linn, ED 60, image 13 of 14, citing NARA microfilm publication T625.

marry, which he did.[61] Their marriage license indicated that Orpha lived at Stockton, where Probate Judge Fry Headlee married them.[62]

The couple removed to California and settled in Fresno shortly after their marriage, and sometime after their son, Lawrence, was born, in Missouri, on September 17, 1923. In the spring of 1930, they were in Fresno renting a $12-a-month apartment on Woodward Street. Their son was age 6 and in school. Both Orpha and Lloyd had good jobs working in a packing plant.[63] They led a comfortable existence in Fresno.

No more children came along. Lawrence was an only child. Meanwhile, John L. White, Lloyd's father, died in 1937, in Cedar County, Missouri, and Lloyd's mother moved to Fresno with her other son, Chancy L. White, the younger brother of Lloyd. The 1940 census found the White family on Fourth Street.

In 1940, Orpha and Lloyd lived in their own modest home valued at $1,000, which they bought some time before 1935. Their only son, Lawrence, was 16 and in his second year of high school. Living in a small house next door were Lloyd's mother, Widow Ellen White, age 60, and her son Chancy L. White, brother of Lloyd. Jobs were plentiful in Fresno in the post-depression era. Lloyd worked in a creamery, putting in 48-hour workweeks and earning $1,284 a year. Orpha worked, too, part-time, to bring in extra money. Chancy, who had a year of high school, worked for the same creamery as Lloyd, earning the same salary.[64]

Chancy White was an interesting member of the White family. In addition to a distinctive first name, at age 38, he entered the draft for World War II on October 10, 1942, enlisting for the duration of the war. Probably due to his age and the circumstances of having a family

---

[61] 1920 US Census, Missouri, Cedar, Linn, ED 60, image 7 of 14, citing NARA microfilm publication T625.

[62] Missouri, County Marriage, Naturalization, and Court Records, 1800-1991, Cedar, Marriage applications and licenses 1919-1922, image 1034 of 1355, image 1035 of 1355, Missouri State Archives, Jefferson City.

[63] 1930 US Census, California, Fresno, Fresno, ED 25, image 97 of 133, citing NARA microfilm publication T626.

[64] 1940 US Census, California, Fresno, Judicial Township 3, Fresno City, 10-55, image 20 of 32, citing Sixteenth Census of the United States, 1940, NARA digital publication T627, Records of the Bureau of the Census, 1790-2007, RG 29, National Archives and Records Administration.

member dependent on him—his mother—he appears to have remained stateside during the War. He returned to Fresno at the War's end and moved back in with his 77-year-old mother, next door to Orpha and Lloyd, then living on 54th Street off Woodbury, [65] He took a job hauling figs to fig packers at a dried fruit packing company.

Mary Ellendar Long White died in the spring of 1951. Chancy accompanied the remains of his mother to Missouri, where her burial was in Gum Springs Cemetery, Cedar County, next to her husband, John L. White, who had died 14 years prior. Chancy went back to California and made his home in Fresno for another decade. Still single, he retired and came home to Missouri. On June 26, 1961, at the age of 56, he married Opal Matilda Sellers of Stockton. They married in Dade County.[66]

Meanwhile, Orpha and Lloyd lived out their lives in Fresno. In 1950, Lloyd still worked at the creamery but now as a machine operator. Orpha worked fulltime as a raisin packer in a raisin packing plant. Lawrence White, their son, was out of the house and living next door at age 26 with his wife, Dorothy, and their two-year-old son, Lawrence, Jr.

Lloyd Lester White died on April 3, 1963, in Fresno.[67] Orpha Baldwin White lived on until November 19, 1985.[68] She died at the age of 84, having made her home in Fresno, California, for 57 years. Her obituary noted that she was a homemaker and a member of Peoples Church. Peoples Church today is a Pentecostal mega church with a weekly attendance exceeding 4,000 worshipers. The church has a reputation for

---

[65] United States World War II Army Enlistment Records, 1938-1946, Chancy L White, enlisted 10 Oct 1942, Fresno, California, United States, citing Electronic Army Serial Number Merged File, ca. 1938-1946, National Archives and Records Administration, 2002, NARA NAID 1263923, National Archives at College Park, Maryland, Serial Number 39684572, Affiliate ARC Identifier 1263923, Box Film Number 14617.32.

[66] Missouri, County Marriage, Naturalization, and Court Records, 1800-1991, image 1 of 1, Missouri State Archives, Jefferson City.

[67] California Death Index, 1940-1997, Lloyd L White, 03 Apr 1963, Department of Public Health Services, Sacramento.

[68] California Death Index, 1940-1997, Orpha May White, 19 Nov 1985, Department of Public Health Services, Sacramento.

its strong use and support of creative arts and technology. Orpha's survivors were her son, Lawrence, Jr., her sister Minnie Baldwin Cornwell and brother Harry Baldwin, of Missouri, and one grandchild.[69] The burials of Orpha and Lloyd were in Belmont Memorial Park, in Fresno, California.[70]

Orpha and Lloyd's only son, Lawrence, Jr., died on February 27, 2006, in Fresno. Lawrence, Jr., worked as an installer for Western Electric.[71] He spent more than 30 years working for Western Electric Telephone Company before retiring to Los Baños, in Merced County, California's San Joaquin Valley. His burial was in Fresno Memorial Gardens, Fresno, California.[72] His gravesite honors his service as a veteran of World War II. He was a corporal in the US Army Air Corps.[73] His wife of many years, Dorothy White, died in 2011. Her burial was beside him in Fresno Memorial Gardens.[74]

Chancy Leroy White, brother of Lloyd, died September 17, 1987, at the Barton County Memorial Hospital, in Lamar, Missouri, at the age of 82. His wife, Opal Sellers, died in 1971. Chancy spent the last years of his life with his beloved friend and companion, Lorene Eggleston. His burial was in Omer Cemetery, Cedar County, near the graves of his parents.[75]

> 19   F   **Minnie Cassie Baldwin** was born on 30 Aug 1902, in Cedar County, Missouri. She died on 24 Mar 1998, in

---

[69] California, Fresno and Napa Counties, Obituaries, 1974-1997, Mrs. Orpha M White, 21 Nov 1985, from Napa Valley Genealogical and Biographical Society, Napa, and Fresno County Public Library, Fresno, California.

[70] Billion Graves record for Orpha M. White (1900-1985), Belmont Memorial Park, Fresno, Fresno, California; Billion Graves record for Lloyd L. White (1901-1963), Belmont Memorial Park, Fresno, Fresno, California.

[71] 1950 US Census, Fresno, Fresno, California, Enumeration District 63-148, p 24.

[72] Find a Grave Memorial ID 13505056.

[73] Department of Veterans Affairs Cemetery: Fresno Memorial Gardens Address: 175 S Cornelia Avenue Fresno, Ca 93706 Phone: (559) 268-7823, US Department of Veterans Affairs.

[74] Find a Grave Memorial ID 157188434.

[75] Find a Grave Memorial ID 132354148, obituary contributed by Pat Faulkner.

Stockton, Cedar County. Her burial was in Gum Springs Cemetery, Linn Township, Cedar County, Missouri.[76]

Minnie married **Lewis Ewing Cornwell**, son of Elisha Leonard Cornwell and Pearl Olive Sanders, on 22 Jul 1933, in M. E. Parsonage, Stockton, Cedar County, Missouri. Lewis was born on 3 Oct 1904, in Cedar County, Missouri. He died on 22 Apr 1992, in Stockton, Cedar County, Missouri. His burial was in Gum Springs Cemetery, Linn Township, Cedar County, Missouri.[77]

MINNIE CASSIE BALDWIN was the 19th child of John Calvin Baldwin, and the youngest daughter of John Calvin and Sarah Cordelia. She was age 5 when John Calvin died.[78] In 1920, she was living with her mother and in school at age 17; nevertheless, records show she had an eighth-grade education and not a high school education, as the 1920 census might suggest.[79]

She turned 27 in 1930. The census for that year found her still living with her mother, Cordelia, on the farm in Linn Township, Cedar County, with brothers Hugh and Harry. Her older brother, William Byron Baldwin, and his family lived next door. Widow Cordelia continued to style herself as a farm laborer at the advanced age of 68, but Minnie claimed no occupation on the census form.[80]

Minnie's age of 27 carried the unfortunate stigma of the unmarried Baldwin girl; that is, "spinster" or "old maid," terms that originated far back in history and carried unfortunately into the early 20th century. However, Minnie's status changed on July 22, 1933, when she married Lewis Cornwell, a 28-year-old Cedar County boy, 5 ft. 8 in. tall, 195 lbs.,

---

[76] Find a Grave Memorial ID 5495563.

[77] Find a Grave Memorial ID 5495573.

[78] 1910 US Census, Linn, Cedar, Missouri, United States, citing enumeration district (ED) ED 57, sheet 4B, family 76, NARA microfilm publication T624, roll 768, FHL microfilm 1,374,781.

[79] 1920 US Census, Missouri, Cedar, Linn, ED 60, image 13 of 14, citing NARA microfilm publication T625.

[80] 1930 US Census, Missouri, Cedar, Linn, ED 10 , image 1 of 22, citing NARA microfilm publication T626.

of ruddy complexion, brown eyes, and black hair.[81] They married at the Methodist Episcopal Parsonage in Stockton, Rev. C. O. Crockett performing the ceremony.[82]

Lewis was one of the more eligible bachelors in Cedar County. He was an eighth-generation descendant of the Cornwells of Virginia who immigrated to America in the early 1600s. Migration of the Cromwell family took them through Tennessee, Alabama, and into Missouri, where they settled in 1853.[83] Lewis was the grandson of Barnett Logan Cornwell, Jr., a Civil War veteran who fought for the Union, 15 Unit, Missouri, Calvary, Company M.[84]

In 1940, Minnie and Lewis lived in a rented house in North Township, Dade County, Missouri. Lewis continued the Cromwell tradition of farming, like almost everyone else in that part of Dade County. Lewis had graduated after four years of high school. The couple chose to make rural Missouri their home for most of their lives, interrupted only by World War II.[85]

On February 14, 1942, Lewis registered for the draft at Arcola, Dade County. We do not know the circumstances of his military service, or if he served. He was 37 in 1942, an age that could excuse men from the

---

[81] Missouri, World War II Draft Registration Cards, 1940-1945, Minnie Cornwell in entry for Lewis Ewing Cornwell, 14 Feb 1942, citing Draft Registration, Arcola, Dade, Missouri, United States, NARA NAID 5833895 Draft Registration Cards for Missouri, 10/16/1940–3/31/1947, National Archives at St. Louis, Missouri, FHL microfilm .

[82] Missouri, County Marriage, Naturalization, and Court Records, 1800-1991, Cedar, Marriage applications and licenses 1933-1936, image 69 of 1014; Missouri State Archives, Jefferson City; Missouri, County Marriage, Naturalization, and Court Records, 1800-1991, Cedar, Marriage licenses 1930-1949 Vol. L, p. 170, image 185 of 500; Missouri State Archives, Jefferson City.

[83] Find a Grave Memorial ID 44109996. Barnett Cornwell, Sr., was originally buried in Miller Cemetery near Greenfield. The Stockton Dam project in the 1960's flooded the area and the interments of Miller Cemetery were moved to Vaughn Cemetery, in Greenfield, Dade County.

[84] Find a Grave Memorial ID 524792.

[85] 1940 US Census, Missouri, Dade, North Township, Arcola, 29-9, image 6 of 17, citing Sixteenth Census of the United States, 1940, NARA digital publication T627.

draft.[86] His lone dependent was Minnie. The government required all men between the ages of 21 and 42 to register for the draft. However, those engaged in agriculture could obtain a deferment, especially if they were older and had dependents.

When Minnie's mother, Cordelia, died in the spring of 1945, she and Lewis took over the farm operation until their retirement.[87]

The 1950 census reiterated the quiet life that Minnie and Lewis enjoyed on the farm in Cedar County, living in their modest home on Highway 39. Farm work was hard work. Lewis worked 60 hours a week in the busy spring and fall seasons, in addition to his own chores, helping and sharing work with the Belchers, Willets, and Deckers, all neighbors living nearby. There were not as many people living in the neighborhood as before 1950. Rural life for some was too hard, and jobs in post-war America were plentiful, as more and more people joined the middle class. Several vacant houses dotted the prairie in 1950.[88]

Minnie always described herself in census records as a homemaker. She never recorded an occupation other than homemaker. We know, however, that she was active in the community, busy helping Lewis on the farm, and tending to her own interests. She was an avid Baldwin family historian and genealogist. Much of what we know and remember about the Baldwin and Cornwell families and their descendants owes to Minnie Baldwin. She gathered a prodigious amount of information and documentation, which she combined with her extensive knowledge of family traditions and lore of the Baldwin family. Baldwin descendants often visited her to reminisce about the Baldwin family.[89] Minnie and Lewis lived in Stockton in their final years. Both lived long lives, married to each other for 58 years. Lewis

---

[86] Missouri, World War II Draft Registration Cards, 1940-1945, Minnie Cornwell in entry for Lewis Ewing Cornwell, 14 Feb 1942, citing Draft Registration, Arcola, Dade, Missouri, United States, NARA NAID 5833895 Draft Registration Cards for Missouri, 10/16/1940–3/31/1947, National Archives at St. Louis, Missouri, FHL microfilm .

[87] Jimmy O. Baldwin, in History of Cedar County.

[88] 1950 US Census, Missouri, Cedar, Linn, p. 2, digital record 108943830, NARA.

[89] Vickie Baldwin Correspondence, Email, 5 Jan 2005.

died in 1992, at the age of 88.[90] Minnie died on March 24, 1998. She was 95 years old. Their burials were in Gum Springs Cemetery, south of Stockton, on Highway 39, just south of the 39 and 215 junction, and not far from where they lived most of their lives on their farm on Highway 39. Minnie and Lewis did not have children.

Minnie Cassie Baldwin. For many years, Minnie was the Baldwin family historian and chronicler of Cedar County. She married Lewis Cornwall and together they took over the Baldwin farm. When she died in 1998, she was the last of the 20 children of John Calvin Baldwin. K. Burchett Photo File.

When Minnie died, she was the last of the children of John Calvin Baldwin to pass. She survived her siblings by nearly a decade. In her long life, she witnessed four wars: World War I, World War II, Korea, and Vietnam; saw the development of the atomic bomb; and lived through the rise and fall of the Soviet Union. She experienced the innovations of technology from horses, wagons, and steam engines to automobiles, jet planes, and computers, to name a few. In the year she died in 1998, Microsoft became the biggest company in the world, and

---

[90] United States Social Security Death Index, Lewis Cornwell, 23 Apr 1992, citing US Social Security Administration, Death Master File.

Google went public. She lived through the Great Depression and the administrations of 17 presidents from Theodore Roosevelt to Bill Clinton. It is safe to say that from her perspective in rural southwest Missouri, many of the events and innovations of the 20th century did not agreeably enthrall Minnie.

> 20 M **Harry Howard Baldwin** was born on 15 Mar 1904 in Cedar County, Missouri. He died on 20 May 1988, at Stockton, Cedar County, Missouri. His burial was in Gum Springs Cemetery, Cedar County, Missouri.[91]
>
> Harry married **Mary Kathryn Haselwood**, daughter of Willis Haselwood and Etta Belle Goforth, about 1933. She was born 18 Feb 1909, in Barnard, White Cloud Township, Nodaway County, Missouri. She died 29 Jul 1976, at Stockton, Cedar County, Missouri. Her burial was in Gum Springs Cemetery, Linn Township, Cedar County, Missouri.[92]

HARRY HOWARD BALDWIN was the youngest of the Baldwin family, the last of 20 children born to John Calvin Baldwin, and the youngest child of Sarah Cordelia Baldwin. Harry's father died when Harry was age four, and his single mother raised him along with his siblings on the family farm in Cedar County, Missouri.[93] He attended school until he was 15, received an eighth-grade education, and learned the trade of farming from his mother and older half-siblings.[94]

He stayed on the family farm for several years. The 1930 census for Linn Township recorded him at the age of 26 living with Cordelia, age 68, his sister Minnie, age 27, and brother Hugh Baldwin, age 35. His older brother, William Byron, lived with his family next door.[95]

---

[91] Find a Grave Memorial ID 5495429

[92] Find a Grave Memorial ID 5495469·

[93] 1910 US Census, Linn, Cedar, Missouri, United States, citing enumeration district (ED) ED 57, sheet 4B, family 76, NARA microfilm publication T624, roll 768, FHL microfilm 1,374,781.

[94] 1920 US Census, Missouri, Cedar, Linn, ED 60, image 13 of 14, citing NARA microfilm publication T625.

[95] 1930 US Census, Missouri, Cedar, Linn, ED 10, image 1 of 22, citing NARA microfilm publication T626.

Harry Howard Baldwin. The youngest of John Calvin Baldwin's 20 children, he was age four when his father died. He worked the family farm and cared for his aging mother until his death in 1944. She died the following year. K. Burchett Photo File.

Sometime around 1932, a new girl moved into the neighborhood. Her name was Mary Kathryn Haselwood, a young woman in her early twenties, recently working as an office girl for a doctor in Barnard, Missouri. She came to Cedar County with her parents from White Cloud Township, in Nodaway County, Missouri.[96] The Haselwoods were farmers in Nodaway County who left their farm at Barnard for the same occupation in North Township, Dade County, Missouri.[97] Rural southwest Missouri was very similar to upstate Missouri. Nodaway County sits on the Iowa border in northwest Missouri. Barnard was a small town of about 300 people in 1930, similar to the village of Arcola near where the Haselwoods settled in Dade County, although not nearly as crowded as Barnard. Arcola never approached a population of 300. Barnard had the historical distinction of being where a local farmer in

---

[96] 1930 US Census, Missouri, Nodaway, White Cloud, ED 37, image 10 of 22, citing NARA microfilm publication T626.

[97] 1940 US Census, Missouri, Dade, North Township, Arcola, 29-9 North Township, Arcola, image 13 of 17, citing Sixteenth Census of the United States, 1940, NARA digital publication T627.

1883 discovered a human skeleton 12 ft. tall with ribs nearly 4 ft. long.[98] The Haselwoods continued to live for many years in Dade County, Missouri.

Harry Baldwin and Mary Kathryn Haselwood married about 1933. No marriage record is available. However, their son Max D. Baldwin was born October 28, 1934. The 1940 census located Harry, age 36, Mary, age 30, and son Max D., age 5, living in the household of Cordelia and Hugh Baldwin. Because of the advanced age of Cordelia, who was no longer able to work, and her son Hugh's assumed disability, Harry and Mary became the main caregivers of the family.[99]

Hugh died in 1944, and Cordelia passed in 1945. Harry and Mary continued to live on the farm one-half mile south of Omer, Missouri, in the Jerico Springs postal district, where they raised Max to adulthood. In 1950, Harry reported to the census enumerator that he worked 60 hours a week on the farm with his helper, Max.[100]

Mary Kathryn Baldwin died in 1976 at the age of 67. Harry died in 1988 at the age of 84.[101] Their shared gravestone marks the site of their burials in Gum Springs Cemetery, Linn Township, Cedar County, Missouri.[102]

Max Duane Baldwin married Shirley Joan Hayward on August 18, 1953. Max was 18 years old; Shirley was 15.[103] Harry gave permission for his son to marry.[104] We assume Shirley's mother or stepfather filed a similar document for Shirley. The young couple did not follow the Baldwin tradition of farming. They removed to Independence, Jackson

---

[98] *Fort Worth Daily Gazette*, August 15, 1883, "A Giant's Skeleton."

[99] 1940 US Census, Linn, Cedar, Missouri, Roll: m-t0627-02095, p. 12A, Enumeration District:20-11.

[100] 1950 US Census, Missouri, Cedar, Linn, p. 2, digital record 108943830, NARA.

[101] United States Social Security Death Index, H. H. Baldwin, 20 May 1988, citing US Social Security Administration, Death Master File.

[102] Find a Grave Memorial ID 5495469·

[103] Missouri, County Marriage, Naturalization, and Court Records, 1800-1991, Max Duane Baldwin and Shirley Joan Hayward, 1953, citing Marriage, Cedar, Missouri, United States, Missouri State Archives, Jefferson City, FHL microfilm 007255180.

[104] Missouri, County Marriage, Naturalization, and Court Records, 1800-1991, Cedar, Marriage applications and licenses 1952-1957, image 285 of 1067, Missouri State Archives, Jefferson City.

County, Missouri, near Kansas City.[105] There, Max spent more than 50 years in the vending machine business. Shirley worked at the Mid-Continent Public Library in Independence for more than 24 years before she retired. Both were members of the Sycamore Hills Baptist Church in Independence, where Max served as a deacon and enjoyed a love of southern gospel music. According to his obituary, his part of the Baldwin family was very musically inclined. Shirley taught Sunday school. Max and Shirley were together for 57 years. Shirley died on January 19, 2011, at the age of 72. Max died on February 18, 2017, at age 82. Their graves are in Lee's Summit Historical Cemetery, Lee's Summit, Missouri.[106]

Baldwin Reunion. Descendants of John Calvin Baldwin and their spouses posed for this family reunion photograph in the summer of 1914. Cordelia Baldwin is the woman dressed in black. In the third row, aligned with the seated baby is Anna Eliza Baldwin Cardwell Biddy McCollum. Baldwin reunions were an annual event, which usually included all members of the Baldwin family who were able to attend. Photo Courtesy of Faye Baldwin.

---

[105] United States Public Records, 1970-2009, Max D. Baldwin, 2008.

[106] Find a Grave Memorial ID 176530387. Obituaries for Max Baldwin and Shirley Baldwin are at Find a Grave. Max and Shirley had three daughters. With the passing of Max Baldwin, the Baldwin surname discordancy of Harry Baldwin went extinct.

Bibliography

A New Map of Indiana with Its Roads and Distances. Philadelphia: S. Augustus Mitchell, 1848.

Abbott, Clayton. *Historical Sketches of Cedar County, Missouri*. Greenfield, Mo.: Vedette, 1967.

Absher, Mrs. W. O. *Wilkes County Court Minutes 1789 1797*, (Vol. 4), Easley, S.C.: Southern Historical Press, 1989.

Adamson, Hans C. *Rebellion in Missouri in 1861: Nathaniel Lyon and His Army of the West*. Philadelphia: Chilton, 1961.

Alderman, John P. Marriages, Grayson County, Virginia, 1793-1853. Richmond, Va.: Virginia State Library, 1975.

Alderman, John Perry. *Carroll 1765-1815, the Settlements: A History of the First Fifty Years of Carroll County*. [S. l.]: Central Virginia Newspapers, 1985.

Anderson, Ephraim M. *Memoirs: Historical and Personal*, St. Louis: Times Print Co., 1868.

Anderson-Green, Paula H. The New River Frontier Settlement on the Virginia-North Carolina Border (1760 1820). *Virginia Magazine of History and Biography*, 86, (Oct, 1978): 413-431.

Andreas, Alfred T. *Map of Wayne County*. Chicago: Baskin, Forster, 1876.

Andrews, Matthew P. *Virginia, the Old Dominion*. New York: Doubleday, Doran, 1937.

Ashmead, Henry G. *History of Delaware County, Pennsylvania*. Philadelphia, Pa.: L. H. Everts, 1884.

Atlas of Henry Co. Illinois to which is Added an Atlas of the United States. Chicago: Warner & Beers, 1875.

Atlas of Illinois, Counties of Sangamon, Macoupin, and Montgomery. Chicago: Warner & Beers, [1872] 1876.

Baldwin, Charles C. *The Baldwin Genealogy from 1500 to 1881*. Cleveland, Ohio: Leader Printing, 1881.

Baldwin, Charles C. *The Baldwin Genealogy Supplement*. Cleveland, Ohio: Leader Printing, 1889.

Baldwin, Frank C. *History of the Baldwins in Europe and England from 672 A. D. to 1640*. Onondaga, Mich.: F. C. Baldwin, 1935.

Baldwin, Jimmy O. [Baldwin]. In *History of Cedar County*, Springfield, Mo.: Greene County Archives and Records Center, 1992, 1998.

Baldwin, John D. *A Record of the Descendants of John Baldwin of Stonington, Conn. with Notices of Other Baldwins Who Settled in America in Early Colony Times*. Worcester Mass.: Tyler & Seagrave, 1880;

Baldwin, Ralph E. *Theophilus Baldwin 1792-1851 and His Descendants, North Carolina-Indiana*. Speedway, Ind.: Author, 1988.

Baldwin, Roy C. *Narrative of the Massacre, by the Savages, of the Wife and Children of Thomas Baldwin*. New-York: Martin & Wood, 1835.

Banks, Charles E. *Topographical Dictionary of 2885 English Emigrants to New England 1620-1650* (3rd ed, edited by Elijah E. Brownell). Baltimore: Genealogical Publishing, [1937] 1963.

Barbour, Philip L. *The Jamestown Voyages under the First Charter, 1606-1609*. London: Hakluyt Society, 1969.

Barns, C. R. *The Commonwealth of Missouri, a Centennial Record*. St. Louis: Bryan, Brand, 1877.

Barrow, John. *New Geographical Dictionary*. London: [N.p.], 1759-60.

Bathe, Basil W. *Seven Centuries of Sea Travel: From the Crusaders to the Cruises*. London: Barrie & Jenkins, 1972.

Binford, J. H. *History of Hancock County, Indiana*. Greenfield, Ind.: King & Binford, 1882.

Blankenbecker, C. C. Pioneer Life in Bates County. In *Old Settlers' History of Bates County, Missouri* by S. L. Tathwell & H. O. Maxey. Amsterdam, Mo.: Tathwell & Maxey, 1897, pp. 139-141.

Blome, Richard. *Britannia or, a Geographical Description of the Kingdoms of England, Scotland, and Ireland, with the Isles and Territories Thereto Belonging*. Printed by Tho. Rycroft, 1673.

Brown, G. W. *Reminiscences of Old John Brown.* Rockford, Ill.: Abraham E. Smith, 1880.

Bruce, H. Addington. *Daniel Boone and the Wilderness Road.* N.Y.: Macmillan, 1911, p 341.

California. County Birth and Death Records, 1800-1994. California State Archives, Sacramento.

California. Death Index, 1940-1997, Department of Public Health Services, Sacramento.

California. Tulare County Sheriff's Office and Jail Records, 1874-1963. California Archives.

Campbell, Robert A. *Campbell's New Atlas of Missouri With Descriptions Historical, Scientific, and Statistical.* St. Louis: R. A. Campbell, 1873.

Canada. Northwest Provinces Census, 1906. Census and Statistics Office. Public Archives, Ottawa, Ontario, Canada.

Canby, Henry S. *The Brandywine.* Exton, Pa.: Schiffer, 1977.

Carlinville Free Democrat. History of Virden. Virden, Macoupin County, Ill.: Author, October 27, 1859.

Carswell, Roger. *The Early Years of Osage County.* North Newton: Mennonite, 1982.

Cawley, Charles. *Medieval Lands: A Prosopography of Medieval European Noble and Royal Families* [Online 4th ed.]. Foundation of Medieval Genealogy, 2006-2001.

Chamberlayne, C. G. Ed. *The Vestry Book of Christ Church Parish, Virginia, 1663-1767.* Greenville, S. C.: Southern Historical Press, 2006.

Clifford, Glenda. *Historical Tours of Cedar County, Missouri.* Stockton, Mo.: Cedar County Historical Society, 1977.

Coale, Charles B. *The Life and Adventures of Wilburn Waters, the Famous Hunter and Trapper of White Top Mountain: Embracing Early History of Southwestern Virginia, Sufferings of the Pioneers, etc.* Richmond: G. W. Gray, 1878.

Coldham, Peter W. *The Complete Book of Emigrants 1607-1660.* Baltimore: Genealogical Publishing, 1987.

Cope, Gilbert, and Ashmead, Henry G. Eds. *Chester and Delaware Counties, Pennsylvania* (Vols. 1 & 2). New York: Lewis Publishing, 1904.

Corbitt, D. L. Congressional Districts of North Carolina, 1789-1934. *The North Carolina Historical Review* 12 (April 1935): 173-188.

Cridlin, William B. *A History of Colonial Virginia: The First Permanent Colony in America, to Which is Added the Genealogy of the Several Shires and Counties and Population in Virginia from the First Spanish Colony to the Present Time.* Richmond, Va.: Williams Printing Co., 1923.

Cutler, William G. *History of the State of Kansas.* Chicago: A. T. Andreas, 1883

Dabney, Virginius. *Virginia, the New Dominion.* Garden City, N.Y., Doubleday, 1971.

Dorrell, Ruth. *Pioneer Ancestors of Members of the Society of Indiana Pioneers.* Indianapolis: Indiana Historical Society, 1983.

Durant, Pliny A., Ed. *The History of Clinton County, Ohio* (Vol. 2). Chicago: W. H. Beers, 1882.

Dyer, Frederick H. *A Compendium of the War of the Rebellion.* Des Moines, Iowa: Dyer Publishing, 1908.

Ellis, Franklin, Ed. *Fayette County Pennsylvania.* Philadelphia: L. H. Everts, 1882.

Finley, Anthony. *Indiana.* Philadelphia: Anthony Finley, 1831.

Fisher, Michelle L. Fisher Family Tree [On-Line].

Fletcher, Arthur L. *Ashe County, a History.* Jefferson, N.C.: McFarland, 1963.

Fletcher, J. F. *A History of the Ashe County, North Carolina, and New River, Virginia Baptist Associations.* Raleigh, N. C.: Commercial Printing, 1935.

Fry, Joshua. *A Map of the Most Inhabited Part of Virginia* [containing parts of Pennsylvania and North Carolina]. London: Thos. Jefferys, [1755].

Futhey, J. Smith, and Cope, Gilbert. *History of Chester County, Pennsylvania.* Philadelphia: Louis H. Everts, 1881.

Gardiner, Samuel R. *School Atlas of English History*. London: Longmans, Green, & Co., 1914.

Gasperini, Antonella, Galli, Daniele, & Nenzi, Laura. The Worldwide Impact of Donati's Comet on Art and Society in the Mid-19th Century [On-line ed.]. Proceedings of the International Astronomical Union, (2009): 340-345.

Georgia. Georgia Marriage Records from Select Counties, 1828-1978. Georgia Archives, Morrow, Georgia.

Gerteis, Lewis S. *Civil War St. Louis*. Lawrence, Kans.: University Press of Kansas, 2001.

Goodspeed's 1888 History of Lawrence County (reprint). Cassville, Mo.: Litho Printers, [1888] 1973.

Grayson County Militia Officers 1793-1812, Antebellum Grayson County, Virginia Militia [On-line New River Notes].

Grayson County, Virginia, Court Order Book, 1810, 1811-1829 [On-line New River Notes].

Grayson County, Virginia, Personal Property Tax List—1794, 1799, 1800, 1805, 1810, 1817, 1825, [Online New River Notes].

Grayson County, Virginia, Superior Court Order Book 1809-1821

Greene, E. B. *Sectional Forces in the History of Illinois (No. 8)*. Indianapolis, Ind.: Publications of the Historical Library of Illinois, 1903.

Grierson, Francis. *The Valley of Shadows*. New York: Houghton Mifflin, 1909.

Hardesty, Thomas C., Baughn, Milton L., and Barrus, Ben M. *A People Called Cumberland Presbyterian*. Memphis: Tenn.: Frontier, 1972.

Heiss, Willard C. *The Census of the Territory of Kansas, February 1855: With Index and Map of Kansas Election Districts in 1854*. Knightstown, Ind.: Eastern Indiana Publishing, 1968.

Herklotz, Hildegarde R. Jayhawkers in Missouri, 1858-1863. *Missouri Historical Review* 17 (April 1923): 266-284.

Herndon, William H., & Weik, Jesse W. *Herndon's Life of Lincoln* (Vols. 2 & 3). Cleveland, Ohio: World Publishing, [2889] 1949.

Hinshaw, William W. *Encyclopedia of American Quaker Genealogy* (Vol. 1). Ann Arbor, Mich.: Edwards Brothers, 1936

History of Macoupin County, Illinois. Philadelphia: Brink, McDonough, 1879.

History of Ross and Highland Counties, Ohio. Cleveland, Ohio: Williams Bros., 1880.

History of Sangamon County, Illinois, Chicago: Interstate Publishing, 1881.

History of Steele and Waseca Counties, Minnesota. Chicago: Union, 1887.

Hodder, Frank H. *The Genesis of the Kansas-Nebraska Act*. Madison, Wis.: State Historical Society of Wisconsin, 1913.

Hotten, John C. *The Original Lists of Persons of Quality* (Reprint ed.). New York: Empire State Book, [1874] 1940.

Humphrey, Grace. *Illinois: The Story of the Prairie State* (Centennial Edition). Indianapolis, Ind.: Bobbs Merrill, 1917.

Illinois. 122nd Illinois Infantry Regiment History, Adjutant General's Report, Illinois [On-line]

Illinois. Statewide Marriage Index, 1763–1900, Illinois, County Marriages, 1810-1940 [Online].

Inman, Henry. *Stories of the Old Santa Fe Trail*. Kansas City, Mo.: Ramsey, Millett, & Hudson, 1881.

Iowa. Death Records, 1904-1951. State Historical Society of Iowa, Des Moines

Isle of Wight County, Va. Records. *William and Mary College Quarterly* 7 (No. 4, 1899): 205.

John Smith's Map of Virginia: With a Description of the Country, the Commodities, People, Government, and Religion. Originally published in 1612.

Josselyn, John. *An Account of Two Voyages to New-England Made during the Years 1638, 1663*. Boston; William Veazie, 1865.

Kansas. Muster Rolls, Kansas State Militia, Adjutant General's Office (Vol. 9), 1864.

Lancaster, Robert B. *A Sketch of the Early History of Hanover County*. Ashland, Va.: Herald Progress, 1957.

Lapp, Dorothy, Trans. *Records of the Courts of Chester County, Pennsylvania* (Vol. 2) Philadelphia, Pa: Patterson & White, 1910.

Lincoln, Abraham. *Abraham Lincoln: Complete Works*, edited by John G. Nicolay & John Hay. New York: Century, 1920.

Lists of the Living and Dead in Virginia, February the 16th, 1623. In John C. Hotten, Ed. *The Original Lists of Persons of Quality*. London: Hotten, 1874.

Lyon County, [Kansas]. Philadelphia: L. H. Everts, 1887.

Map of Cedar Co., Missouri. [St. Louis]: Reily & Co., 1879.

Map of Hancock County. Chicago: Baskin, Forster, 1876.

Marshall, John. *A History of the Colonies Planted by the English on the Continent of North America*. Philadelphia: A. Small, 1824.

Martin, George W. Lincoln in Kansas. In *Transactions of the Kansas State Historical Society, 1901-1902* (Vol. 7). London: Forgotten Books, 2016.

Martin, John H. *Chester (and Its Vicinity,) Delaware County, in Pennsylvania: with Genealogical Sketches of Some Old Families*, Philadelphia: W. H. Pile & Sons, 1877.

Martinez-Hidalgo, José M. *Columbus's Ships*, Barre, Mass.: Barre Publishers, 1966.

McElroy, John. *The Struggle for Missouri*. Washington, D. C.: National Tribune, 1909.

McFarlane, Anthony. *The British in the Americas, 1480-1815*. New York: Longman, 1994.

McGrane, Reginald. *The Panic of 1837: Some Financial Problems of the Jacksonian Era*. New York: Russell & Russell, 1965.

Merlan, Matthäus. *De magna clade, quam Angli anno 1622. Martiij in Virginia Acceperunt*. Frankfurt am Main, 1634, after Edward Waterhouse. *A Declaration of the State of the Colony and Affaires in Virginia*, 1622.

Missouri. County Marriage, Naturalization, and Court Records, 1800-1991. Missouri State Archives, Jefferson City, Mo.

Missouri. County Marriage, Naturalization, and Court Records, 1800-1991. Missouri State Archives, Jefferson City.

Missouri. General Assembly. *Journal of the House of the State of Missouri.* Missouri Secretary of State [On-line]

Missouri. Marriage Records, 1805-2002. Missouri State Archives, Jefferson City, Mo.

Missouri. Standard Certificate of Death. Missouri State Board of Health, Bureau of Vital Statistics.

Missouri. World War II Draft Registration Cards, National Archives at St. Louis, Missouri.

Mitchell, Samuel A., and Young, James H. *Indiana.* Philadelphia: S. Augustus Mitchell, 1834.

Mobley, Joe A., Fenn, Elizabeth A., et al. Eds. *The Way We Lived in North Carolina.* Chapel Hill, N.C.: University of North Carolina Press, 2003.

Morrison, E. M. *A Brief History of Isle of Wight County, Virginia 1608-1907.* [Norfolk, Va.]: Library of Congress, 1907.

Moser, Arthur P. *A Directory of Towns, Villages, and Hamlets Past and Present of Cedar County, Missouri.* [s.n.], 1975.

Nicolay, John G., & Hay, John, Eds. *Herndon's Lincoln: The True Story of a Great Life...The History and Personal Recollections of Abraham Lincoln* (Vols. 2 & 3). Chicago: Belford, Clarke, 1889 & Springfield, Ill.: Herndon's Lincoln Publishing, 1921.

North Carolina. State Archives of North Carolina, Raleigh, North Carolina.

Observations on the Prehistoric Earthworks of Wayne County, Indiana. *Eighth Annual Report of the Geological Survey of Indiana.* Indianapolis: Indianapolis Journal Company, 1876.

Official Records of the War of the Rebellion. National Archives, Washington, D.C.

Ogden, John W. *The History of Champaign County, Ohio.* Chicago: W. H. Beers, 1881.

Ohio. County Marriages, 1789-2016. National Archives, Washington, D.C.

Pennsylvania, Historical Society of Pennsylvania, Marriage Records, 1512-1989; Pennsylvania, Church Marriages, 1682-1976; Marriage Record of St. Paul's Episcopal Church, Chester, Pa. 1704 1733, Pennsylvania Archives, Second Series, Volume 8.

Pension Applications, National Archives and Library of Congress.

Perry, Arthur C. *American History*. New York: American Book Company, 1913.

Pollard, Edward A. *Southern History of the War: The First Year of the War*. New York: C. B. Richardson, 1863.

Powell, William S. Ed. *Encyclopedia of North Carolina*. Chapel Hill, N.C.: University of North Carolina Press, 2006.

Prentis, Noble. *History of Kansas*. Winfield: E. P. Greer, 1899.

Ream, Robert L. *Sectional Map of the Territory of Kansas*. St. Louis: John Halsall, 1858.

Record of the courts of Chester County, Pennsylvania, 1681-1697. Philadelphia: Colonial Society of Pennsylvania, 1910.

Richardson, Albert D. *Beyond the Mississippi; from the Great River to the Great Ocean*. Hartford, Conn.: American Publishing, 1867.

Richman, George J. *History of Hancock County, Indiana, Its People, Industries, and Institutions*. Indianapolis, Ind.: Federal, 1916.

Ricks, Donald M. *The Descendants of Jonas Ricks and Other Ricks Families in America*. Dexter, Mich.: Donald M. Ricks, 1998.

Ricks, Howard, Ed. *History and Genealogy of the Ricks Family of America* (Rev. ed.). Salt Lake City, Utah: Ricks Family Association, [1908] 1957.

Roosevelt, Theodore. *The Winning of the West* (Vol. 1). New York: Current Literature Publishing, 1905.

Rummel, Merle C. The Kanawha Trace Way Bill, 1998. Maggie Stewart Zimmerman [On-line].

Rutman, Darrett B., and Rutman, Anita. *A Place in Time: Middlesex County, Virginia, 1650-1750*. New York: Norton, 1984.

Sanborn, F. B. Ed. *The Life and Letters of John Brown, Liberator of Kansas, and Martyr of Virginia*. Boston: Roberts Bros., [1885].

Sanchez-Saavedra, E. M. *A Guide to Virginia Military Organizations American Revolution, 1774-1787*. Richmond, Va.: Virginia State Library, 1978.

Schrader, Christian. *Indianapolis Remembered: Christian Schrader's Sketches of Early Indianapolis*. Indianapolis, Ind.: Indiana Historical Bureau, 1987.

Schrader, William H. Reminiscences, [Online collection C1519]. State Historical Society of Missouri.

Shourds, *Thomas. History and Genealogy of Fenwick's Colony.* New Jersey. Bridgeton, N.J., G. F. Nixon, 1876.

Smith, Abbot E. *Colonists in Bondage: White Servitude and Convict Labor in America, 1607-1776.* New York: Norton, 1971.

Smith, George. *History of Delaware County, Pennsylvania: from the Discovery of the Territory Included Within Its Limit to the Present Time; With a Notice of the Geology of the County, and Catalogues of Its Minerals, Plants, Quadrupeds, and Birds.* Philadelphia: H. B. Ashmead, 1862.

Snead, Thomas L. *The Fight for Missouri, from the Election of Lincoln to the Death of Lyon.* New York: C. Scribner's Sons, 1886.

Stevens, Walter B. *Centennial History of Missouri, (the Center State) One Hundred Years in the Union, 1820-1921.* St. Louis: S. J. Clarke, 1921.

Stevens, Walter B. *Lincoln and Missouri.* Columbia, Mo.: State Historical Society, 1916.

Story of Macoupin County, edited by Lucy P. Purdom. Carlinville, Ill.: Sesquicentennial Historic Committee. 1979.

Swaim, Jean N. *The Era of the One-Room Rural Schools of Cedar County, Missouri.* [s. n.], 1988.

Switzler, William F. *Switzler's Illustrated History of Missouri, from 1541 to 1881.* St. Louis: C. R. Barns, 1881.

Symons, Thomas W. *Report of an Examination of the Upper Columbia River.* Washington, D.C.: Government Printing Office, 1882.

Tabler, Dave. The Lost Provinces. [On-line Appalachian History.Net]. Retrieved February 4, 2018.

United States. Agriculture Schedule, 1860. National Archives and Records Administration

United States. Appointments of U.S. Postmasters, 1832-1971. National Archives.

United States. Bureau of Land Management (BLM), General Land Office (GLO) Records, Land Records. National Archives.

United States. Census Records of the Bureau of the Census. National Archives and Records Administration, Washington, D.C. 1790-1950.

United States. Civil War Pension Index: General Index to Pension Files, 1861-1934. National Archives;

United States. Congress. House of Representatives. *Report of the Special Committee Appointed to Investigate the Troubles in Kansas.* Washington, D.C.: Wendell, 1856.

United States. Department of Veterans Affairs. Department of Veterans Affairs Cemetery: Fresno Memorial Gardens.

United States. Department of State. *Return of the Whole Number of Persons within the Several Districts of the United States.* Philadelphia: Childs & Swaine, 1791.

United States. Passenger Arrival Records of Immigration Ships [On-line].

United States. Register of Civil, Military, and Naval Service, 1863-1959 (Vol. 2). National Archives.

United States. Social Security Death Index. U.S. Social Security Administration. National Archives.

United States. Special Census (Veterans of the Civil War Still Living in 1890), Enumerating Union Veterans and Widows of Union Veterans of the Civil War; Series Number: M123, Records of the Department of Veterans Affairs; Record Group Number: 15. National Archives.

United States. Special Schedules of the Eleventh Census Enumerating Union Veterans and Widows of Union Veterans of the Civil War, Series No. M123, Record Group No. 15 Records of the Department of Veterans Affairs, Census Year 1890. National Archives.

United States. Veterans Administration Master Index, 1917-1940. St. Louis: National Archives and Records Administration, 1985.

United States. World War I Draft Registration Cards, 1917-1918. National Archives.

United States. World War II Army Enlistment Records, 1938-1946. National Archives and Records Administration, 2002; NARA NAID 1263923, National Archives at College Park,

United States. Revolutionary War Service Records, No. M881 Record Group 93. National Archives.

Valley Forge Muster Roll [On-line]. Valley Forge, Pa.: Valley Forge Park Alliance, 2025.

Van Schreevan, William J., et al. *Revolutionary Virginia, the Road to Independence* (Vol. 1). University Press of Virginia, 1973.

Vandermaelen, Philippe. *Parties des États-Unis* (Amer. Sep. 50). Bruxelles: Vandermaelen, 1827.

Virginia. Executive Department. Office of the Governor (RG#3 Bounty Warrants). Archives at the Library of Virginia

Virginia. Virginia State Land Office. Grants 125-, reel 369. Library of Virginia Archives.

Virginia. Wythe County Personal Property Tax List 1793 [On-line New River Notes].

Virginia's Soldiers in the Revolution. *The Virginia Magazine of History and Biography* 19 (Oct., 1911): 402-414.

Waldenmaier, Nellie P., Ed. *Some of the Earliest Oaths of Allegiance to the United States of America.* Lancaster, Pa.: Author, 1944.

Walker, Charles A. *History of Macoupin County, Illinois: Biographical and Pictorial.* Chicago: S. J. Clarke, 1911.

Walker, Virgil L. *New Map of Cedar Co. Missouri.* Philadelphia: E. P. Noll, 1897.

Wardens and Vestrymen of St. Paul's Episcopal Church (1704 1727); Chester County, Pa. [Online].

Ware, Eugene F., *The Lyon Campaign in Missouri.* Topeka, Kans.: Crane & Company, 1907.

Washington. Washington Death Certificates, 1907-1960. Bureau of Vital Statistics, Olympia, Washington.

Washington. Washington County Marriages, 1855-2008. Bureau of Vital Statistics, Olympia, Washington.

Wheeler, John H. *Historical sketches of North Carolina, from 1584 to 1851.* Philadelphia: Lippincott, Grambo, 1851.

Williams, Dorothy J., & Williams, Thomas E. *A History of Hancock County, Indiana, in the Twentieth Century.* Greenfield, Ind.: T. E. Williams, 1995.

Williams, F. Marion. *Early Days in Cedar County*. Kansas City: Punton-Clark, 1908.

Williams, Walter. *State of Missouri*. Columbia, Mo.: E. W. Stephens, 1904.

Wingfield, Marshall. *A History of Caroline County. Virginia*. Baltimore: Regional Publishing, 1975.

Woodruff, Mrs. Howard W. *Marriage Records, Dade County, Missouri: Books A and B, 1863 1872, and Abstracts of Wills and Admins. A, 1841-1867*. Kansas City, Mo.: Author, 1971.

Worsham, Gibson. *A Survey of Historic Architecture in Grayson County, Virginia*. Richmond, Va.: Virginia Department of Historic Resources, 2002.

Wright, Robert K., Jr. *The Continental Army*. Washington, D.C.: Center of Military History, United States Army, 1983.

Young, Andrew W. *History of Wayne County, Indiana, from Its First Settlement to the Present Time*. Cincinnati: Robert Clarke, 1872.

Index

www.ingramcontent.com/pod-product-compliance
Lightning Source LLC
Chambersburg PA
CBHW081356270326
41930CB00015B/3320